QUE®

Using

Using the Internet Starter Kit

Galen Grimes

Using

the Internet

Starter Kit

using

Library of Congress Catalog No.: 97-69187

ISBN: 0-7897-1480-9

99 98 97 6 5 4 3 2 1

Interpretation of the printing code: the rightmost double-digit number is the year of the book's printing; the rightmost single-digit number, the number of the book's printing. For example, a printing code of 97-1 shows that the first printing of the book occurred in 1997.

Screen reproductions in this book were created using Collage Plus from Inner Media, Inc., Hollis, NH.

Contents at a Glance

Table of Contents

Credits

PRESIDENT
Roland Elgey

SENIOR VICE PRESIDENT/PUBLISHING
Don Fowley

PUBLISHER
Stacy Hiquet

GENERAL MANAGER
Joe Muldoon

MANAGER OF PUBLISHING OPERATIONS
Linda H. Buehler

PUBLISHING MANAGER
Jim Minatel

MANAGING EDITOR
Thomas F. Hayes

DIRECTOR OF ACQUISITIONS
Cheryl D. Willoughby

ACQUISITIONS EDITOR
Jill Byus

SENIOR PRODUCT DIRECTOR
Lisa D. Wagner

PRODUCT DIRECTOR
Mark Cierzniak

PRODUCTION EDITOR
Sean Medlock

EDITORS
Sean Dixon
Patricia Kinyon

PRODUCT MARKETING MANAGER
Kourtnaye Sturgeon

ASSISTANT PRODUCT MARKETING MANAGER
Gretchen Schlesinger

TECHNICAL EDITOR
Bill Bruns

ACQUISITIONS COORDINATOR
Tracy M. Williams

SOFTWARE RELATIONS COORDINATOR
Susan D. Gallagher

EDITORIAL ASSISTANT
Virginia Stoller

BOOK DESIGNER
Ruth Harvey

COVER DESIGNER
Dan Armstrong

PRODUCTION TEAM
Erin M. Danielson
Jenny Earhart
Bryan Flores
Brian Grossman
Julie Searls
Lisa Stumpf

INDEXER
Chris Cleveland

Composed in *Century Old Style* and *ITC Franklin Gothic* by Que Corporation.

We'd Like to Hear from You!

As part of our continuing effort to produce books of the highest possible quality, Que would like to hear your comments. To stay competitive, we *really* want you, as a computer book reader and user, to let us know what you like or dislike most about this book or other Que products.

You can mail comments, ideas, or suggestions for improving future editions to the address below, or send us a fax at (317) 581-4663. For the online inclined, Macmillan Computer Publishing has a forum on CompuServe (type **GO QUEBOOKS** at any prompt) through which our staff and authors are available for questions and comments. The address of our Internet site is **http://www.mcp.com** (World Wide Web).

In addition to exploring our forum, please feel free to contact me personally to discuss your opinions of this book: I'm **MCierzniak@que.mcp.com** on the Internet.

Thanks in advance—your comments will help us to continue publishing the best books available on computer topics in today's market.

Mark Cierzniak
Product Development Specialist
Que Corporation
201 W. 103rd Street
Indianapolis, Indiana 46290
USA

Introduction

By now, you already understand the significance of the Internet. How can you help it—you're bombarded with the thing everyday on the TV and radio; by your friends and coworkers; in newsprint and roadside billboards. Do you really have a full picture of what you can *do* on the Internet, though?

- Read current news, weather, and sports information. You can look for this information on the Web, or you can have it delivered directly to our desktop.
- Look up the home address and phone number for any person or business that is listed in a phone book. Then, display an online map that shows you how to get there.
- Research. Whether you're researching your business competition or the mating habits of presidents, you'll find the information you want on the Internet.
- Shop till you drop. You can purchase just about anything on the Internet: software, home electronics, clothing, flowers, and plane tickets. Shopping on the Internet is quite a safe thing to do these days, too.

You and This Book

I wrote *Using the Internet Starter Kit* with the beginner in mind. You don't have to know anything about the Internet. TCP/IP? Domain names? Phooey. You don't need to know how any of it works before using this book. You'll fare better if you do learn a few basics, though; but I promise not to swamp you with more details than you need. You just want to use the Internet, right? So, this book leaves out a lot of the Internet jargon that you don't need to know right away.

Why Should I Learn about the Internet?

Tough question. Everyone's situation is a bit different. For now, the most important reason that you should learn about the Internet is that it's great fun.

Beyond getting your jollies on the Internet, I believe that, in the very near future, the Internet will have important social and economic impact—impact that affects you directly. It's going to become a very important part of your life. It will change how you work, play, and relate to other people. It's happening already, too, as you can see in the following examples:

- Shop your local markets on the Internet. A major grocery chain in the Dallas area will accept your shopping list via the Internet. They'll bag your groceries and deliver them right to your doorstep. All for a fee, of course, but it's worth it if you spend less time at the grocery store and less money on gas. Oh, yea, no checkout lines—yippee!
- Use the Internet for research. For example, students in my local school system get extra credit on their homework if they can show that they researched it on the Internet. Students who have Internet connections at home fare much better than those who have to wait in line to use the computer lab.
- Improve communication in your office. For professionals in a national company for whom I consulted, Internet mail is replacing the telephone as the communication tool of choice. It's quicker to use and makes tracking people down easier. You're much more likely to get a reply to your queries if you fire off an Internet mail message than if you leave other types of messages. Internet mail also gives you a better paper trail so that when someone tries to tell you that he didn't get your message, you can say "Phooey."

- Work at home. Many companies in the Dallas area have found that they don't have enough cubicles in which to stuff their employees. Thus, they're gradually allowing employees to work at home, using the Internet to connect to the office (Dilbert would be proud). The result is lower costs and, I hope, more productive employees.
- You can increase your odds of landing a great job by learning how to use the Internet. A number of technological companies in the Dallas area give preference to candidates who have experience using the Internet. Why? A huge number of online resources are now available only on the Internet. If you're a Windows programmer, for example, the only place to go for support is the Internet. Besides, learning the Internet also makes you look more technically hip and up-to-date.

Sold. What Do I Need before Using This Book?

You need to have two things before you can put this book to good use: a basic computer system and a little bit of knowledge. First, the computer system. This book is predominantly for Windows users: Windows 3.1 or Windows 95. It doesn't matter which flavor you prefer, but you must have a computer running one of the Windows platforms before you can follow the examples in this book.

NOTE The CD-ROM included with the book contains software that is discussed throughout the book in each chapter. These programs are for trial use only and time out after a certain period of time. After the trial period expires, you can contact the company who makes the full version of the program you're interested in. This does **not** apply to Internet Explorer with AT&T and Netscape with Earthlink. Those programs are already full versions.

And the knowledge? This book requires that you understand a handful of really basic topics. You should understand how to use the different parts of Windows. In Windows 3.1, for example, you should understand how to use the Program Manager. Likewise, in Windows 95, you should understand the taskbar, Start menu, and desktop. You also should understand how to use windows, menus, and dialog boxes. If you're not familiar with Windows or your computer, take a look at some of these Que resources to help you get going:

Using Windows 3.1

Using Windows 95, Second Edition

Using Your PC, Fourth Edition

How This Book Is Organized

Using the Internet Starter Kit has 3 major parts, 18 chapters, 1 appendix, and an index.

- Part I, "Get Connected to the Internet," helps you choose the right type of Internet connection. You can connect via a commercial online service (AOL) or an Internet server provider (ISP), like AT&T and Earthlink. This part also shows you how to configure your computer, download and install the software you need, and troubleshoot your Internet connection.

- Part II, "Use Your Internet Connection," is the meatiest part of this book. It shows you how to use each major Internet service (World Wide Web, Internet mail, Usenet newsgroups, chat, and so forth).
- Part III, "Web Tools and Utilities," focuses on showing you how to use various software (included on the CD-ROM) to browse offline, print Web pages, make phone calls, protect your children, add plug-ins, and more.

Information That's Easy to Understand

This book contains a variety of special features to help you find the information you need. For example, it uses formatting conventions to make important keywords or special text obvious and it uses specific language to make keyboard and mouse actions clear.

Chapter Roadmaps

Each chapter begins with a brief introduction and a list of the topics that each chapter covers. You know what you'll be reading about before you start.

Tips, Notes, Cautions, ...

You'll find a number of special elements and conventions in this book that jump right off the page. These elements provide just-in-time information.

Tips point out things that you can do to get the most out of the Internet. Often, these tips are not found in books or online help, but come from personal experience instead.

NOTE Notes are chunks of information that don't necessarily fit in the surrounding text but could be valuable nonetheless.

CAUTION

Cautions warn you of possible trouble. They warn you about things that you should avoid or things that you need to do to protect yourself or your computer.

Sidebars are "oh-by-the-ways"

Sidebars provide useful and interesting information that doesn't really fit in the text. They also provide information of a more technical nature.

TROUBLESHOOTING

What are troubleshooting sections? These elements anticipate your questions and provide advice about how to solve problems or avoid bad situations.

Keyboard Conventions

In addition to the special features that help you find what you need, this book uses some special conventions that make it easier to understand:

Element	Convention
Hot keys	Hot keys are underlined in this book, just as they appear in Windows menus and dialog boxes. To use a hot key, press Alt and the underlined letter. The F in File is a hot key that represents the File menu, for example (so, Alt+F).
Key combinations	Key combinations that you must press together are separated by plus signs. For example, "Press Ctrl+Alt+D" means that you press and hold down the Ctrl key, then press and hold down the Alt key, and then press and release the D key. Always press and release, rather than hold, the last key in a key combination.
Menu commands	A comma is used to separate the parts of a pull-down menu command. For example, "Choose File, New" means to open the File menu and select the New option.

In most cases, special-purpose keys are designated by the text that actually appears on them on a standard 101-key keyboard. For example, press "Esc" or press "F1" or press "Enter." Some of the keys on your keyboard don't actually have words on them. So, here are the conventions used in this book for those keys:

- The Backspace key, which is labeled with a left arrow, usually is located directly above the Enter key. The Tab key usually is labeled with two arrows pointing to lines, with one arrow pointing right and the other arrow pointing left.
- The cursor keys, labeled on most keyboards with arrows pointing up, down, right, and left, are called the up-arrow key, down-arrow key, right-arrow key, and left-arrow key.
- Case is not important unless explicitly stated. So "Press A" and "Press a" mean the same thing. This book always uses the uppercase version, though.

Mouse Conventions

In this book, the following phrases tell you how to operate your mouse within Windows:

- **Click.** Position the mouse pointer in the area of the screen specified and press the left mouse button. (If you've reversed these buttons—as many left-handed people like to do—whenever the instructions say to press the left button, press the right button instead.
- **Double-click.** Press the left mouse button twice rapidly without moving the mouse between clicks.
- **Drag.** Press and hold down the left mouse button while you're moving the mouse pointer. You see an outline of the object as you drag the mouse pointer.
- **Drop.** Release the mouse button after a drag operation.

Typeface Conventions

This book also uses some special typeface conventions that make it easier to read:

Element	Convention
Bold	**Bold indicates Internet addresses and text that you type.**
Italic	*Italic indicates placeholders, which you substitute with appropriate text or new terms.*
`Monospace`	`Monospace indicates file names and text you see on-screen.`

PART I

Part I Get Connected to the Internet

CHAPTER 1

Here's How the Internet Works

You can use the Internet to its fullest potential if you know a few vital details. This chapter helps you cut through all the nonsense and get online straight away. ■

What Are Hosts and Clients

Every computer on the Internet is called a *host* computer. Some hosts serve up content or applications to other host computers; they're called *servers*. Other computers, like yours, consume or utilize the content and information served by a server. These computers are called *client* computers. This relationship is called *client/server* computing.

The same terminology applies to the programs running on computers connected to the Internet.

- A *client program* is a program that has a user-friendly interface and runs on your computer and accesses resources on the Internet. When the client program needs something from the Internet, it seeks out a server program.
- A *server program* sends back a suitable reply to the client program. For example, your Web browser is a client program and each Web server on the Internet is a server program.

Each server program requires a client program that talks the same language; for example, you need an FTP client program to talk with an FTP server. All client and server programs on the Internet have a *protocol,* or rules governing the exchange of information:

- FTP client programs and servers use the *File Transfer Protocol (FTP)*.
- E-mail client programs and servers communicate via the *Simple Mail Transfer Protocol (SMTP)*.
- Web client programs and Web servers use the *Hypertext Transport Protocol (HTTP)*.

TCP/IP Addresses Every Computer on the Internet

Every computer on the Internet (including Windows, Macs, UNIX, Amiga, huge mainframes, and even tiny PDAs with Windows CE and pagers) must support TCP/IP in order to communicate with other computers. The TCP/IP protocol standardizes how one host computer communicates with another by defining how the computer packages the data and how the package finds its way to the remote computer.

TCP/IP, however, is really two different protocols, joined at the hip:

- **IP**. Special computers, called *routers*, use the *Internet Protocol* to move bits of information around the Internet. Every *packet* of information has the IP address of the computer that sent it and the computer to which it's going. An *IP address* is the unique identification number of the computer, as the other computers on the Internet know it. IP addresses are four numbers, separated by dots. Que's host computer, for example, has the IP address **206.246.150.10**.
- **TCP**. The *Transmission Control Protocol* defines how the information will be broken up into packets and sent across the Internet. Imagine ripping the first three pages out of this book and sending them to a friend. If you put the first page on a bus, mailed the second at the Post Office, and sent the last via Federal Express, the pages would get to your

friend at different times and in the wrong order. Your friend would have to check the page numbers to put the pages in a readable order. TCP handles packets of information in a similar way. It can't always guarantee that information arrives all at once, so it makes sure that each packet is recombined in the correct order. (It also checks each packet for errors.)

Understanding Domain Names

As you just learned, every single computer on the Internet has an IP address. I'd hate to try to remember the IP address of every computer, though. Thankfully, there's a friendlier way to address a computer, called a *domain name.* Remember Que's IP address (**206.246.150.10**)? The domain name for that host is **www.mcp.com**—a lot easier, eh?

A *domain name* consists of two or more words separated by dots, like this: *host.second-level.first-level*. You'll see first-level domains, like **com** or **uk**, which indicate the type or organization or even the country in which the organization exists. Table b.1 describes the first-level domains you find in use in the United States. The second-level domain identifies the organization. The only information that the Internet needs in order to route information to the host computer is the first and second-level domains. The host computer might use the host part of the domain to route information to other computers on the network, though.

Table 1.1 First-Level Domain Names

Name	Description
COM	Commercial and for-profit organizations
ORG	Miscellaneous and nonprofit organizations
NET	Internet infrastructure and service providers
EDU	Universities that grant 4-year degrees
GOV	Federal government agencies

NOTE In the future, you'll see more top-level domains with endings like **WEB**, **BIZ**, and so on. ■

Understanding PPP and SLIP

To connect your computer to an Internet Service Provider, you use one of two *connection protocols:* PPP or SLIP. PPP stands for *Point to Point Protocol* and SLIP stands for *Serial Line Interface Protocol.* Most Internet Service Providers use PPP. A connection protocol like PPP lets your computer communicate with the service provider's network computer so that your operating system thinks that it's physically connected. The networking protocols that work on top of PPP, like TCP/IP, don't even realize that they're using a serial connection to the network instead of a plain old network adapter card.

Connecting to the Internet with a Modem

Most folks use a modem to make a PPP connection to an Internet Service Provider through the telephone line. A modem takes digital data and transmits it as an analog signal through the telephone line (*modulation*). A modem on the other end of the line takes the analog signal off the telephone line and turns it back into digital data (*demodulation*). External modems, which come in a separate box that you connect to your computer's serial port with a serial cable, and internal modems, which are cards that you plug into one of your computer's open expansion slots, both are popular.

Modems come with a variety of capabilities. Most modems sold these days are 33.6Kbps or 56Kbps (bits per second), but slower modems like 28.8Kbps still exist. Buy a 56Kbps modem if you can afford it. Many Internet Service Providers still don't support 56Kbps modems, but you can bet that your service provider will get up-to-speed in short order. Make sure that any modem you buy is "Hayes Compatible," which means that the modem understands a standard set of instructions that most every communication program uses.

Ask your Internet Service Provider what type of modem they recommend. You'll be better off if you match your modem to their modems so that you can avoid any incompatibilities. Some modems just don't talk well together.

Connecting to the Internet with ISDN

ISDN stands for *Integrated Services Digital Network*. It's a relatively high-speed connection to the Internet. You can connect at 64Kbps (one bearer channel, or 1B) or 128Kbps (two bearer channels, or 2B). ISDN requires special service from your telephone company, an ISDN terminal adapter (like a modem), and ISDN service from your Internet Service Provider.

ISDN isn't quite what it's cracked up to be. First, it can be terribly expensive. Some telephone companies have the nerve to charge a per-minute fee for using ISDN. And if you don't live in an area that's directly serviced by ISDN, you have to pay additional monthly fees. Not only is ISDN expensive, it's sometimes difficult to install, even for the phone company.

If you want to try ISDN service, arrange installation through your Internet Service Provider. The service provider can set up installation at your site with the telephone company, sell you the hardware, and provide you an ISDN connection on their end. Better still, most service providers have worked out special deals with the local telephone companies to give consumers a break.

Watch for *ADSL* (Digital Subscriber Loop). Whereas ISDN uses 90 year-old technology to deliver digital data, ADSL uses technology that was invented to provide video-on-demand. It's new and it's fast.

Connecting to the Internet via Your Cable Company

In some parts of the United States, television cable companies are providing Internet access. Internet access via the cable network is still experimental, though. Check with your local cable company to see if they do offer or intend to offer this service in your area.

Here's how it works. The cable company comes to your home and installs some special equipment and additional cables. The equipment splits the cable signal into two parts: one goes to the TV and the other to your computer. Then, they install a special network card in your computer and configure your computer to access the Internet via that network card.

You might be able to access the Internet via your Digital Satellite System (check with your DSS broadcaster). If so, you can receive information from the Internet at lightning fast speeds via your satellite receiver, while transmitting information at slower speeds via your telephone line.

Using an Internet Shell Account

You can access an Internet shell account by using terminal emulation software such as HyperTerminal, which Windows 95 provides. A shell account lets you execute commands on a computer that's directly connected to the Internet. Your computer is a dumb terminal, however, in that all it does is feed keystrokes to the remote computer and display the text (on your screen) that the remote computer sends back.

Shell accounts are completely text-based. They don't give you any menus or icons to click—just some archaic commands that you type on a UNIX command line. Downloading files is even painful on a shell account because you have to transfer it to your home directory on the remote computer first, and then download it from the remote computer to your computer. Using the Lynx Web browser, to which you have access via your shell account, is almost fruitless because it doesn't support graphics and supports few, if any, of the HTML extensions commonly used these days.

A shell account should be your last resort when seeking Internet access. If you currently rely on a shell account as your only means of Internet access, ditch it in favor of PPP access. If you currently have PPP access, though, check to see if you do have shell access as well. Shell access is a good complement to PPP access because it gives you an easy way to check your Internet mail while you're traveling.

Which Windows Do You Use?

If you're using Windows 3.1 and you can afford to upgrade to Windows 95, I strongly recommend it. Here's why:

- Windows 95 has Internet access built right in, whereas Windows 3.1 requires you to go outside the operating system to get onto the Internet.

- If you use Windows 3.1, you don't have access to all the resources available to Windows 95 and Windows NT users because some programs and features are available only on those platforms.

Here's some of the ways Windows 95 supports the Internet:

- Windows 95 is a networking operating system, which includes support for a variety of network adapters and protocols, such as TCP/IP.
- Windows 95 includes Dial-Up Networking, which allows you to connect to a network, such as the Internet, via the phone lines.
- Windows 95 includes plenty of other Internet utilities, such as a Web browser, FTP, and Telnet, to get you started.

Pick Your Internet Service

This book and CD-ROM comes complete with the nationally known Internet Service Providers: Earth Link Network and AT&T World Net Service. Both are discussed in Chapters 2 and 3.

CHAPTER 2

Connecting to the Internet with AT&T WorldNet℠ Service

- Installing AT&T WorldNet Service
- Connecting to AT&T WorldNet Service
- Browsing the Web with AT&T WorldNet Service
- Sending and receiving e-mail with AT&T WorldNet Service
- Accessing newsgroups with AT&T WorldNet Service

The Internet is fast becoming one of the communication tools of choice in both today's business and personal world. It seems that it's more important than ever to have your own connection to the Internet.

Personal and professional contacts want to send you e-mail. A colleague tells you about a great new Web site where he found cheap airline tickets for his upcoming vacation. You hear about an online chat group that has been having some very lively discussions concerning your favorite hobby.

A number of online services and Internet Service Providers exist that can get you online. One of the newest entries into this market is AT&T WorldNet Service. All you need to connect to this service is a modem and the software included with this book. AT&T WorldNet Service provides you with access to all the popular Internet information routes, such as World Wide Web browsing, Internet e-mail, and Internet newsgroups. ■

Installing AT&T WorldNet Service

The latest edition of AT&T WorldNet Service software is included on the CD-ROM that accompanies this book. To install the software and connect to AT&T WorldNet Service, place the CD in your CD-ROM drive.

1. Click the Start button and choose Run from the menu. In the Run box, type **D:\s121ie**. Then click OK.

Your CD-ROM drive may be designated as a different drive letter, so be sure to reference the correct drive when running the file in step 1.

2. The file supplied is a compressed archive and contains all the files you need to get the AT&T WorldNet Service software up and running. The WinZip Self Extractor Window opens. Click OK to continue.
3. The Self Extractor unzips all the files that are necessary to continue the installation process. The files are temporarily held in your C:\TEMP directory; click Unzip to continue.

If you want to extract the files to another directory, change the directory name and location in the Self Extractor's directory box.

4. After the files are unzipped and you are notified that the process is complete, click OK to close the notification box. To close the Self Extractor box, click Close.
5. Now you are ready to run the installation files for AT&T WorldNet Service. Click the Start button and then click Run. In the Run box, type **C:\TEMP\setup** (and be sure to designate the directory to which you unzipped the files), and then click OK.
6. The AT&T WorldNet Setup window appears, as shown in Figure 2.1. You can click the Browse button to change the folder in which the files should be installed. If you want to go with the default folder, click the OK button.

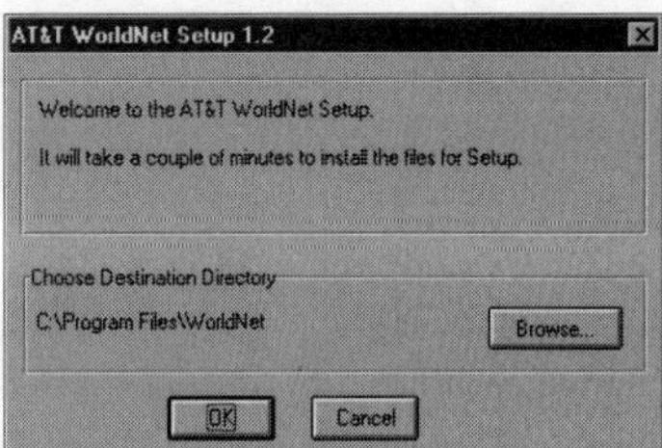

FIG. 2.1
The AT&T WorldNet Setup screen allows you to select the directory in which you want the AT&T WorldNet files placed.

7. The software is installed in the selected folder and the AT&T WorldNet Service Setup window opens.

The setup program walks you through three different sets of steps. You will

- Set up your modem to work with AT&T WorldNet Service
- Register your account with AT&T WorldNet Service
- Install a Web browser for use with the service

NOTE A customized version of Internet Explorer 3 comes with the AT&T WorldNet Service software included in the CD-ROM.

Setting Up Your Modem

The first step in configuring AT&T WorldNet Service for use on your computer is to set up your modem. Your modem needs to dial into AT&T WorldNet Service for you to connect to the Internet.

1. At the first screen of the AT&T WorldNet Service Setup screen (see Figure 2.2), click the Next button.

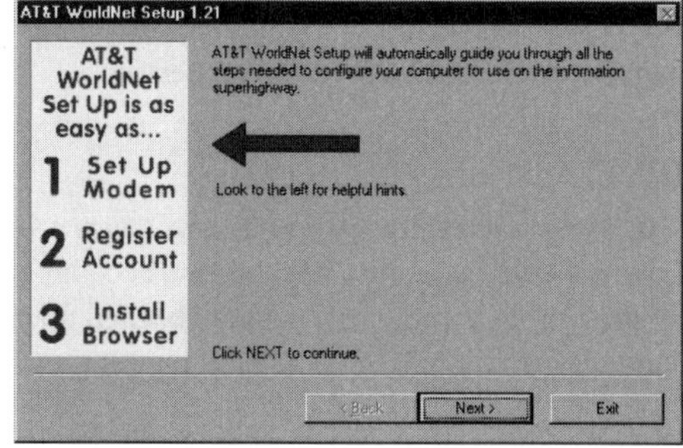

FIG. 2.2
The AT&T WorldNet Setup program helps you configure your modem, your AT&T WorldNet account, and your Web browser.

2. A list of the modems installed on your PC appears on the next screen. Select the modem that you want to use to connect to the service. In most cases, you will have only one modem installed on your computer. Click Next to continue.
3. In the next step, you are prompted to provide the phone number that you are calling from. This allows the Setup program to identify a local number that you can use to dial into the service. Provide your phone number, as shown in Figure 2.3, and then click Next.

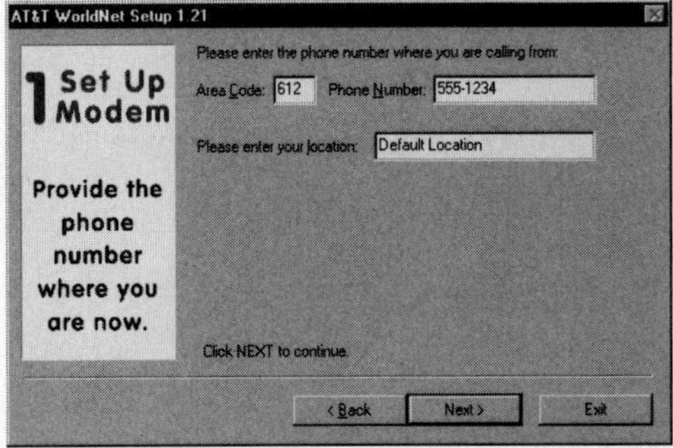

FIG. 2.3
Providing your area code and phone number helps the Setup program identify a local number that you can use to access the AT&T WorldNet Service.

4. The Next screen asks you to designate the type of dialing you use (tone or pulse), as well as other dialing parameters, such as dialing a 1 before a long distance number or any number you may have to dial to access an outside line (if you call from an office). Designate the appropriate responses by clicking the radio dial button for each selection. When you finish making your choices, click Next to continue.

After you designate your modem and the dial-in properties that you want to use, you are done with the first part of the AT&T WorldNet Service configuration. In the second part of the setup process, you register a new account for AT&T WorldNet Service.

Registering Your Account

The account portion of the Setup process allows you to start a new account or transfer an existing AT&T WorldNet account to your computer. The existing account can be an account that you used on another computer or an account that you had backed up on the current computer but lost as a result of a hard disk problem.

1. Select the type of account you want to install on the computer: a new account, an account from another computer, or an account from a backup file. Use the radio dial buttons, as shown in Figure 2.4, to make your choice, and then click the Next button to continue.

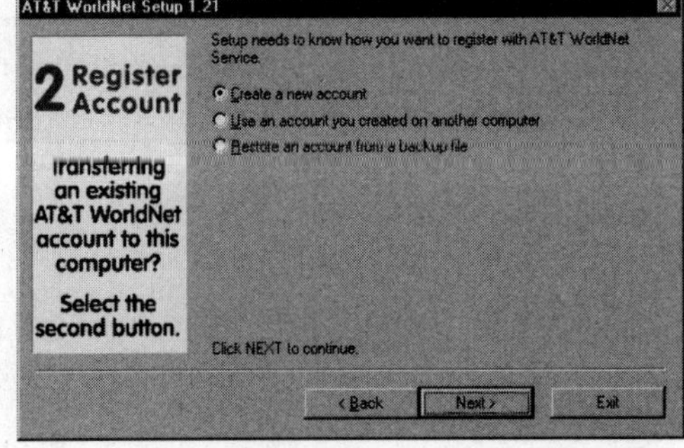

FIG. 2.4
The AT&T WorldNet Setup program allows you to start a new AT&T WorldNet account or install a previous account to your computer.

2. The Setup program dials a toll-free number to start the new account process. Make sure that you have a credit card and a blank disk ready. Then click the Next button.
3. The Setup software uses the toll-free number to connect. Once connected, you see a list of local numbers (based on the dialing information you provided in the first part of the setup procedure) for your use in connecting with AT&T WorldNet Service. Select a local number and then click Next.

If a local number does not exist for your calling area, you can select the toll-free number that appears in the list.

4. In the next step in the process, you are given the option of selecting a backup number for use when connecting to the service. You can choose to have the primary number serve as the backup, or you can select a second number from the numbers listed as your backup. Use the radio buttons to make your choice, and then click Next.
5. The choices that you have been made are recorded and you are taken to a screen where you can become a new member of the service or activate a previously existing account (there is also a button to hang up). Click the appropriate button, such as "I want to be a new member."
6. The Next screen asks you to enter your registration code, which is listed in the appendix of this book. After you enter the code, click Next to continue.
7. You are then asked to accept the AT&T WorldNet Service agreement before continuing. Scroll down to read the agreement, and then click the Yes radio button. Click Next to continue.
8. The next screen asks you to specify whether you use AT&T as your long distance phone company. Click the Yes or No radio button and then click Next.
9. The next screen asks you to choose a pricing plan for your service. Choose one of two price plans: unlimited usuage access or hourly usage access. Make your choice as shown in Figure 2.5, and then click Next.

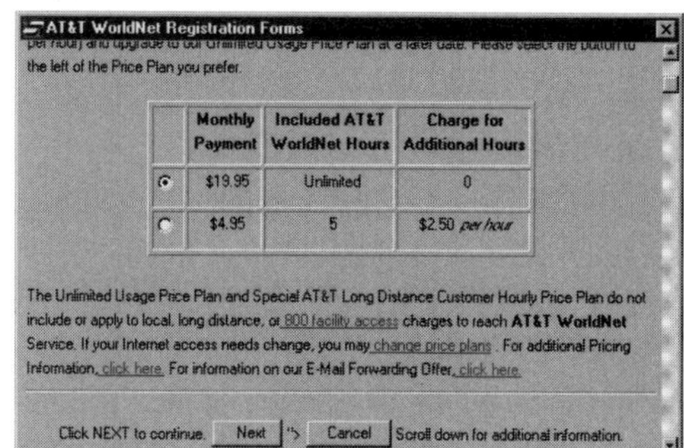

FIG. 2.5
The AT&T WorldNet Service provides more than one price plan for all members.

10. The next screen asks you for your name, address, and other personal information. Fill out the appropriate boxes and then click the Next button.

It's easy to move from text box to text box on the registration screen by using the Tab key to move forward and Shift+Tab to move backward.

11. The next screen asks you to enter your credit card information. After doing so, click Next.
12. You are asked to provide the e-mail name that you will use with AT&T WorldNet Service. You can use up to 46 characters (no spaces). You can use your name, a nickname, or whatever you like. You also are asked to designate a password to use to connect to your e-mail account. Choose something that you can remember, but not something that is easy for others to guess. After you choose the e-mail name and password, click Next.

NOTE The e-mail name that you choose will be part of your e-mail address only on AT&T WorldNet Service. Your e-mail address will actually look like **yourname@worldnet.att.net**.

13. The next screen asks you to choose a password to use when you connect to AT&T WorldNet Service. The password can be up to 16 characters and, again, should be something that you can remember but others can't guess. After you enter your password, click Next.
14. AT&T WorldNet Service includes you in a member directory if you want. Click Yes to be included in the directory (and No if you do not want to be included), and then click Next.
15. The last screen in the registration process shows you your e-mail name, your e-mail password, and your security sign-on password. If these are all correct, click Register Now to complete the registration process.
16. Setup then offers to back up your registration information to a floppy disk if you want. Click the "Your account information will be saved to" check box and then specify your floppy drive. Insert a disk in your drive and click Next.

The last part of the AT&T WorldNet Setup entails installing your Internet software, such as your Web browser.

Installing Your Web Browser

AT&T WorldNet Service software comes with a customized Web browser, Microsoft Internet Explorer. If you do not currently have Explorer on your computer, you will want to install the software now. If the software is already on your computer, AT&T WorldNet Service can configure the Web browser to work with the AT&T WorldNet Service.

1. Choose whether to install the AT&T WorldNet Service customized Internet Explorer browser or to configure the current copy of Internet Explorer on your PC. These steps assume a fresh install. After you make your selection, click Next.

CAUTION

If you already have an Internet Service Provider (ISP) set up on your computer, AT&T WorldNet Service Setup program overwrites your current settings. To restore the old ISP settings, use the Restore Previous ISP settings in the AT&T WorldNet Program group on the Start menu.

2. The Internet Explorer files are then extracted. You are prompted to specify a folder for the Internet Explorer software, as shown in Figure 2.6. If you want to choose the default, C:\Program Files, click OK.

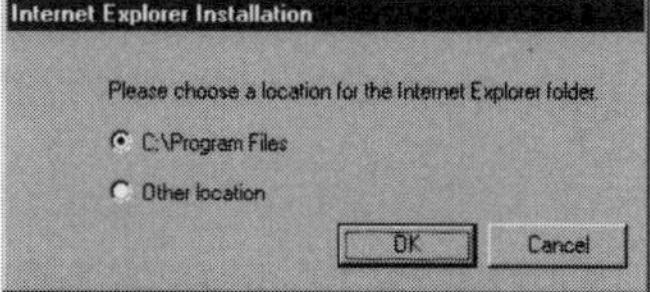

FIG. 2.6
You can specify the folder in which you would like to have the Internet Explorer software placed.

3. The Internet Explorer software (including Internet Mail and Internet News) is installed on your computer. To complete the installation, click Yes to restart your computer.
4. After your computer restarts, the final screen of the setup program appears. Click Finish to complete the process.

Connecting to AT&T WorldNet Service

When you install AT&T WorldNet Service on your PC, it places a shortcut for the service on your desktop. You can start the service via clicking the icon or by accessing the AT&T WorldNet Program group on your Start menu.

1. Double-click the AT&T WorldNet icon on your desktop. The AT&T WorldNet Connection Manager appears, as shown in Figure 2.7. Click Connect.
2. The local access number for AT&T WorldNet Service is dialed and your modem connects to the service. A dialog box appears, showing the connection speed, time online, and the connection number. The dialog box also provides you with a Disconnect button, which you can use to log off from the service.

FIG. 2.7
The AT&T WorldNet Connection Manager uses your modem to get you online.

As soon as the Connection Manager appears, Microsoft Internet Explorer is loaded. You are now ready to browse the Web using the AT&T WorldNet Service.

Browsing the Web with AT&T WorldNet Service

When you're online with AT&T WorldNet Service and your browser is up and running, you're ready to take advantage of all the connections on the World Wide Web. AT&T WorldNet Service uses a customized version of Microsoft Internet Explorer 3.01 as its Web browser.

When you connect to AT&T WorldNet Service and Internet Explorer opens, you are taken to the AT&T WorldNet Service home page. This page gives members access to links that offer special content as well as links to hot spots on the Web. You can also get information on your account as well as help troubleshooting your connection with AT&T WorldNet Service (see Figure 2.8).

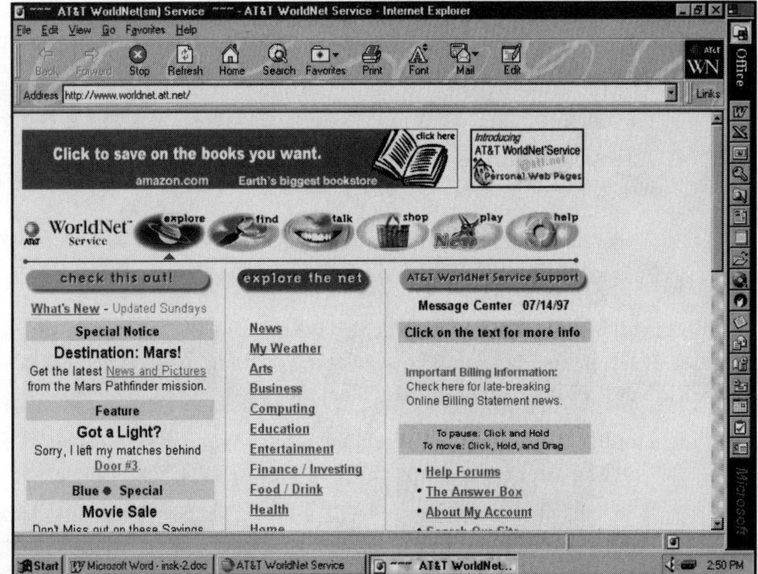

FIG. 2.8 AT&T WorldNet Service provides you with all the features of the powerful and easy-to-use Web browser, Microsoft Internet Explorer.

The AT&T WorldNet home page offers quick links to Web search engines, Internet directories, and Chat, as well as access to online shopping through AT&T Market Square®. AT&T WorldNet Service also provides its members the opportunity to create and publish their own AT&T WorldNet personal Web page.

1. To search the Web, click the find icon at the top of the AT&T WorldNet home page. You can access all the popular Web search engines from this page. Select your favorite search engine, type in your search string, and click the Search button, as shown in Figure 2.9.

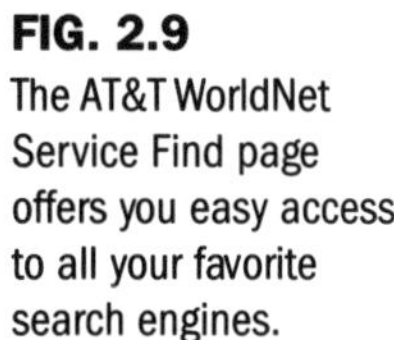

FIG. 2.9
The AT&T WorldNet Service Find page offers you easy access to all your favorite search engines.

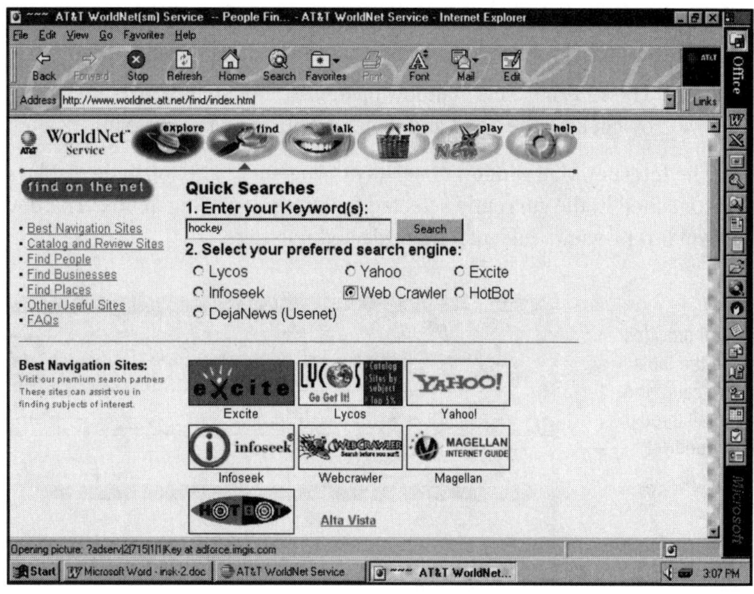

TIP The AT&T WorldNet Find page also offers links to sites that you can use to find people, business, and places.

2. Your search results page appears in the Web browser window. Click any of the links to explore the results of your search.

Sending and Receiving E-Mail with the AT&T WorldNet Service

Sending e-mail with AT&T WorldNet Service is very straightforward and quite easy. Internet Explorer has an integrated e-mail client called Internet Mail. You can access the e-mail client directly from the Internet Explorer window, or you can start the Internet Mail software from its icon on the Start menu.

Internet Mail was configured for your AT&T WorldNet Service e-mail account during the AT&T WorldNet Service installation process. That means it's ready to start sending and receiving e-mail. Internet Mail provides such features as a spell checker, as well as an address book that you can use to keep track of all your important e-mail contacts.

Accessing Internet Mail via Explorer

Since Internet Explorer has an integrated e-mail client—Internet Mail—you can send and receive e-mail while you browse the Web. You just have to be connected to AT&T WorldNet Service and have Internet Explorer up and running.

1. With the Internet Explorer window open, click the Mail and News icon on the Explorer toolbar. From the drop-down list, select Read Mail.
2. The Internet Mail Window opens, as shown in Figure 2.10. You can check for new e-mail by clicking the Send and Receive button on the toolbar.

The Internet Mail window consists of two panes. The top pane displays the messages that are contained in the currently selected folder, such as your Inbox. The bottom pane of the mail window previews the currently selected message.

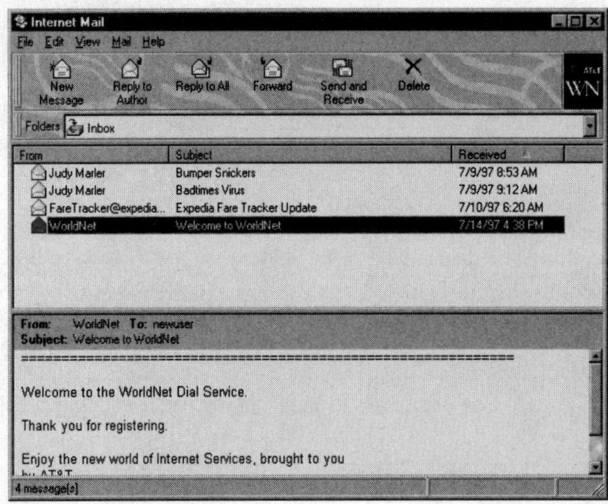

FIG. 2.10
Internet Mail provides you with all the tools you need to send and receive e-mail through your AT&T WorldNet account.

Internet Mail typically opens to your Inbox; this is where your new e-mail appears when you click the Send and Receive button. The drop-down folder box also allows you to switch from your Inbox and view other folders, such as your Deleted Items, Sent, and Outbox folders.

The Internet Mail toolbar not only allows you to check for new e-mail and send the e-mail that you compose, but it also gives you the ability to easily create new messages, reply to messages that you receive, and forward messages to other e-mail addresses.

To forward a message to another e-mail address, click the Forward button, and then supply the new e-mail address in the To: box. Click Send and the message is on its way.

Reading Your New Mail

New mail messages appear in the Inbox in bold. The mail icon to the left of the message's subject line is also closed. To read the new message, you can

1. Click the message to read it in the preview pane. Scroll down through the message as necessary.
2. You can also open a separate window to view the message. Double-click the message. A message window appears, as shown in Figure 2.11.

3. When you are in the message window, you can reply to the message, forward the message, or delete the message, by using the buttons on the toolbar.
4. To close the message window, click its Close button.

FIG. 2.11
Double-click to open a separate window for your newly received e-mail message.

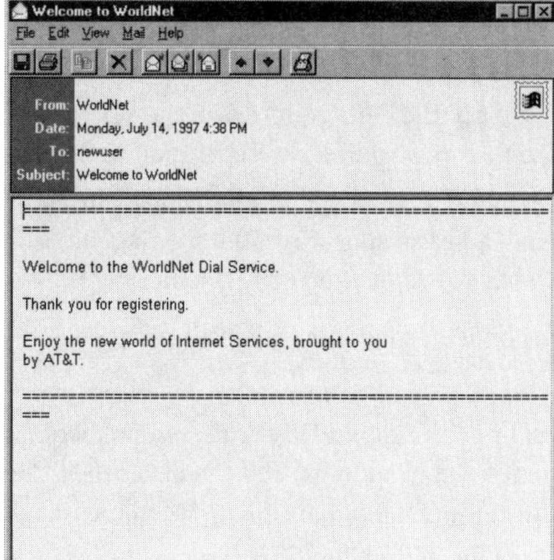

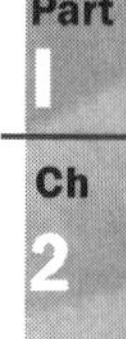

Sending New Mail

Composing and sending new e-mail using Internet Explorer is also a snap. You can even spell-check your new messages before you send them.

In the main Internet Mail window, click the New Message button. A window appears for your new message, as shown in Figure 2.12.

FIG. 2.12
Before you compose your new e-mail message, be sure to address it and give it a subject.

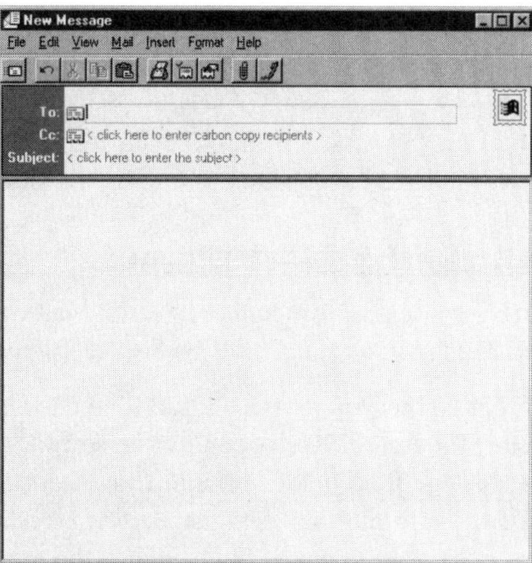

After you open the new message window, you can address the e-mail, give it a subject, and actually compose the message itself. The new message window is divided into two distinct panes: the Address pane and the Message pane.

The Address pane is where you designate the e-mail address (or addresses) to which you want to send the message and specify the subject of the e-mail message. You can actually send your message to e-mail addresses in two different ways:

- **To:** This is where you place the e-mail address of the primary recipient of the message. You can include more than one address by separating them with a space.
- **CC:** This allows you copy (CC stands for carbon copy) the message to another e-mail address. The CC e-mail address appears on the message that the primary recipient receives, as well as others to whom you copy the message.

An e-mail message requires only a To: address before it may be sent. To address and give your new message a subject:

1. Place the insertion point to the right of the address book icon in the To: box, and then type the main recipient's e-mail address. You can also select the address from your address book; click the Address Book icon. Double-click the address that you want to select in the Address Book, and then click OK.
2. Place e-mail addresses in the CC: if appropriate. You can move to the CC: box by clicking it or by pressing the Tab key.
3. After you address the message, be sure to type a subject in the subject box. When other people receive your e-mail messages, the subject line appears in their Inboxes. If you don't include a subject line, it makes your message to them mysterious and nondescript.
4. Compose your message in the message pane of the window. After you complete the address, subject, and message, click the Send button. The message is then placed in your Outbox.

If you're online (which you probably are if you started Internet Mail via the Internet Explorer toolbar), click the Send and Receive button to send your e-mail to the AT&T WorldNet mail server. A status box shows you the progress of the sending of your message. After the message is sent, you will find that a copy of it has been placed in your Sent box. Just click the Folder button in the Internet Mail window to check your Sent messages.

Accessing Internet Mail via the Start Menu

You can also send and receive new e-mail by opening Internet Mail via the Windows Start menu. So, you don't necessarily have to launch Internet Explorer to use your e-mail client.

Just click the Start menu, point at the Programs icon, and then click Internet Mail on the Program menu. If you didn't start the AT&T Service connection software by double-clicking the desktop icon, you can now work in Internet Mail offline. This means that you can read any messages that you received earlier while you were connected to AT&T WorldNet Service. You can also compose new messages while you are offline. Follow the same steps that you used earlier in this chapter to compose and send a new message.

The only major difference between working online and offline is what happens when you click the Send and Receive button. When you are online, Internet Mail connects immediately to the AT&T WorldNet mail server and receives your new e-mail and sends any messages that you had in your Outbox.

When you are working offline and click the Send and Receive button on the Internet Mail toolbar, the AT&T WorldNet connection box opens as shown in Figure 2.13. All you have to do is click OK.

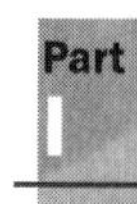

FIG. 2.13
The AT&T WorldNet Connection Manager connects you to your e-mail server when you click Send and Receive while offline.

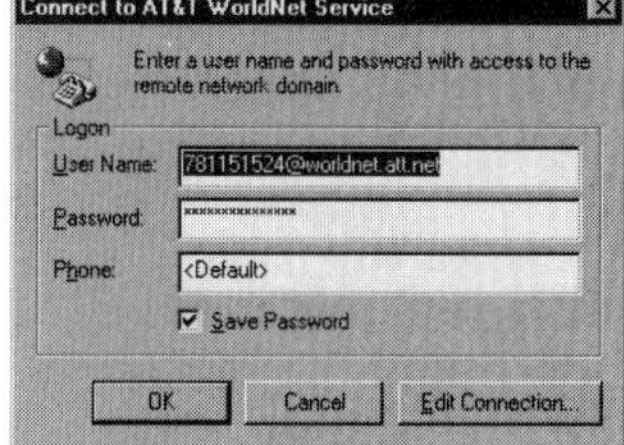

You are connected to the AT&T WorldNet Service and any new e-mail waiting for you on the mail server is placed in your Inbox. Messages that you have placed in your Outbox are sent on to the mail server and the various recipients on the Internet.

Accessing Newsgroups with AT&T WorldNet Service

You can also access Internet Usenet Newsgroups via the AT&T WorldNet Service. Newsgroups are very much like electronic bulletin boards where you can post and read messages that others have posted about a particular subject or area of interest. Huge numbers of newsgroups exist, focusing on everything from skydiving to Barney the dinosaur.

AT&T WorldNet Service offers thousands of newsgroups for your perusal. The Internet Explorer installation provided you with a newsreader—Microsoft's Internet News reader. The reader is integrated with Internet Explorer, just as the Internet Mail client was.

This means that you can read your newsgroups by using Internet News while you're browsing the Web with Explorer, or you can start Internet News by itself via the Start button.

Launching Internet News from Explorer

When you are connected to AT&T WorldNet Service and browsing the Web using Internet Explorer, you can quickly launch the Internet News reader and connect to the newsgroups that AT&T WorldNet Service subscribes to.

N O T E Your Internet News reader is configured for the AT&T WorldNet News service when you install the service and Internet Explorer.

1. Click the Mail button on the Internet Explorer toolbar.
2. Select Read News from the menu that appears, to start the Internet News reader.

The first time that you start the newsreader, it connects to the AT&T WorldNet News server and downloads a list of all the newsgroups that are available, as shown in Figure 2.14. You can subscribe to a newsgroup by selecting it on the list and then clicking the Subscribe button.

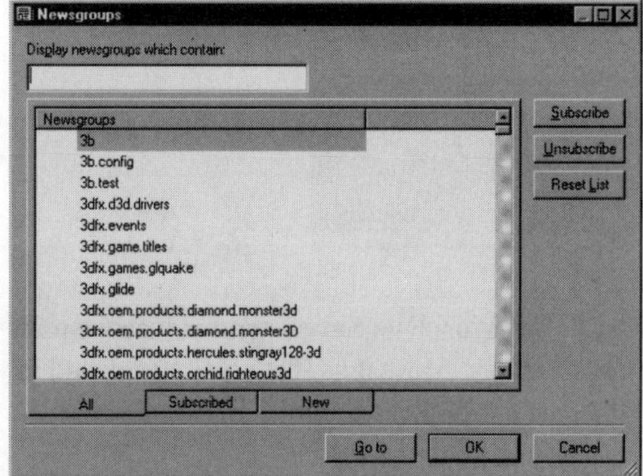

FIG. 2.14
Your newsreaders lists all the newsgroups available on the AT&T WorldNet News server.

By subscribing to groups, you can view a much smaller subset of all the newsgroups that the reader lists. To view your the groups that you have subscribed to, click the Subscribed tab in the Newsgroups window.

Reading Newsgroup Postings

To read the postings in a particular newsgroup on the list or in the subscribed to list, just select the particular group and then click GoTo.

The most current posts are downloaded for the groups and displayed in the Reader window. To read a particular post, scroll down through the list and then click that post.

You can also view a post in a separate window by double-clicking a particular posting in the Reader window.

The actual post message appears in the Preview pane of the Reader window, as shown in Figure 2.15. You can respond to the post by clicking the Reply to Group button on the toolbar. You can reply directly to the author of the post by clicking the Reply to Author button.

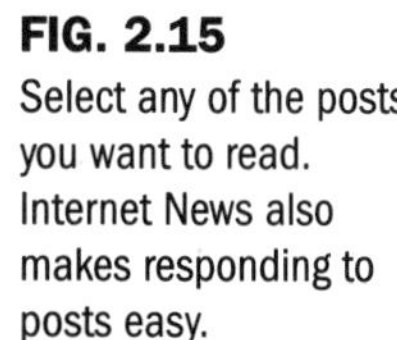

FIG. 2.15
Select any of the posts you want to read. Internet News also makes responding to posts easy.

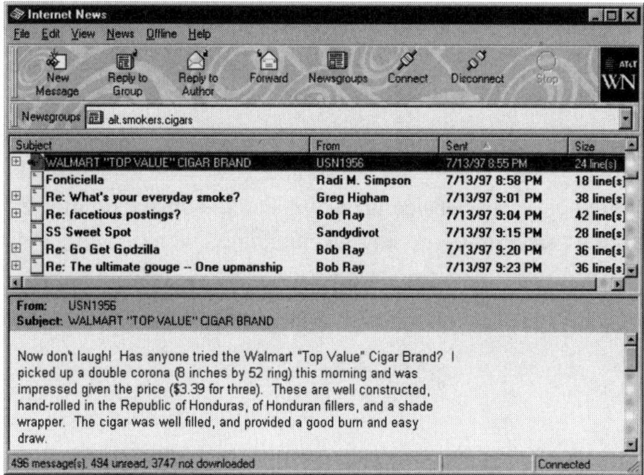

CAUTION

You might want to read the posts in a newsgroup for a period of time before participating in posts and responses to authors of other posts via e-mail. Newsgroups can be very unusual places and it's best to be a *lurker* (a non-responding reader) for a while, until you get an idea of what a given group is all about and what its particular "rules of engagement" are.

You can switch between the groups that you have subscribed to via the Newsgroup drop-down box. Click the drop-down arrow and select from the list of groups shown.

Connecting to the News Reader via the Start Menu

You can also connect to the Internet News software without double-clicking the AT&T WorldNet icon on the desktop. Click the Start button, point at Programs, and then click the Internet News icon on the Program menu.

Internet News starts and immediately brings up the AT&T WorldNet Connection Manager. Click on Connect and you are connected to the service. The latest posts are downloaded for the active newsgroup on the News reader. This means that the group you were perusing the last time you used the News reader is updated with any new posts that have occurred.

It's easy to tell the new posts from the posts that you have read. New posts display in bold, whereas read messages do not. Internet News allows you to print and save the posts. Select the message that you want to save or post, and then click the Reader's File menu.

A menu choice exists for Save Message and for Print. Make the appropriate selection and you can have a hard copy of a posting or save a posting to a special folder for later consideration. After you finish reading the posts in the various newsgroups, close the newsreader via the Close button.

Newsgroup posts are updated each time you connect to the service. Old posts eventually are deleted; so, if you see a post that you may want to refer to later, either print or save that post.

AT&T WorldNet Service's connection also allows you to connect to Internet Relay Chat conferences and other typical Internet information highway services—all the things that you would expect from your Internet Service Provider. The best place on the Web to get more information about what the AT&T WorldNet Service can do and what it offers you as an Internet Service Provider is **http://www.worldnet.att.net/**. ●

CHAPTER 3

Connecting to the Internet with EarthLink Network and Netscape

- What EarthLink Network is, and what Internet Service Providers like EarthLink actually do
- How your computer, modem, software, and phone connection work together to get you online
- Installing EarthLink's TotalAccess software on your operating system
- Troubleshooting your Internet connection and contacting EarthLink for assistance

The CD-ROM that accompanies this book includes an installer for EarthLink Network Total Access software. With this software, you can sign up for an Internet account with EarthLink and begin surfing the World Wide Web, sending e-mail, collecting free software programs and games, and generally, gaining access to the wealth of information and services that the Internet provides. ■

What Is EarthLink Network?

EarthLink Network is an ISP, and ISPs like EarthLink are in the business of connecting people to the Net. Companies like EarthLink sell access to the Internet, somewhat like telephone companies sell access to the phone system. Internet service providers maintain large, powerful computers called *servers*; on these computers, ISPs maintain e-mail boxes for their customers, store UseNet news articles, and house Web sites and FTP archives, and they provide customers with access to the fast-growing, global computer network known as the Internet.

EarthLink Network was founded in 1994 by a young entrepreneur named Sky Dayton. Initially, the company provided Internet access within Los Angeles and the Southern California region. However, in the years since its founding, the company has grown phenomenally (as have many Internet service providers—the Internet is nothing if not popular!), and EarthLink now offers access throughout the United States and Canada. The company has designed its own easy-to-use Internet software, which goes by the name of EarthLink TotalAccess (the very product included on your CD-ROM). EarthLink has also developed an extensive program of customer support and education: The company maintains a large Web site at **http://www.earthlink.net**, where customers can find information on a variety of Internet subjects, technical and otherwise. The EarthLink Web site also includes a daily Webzine called the *Daily bLink*. EarthLink provides customers with printed support materials, including a frequent newsletter, and a booklet distributed to new Internet users.

Why Choose EarthLink?

Well, first of all, you need an address on the Information Superhighway, if you want people to stop and visit! The Internet account that you obtain from an ISP identifies you to other Internet users and provides you with an address so you can send and receive electronic mail.

Before you can start traveling, you need to find a way onto the darned highway itself. The Internet is a computer network, remember; you have to find a way into a computer on that network before you can move around! Your home computer isn't connected to the Internet—it's connected to a modem, which is connected to a telephone line. All that hardware doesn't get you onto the Internet—it only gets you into the phone system. And the phone system is not the Internet!

Somehow, the computer signal you send into the phone system has to hop out off the phone line someplace, and hop onto the computer network of the Internet. This is where ISPs come in. They provide the missing link, by maintaining computer connections to the Internet and selling access to these connections. You might think of the ISP as the "on-ramp" to the Information Superhighway.

How Modem Signals Work

To put it simply, your computer creates electronic information in digital form. Unfortunately, electronic information must be in analog form to travel through telephone lines. A small device called a *modem* resolves the conflict, transforming the digital information coming from your computer—*modulating* it—so that it can travel across phone lines. The modem also processes analog data coming back to your computer from the phone line—*demodulating* it—so that your computer can make sense of the information it receives. (It is from this process—modulation/demodulation—that the modem gets its name.)

Digital information is composed of scores of separate *bits*, with each bit being read as either "on" or "off." Thousands, even millions, of these on/off bits compose a typical computer message. Analog information, on the other hand, takes the form of a continuously varying stream. (Picture the difference between musical reproduction on CDs versus music reproduction on record albums, and you get something of the idea.)

All right! So what does all this mumbo-jumbo tell us about Internet service providers? Well, just as your computer needs a modem to send signals back and forth between your computer and the telephone system, the computers that make up the Internet must also be connected to modems, so that the information they receive from telephone lines can be transformed, one more time, back into digital information that Internet computers can understand.

ISPs provide access to these modems at the other end of the telephone line. (Generally speaking, other people—schools, governments, companies—shoulder the main responsibility for maintaining the computers that comprise the Internet itself.) When an Internet service provider gives you a *dial-up number*—the telephone number that your modem uses to "call the Internet"—you are actually calling the phone number of a modem at the other end of the phone line, one that is translating for an Internet computer. You really can't get into the Internet without passing through these modems (unless you have access to the Net at work or at school, or unless you have a special high-speed connection). That is why you need an Internet service provider.

Points of Presence

Let's say that you live in Chicago. When you are at home, you make a local call to your Internet service provider and connect to the modems they maintain. But what do you do if you travel to New York City? You certainly can't call Chicago, long-distance, to connect to your ISP's modems back home. But you would like to have access to the Internet while you are in New York, to send e-mail and conduct business.

But the modem pools in New York—or in any other city, for that matter—aren't free! You can't just call up and connect. If you are in luck, your ISP maintains a modem pool in New York City, too. Otherwise, you must go to an Internet service provider in New York, and pay for an entirely new account.

Thankfully, most of the larger ISPs do in fact maintain a presence throughout the country. EarthLink is one such company, offering POPs (or *points-of-presence*, industry lingo for *local modem pools*) in almost every major city in the United States and Canada. After you establish an account with EarthLink, you can use your account to gain access to any POP the company operates. If you would like to see just how many POPs are available through EarthLink, you can take a look at their list, available at **http://www.earthlink.net/priv/dialuplist.html**.

POP, the abbreviation of "point of presence," is pronounced just the way it looks: pop.

That's the good news. The bad news is that not all POPs are of equal quality. In fact, a great many POPs aren't even maintained by the company that provides them. Most ISPs, including EarthLink, actually resell space on POPs that they themselves lease from a third-party, a company that is really in the business of maintaining modem banks. Given the great expense of setting up and maintaining modems, this arrangement is the only way that most ISPs can provide national service. Even that giant Internet content provider, America Online, leases POP access from third-parties.

This means that the specific quality of your Internet service depends, not only on the quality of the ISP to which you belong, but also on the specific quality of the modem banks in your town. A given company's service in Kansas may be dramatically different from that same company's service in Seattle. Quality may even vary between the local calling areas of a single city! (As a resident of Los Angeles, I can tell you that is certainly the case here!)

Installing EarthLink Network TotalAccess™ Software

The POP you use isn't the only factor that determines the quality of your Internet connection. The quality of the software that you use to connect to the Internet also plays a substantial role. EarthLink Network provides its customers with TotalAccess, Internet connection software designed by the company.

The CD-ROM included with this book contains the installation files you will need to get EarthLink Network TotalAccess™ software running on your computer. The CD-ROM includes software for the Windows 95 and Windows 3.x operating systems. The following steps describe the installation on Windows 95.

To begin the installation of TotalAccess, do the following:

1. Insert the CD-ROM into your drive.
2. Open the EarthLink folder.
3. Open the folder named for your operating system (in this case, the folder called Win95).
4. Open the file called Setup to begin the installation.

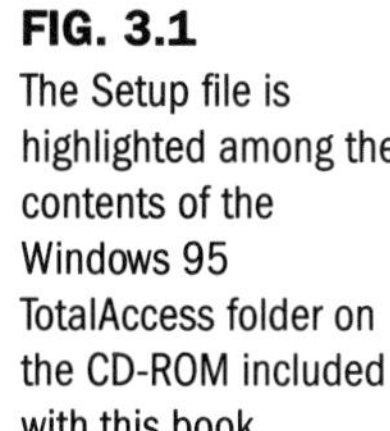

FIG. 3.1
The Setup file is highlighted among the contents of the Windows 95 TotalAccess folder on the CD-ROM included with this book.

After you open the Setup file, you are presented with a screen welcoming you to TotalAccess. Click OK to continue installation. The next screen tells you what you need to install the software:

- 15M of free disk space on your computer
- A modem connected to a phone line
- The credit card to which you want to bill your account
- Your original Windows 95 disks or CD-ROM, in case your computer needs any Win95 files during the installation

And, although the screen doesn't tell you this, you need at least 8M of RAM in your computer to operate TotalAccess.

Click Next. A screen asks you where you want to install TotalAccess. Pick a directory on your hard drive, and click Next. The installation software will then be placed onto your computer.

After TotalAccess transfers from the CD-ROM to your computer, a TotalAccess folder opens on your desktop. This folder includes

- A Read Me document for you to look at, if you like
- An EarthLink Internet Guide, in PDF format
- An Adobe Acrobat Setup installer, which installs the PDF reader you need to open the Internet Guide
- A Registration and Utilities program

A second window also opens, asking you if you want to set up an account. Click Yes. A general information form appears. Fill this out and click Next.

A new window appears, asking you to choose a username and a password for your Internet account.

Your username is your Internet "handle." It identifies you to everyone you encounter on the Internet. Your username can be anything you want, really, although there are certain restrictions you need to respect:

- It can consist only of letters and numbers—no punctuation marks or anything else out of the ordinary.
- It can be no longer than 12 characters in length.
- Many people use their first or last name as their username, or a combination of the two. As long as no one else who subscribes to your ISP is using the name you request, you generally get it.

You also are asked to select a password at this point in time. Again, you can choose anything you want. The real skill here is in choosing something fairly easy to remember but that no one else can figure out. The best passwords are six characters or longer, composed of letters and numbers. And whatever you do, don't use your name for a password, or something obvious, like the word "password."

Next, you are prompted to choose between two EarthLink pricing plans:

- TotalAccess USA, which costs $19.95 per month for unlimited Internet access, with no setup fee, and with 15 free days.
- TotalAccess800, for access over a 1-800 number. You should only select this plan if there is no local EarthLink POP for you to use. This option is more expensive: $24.95 per month for 5 hours of access, with an additional charge of $4.95 for each additional hour, with no setup fee.

From this setup window, you can also view the list of dial-up numbers that are available to you as an EarthLink subscriber.

Hang in there! We're almost done. The next screen asks you for your credit card information. After you enter it and click Next, TotalAccess automatically connects you to EarthLink via a toll-free number. Your account is registered and your modem is configured automatically. During this last part of the registration process, you also are asked to choose an EarthLink POP number for your local dial-up access.

Connecting to EarthLink

Now you are ready to start surfing the Internet! Whenever you want to connect to EarthLink, just turn on your modem, open up My Computer on your desktop, open the Dial-Up Networking folder, click the EarthLink entry, check your username and password, and click Connect. When you want to disconnect from the Internet, click Disconnect.

For Windows 3.x users, the process is a little, different. Open the TotalAccess folder installed on your computer, click the Internet Dialer, make sure that your username appears, and then click Connect. When you want to disconnect from the Internet, click Disconnect.

Changing Your Dial-Up Number

As mentioned earlier, EarthLink maintains POPs all across the United States and Canada that all of their subscribers can use to connect to the Internet. TotalAccess registration, however, configures your software to dial up your local number, and you have to change this number if you need to connect through a different POP.

To change your dial-up number:

1. Open the TotalAccess folder on your computer.
2. Click Registration & Utilities.
3. Select Dial-Up, and then Number.
4. A full list of access numbers will appear. Pick the one you want.

Then connect to EarthLink the way you normally would. Your computer dials the new number you have chosen.

You can also review EarthLink's entire list of POPs online, at the company's Web site. You may want to do this in advance, to get the most up-to-date numbers possible before your trip.

You'll find the list at **http://www.earthlink.net/priv/dialuplist.html**.

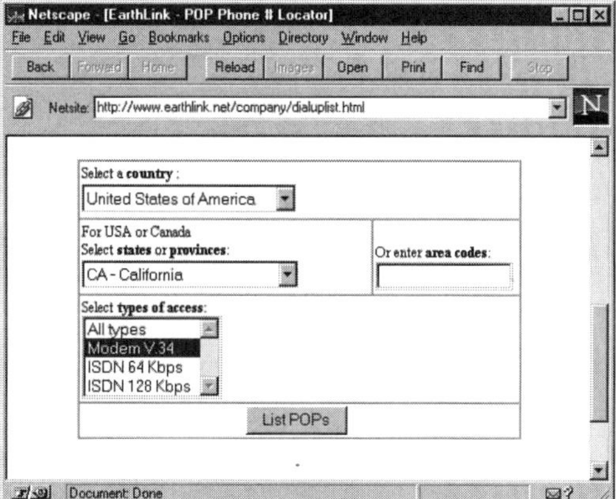

FIG. 3.2
The dial-up list available at EarthLink's Web site.

Updating Your EarthLink Account

Have you changed your address? Your phone number? Perhaps you want to charge your monthly bill to a different credit card number. Whatever change you want to make in your account, you can do easily with EarthLink's TotalAccess. Make sure that your modem is turned on, and then:

- Open the TotalAccess folder on your computer.
- Click Registration & Utilities.

- Click Account.
- Click Update.
- TotalAccess connects to EarthLink's registration server via a toll-free number. Change the information you want—you can even use this resource to change your password.

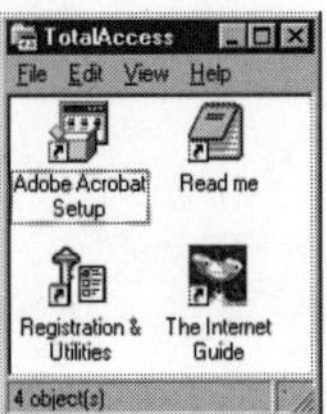

FIG. 3.3
The TotalAccess folder, including the Registration & Utilities file.

Troubleshooting Your Connection

Sometimes, even in the most perfectly planned computer applications, problems occur. TotalAccess is no exception. There are so many variables in the relationship between your computer's operating system, your modem, your phone company, and TotalAccess, that you may encounter some difficulties.

Luckily, technical support from EarthLink is easy to come by. If you indeed can get online, the company provides an extensive Web site (and it has real, live, non-technical content in addition to technical support.), at **http://www.earthlink.net/**. You can contact EarthLink Technical Support, as well as the company's billing and customer service operations, via the site, **http://www.earthlink.net/assistance/**. You can also get a live person to speak with, 24 hours a day, 7 days a week, by calling 1-800-395-8410. This number also connects you with the company's Fax-on-Demand system, if you think your problem can be solved through that resource. And, of course, you should also take a look at EarthLink's Internet Guide, which was installed in PDF format in your TotalAccess folder.

There are, however, some common problems that are easy to fix. Several of them are outlined in the following:

You get an error message that says: `Can't initialize your modem.`

First of all, make sure that your modem is turned on. If your modem is already on, try turning it off for a minute and turning it back on. If your modem is built into your computer, turn your entire computer off and then back on.

Windows 3.x users also should check to make sure that their modem is properly named in Modem Information.

You get an error message that says: `Modem already in use.`

Make sure your modem isn't being used by another program. Check as well to make sure you have assigned the correct COM port number to your modem. To check this

1. Open My Computer.
2. Open Control Panels.
3. Open Modems, and then Select Modem.
4. Open Properties.
5. Choose Port.

Windows 3.x users can find this information in Modem Information.

Your computer keeps locking up during registration connection via the toll-free number.

To fix this, you may have to lower the speed of your modem temporarily. It works more slowly during the registration, but it does work. To lower your modem speed

1. Open My Computer.
2. Open Control Panels.
3. Open Modems, and then Select Modem.
4. Open Properties.
5. Open Port, and set the Maximum Speed of the modem at 2400.
6. Remember to reset your modem's speed back to its original configuration after you have completed the registration process.

CHAPTER 4

Connecting to the Internet with AOL

- What kind of service AOL is
- How you can obtain AOL
- How you can connect to AOL through your existing Internet service provider
- How you can use AOL to access the resources of the Internet

In just seven short years, America Online has developed into the largest privately owned online service in the world. This chapter provides you with an overview of this monster company, placing particular emphasis on its Internet-based capabilities.

You will see that although AOL might not be the best way to access the Internet, it can serve as a good tool for learning how to navigate the online world. ■

Exploring AOL

America Online is an online service, providing a wide range of content to subscribers. However, AOL is not an Internet service provider, or ISP. Although AOL offers its subscribers a gateway to the Internet (primarily through e-mail and through the company's proprietary Web browser), Internet access is not AOL's primary aim. Rather, AOL strives to be a first-rate source of news, information, games, software, and other services.

AOL's easy to understand graphical interface makes online experience as simple as possible for its subscribers. One glance at AOL's opening screen says it all—here's a computer resource that you can negotiate just by clicking a mouse!

Online chat between AOL users remains one of the biggest draws on AOL, with the service hosting an array of chatrooms that range from the sublime to the ridiculous, and which provide opportunities to communicate for many special interest groups. Online shopping also is a significant source of interest on AOL, as it is now on the Internet generally.

Figure 4.1 shows the opening AOL screen.

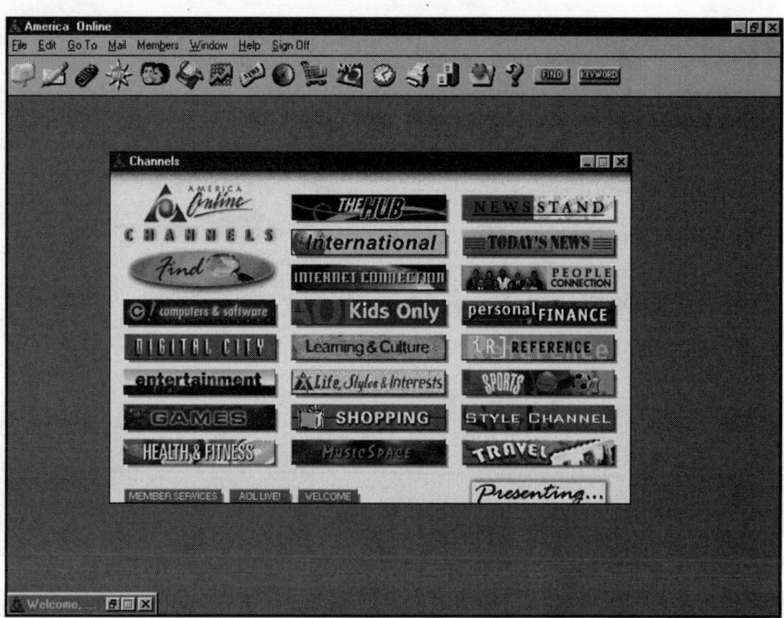

FIG. 4.1
The main AOL screen lists many popular areas, accessible with a quick click of a mouse.

You can reach the many different areas of the AOL site quickly by using online shortcuts called *keywords*. To reach the keyword window, you press Ctrl+K on a PC keyboard or Command+K on a Mac. Enter the keyword for the area that you want to reach on AOL, click Go, and you're there! If you want, just type "keyword" into this window to get a list of all the keywords and where they take you.

Let's visit some of the more popular areas on AOL:

- **People Connection (PC).** People Connection is a large collection of chat lobbies and public rooms. You can talk about any subject under the sun, from aviation, to your local town, to... well, take a look and see!
- **The Shopping Area, keyword Shopping.** Coffee fans can buy coffee-related items from Starbucks, flowers from 1-800-FLOWERS, or cosmetics from Avon.
- **Files, Files, Files, keyword Filesearch.** This area is the reason that I use AOL. It has a very large file base of freeware and shareware, not to mention software of the more expensive variety—along with a very good search engine to help you find what you need.
- **Internet on AOL, keyword Internet.** The Internet-related features of AOL still work more slowly than they do if you have a "real" connection to the Internet (through an ISP), but you still can get online.

This short list is intended merely to suggest to you all that AOL has to offer. Of course, amidst all this plenty, AOL does have a downside. As most people probably know, the company has been struggling since late 1996, when it began charging users a low monthly fee instead of an hourly rate. AOL usage increased so much under this new pricing plan that people had trouble even getting online, and service plummeted; however, AOL's health is improving.

NOTE If you enjoy chatting online, remember that AOL does not grant absolute free speech to its chat room users. Unlike true Internet chat (such as IRC), AOL chat is monitored, by roving "Guides." If a Guide catches you using "inappropriate" language, you can have your service terminated.

Installing AOL

If you want to subscribe to AOL, you can call them at 1-800-827-6364, or you can use one of the many disks circulated widely by the company through direct mail and magazines. If you have a friend who uses AOL, get them to sign you on (through the keyword Friend)—if you do, they get a $20 credit!

Of course, the quickest way to join AOL is to download the software directly from their sign-up page:

http://www.aol.com/try/

After you download AOL, you have to double-click the AOL setup95.exe file (in Windows), or an Install AOL icon (in Macintosh) to start the installation. When you install from a disk (or from a CD-ROM), you simply open the disk (or CD-ROM) and double-click the install file.

Now, you are ready to set up your connection to AOL. First, the ***install/setup*** program prompts you to choose a local phone number. At the AOL Web site, the download page also features a way for you to search for the number that would best serve your needs. Figure 4.2 shows the results of one such search. You can type in your state, town, or area code to generate a list of local phone numbers.

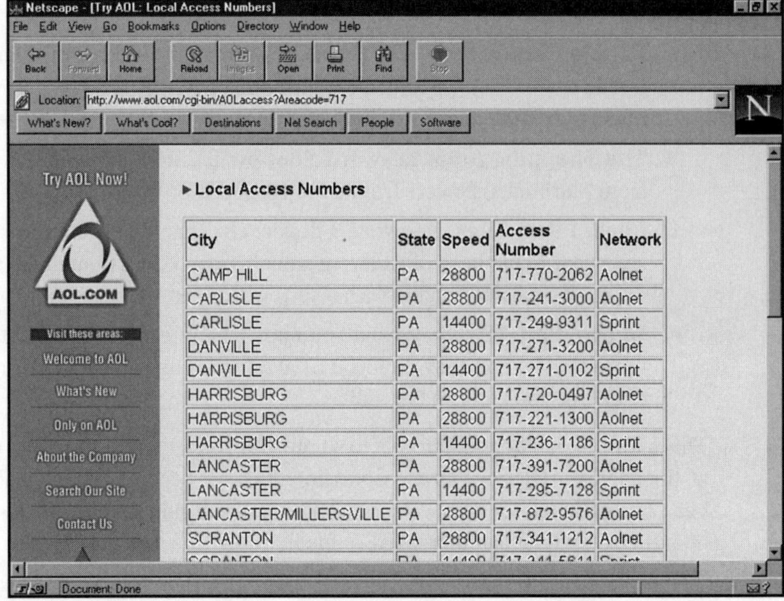

FIG. 4.2
The Web-based local phone search quickly lets you know if you can access AOL without incurring a toll call.

After you figure out your local number, you're already halfway there. Here are the steps to complete your installation of AOL. Figure 4.3. shows the AOL setup screen.

1. Obtain a second number from the list to use as a backup. Write both numbers down.
2. Select the Setup option from the main menu.
3. Click the Edit Location button.

Fill out the information that AOL requests. You want to use as your primary number the one that connects at the highest speed. If a problem ever occurs with that number, you can click the Swap Phone Numbers button and attempt to dial in using the slower secondary number.

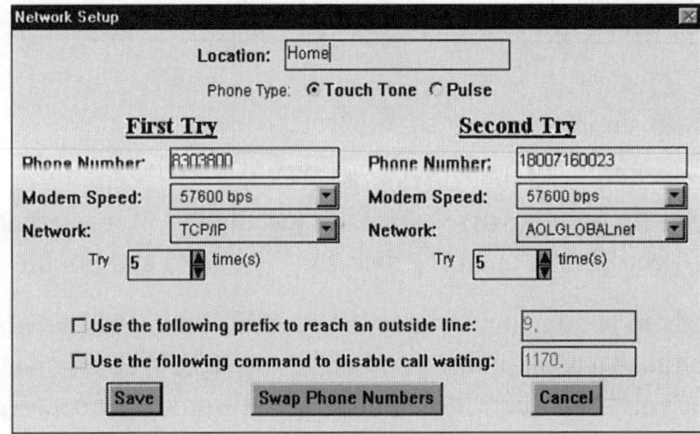

FIG. 4.3
The setup screen on AOL is easy to fill out after you determine your primary and secondary dial-in numbers.

Now you are ready to connect. The first time that you connect to AOL, you have to provide a credit card number and billing address, so that when your trial period ends, AOL can begin charging you.

NOTE If you live in a *black zone*, (that is, an area in which no local AOL numbers are available), you can use a surcharged 1-888 access number (1-888-245-0113). Using this number, however, costs an additional ten cents a minute, or $6 an hour.

Before you begin exploring AOL, you need to choose one last item from the AOL sign-up screen: the specific billing plan that you want to use. The next section of this chapter discusses various payment options available to AOL users, and how to determine which payment scheme is the right one for you.

Choosing One of AOL's Pricing Plans

America Online has several plans from which you can choose. In the "old days" of AOL, everyone had to pay about $20 a month, as well as an additional surcharge between $4 to $6, depending on the time of day at which they connected to AOL. Such high rates are no longer good business, because ISPs offer a greater wealth of information for much less money.

AOL offers a variety of packages, which can prove to be a bit confusing. Let's take a look at each plan in more detail.

AOL has five basic pricing plans:

- A "standard plan" charging $19.95 per month for unlimited use of AOL.
- An "advance renewal rate" of $17.95 per month for those who pay for a full year of AOL in advance.
- A "bring your own access" rate of $9.95 per month for those who connect to AOL through their local Internet service provider.
- A "light usage program" offering 3 hours of AOL for $4.95 per month, with additional time priced at $2.50 per hour.
- A "limited usage" plan charging $9.95 per month for 5 hours of AOL, with additional time priced at $2.95 per hour.

The following sections examine these plans in more detail so that you can determine which one is best for you.

The Standard Plan

The standard plan is AOL's "default" pricing plan. It's simple—you pay $19.95 a month for full, unlimited access to AOL. This rate is comparable to that of many ISPs. It's a good plan for people who are just learning about the online world, or for those who don't have an ISP within local calling range (and who thus need AOL as their main gateway to the Internet).

NOTE The term "unlimited" is not quite what it seems. Depending on the phone number that you use, and the AOL traffic in the area, people are sometimes forcefully disconnected ("booted") from AOL after 46 minutes online, to allow other people to connect. The company claims that it has discontinued this practice. ■

The Advance Renewal Rate Plan

This plan offers the same features of the standard plan; it differs only in the manner in which you pay. Under this plan, AOL gets additional capital up front (remember, you have to pay for an entire year, in advance), while the user gets a slightly less expensive rate of $17.95 per month, saving $2 a month. Use this plan only if you are certain that you are going to stay with the service for a full year!

NOTE Interestingly enough, annual turnover of AOL customers is around 50 percent. Although the company has millions of users, only half stay with AOL a full year. Most other online services have similar customer turnover statistics. ■

The Bring Your Own Access Plan

If you already have, or plan to get, a direct connection to the Internet via an ISP, I recommend this plan for you. You pay only $9.95 a month for unlimited access, but you don't—actually, you can't—connect to AOL using the company's network of local dial-in numbers. Instead, you first log on to your ISP, and then connect to AOL via the Internet itself. See the "Configuring AOL for TCP/IP" section of this chapter for a full description of how this is accomplished.

Light Usage Plan

The light usage plan offers access to AOL for users who don't expect to need much online time. Under this plan, you pay a monthly fee of $4.95, and you are limited to three hours online per month. After that, additional hours are charged at a rate of $2.50 per hour. You may not think that $2.50 is much of an hourly fee, but time online can get away from you! If you were to spend 20 hours online in a given month under this plan, you would be charged $47.45. So choose this option with caution!

Limited Usage Plan

The limited usage plan is similar to the light usage plan but is intended for people who need a little more time online. After paying $9.95 per month for 5 hours, you are charged an additional $2.95 for every hour you spend online. Oddly enough, in the scenario sketched out in the last paragraph—20 hours online in a given month—you would owe $54.20 under this plan. As with the light usage plan, sign up for this plan only if you know you won't be using AOL very much.

Setting Up and Connecting with TCP/IP

Now that we have shown you how to sign up, we can focus on telling you how to use AOL for the Internet, which is, after all, the subject of this book. For the purposes of this section, we assume that you are going to sign up with an ISP, and that you will join AOL under the "bring your own access" plan.

Using Your ISP Connection

The great thing about using your ISP to connect to AOL is that you do not need to do anything special before going online with AOL. You are just a couple of settings away.

For the most reliable connection to AOL, connect to your Internet service provider using the TCP/IP function built into Windows95/NT and the latest Macintosh operating systems. During all of AOL's much publicized problems in late 1996, I was able to get online in this way well over 90 percent of the time. These connections also do not get bumped for inactivity after 46 minutes!

Configuring AOL for TCP/IP

The current version of AOL (3.x) supports the TCP/IP connection very well. (On the other hand, older versions of AOL are practically incompatible with TCP/IP connections).

To configure AOL for your TCP/IP connection, go to your AOL sign-in screen.

On your PC:

- Choose the Setup button on your sign-in screen.
- Click the Edit Location button.
- Click the Network drop-down box.
- Select TCP/IP.
- Click the Save button.

On your Macintosh:

- Set the Select Location pull-down menu to TCP (for LAN or ISP).
- Click the Setup button.
- Choose Connect Method, First Profile, TCP.
- Choose Connect Method, Second Profile, TCP.
- Click the Save button.

You now are ready to connect to AOL via TCP/IP. Connect to your ISP as you normally would (or if you are on a LAN, say, at your office, just skip this step). After you open your Internet connection in this fashion, start AOL and click the Sign On button.

You should see the progress screen move through its connecting steps pretty quickly. These steps are

1. Initializing your TCP/IP connection (or your modem connection, when you dial in directly)
2. Connecting to your AOL host
3. Checking and accepting your password

When you see the lightning icon (the screen indicator for the second step) highlighted, you know that the connection is going well. Figure 4.4 shows the connection progress screen.

When the connection is fully established, you hear AOL's eager "Welcome" emanate from your computer. From this point, it's America Online as usual.

FIG. 4.4 The connection status screen is a simple and useful diagnostic tool for testing a connection.

Using AOL on the Internet

Is AOL really the Internet? No, it's not. It's a content provider that also allows access to the Internet, absent many of the features of an ISP account. You can spend a large amount of time surfing the Web via AOL, but you are not going to catch the ultimate cyberwave there.

Because you have a TCP/IP connection to AOL, you also have an ISP connection, and you may just want to use your ISP connection and a browser of your choice, to surf the Web. Sometimes, though, you may prefer to use the AOL gateway for your Internet access. This section describes some of the most popular AOL Internet tools and how to use them.

E-Mail

Just as it is on the Internet, e-mail is one of the most important features available on AOL.

Remember: If you are sending e-mail to another AOL user from within AOL, you can simply address the e-mail to that person's user name. For example, you can use "StacieLndo" as an address, instead of "StacieLndo@aol.com". If you are sending e-mail across the Internet to someone outside AOL, however, you still need to use a fully qualified e-mail address, like "eric@rconsult.com".

Sending e-mail with AOL is easy. Just follow these steps:

1. Choose the Mail menu, and then select the Compose Mail option.
2. In the To: box of the e-mail form, place the address of the person to whom you are sending the e-mail message. If you want to send a courtesy copy of the message to someone else, go to the CC: box and place the correct address there.
3. Enter an appropriate subject line, and then write your message in the body of the e-mail (see Figure 4.5).
4. If you want to send a separate file along with your message, click the Attach Files button, and then select the file that you want to send.
5. Click the Send Now button, and the message will be sent.

That's all there is to it. AOL e-mail is designed to be easy to use. To read e-mail that you receive, simply click the e-mail button on the welcome screen, or use the Mail menu. Whenever e-mail arrives in your mailbox, a computer voice tells you that "You've Got Mail!"

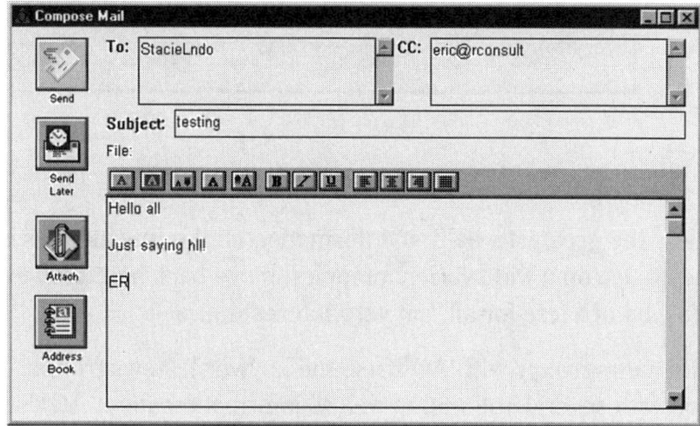

FIG. 4.5
Sending e-mail is an easy task, because of AOL's well-designed interface.

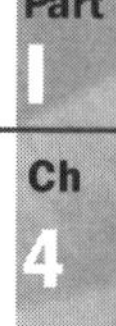

Gopher

Although interest in Gopher has dropped off tremendously over the past five years because of the growth of the World Wide Web, it remains a useful way to obtain data from the Internet. AOL does support Gopher, and it might be a good idea for you to become familiar with it. To access the AOL Gopher, use the keyword, Gopher. The AOL Gopher interface is straightforward—after you select a Gopher site to explore, you connect to it via AOL's Web browser. The Gopher Directory includes a link to the University of Minnesota (which is the birthplace, and namesake, of this Net rodent), where you can find a comprehensive listing of every Gopher site in the world.

When using Gopher, you search through successive levels of directories, narrowing your search at each level. Figure 4.6 shows the Penn State Gopher phone book, as viewed through AOL.

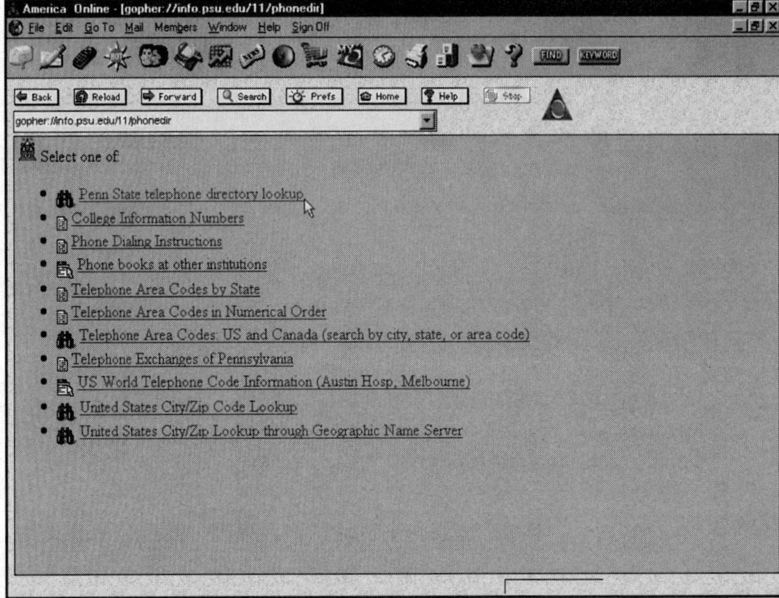

FIG. 4.6
Using Gopher is simple in AOL. When you click the directory or file you want, the information appears on your screen.

Newsgroups

In my opinion, the greatest wealth of information on the Internet lies in newsgroups. Thousands of messages, on a wide variety of topics, move back and forth every day between scores of users. It's a bit of a free-for-all, but very interesting.

To access the newsgroups with AOL, use the keyword, Newsgroups. The Newsgroups screen presents you with several options, as well as information about AOL's newsgroup policies.

The AOL news reader has some nice features:

- It allows you to search for a specific area of interest.
- It decodes binary files automatically.
- It has an easy-to-use interface (see Figure 4.7).

To read newsgroups on AOL, follow these steps:

1. From within AOL, press Ctrl+K (on a PC) or Command+K on a Macintosh, and then enter the keyword, **Newsgroups**.
2. Click the Read My Newsgroups icon.
3. Double-click the newsgroup that you want to read, and the news reader displays that group's posts for you.
4. To read a specific message, just double-click the post that interests you.

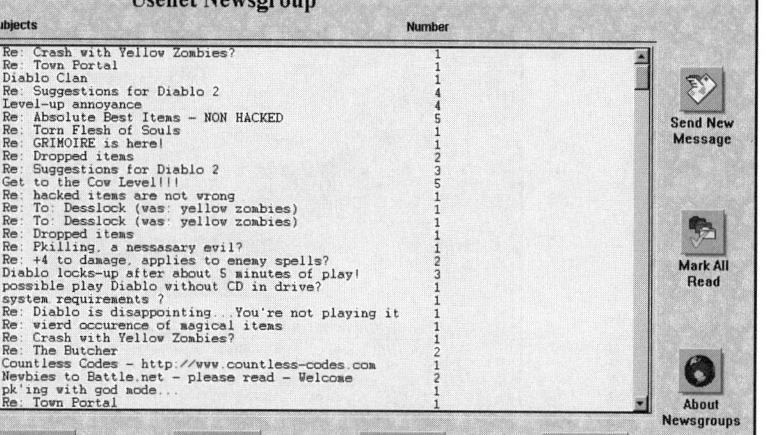

FIG. 4.7
AOL's news reader displays individual posts in such a way that you can easily pick the one that you want to read.

Remember that AOL does not allow access to all existing newsgroups. This is to "keep potentially offensive material off the AOL system," according to the company. Of course, thousands of interesting newsgroups are still accessible to AOL users, so fear not.

Browsing the Web

Millions of people have begun to use the Internet in recent years, and the World Wide Web is a primary factor behind this development. AOL began to realize that they had to make the Web available to their users, so the service created its own browser. To get to the AOL browser, enter the keyword, Web. Figure 4.8 shows the AOL browser.

Here are some basic instructions for using the AOL Web browser:

- To follow a link, click any highlighted, underlined text. (The mouse pointer turns into a pointing hand when it passes over a linked text.)
- To set up the browser to your specifications, click the Prefs button, and then make your choices in the Preferences window that appears.
- To move forward or back to other Web pages you have already browsed, use the Forward and Back arrow buttons on the browser toolbar.
- To go to a specific Web site, type the URL that you want to visit into the Address window. Another way to specify the Web site that you can visit is to type the complete URL into any Keyword entry box.

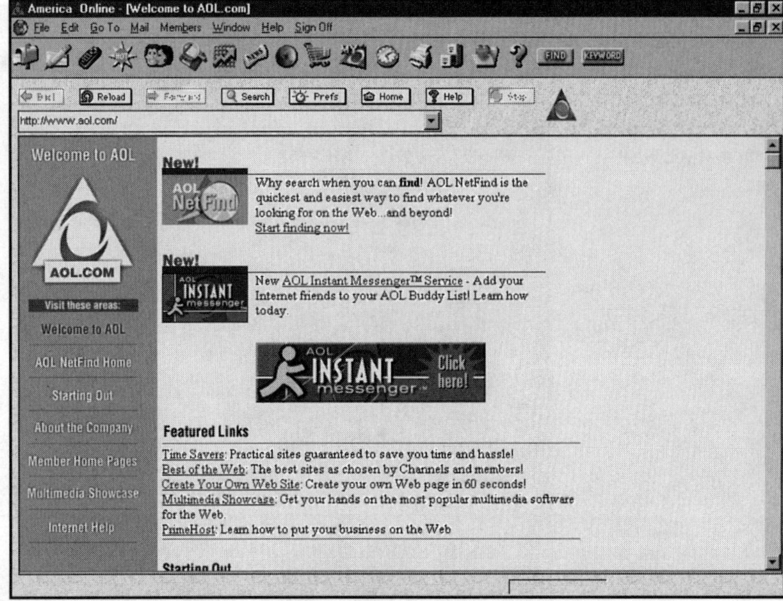

FIG. 4.8
The AOL Web interface is similar to most other Web browsers.

If you have experience with other browsers, you will find the AOL Web browser very familiar.

NOTE AOL is improving its Web browser, but it still is not equal to the Microsoft Internet Explorer or Netscape Navigator. Hopefully, AOL will remedy this, but in the end, you may prefer surfing the Net through your ISP connection with one of these other browsers.

AOL also provides each user with 2 megabytes of Webspace on the AOL server. This means that each AOL member can create their own Web page should they so desire. You can peruse the AOL home pages of those members who have taken AOL up on this offer, at **http://members.aol.com/**. These pages provide an interesting glimpse at an online community.

America Online will surely continue to grow. Currently, AOL boasts nearly ten million users worldwide. The hallmark of this service is its ease of use, although it has been much maligned for recent problems, many of which are being resolved. America Online remains a good way to test the waters of the online world. Millions of people have been exposed to the Internet via AOL, before moving on to more sophisticated surfing via their ISPs. If nothing else, AOL is the best (and least expensive!) way to teach yourself about the electronic online community.

PART II

Part II Using Your Internet Connection

CHAPTER 5

Browsing the Web with Netscape

Some people characterize the Web as confusing. They complain that it's not linear. It doesn't present you with a logical sequence of choices that you must make in order to move forward. You'll find through your own experience, however, that this is precisely why the Web is so intuitively easy. It's free-form, not linear. It more closely matches how people think: jumping from topic to topic as we see fit, as opposed to having order forced upon us.

Do you watch television, read the news, or listen to your technically adept friends talk about the Web? If so, you've probably encountered a variety of metaphors that people use to explain how the Web works. Here are two examples:

- The Web is like our national highway system. It connects countless destinations together in a web.
- The Web is similar to a spider's web. Nodes are joined together by tiny strands of silk.

The one concept that both of these metaphors have in common is that of joining, or linking, things together. This is, in fact, what the Web is all about, and represents one of the most important things you need to know about it. For example, you need to know that you can jump from one Web page to another by clicking a link. You also need to know some other ways to get to a Web page without using links.

In this chapter, you learn about all these things and much more, including:

- Understanding how links work and how they look
- Learning about what a link can do
- Getting around with and without links
- Making Netscape load Web pages faster
- Configuring the way Netscape works with links

Understanding Links

By now, you've noticed the references in the margins of this book. They serve a similar purpose as links do on a Web page—albeit a little low-tech. They refer you to other places in this book that might be useful or interesting to read. Without these references, you would have to resort to flipping through the pages looking for what you need.

Links on a Web page are even more vital. You have all the pages of this book right in front of you. At least you would know where to start looking. On the other hand, you have no idea where to find all the Web pages on the Internet. And there are too many to keep track of, anyway. Therefore, links are the only reasonable way to go from one Web page to another related Web page.

NOTE Hypertext and hypermedia are two terms you'll frequently hear associated with the Web. A hypertext document is a document that contains links to other documents–allowing you to jump between them by clicking the links. Hypermedia contains more than text, it contains multimedia such as pictures, videos, and sounds, too. In hypermedia documents, pictures are frequently used as links to other documents.

A link really has two different parts. First, there's the part that you see on the Web page—called an anchor. There's also the part that tells Netscape what to do if you click that link—called the URL reference. When you click a link's anchor, Netscape loads the Web page given by the link's corresponding URL reference. You'll learn about both parts of a link in the following sections. You'll also learn about the different resources to which a link can point.

Anchors

A link's anchor can be a word, a group of words, or a picture. Exactly how an anchor looks in Netscape depends largely on what type of anchor it is, and how the person who created the Web page used it. There are only two types of anchors though: text and graphical. You'll learn about both types in this section.

TIP When you move the mouse cursor over a link's anchor, it changes from a pointer to a hand.

Text Anchors Most text anchors look somewhat the same. A text anchor is one or more words that Netscape underlines to indicate that it represents a link. Netscape also displays a text anchor using a different color than the rest of the text around it.

TIP Click and drag a link's text anchor onto your desktop. You can return quickly to that Web page by double-clicking the shortcut.

Figure 5.1 shows a Web page that contains three text anchors. In particular, notice how the text anchors on this Web page are embedded in the text. That is, they aren't set apart from the text, like the references in this book, but are actually an integral part of it. Clicking one of these links will load a Web page that is related to the link. You'll find many text anchors used this way.

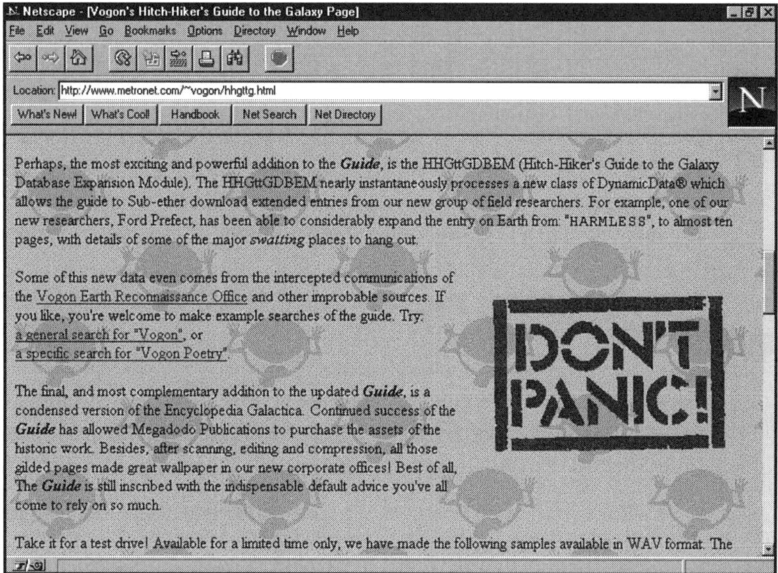

FIG. 5.1
You'll find Vogon's Hitch-Hiker's Guide to the Galaxy Page at **http://www.metronet.com/~vogon/hhgttg.html**.

Figure 5.2 shows another Web page with a lot of text anchors. These anchors aren't embedded in the text, however. They are presented as a list or index of links from which you can choose. Web page authors frequently use this method to present collections of related links.

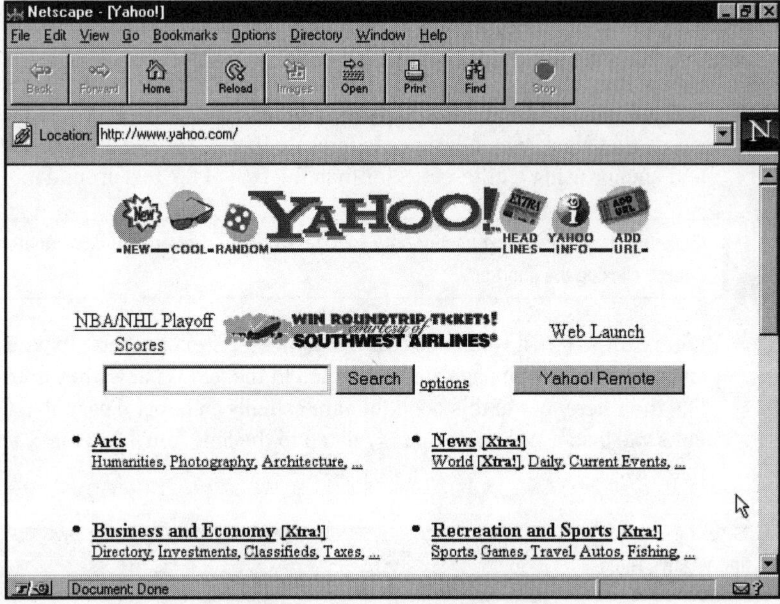

FIG. 5.2
Yahoo (**http://www.yahoo.com**) is one of the most popular indexes on the Web.

Graphical Anchors A graphical anchor is similar to a text anchor. When you click a link's graphical anchor, Netscape loads the Web page that the link references. Graphical anchors aren't underlined or displayed in a different color. And no two graphical anchors need to look the same. It depends entirely on the picture that the Web page's author chose to use.

Right-click a graphical anchor, and choose Save This Image As to save the image in a file on your computer.

Versatility is the strong suit of graphical anchors. Web page authors effectively use them for a variety of reasons. Here are some examples of the ways you'll find graphical anchors used on a Web page:

- Bullets. Graphical anchors are frequently used as list bullets. You can click the picture to go to the Web page described by that list item. Frequently, the text in the list item is also a link. You can click either the picture or the text.
- Icons. Many Web sites use graphical anchors in a similar manner to the way Windows 95 uses icons. They are common on home pages, and represent a variety of Web pages available through that site. Figure 5.3 shows a Web site that uses graphical anchors in this manner. Click the ProShop icon to open the ProShop Web page, for example.
- Advertisements. Many Web sites have sponsors that pay to advertise on the site. This keeps the Web site free to you and me, while the site continues to make money. You'll usually find advertisements, such as the one shown in Figure 5.4, at the top of a Web page. Click the advertisement, and Netscape will load the sponsor's Web page.

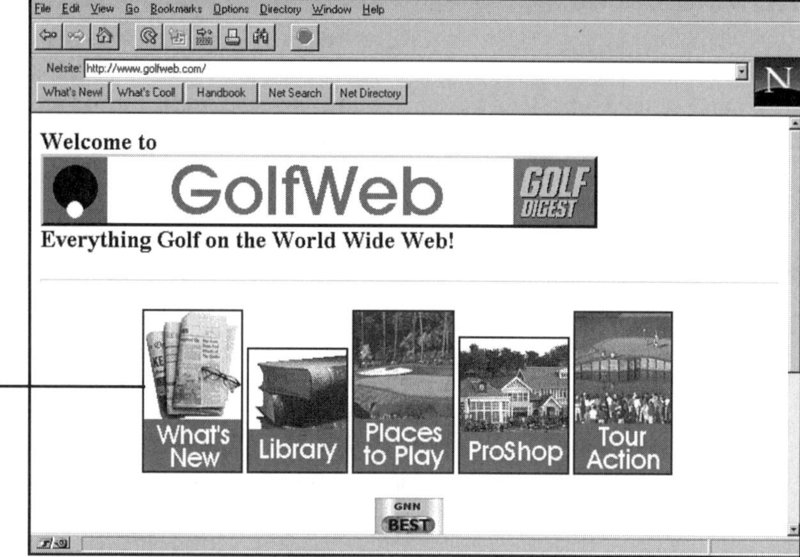

FIG. 5.3
You'll find GolfWeb at **http://www.golfweb.com**. GolfWeb's home page uses graphical anchors to represent a variety of its pages you can load.

Graphical anchors used as icons

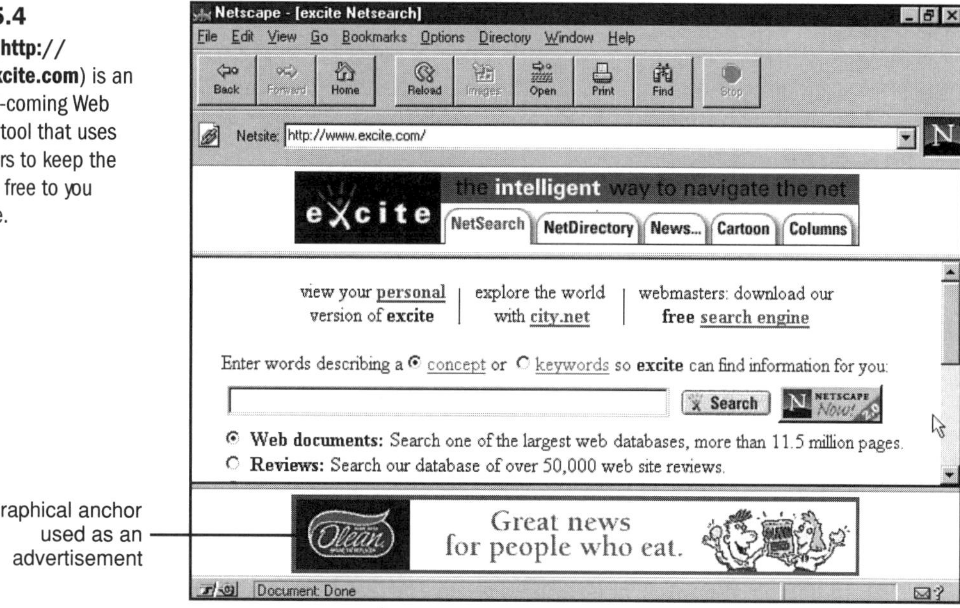

FIG. 5.4
Excite (**http://www.excite.com**) is an up-and-coming Web search tool that uses sponsors to keep the service free to you and me.

Graphical anchor used as an advertisement

URL References

The other part of a link is the URL reference. This is the address of the Web page that Netscape will load if you click the link. Every type of link, whether it uses a text or graphical anchor, uses either a relative or absolute reference. You'll learn about each type in this section, but when you're "surfing" the Web it really doesn't matter which type of URL reference a link is using—as long as Netscape loads the Web page you want.

Choose View, Document Source to tell for sure if a link is using relative references.

An URL reference to a file on the same computer is also known as a relative reference. It means that the URL is relative to the computer and directory from which Netscape originally loaded the Web page. If Netscape loads a page at http://www.mysite.com/page, for example, then a relative reference to /picture would actually refer to the URL http://www.mysite.com/page/picture. Relative references are commonly used to refer to Web pages on the same computer. Figure 5.5 shows a Web page that contains relative references to other Web pages on that site.

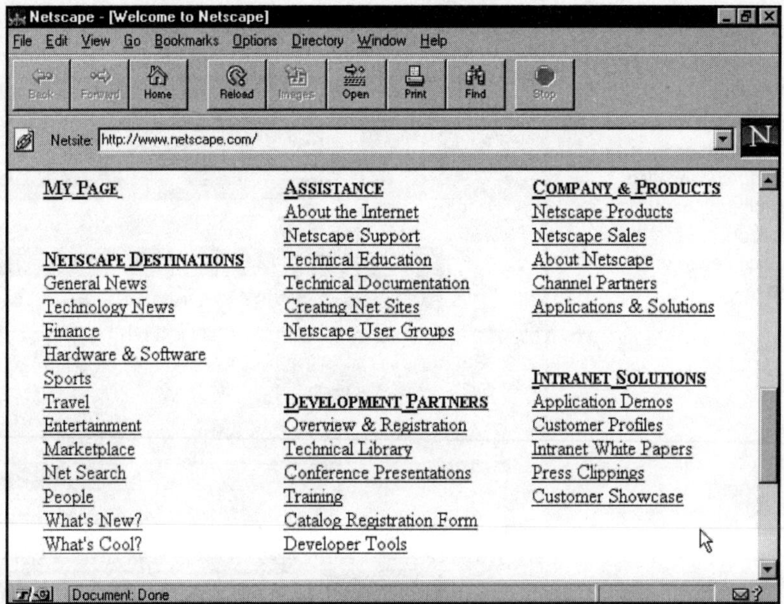

FIG. 5.5 Netscape's Web site is at **http://www.netscape.com**. You can find various information about Netscape and its products.

The primary reason Web authors use a relative reference is convenience. It's much simpler to just type the file name instead of the entire URL. It also makes it easier to move Web pages around on a server. Since the URL references are relative to the Web page's computer and directory, the author doesn't have to change all the links in the Web page every time the files move to a different location.

Corporate Bulletin Boards

Many corporations, such as Hewlett Packard, have created corporate bulletin boards that their associates view with Web browsers such as Netscape. These Web pages aren't on the Web, however. They're stored on the companies' internal network servers. They contain a variety of information that is useful to their associates such as the following:

- Meeting schedules and meeting room availability
- Announcements about corporate events
- Information about policies and benefits
- Recent press releases and financial statements
- Technological information

Absolute References An URL reference that specifies the exact computer, directory, and file for a Web page is an absolute reference. Whereas relative references are common for links to Web pages on the same computer, absolute references are necessary for links to Web pages on other computers.

Hold your mouse over a link and look at Netscape's status line to see its URL reference.

Resources to Which Links Can Point

Links can point to more than just Web pages. They can point to a variety of files and other Internet resources, too. A link can point to a video, pictures, or even a plain text file. It can also point to an FTP server, Gopher server, or a UseNet newsgroup. Table 5.1 describes the other types of things a link can point to, and shows you what the URL looks like.

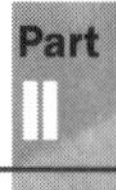

Table 5.1 Resources to Which a Link Can Point

Type	Sample URL
Web Page	**http://www.mysite.com/page.html**
Files	**file://C:/picture.bmp**
Multimedia	**http://www.mysite.com/video.avi**
E-mail	**mailto:info@netscape.com**
FTP	**ftp://ftp.mysite.com**
Gopher	**gopher://gopher.mysite.com**
Newsgroup	**news:alt.fan.que**
Telnet	**telnet://mysite.com**

How to Move Around the Web

You didn't buy this book to learn how to load a Web page in Netscape, then sit back and look at it all day. You want to "surf" the Web—jumping from Web page to Web page, looking for entertaining and useful information.

In fact, surfing is such an important part of the Web that both Netscape and the Web itself provide many different ways to navigate. You can use the links and imagemaps that you find on a Web page, for example. You can go directly to a Web page if you know its URL. You can also use some of the more advanced Netscape features such as bookmarks and frames. In this section, you'll learn how to use those features to move around the Web like a pro.

Clicking a Link

You learned about links earlier in this chapter. They are the primary method you use to go from the Web page you're viewing to another related Web page. All these links are provided by the Web page's author, and are usually accurately related to the context in which you found it (see Figure 5.6).

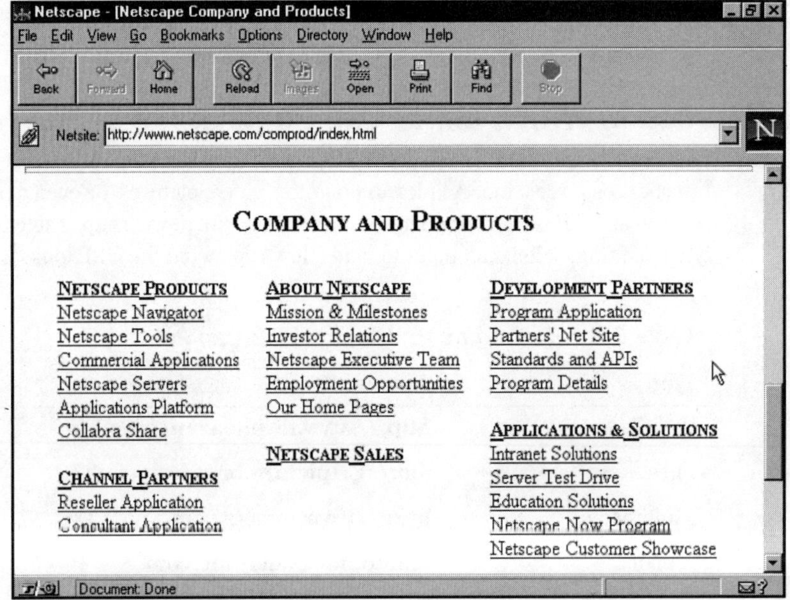

FIG. 5.6
This Web page (**http://www.netscape.com/comprod/index.html**) has a complete list of Netscape products and services at the bottom.

Client Pull On The Web

You'll eventually run across a Web page that says something like "We've moved" or "This Web page has a new location." It'll display a link that loads the Web page at its new location if you click it. If you wait long enough, however, Netscape may automatically load the Web page at its new location.

Client pull is the technology behind this behavior. Client pull allows the Web server to tell Netscape to reload the current Web page or load a different Web page after a set amount of time. One of the most common uses for client pull is the situation described previously. It's also used for simple sequences of Web pages, however, that work just like slide shows.

Clicking an Imagemap

Imagemaps are similar to graphical anchors, in that if you click an imagemap, Netscape will load another Web page. Imagemaps can load more than one Web page, however, depending on what part of the image you click. The image itself usually indicates the areas you can click to load a particular Web page.

Figure 5.7, for example, shows the imagemap that Microsoft uses at its Web site. Each region of the imagemap is clearly defined so that you know where you need to click, and you know what Web page Netscape will load as a result.

FIG. 5.7
Microsoft's Web site is at **http://www.microsoft.com**.

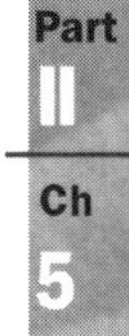

TIP If you're having trouble deciphering a button bar, look for text links just below it.

A common use for imagemaps on the Web is button bars. Button bars are similar to the toolbars you've used in Windows 95 and other windowing environments. They don't appear to toggle in and out like buttons, however. They are, after all, just imagemaps. You'll find them at the top or, more fre¡uently, the bottom of a Web page. Figure 5.8 shows a button bar from Netscape's Web site. Just like any other imagemap, each area you can click is clearly defined.

You can click different areas to load different Web pages. You can click the Netscape Search button to search Netscape's Web site, or you can click the Table of Contents button to get a roadmap of Netscape's site.

FIG. 5.8 You'll find this button bar at the bottom of all Netscape Web pages.

Going Directly to a Resource

Which came first, the link or the Web page? If the only way to load a Web page was by clicking a link, you'd never get anywhere. If a friend gives you an URL, for example, you need a way to tell Netscape to open that Web page without having to use a link. That's why Netscape lets you go directly to a Web page by specifying its URL in either the location bar or Open Location dialog box.

TIP URLs are case sensitive. If you can't open a Web page, check for strangely capitalized letters such as **http://www.MywEbsiTe.com**.

Figure 5.9 shows the Netscape location bar with the drop-down list open. Type the URL of a Web page in Netscape's location bar, and Netscape will load the Web page. Netscape keeps the addresses of all the Web pages you've opened this way in the location bar's drop-down list. It keeps this list from session to session, too. That way you can always go back to a previous site by dropping down the list, and clicking the Web page's URL.

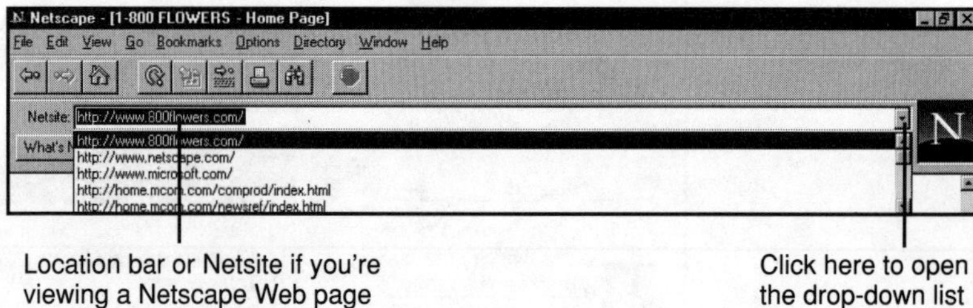

FIG. 5.9 The drop-down list keeps track of only those Web pages you've opened using the location bar.

NOTE You don't have to type the http:// part of an URL for a Web address in the location bar, because Netscape will add this for you. ■

The Open button requires a few more mouse clicks, but it's just as easy to use. Click the Open button on the Netscape toolbar. Type the URL of a Web page in the Open Location dialog box, and click Open. Netscape loads the Web page that you specified.

Moving Forward and Backward

After you've clicked a few links and opened a few Web pages, you may want to go back to a Web page you looked at earlier. Maybe you forgot something you just read, or something didn't seem that interesting then, but it does now. Netscape provides two useful features to look at previously viewed Web pages: the history list and the Back/Forward buttons on the toolbar.

In the History window, select a Web site from the list, and click Create Bookmark to add it to your bookmarks.

- The history list keeps track of all the Web pages that you've visited during the current session. You can access the history list in one of two places: the Go menu, shown in Figure 5.10, shows the last 15 Web pages that you've loaded in Netscape. Choose Go from the Netscape main menu, and then choose any of the Web pages on the menu. If you want to see a list of all the Web pages that you've visited during the current session, choose Window, History from the Netscape main menu. Figure 5.11 shows the History window. You can scroll up and down the list, and double-click a Web page to open it in Netscape.

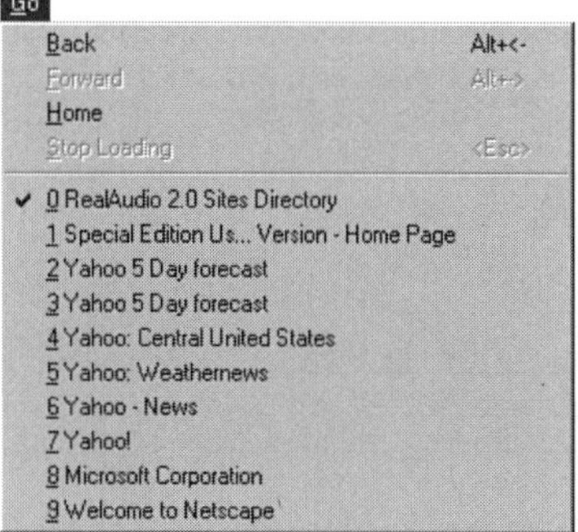

FIG. 5.10
The checkmark in this menu indicates the current Web page.

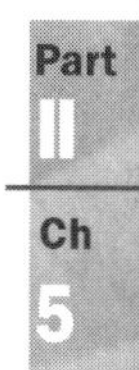

- The Forward and Back buttons move you up and down the history list shown in Figure 5.11. If you click the Back button, Netscape moves the highlight down the list and opens that Web page. If you click the Forward button, Netscape moves the highlight up the list, and opens that Web page. Once you've reached the bottom of the list, the Back button is disabled. Likewise, when you reach the top of the list, the Forward button is disabled.

Going to Your Home Page

If you start feeling a bit lost, it's sometimes easier to get your bearings by going back to your home page. Netscape lets you configure a home page that it uses for two purposes:

- Netscape loads your home page every time Netscape starts. It usually loads it from the cache so that you don't have to wait for Netscape to transfer it from the Internet.
- At any time, you can click the Home button on the Netscape toolbar to return to your home page.

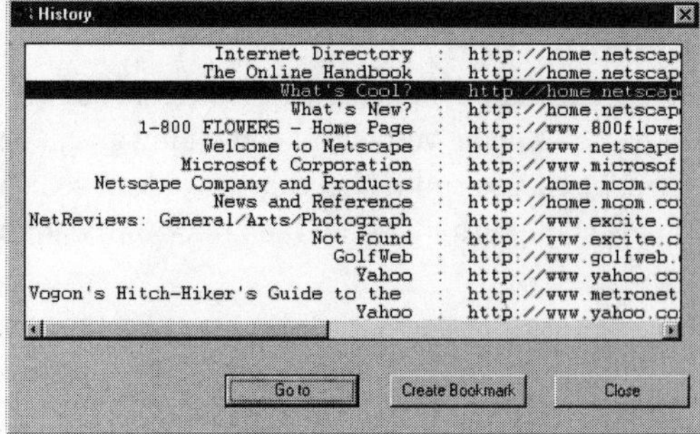

FIG. 5.11
The highlight in this list indicates the current Web page.

TIP Configure your home page to point to your favorite Web index such as www.excite.com. Then it'll be only one click away.

Here's how to change your home page in Netscape:

1. Choose Options, General Preferences from the Netscape main menu.
2. Click the Appearance tab, and Netscape displays the dialog box shown in Figure 5.12.

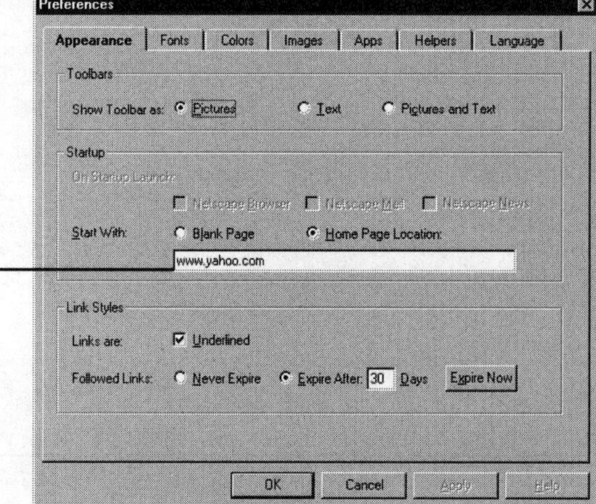

Type your home page URL here

FIG. 5.12
See the section "Changing the Way Netscape Works with Links" later in this chapter to learn more about this dialog box.

3. Select Home Page Location, and type the URL of your home page as shown in Figure 5.12.
4. Click OK to save your changes.

NOTE The term home page has two different meanings these days. First, a home page is usually a personal Web page where you would store links to your favorite Web pages, and maybe express yourself a bit. Second, many people refer to the opening page of a Web site as that site's home page. Hewlett Packard's home page contains links for computers and peripherals, for example. ■

Saving Bookmarks to Web Pages

The easiest way to get back to a Web page that you visit frequently is to use Netscape bookmarks. Bookmarks let you save and organize links to your favorite Web pages. Unlike Netscape's history list, the bookmarks hang around from session to session. They are always easily accessible. Choose Bookmarks from the Netscape main menu. Figure 5.13 shows you what the Bookmarks menu looks like.

FIG. 5.13
Open a submenu or click a Web site to load it in Netscape.

Navigating a Web Site with Frames

Frames are a feature that is currently specific to Netscape. They allow the Netscape window to be split into multiple sections. Each frame on the window can point to a different URL. Figure 5.14 shows a Web page that uses a frame to present a button bar that's always available to you.

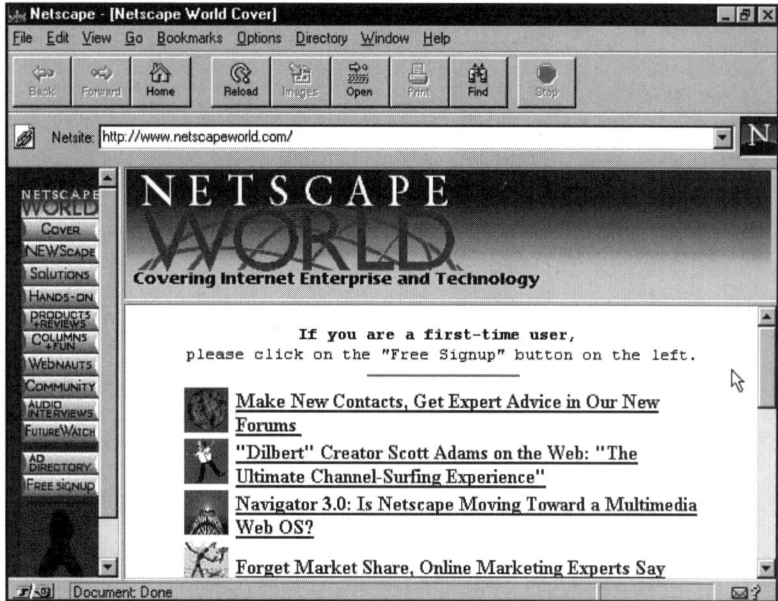

FIG. 5.14
At this site, the button bar will always be available in the left frame, regardless of which Web page the right frame is displaying.

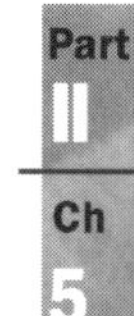

With the addition of frames, Netscape added an extra bit of complexity in navigation. Each frame was treated independent of each other, which meant that you couldn't easily go to a previous frame. With Netscape 2.0, you had to put your mouse cursor in a particular frame, click the right mouse button, then select Back in Frame. If you had pressed the Back button, it would've loaded the previous complete page. Netscape Atlas greatly simplifies navigation with frames by making the Back button smarter. Now, when you press it, you automatically go back to the most recently modified frame.

NOTE You'll run across many Web sites that say "Netscape Enhanced," "Best Viewed with Netscape," or something similar. They mean it. Many Web sites implement Netscape specific features that can't be viewed with other Web browsers. Frames are a typical example.

Many Windows 95 programs divide their windows into panes. They do it to make the organization of the windows' contents more obvious. A program that makes the résumés of a list of people available might have two panes: one to display a list of people and another to display the résumé of the currently selected person. Netscape frames can serve a similar purpose as well. Figure 5.15 shows a Web page that does the same thing as the résumé program. It has three frames: one that shows a list of people, another for the résumé of the currently selected individual, and a pane at the bottom to select a category.

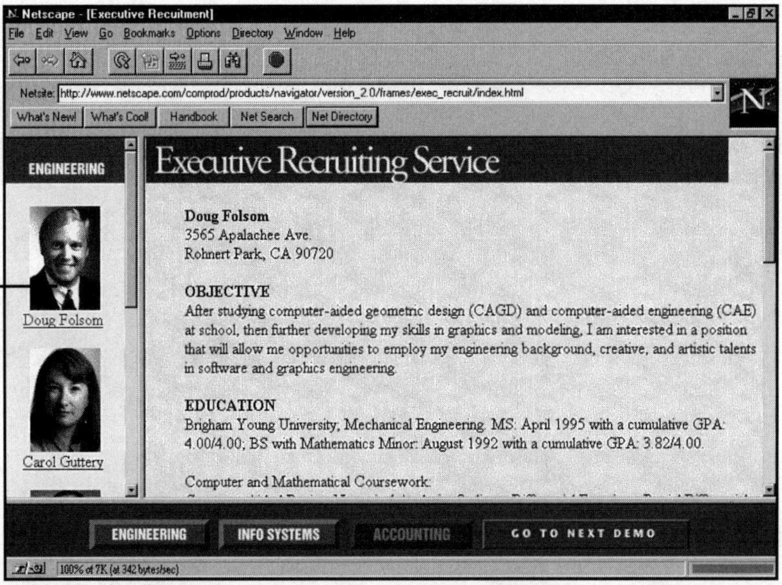

FIG. 5.15
Frames make a Web site easier to use by organizing its contents in a logical fashion.

Résumé of selected person

Watching Netscape's Status

Netscape gives you a lot of feedback about what's happening after you click a link or open an URL. Stars shoot past the Netscape logo while Netscape is transferring a Web page or file, for example. It also updates the status bar with information that'll help you keep track of what Netscape is doing. Here are some of the messages you'll see in the status bar:

Message	Description
http://server/file	The URL reference of the link to which you are currently pointing.
X% of YK	Netscape has completed X percent of a Y kilobyte transfer.
Contacting hostserver:	Netscape is trying to contact the given server.
Connect:	Netscape has contacted the server and is waiting for a reply.
Document: Done.	The Web page is finished loading.

Getting Around Faster

If you're using a 14.4Kbps or slower modem, you'll eventually become frustrated with how long it takes to load some Web pages. Many Web pages have very large graphics that take a long time to download. Unfortunately, the use of large graphics is becoming more common as Web authors take it for granted that everyone on the Internet is using at least a 28.8Kbps modem.

Many Web sites provide links to text-only versions. Look for a text link that says "Text Only."

Fight back. Netscape provides a few features that make Web pages containing too many graphics more tolerable:

- You don't have to wait for the entire Web page to finish loading before you can click a link. Click the Stop button, and Netscape will stop transferring the Web page. If you change your mind and want to reload the page, click the Reload button. Also, most of the text links are available before Netscape has finished transferring the images for the Web page. You can click any of these links. Netscape will stop loading the current page, and start loading the Web page referenced by the link.
- Most of your time is spent waiting for inline images to load. The irony is that the images on many Web pages aren't really worth the time if you have a slow connection. If you don't want Netscape to automatically load inline images, make sure that Options, Auto Load Images is not checked. If you want to view the images on a particular Web page, and you've disabled Auto Load Images, click the Load Images button on the Netscape toolbar. Figure 5.16 shows what a Web page looks like when it's loaded without inline images. Notice that Netscape displays placeholders where it normally displays the images. Netscape also displays alternative text to help you figure out what the link points to.

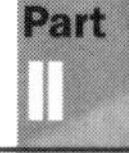

Changing the Way Netscape Works with Links

Netscape gives you a bit of control over how it displays links. It lets you choose whether or not they're underlined and what color it uses to display them.

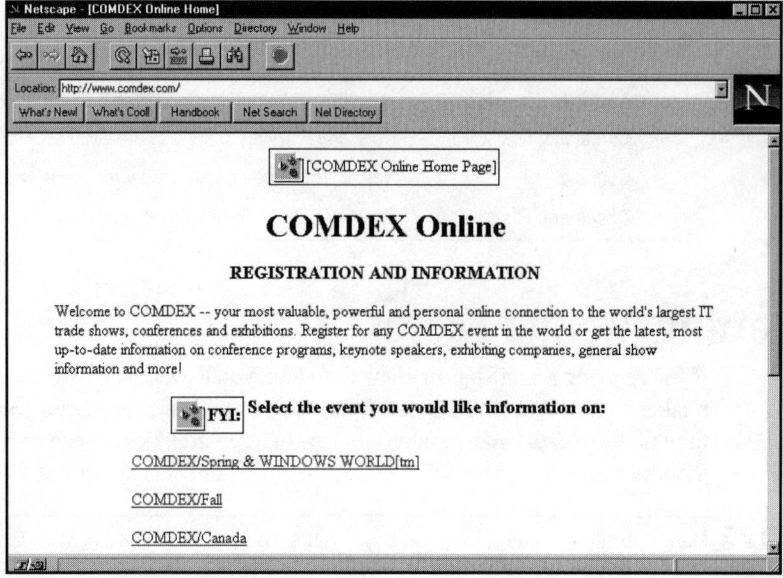

FIG. 5.16
You can click one of the placeholders to load the Web page it refers to, or you can click the Load Images button to see the inline images.

Underlining Links

You learned earlier in this chapter that Netscape underlines a link's text anchor on a Web page. You can change that. Here's how to configure Netscape so that it doesn't underline a link's text anchor:

1. Choose Options, General from the Netscape main menu.
2. Click the Appearance tab, and Netscape displays the dialog box shown in Figure 5.17.
3. Deselect Underlined, and click OK.

Beginning with the next Web page that Netscape loads, text anchors won't be underlined. You can still figure out where the links are, however, because they are displayed in a different color than the text around them.

Using a Different Color for Links

If you don't like the colors that Netscape uses for links, you can change them. If the default colors are hard to tell apart on your computer, for example, you'll want to change the colors so you can easily see the links. Use the following steps to change the colors Netscape uses for a text link's anchor:

1. Choose Options, General from the Netscape main menu.
2. Click the Colors tab, and Netscape displays the dialog box shown in Figure 5.18.
3. Select Links, and click the corresponding Choose Color button. Choose a color from the Color dialog box, and click OK.

FIG. 5.17
The Appearance box allows you to change the toolbar, start up options, and link styles.

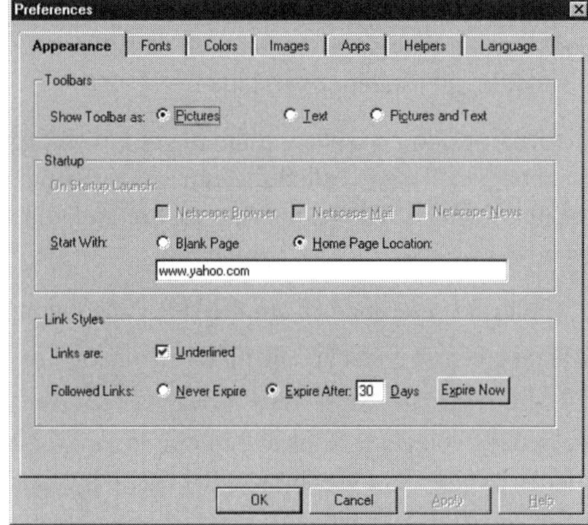

FIG. 5.18
Most of Netscape's options can be configured on one of this dialog box's tabs.

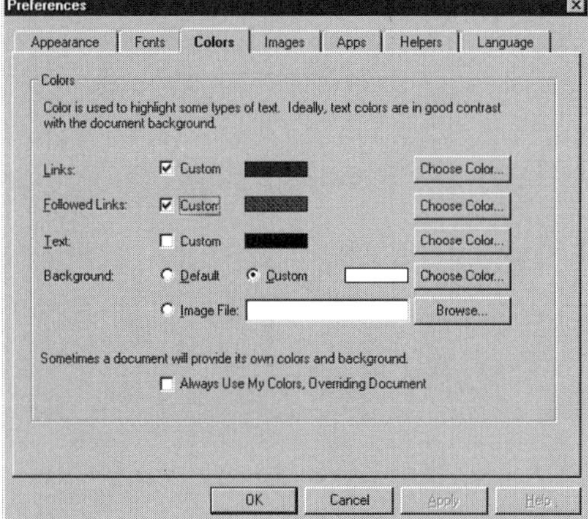

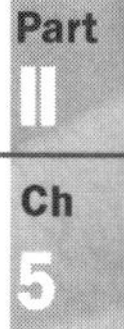

4. Select Followed Links, and click the corresponding Choose Color button. Choose a color from the Color dialog box, and click OK.
5. Click OK to save your changes.

Beginning with the next Web page that Netscape loads, Netscape will display text anchors that you've never visited using the color you chose in Links, and text anchors that you've already visited using the color you chose in Followed Links.

Controlling Link Expiration

Netscape caches Web pages so they'll load faster the next time you visit that Web page. It takes much longer to load a Web page from the Internet than it takes to load it from the hard drive. So, Netscape stores every Web page it loads to your hard drive. The next time you point Netscape to that URL, it loads it from the hard drive instead of the Internet.

The problem is that if Netscape is loading Web pages from your hard drive instead of the Internet, you may be looking at a Web page that's out of date. Even if the Web page's author changes it, you'll still be looking at the older version.

Netscape lets you configure how long it will continue to get a Web page from the cache before it loads it from the Internet again. This is called the expiration. By default, Netscape expires a link after 30 days. If you find that the Web pages you use are updated more frequently, you can easily change it. Here's how:

1. Choose Options, General Preferences from the Netscape main menu.
2. Click the Appearance tab, and Netscape displays the dialog box shown earlier in Figure 5.17.
3. Type the number of days you want Netscape to wait before expiring each link in Days. Alternatively, you can expire all of the links in the cache by clicking Expire Now.
4. Click OK to save your changes.

CHAPTER 6

Browsing the Web with Internet Explorer

- How do hypertext links work?
- What can hypertext links do?
- How do you configure Internet Explorer 3 to work with links?

One of the fascinating features of the World Wide Web, the aspect that makes "Web surfing" possible, is the sheer diversity of information, organized in an intuitive rather than logical way. The Web is not like an encyclopedia, calmly presenting its information from A to Z. It's free-form, not linear. It more closely matches how people think: jumping from topic to topic as we see fit, as opposed to having order forced upon us.

Thus, the metaphor of the "Web" itself is born. Like a spider's web, the Web reaches out across the world, joining computer to computer and node to node. By getting out there on the Web with a Web browser such as Internet Explorer, you can trek through a vast landscape of information, one bit linked to another to another. These links are, in fact, what the Web is all about, and they represent one of the most important things you need to know about the Web. For example, you need to know that you can jump from one Web page to another by clicking a link. You also need to know some other ways to get to a Web page without using links. ■

Understanding Links

Links on a Web page are even more vital. You have all the pages of this book right in front of you. At least you would know where to start looking. On the other hand, you have no idea where to find all the Web pages on the Internet. And it has too many to keep track of, anyway. Therefore, links are the only reasonable way to go from one Web page to another related Web page.

NOTE *Hypertext* and *hypermedia* are two terms you frequently hear associated with the Web. A hypertext document is a document that contains links to other documents—allowing you to jump between them by clicking the links. Hypermedia can contain more than text; it can contain multimedia such as pictures, videos, and sounds, too. In hypermedia documents, pictures are frequently used as links to other documents. ■

A link really has two different parts. First is the part that you see on the Web page—called an *anchor.* The other part tells Internet Explorer 3 what to do if you click that anchor—called the *URL reference*. When you click a link's anchor, Internet Explorer 3 loads the Web page given by the link's corresponding URL reference. You learn about both parts of a link in the following sections. You also learn about the different resources to which a link can point.

Anchors

A link's anchor can be a word, a group of words, or a picture. Exactly how an anchor looks in Internet Explorer 3 depends largely on what type of anchor it is and how the person who created the Web page used it. You can have only two types of anchors, though: text and graphical. You learn about both types in this section.

When you move the mouse cursor over a link's anchor, the cursor changes from a pointer to a hand.

Text Anchors Most text anchors look somewhat the same. A text anchor is one or more words that Internet Explorer 3 underlines to indicate that it represents a link. Internet Explorer also displays a text anchor using a different color than the rest of the text around it.

Click and drag a link's text anchor onto your desktop. You can return quickly to that Web page by double-clicking the shortcut.

Figure 6.1 shows a Web page that contains several text anchors. In particular, notice how the text anchors on this Web page are embedded in the text. That is, they aren't set apart from the text but are actually an integral part of it. Clicking one of these links loads a Web page that is related to the link. You can find many text anchors used this way.

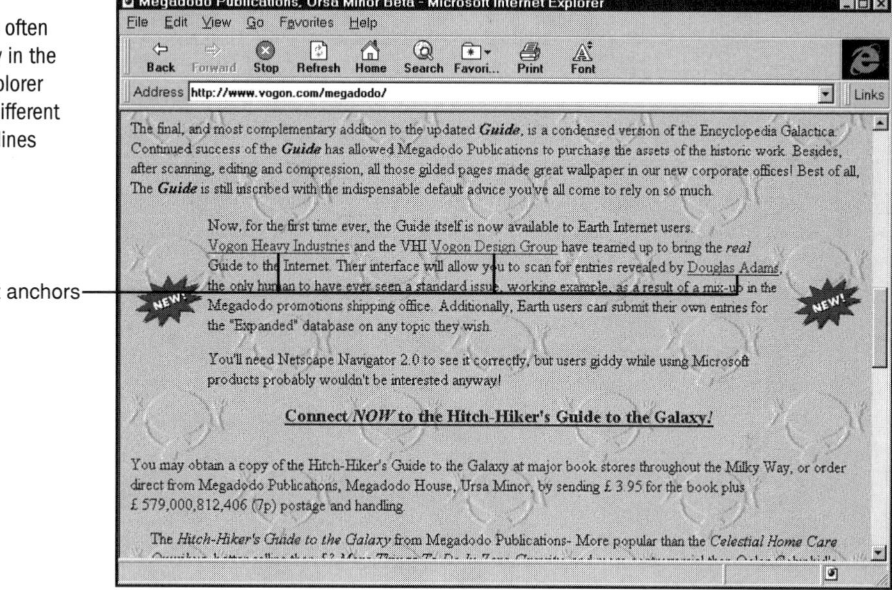

FIG. 6.1
Text anchors are often included directly in the text; Internet Explorer makes them a different color and underlines them.

Figure 6.2 shows another Web page with several text anchors. These anchors aren't embedded in the text, however. They are presented as a list or index of links from which you can choose. Web page authors frequently use this method to present collections of related links.

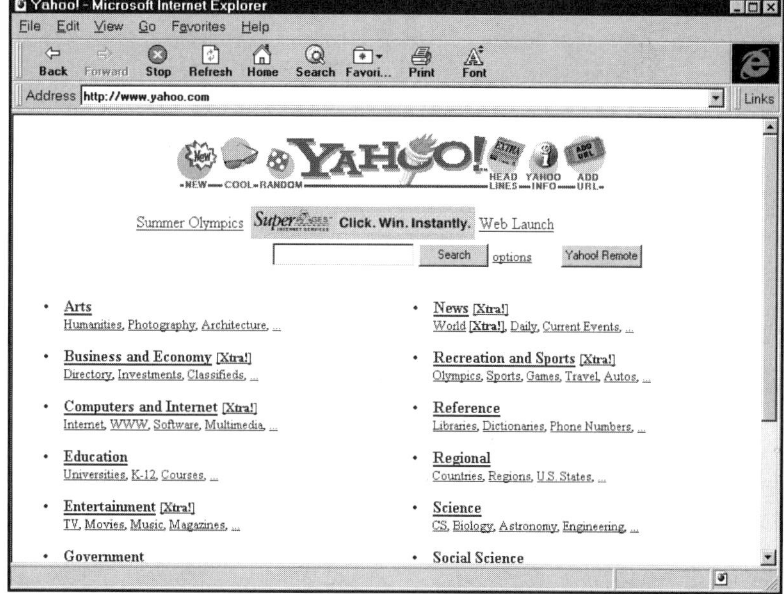

FIG. 6.2
Text anchors can also be presented in HTML lists and tables.

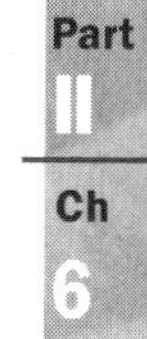

Graphical Anchors A graphical anchor is similar to a text anchor. When you click a link's graphical anchor, Internet Explorer 3 loads the Web page that the link references. Graphical anchors aren't underlined or displayed in a different color, however, though they are usually given a border the same color as text anchors. And no two graphical anchors need to look the same, either. The look depends entirely on the picture that the Web page's author chose to use.

Right-click a graphical anchor, and choose Save Picture As to save the image in a file on your computer.

CAUTION

If you download copyrighted graphics from the Web—for example, cartoon characters, trademarked symbols, or logos—be careful how you use them. You don't want to get in trouble for violating anyone's copyright!

Versatility is the strong suit of graphical anchors. Web page authors effectively use them for a variety of reasons. Here are some examples of the ways you might find graphical anchors used on a Web page:

- **Bullets**—Graphical anchors are frequently used as list bullets. You can click the picture to go to the Web page described by that list item. Frequently, the text in the list item is also a link. You can click either the picture or the text.
- **Icons**—Many Web sites use graphical anchors in a similar manner to the way Windows 95 uses icons. They are common on home pages, and represent a variety of Web pages available at that site. Figure 6.3 shows a Web site that uses graphical anchors in this manner. Click the ProShop icon to open the ProShop Web page, for example.
- **Advertisements**—Many Web sites have sponsors that pay to advertise on the site. Sponsorships keep the Web site free to you and me, while the site continues to make money. You usually find advertisements, such as the one shown in Figure 6.4, at the top of Web pages. Click the advertisement, and Internet Explorer 3 loads the sponsor's Web page.

URL References

The other part of a link is the URL reference. It is usually the address of the Web page that Internet Explorer 3 loads if you click the link. Every type of link, whether it uses a text or graphical anchor, uses either a relative or absolute reference. You learn about each type in this section, but when you're surfing the Web, it really doesn't matter which type of URL reference a link is using—as long as Internet Explorer 3 loads the Web page you want.

Relative References A URL reference to a file on the same computer is also known as a *relative reference*. It means that the URL is relative to the computer and directory from which Internet Explorer 3 originally loaded the Web page. If Internet Explorer 3 loads a page at **http://www.mysite.com/page**, for example, then a relative reference to **/picture** would actually refer to the URL **http://www.mysite.com/page/picture**. Relative references are used to refer to Web pages on the same computer. Figure 6.5 shows a Web page that contains relative references to other Web pages on that site.

FIG. 6.3
GolfWeb's home page uses graphical anchors to represent a variety of pages you can load.

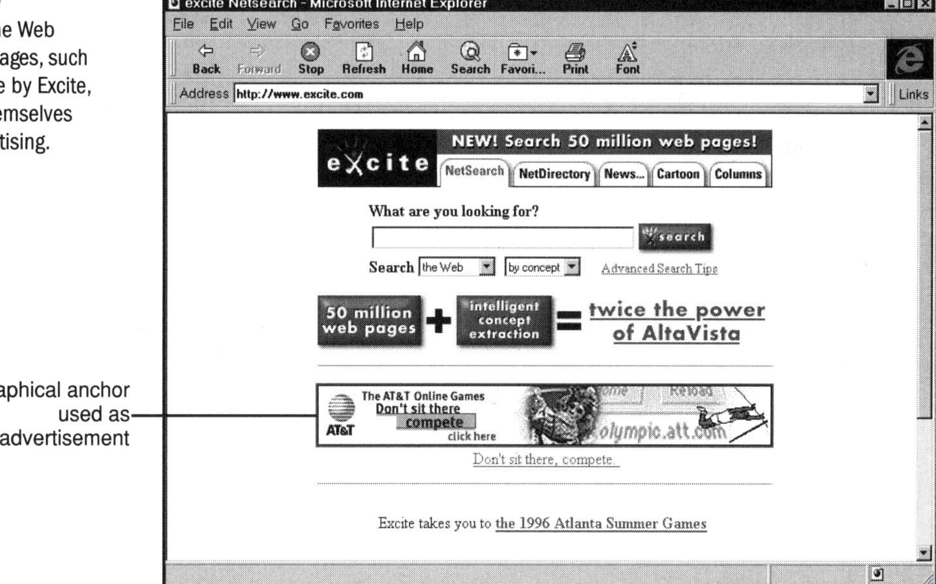

FIG. 6.4
Many of the Web services pages, such as this one by Excite, pay for themselves with advertising.

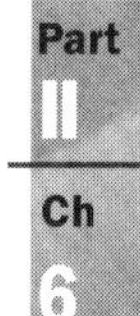

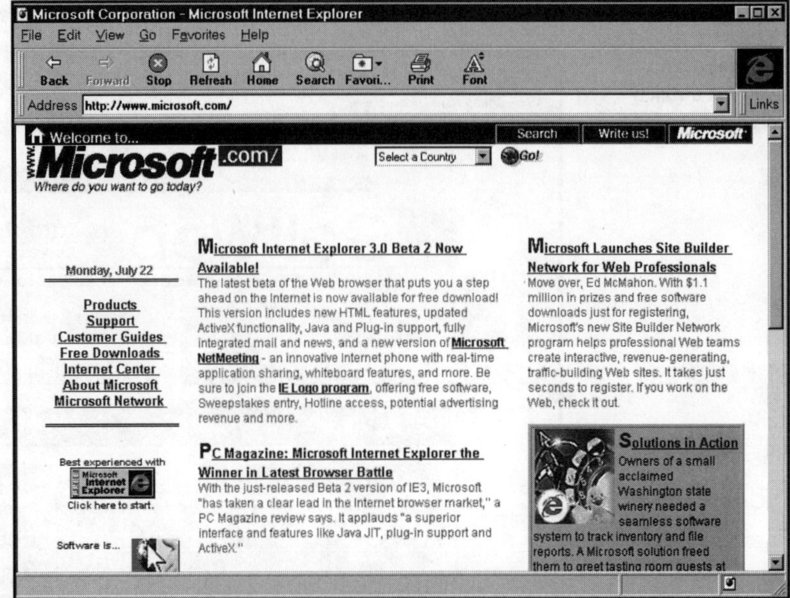

FIG. 6.5
Microsoft's home page contains many relative references to other Web pages at Microsoft.

The primary reason Web authors use a relative reference rather than an absolute reference is convenience. Just typing the filename, instead of the entire URL, is much simpler. This way, moving Web pages around on a server is also easier. Since the URL references are relative to the Web page's computer and directory, the author doesn't have to change all the links in the Web page every time the files move to a different location.

Corporate Bulletin Boards

Many corporations such as Hewlett Packard have created corporate bulletin boards that their associates view with Web browsers such as Internet Explorer 3. These Web pages aren't on the Web, however. They're stored on the companies' internal network servers. They contain a variety of information that is useful to their associates such as the following:

- Meeting schedules and meeting room availability
- Announcements about corporate events
- Information about policies and benefits
- Recent press releases and financial statements
- Technological information

You can easily create a bulletin board for the corporation you work for, too. The only difference between that and building a corporate bulletin board is in the type of information you choose to include on the page.

Absolute References A URL reference that specifies the exact computer, directory, and file for a Web page is an absolute reference. Whereas relative references are common for links to Web pages on the same computer, absolute references are necessary for links to Web pages on other computers.

Hold your mouse cursor over a link and look at Internet Explorer's status line to see its URL reference.

What Types of Resources Links Can Point To

Links can point to more than just Web pages. They can point to a variety of files and other Internet resources, too. A link can point to a video, pictures, or even a plain text file, for example. It can also point to an FTP server, Gopher server, or a UseNet newsgroup. Table 6.1 describes the other types of things a link can point to and shows you what the URL looks like.

Table 6.1 Resources to Which a Link Can Point

Type	Sample URL
Web page	**http://www.mysite.com/page.html**
Files	**file://C:/picture.bmp**
Multimedia	**http://www.mysite.com/video.avi**
E-mail	**mailto:odonnj@rpi.edu**
FTP	**ftp://ftp.mysite.com**
Gopher	**gopher://gopher.mysite.com**
Newsgroup	**news:alt.fan.que**
Telnet	**telnet://mysite.com**

How to Move Around the Web

You didn't buy this book to learn how to load a Web page in Internet Explorer, sit back, and look at it all day. You want to surf the Web—jumping from Web page to Web page looking for entertaining and useful information.

In fact, surfing is such an important part of the Web that both Internet Explorer and the Web itself provide many different ways to navigate. You can use the links and imagemaps—graphics with embedded hypertext links—that you find on a Web page, for example. You can go directly to a Web page if you know its URL. You can also use some of the more advanced Internet Explorer features such as favorite places and frames. In this section, you learn how to use those features to move around the Web like a pro.

Clicking a Link

You learned about links previously in this chapter. They are the primary method you use to go from the Web page you're viewing to another related Web page. All these links are provided by the Web page's author, and are usually accurately related to the context in which you find them.

Figure 6.6 shows a Web page with both text and graphical links. You can click the Big Yellow graphic to go to its Web site. If you use a text link, the next time you see it, its color will change, indicating that you've been there before. This color-changing helps you keep track of the links you haven't visited, so you don't waste any time.

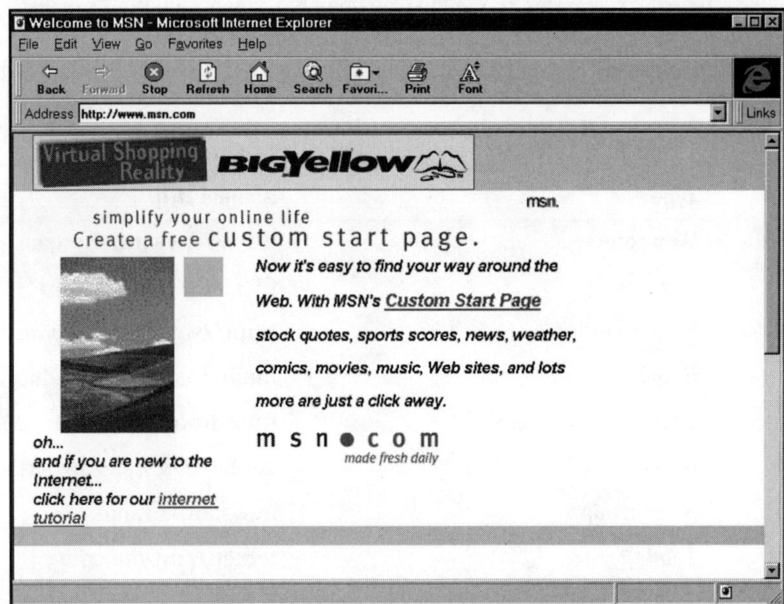

FIG. 6.6
The Microsoft Network home page has both text and graphical anchors for navigating through its Web pages.

Client Pull on the Web

You may eventually run across a Web page that says something like "We've moved" or "This Web page has a new location." It displays a link that loads the Web page at its new location if you click it. If you wait long enough, however, Internet Explorer may automatically load the Web page at its new location.

Client pull is the technology behind this behavior. Client pull allows the Web server to tell Internet Explorer 3 to reload the current Web page or load a different Web page after a set amount of time. One of the most common uses for client pull is the situation described previously. It's also used for simple sequences of Web pages, however, that work just like slide shows.

Clicking an Imagemap

Imagemaps are similar to graphical anchors, in that if you click an imagemap, Internet Explorer 3 loads another Web page. Imagemaps can load more than one Web page, however, depending on what part of the image you click. The image itself usually indicates the areas you can click to load a particular Web page.

Figure 6.7, for example, shows the imagemap that **Windows95.com** uses at its Web site. Each region of the imagemap is clearly defined so that you know where you need to click, and you know what Web page Internet Explorer 3 will load as a result. Click the Win95 Magazine icon, and Internet Explorer 3 loads a Web page containing the latest issue of the *Windows95.com* online magazine. Click the 32-bit Shareware icon, and Internet Explorer 3 loads the shareware Web page.

NOTE Incidentally, the Windows95.com Web page is enhanced especially for Internet Explorer. If you browse the site and have a sound card and speakers hooked up, get ready for a great background, MIDI sound to play as well!

FIG. 6.7 The Windows95.com home page uses an imagemap to navigate through the different parts of its Web site.

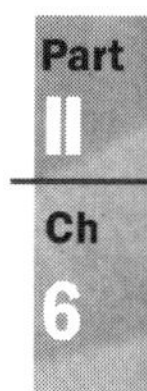

A common use for imagemaps and graphics images arrayed in a row using tables in a Web page is button bars. *Button bars* are similar to the toolbars you've used in Windows 95 and other windowing environments. They don't appear to click in and out like buttons, however. They are, after all, just graphics. You find them at the top or, more frequently, the bottom of

Web pages. Figure 6.8 shows the button bar from the Windows95.com Web site. Notice that each area you can click is clearly defined. You can click different areas to load different Web pages. You can click the Search button to search the Windows95.com, or you can click the Shareware button to check out their shareware collection.

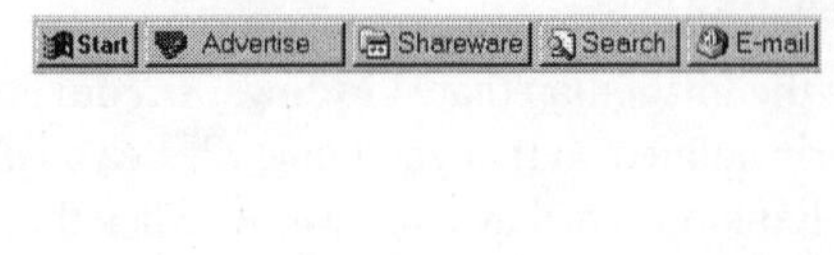

FIG. 6.8
Graphical button bars are popular navigation aids many Web authors include in their Web pages.

If you're having trouble deciphering a button bar, look for text links just below it.

Going Directly to a Resource

Which came first, the link or the Web page? If the only way you could load a Web page was by clicking a link, you would never get anywhere. If a friend gives you a URL, for example, you need a way to tell Internet Explorer 3 to open that Web page without having to use a link. That's why Internet Explorer 3 lets you go directly to a Web page by specifying its URL in the location bar.

URLs are case sensitive. If you can't open a Web page, check for strangely capitalized letters such as **http://www.MywEbsiTe.com**.

Figure 6.9 shows the Internet Explorer location bar with the drop-down list open. Type the URL of a Web page in Internet Explorer's location bar, and Internet Explorer loads the Web page. Internet Explorer keeps the addresses of all the Web pages you've opened this way in the location bar's drop-down list. It keeps this list from session to session, too. That way, you can always go back to that site by dropping down the list and clicking the Web page's URL.

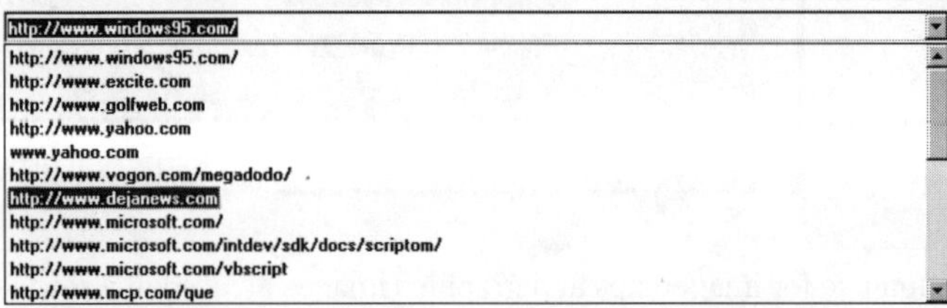

FIG. 6.9
The drop-down list keeps track of the Web sites you have visited during the current session.

You don't have to type the **http://** part of a URL in the location bar because Internet Explorer 3 adds it for you.

NOTE Internet Explorer 3 gives you a lot of feedback about what's happening after you click a link or open a URL. The Internet Explorer 3 logo seems to rotate in the upper-right corner as it transfers a Web page or file, for example. It also updates the status bar with information that helps you keep track of what Internet Explorer 3 is doing.

Moving Forward and Backward

After you've clicked a few links and opened a few Web pages, you may want to go back to a Web page you looked at earlier. Maybe you forgot something you just read, or something didn't seem that interesting then, but it does now. Internet Explorer 3 provides the following two useful features for looking at previously viewed Web pages:

- **The history list**—This keeps track of all the Web pages that you've visited during the current session. You can get at the history list by choosing Go, which shows the most recent Web pages that you've loaded in Internet Explorer (see Figure 6.10). Or, you can get the history list by choosing the Open History Folder at the bottom of the history list. Choosing this option shows the History folder (see Figure 6.11). You can scroll through the list and double-click a Web page to open it in Internet Explorer.

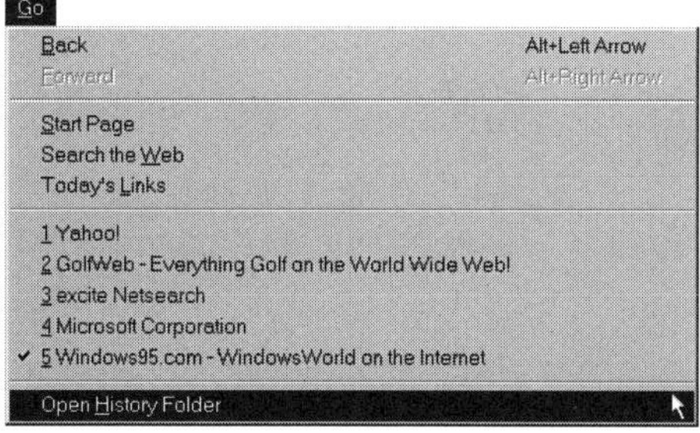

FIG. 6.10
The checkmark in this menu indicates the current Web page.

- **The Forward and Back buttons**—These move you up and down the history list shown in Figure 6.10. If you click the Back button, Internet Explorer 3 loads the previous page from the History list. If you click the Forward button, Internet Explorer 3 loads the next one. Once you've reached the bottom of the list, the Back button is disabled. Likewise, when you reach the top of the list, the Forward button is disabled.

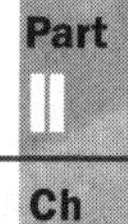

To completely empty your History folder, choose View, Options, select the Navigation tab, and click Clear History.

FIG. 6.11
Opening the History folder shows you a history of all of the sites you've ever visited (since the last time you emptied the folder).

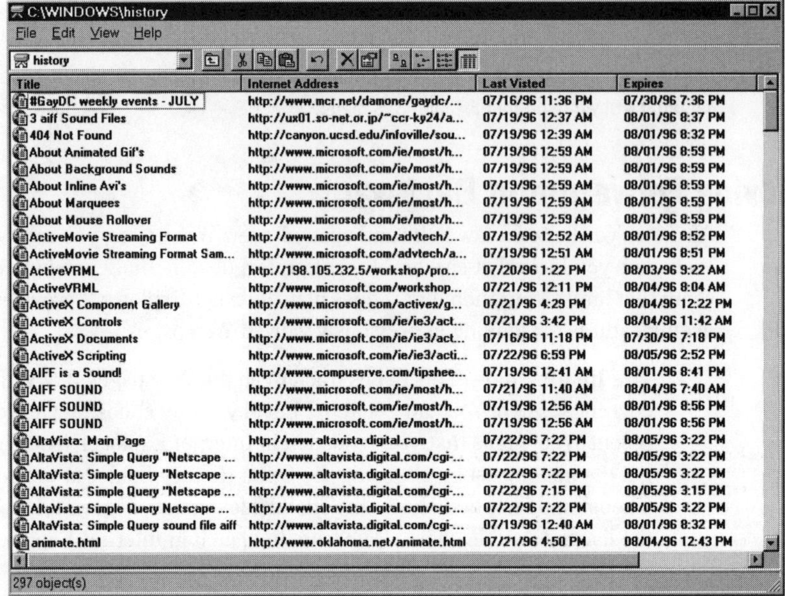

Title	Internet Address	Last Visited	Expires
#GayDC weekly events - JULY	http://www.mcr.net/damone/gaydc/...	07/16/96 11:36 PM	07/30/96 7:36 PM
3 aiff Sound Files	http://ux01.so-net.or.jp/~ccr-ky24/a...	07/19/96 12:37 AM	08/01/96 8:37 PM
404 Not Found	http://canyon.ucsd.edu/infoville/sou...	07/19/96 12:39 AM	08/01/96 8:32 PM
About Animated Gif's	http://www.microsoft.com/ie/most/h...	07/19/96 12:59 AM	08/01/96 8:59 PM
About Background Sounds	http://www.microsoft.com/ie/most/h...	07/19/96 12:59 AM	08/01/96 8:59 PM
About Inline Avi's	http://www.microsoft.com/ie/most/h...	07/19/96 12:59 AM	08/01/96 8:59 PM
About Marquees	http://www.microsoft.com/ie/most/h...	07/19/96 12:59 AM	08/01/96 8:59 PM
About Mouse Rollover	http://www.microsoft.com/ie/most/h...	07/19/96 12:59 AM	08/01/96 8:59 PM
ActiveMovie Streaming Format	http://www.microsoft.com/advtech/...	07/19/96 12:52 AM	08/01/96 8:52 PM
ActiveMovie Streaming Format Sam...	http://www.microsoft.com/advtech/a...	07/19/96 12:51 AM	08/01/96 8:51 PM
ActiveVRML	http://198.105.232.5/workshop/pro...	07/20/96 1:22 PM	08/03/96 9:22 AM
ActiveVRML	http://www.microsoft.com/workshop...	07/21/96 12:11 PM	08/04/96 8:04 AM
ActiveX Component Gallery	http://www.microsoft.com/activex/g...	07/21/96 4:29 PM	08/04/96 12:22 PM
ActiveX Controls	http://www.microsoft.com/ie/ie3/act...	07/21/96 3:42 PM	08/04/96 11:42 AM
ActiveX Documents	http://www.microsoft.com/ie/ie3/act...	07/16/96 11:18 PM	07/30/96 7:18 PM
ActiveX Scripting	http://www.microsoft.com/ie/ie3/acti...	07/22/96 6:59 PM	08/05/96 2:52 PM
AIFF is a Sound!	http://www.compuserve.com/tipshee...	07/19/96 12:41 AM	08/01/96 8:41 PM
AIFF SOUND	http://www.microsoft.com/ie/most/h...	07/21/96 11:40 AM	08/04/96 7:40 AM
AIFF SOUND	http://www.microsoft.com/ie/most/h...	07/19/96 12:56 AM	08/01/96 8:56 PM
AIFF SOUND	http://www.microsoft.com/ie/most/h...	07/19/96 12:56 AM	08/01/96 8:56 PM
AltaVista: Main Page	http://www.altavista.digital.com	07/22/96 7:22 PM	08/05/96 3:22 PM
AltaVista: Simple Query "Netscape ...	http://www.altavista.digital.com/cgi-...	07/22/96 7:22 PM	08/05/96 3:22 PM
AltaVista: Simple Query "Netscape ...	http://www.altavista.digital.com/cgi-...	07/22/96 7:22 PM	08/05/96 3:22 PM
AltaVista: Simple Query "Netscape ...	http://www.altavista.digital.com/cgi-...	07/22/96 7:15 PM	08/05/96 3:15 PM
AltaVista: Simple Query Netscape ...	http://www.altavista.digital.com/cgi-...	07/22/96 7:22 PM	08/05/96 3:22 PM
AltaVista: Simple Query sound file aiff	http://www.altavista.digital.com/cgi-...	07/19/96 12:40 AM	08/01/96 8:32 PM
animate.html	http://www.oklahoma.net/animate.html	07/21/96 4:50 PM	08/04/96 12:43 PM

Going to Your Start Page

If you start feeling a bit lost, getting your bearings is sometimes easier if you go back to your start page—starting over. Internet Explorer 3 lets you configure a start page that it uses for two purposes:

- Internet Explorer 3 loads your start page every time it starts.

- At any time, you can click the Home button on the Internet Explorer 3 toolbar to return to your start page.

Configure your start page to point to a file on your local computer. Then your start page always loads quickly.

To change your start page in Internet Explorer, follow these steps:

1. Load the Web page that you would like to be your start page into Internet Explorer.
2. Choose View, Options from the Internet Explorer main menu. The Options dialog box appears.
3. Click the Navigation tab (see Figure 6.12).
4. Select Start Page from the drop-down list box, and click the Use Current button, or type the URL in the Address field.
5. Click OK to save your changes.

FIG. 6.12
Internet Explorer allows you to change the Web page that is loaded when you click the Home or Search toolbar buttons, or any of the Quick Links.

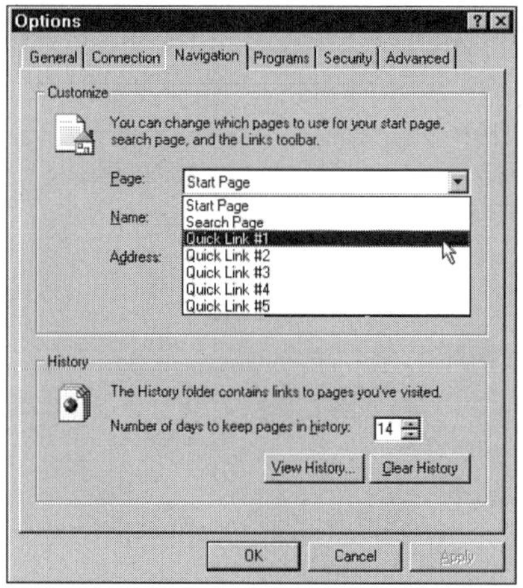

You can use the same procedure to change the page that is loaded when you click the Search button on the toolbar, or the Links buttons.

NOTE Microsoft usually uses the term *start page* to refer to the first Web page your Web browser opens—another term that many people also use for this is *home page*. The term *home page*, though, also has another meaning. Many people refer to the opening page of a Web site as that site's home page. Hewlett Packard's home page contains links for computers and peripherals, for example.

Quick Links

Internet Explorer 3 also features a row of toolbar buttons called Links. When clicked, these buttons can quickly connect you to a variety of Web sites. The default collection of links takes you to various places on the Microsoft Web site. However, in the same way that you can change the start and search pages, you can also change each of these links. Figure 6.13 shows an example of configuring the first link. After it is changed, the first link on the Links section of the toolbar will take me to my home page (which, on my system, is different than my start page).

Saving Web Pages as Favorite Places

The easiest way to get back to a Web page that you visit frequently is to use Internet Explorer 3's Favorites menu. By using favorite places, you can save and organize links to your favorite Web pages. Choose Favorites, Open Favorites Folder from the Internet Explorer 3 main menu, or click the Favorite Places toolbar button to open the favorites list (see Figure 6.14).

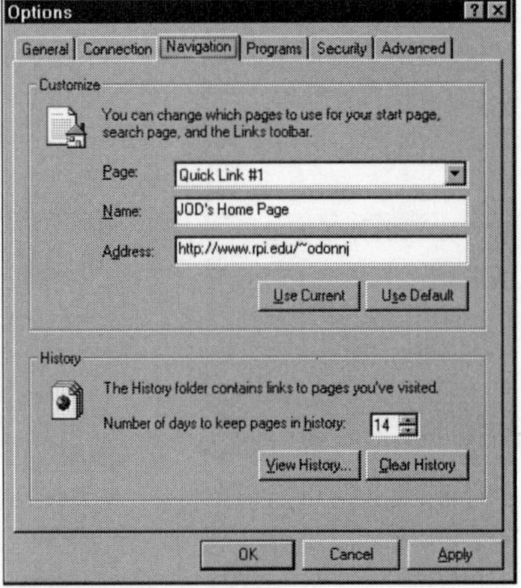

FIG. 6.13
Internet Explorer allows you to configure the five buttons in the Links area of the toolbar to quickly send you wherever on the Web you would like to go.

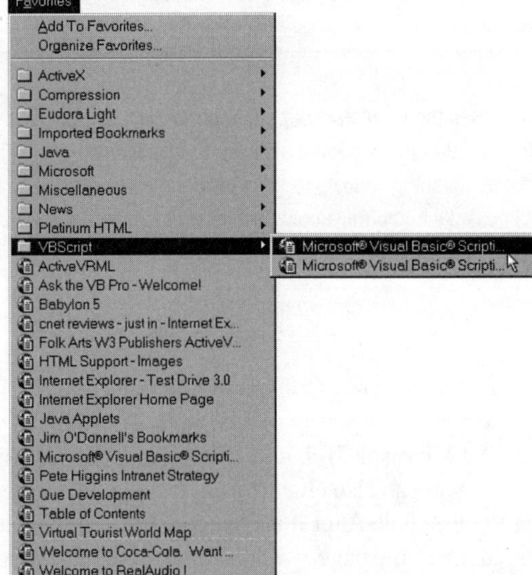

FIG. 6.14
Open a submenu or click a Web site to load it in Internet Explorer.

Navigating a Web Site with Frames

Frames, a feature originally introduced by Netscape, are supported by Internet Explorer 3. They allow you to split the Internet Explorer 3 window into multiple sections. Each frame on the window can point to a different URL. Figure 6.15 shows a Web page that uses a frame to present a button bar that's always available to you. Note that Microsoft has itself enhanced Netscape frames, giving the Web author more control over the appearance of each frame. In Figure 6.15, you can see three frames, but the Web author has chosen to leave out the telltale gray borders normally present.

Many Windows 95 programs divide their windows into panes. They do so to make the organization of the windows' contents more obvious. A program that performs searches might have two panes: one to display a list of general topics and another for the entry of more specific information. Internet Explorer 3 frames can serve a similar purpose, as well.

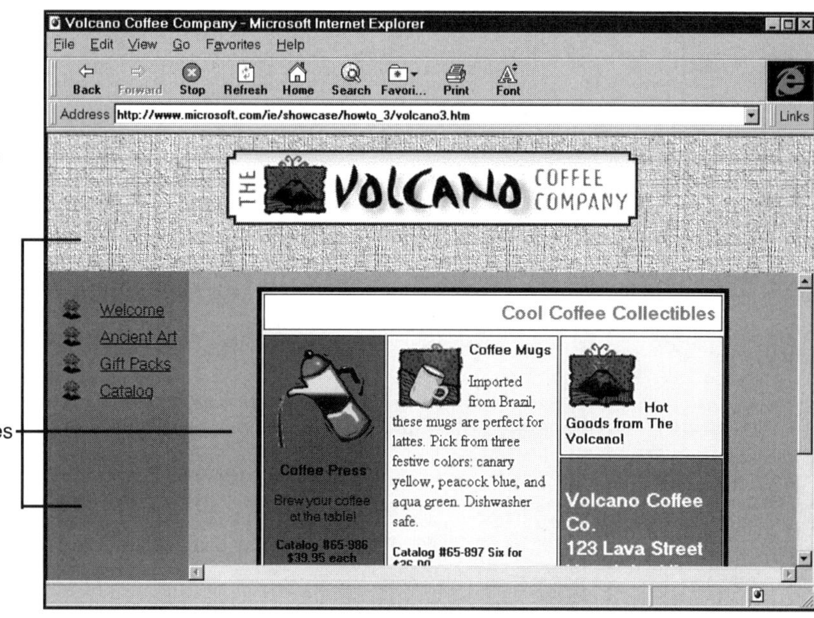

FIG. 6.15
At this site, the showcase site for the capabilities of Internet Explorer 3, the Volcano Coffee Company banner and the table of contents at the left are always available, regardless of what is being shown in the lower-right frame.

Getting Around Faster

If you're using a 14.4 Kbps or slower modem, you may eventually become frustrated with how long it takes to load some Web pages. Many Web pages have very large graphics that take a long time to download. Unfortunately, the use of large graphics is becoming more common as Web authors take it for granted that everyone on the Internet is using at least a 28.8 Kbps modem.

Many Web sites provide links to text-only versions. Look for a text link that says "Text Only."

If you're having trouble with slow connections, Internet Explorer 3 provides a few features that make Web pages containing too many graphics more tolerable:

- You don't have to wait for the entire Web page to finish loading before you can click a link. Click the Stop button, and Internet Explorer 3 stops transferring the Web page. If you change your mind and want to reload the page, click the Reload button. Also, most of the text links are available before Internet Explorer 3 has finished transferring the images for the Web page. You can click any of these links. Internet Explorer 3 stops loading the current page and starts loading the Web page referenced by the link.

- Most of your time is spent waiting for inline images to load. The irony is that the images on many Web pages aren't really worth the time if you have a slow connection. If you don't want Internet Explorer 3 to load inline images automatically, make sure the Show Pictures box under the General tab in the Options dialog box is not checked. If you want to view a particular image, and you've disabled showing the pictures, click the image placeholder. Figure 6.16 shows what a Web page looks like when it's loaded without inline images. Notice that Internet Explorer 3 displays placeholders where it normally displays the images. Internet Explorer 3 also displays alternative text to help you figure out to what the link points. Figure 6.17 shows the same page with all the images loaded.

FIG. 6.16
You can click one of the placeholders to either load the Web page it refers to, if it's a graphical anchor, or to load the image.

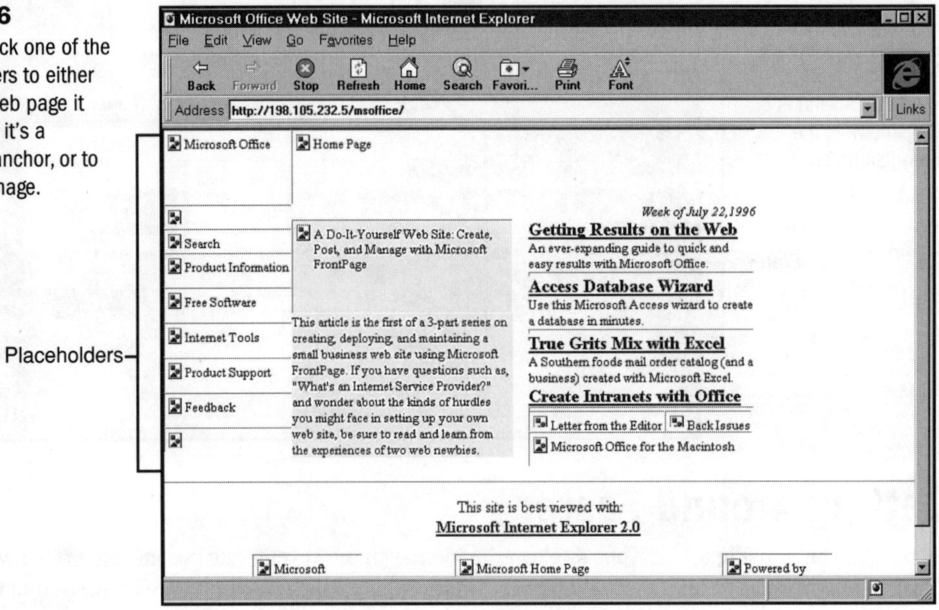

Changing the Way Internet Explorer 3 Works with Links

Internet Explorer 3 gives you a bit of control over how it displays links. It lets you choose whether they're underlined and what color it uses to display them.

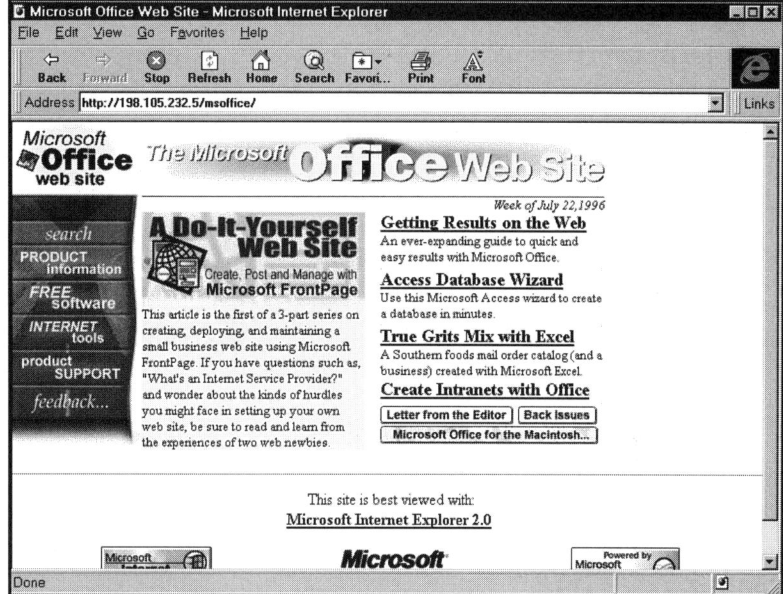

FIG. 6.17
When the inline images are loaded, the Web page looks much more complete but has much the same information.

Underlining Links

You learned previously in this chapter that Internet Explorer 3 underlines a link's text anchor on a Web page. You can change that. Here's how to configure Internet Explorer 3 so that it doesn't underline a link's text anchor:

1. Choose View, Options from the Internet Explorer 3 main menu. The Internet Properties dialog box appears.
2. Click the General tab.
3. Deselect Underline links, and click OK.

Beginning with the next Web page that Internet Explorer 3 loads, text anchors are not underlined. You can still figure out where the links are, however, because they are displayed in a different color than the text around them.

Using a Different Color for Links

If you don't like the colors that Internet Explorer 3 uses for links, you can change them. If the default colors are hard to tell apart on your computer, for example, you may want to change the colors so that you can easily see the links. You can change the colors Internet Explorer 3 uses for a text link's anchor, by selecting the General tab from the Options dialog box. By clicking the two buttons for Visited links and/or Unvisited links, you can change their colors.

Beginning with the next Web page that Internet Explorer 3 loads, it will display text anchors in the selected color, depending on whether or not you have visited them recently. The period of time considered "recently" can be set by selecting the Navigation tab in the Options dialog box and setting the number of days under Number of Days to Keep Pages in History. ●

CHAPTER 7

E-Mail with Netscape

- Configure Netscape 3.0's e-mail servers and preferences
- Send and receive mail
- Organize your mail using folders
- Create an address book to speed your correspondence

Netscape started life as a dedicated Web browser, and there's never been a doubt that it's a superior piece of software for that purpose. Netscape has also bent over backwards, for the most part successfully, to make other Internet services like FTP and Gopher accessible from Netscape.

But in one key area—e-mail—Netscape fell short. Early, 1.x versions of Netscape provided only the most rudimentary capability to access the Internet's most popular service. Users could only send mail with Netscape; they couldn't receive it. Needless to say, the designers of dedicated e-mail managers didn't find Netscape a threat to their business.

This is changing fast. In a bid to make its flagship program a full-service Internet client, Netscape has given version 3.0 a powerful mail manager that many users—particularly those at home—may find suits their needs. ■

Netscape's New E-Mail Manager

In their first attempt to make their Web browser a full-service Internet client, Netscape's programmers have done a pretty fair job. The new e-mail manager provides most of the functionality that veteran Net users have come to expect from their software. It also offers a couple of very useful, Netscape-only twists.

The feature that, above all others, sets Netscape's mail package apart from its established competitors is the fact that it treats incoming messages basically as HTML documents. The mail reader is able to detect any URL mentioned in the text of a message and highlight it for one-click access by the user. Your mail becomes a separate, hotlinked gateway to the World Wide Web and the rest of the Internet.

Netscape doesn't stint on the standard stuff, either. You've always been able to use it to write and send messages, but now you'll find that you can easily reply to, forward, and carbon copy messages, just as users of third-party mail packages can. Message management is a snap because you have the ability to transfer your traffic to a set of custom, user-defined mail folders. Within those folders, you can tell Netscape to sort your mail by subject, sender, or date. You can also keep and maintain a list of your most frequently used addresses.

If you're a casual e-mail user, you'll likely find that Netscape's new built-in mail capabilities are all you need. And if it's important that you have the ability to tap into the Web directly from your message traffic, you'll find Netscape's mail manager indispensable.

But if you're accustomed to using other mail packages, programs like Eudora and cc:Mail, you'll soon see that Netscape's package isn't quite complete. Although some rough edges present in the Address Book and file attachment features of Netscape's early betas have been smoothed over, power users will miss high-end features like automatic message filtering.

All in all, if you're happy with your current mail program, you'll have to make the call as to whether you want to switch to Netscape just yet. You'd be well-advised, however, to watch carefully as it evolves in the future. It's quite clear that Netscape is serious about making its leading program the only Internet client most people will ever need.

But if you're a new mail user, or if you haven't found a package quite to your liking just yet, you'll probably want to give Netscape's e-mail facility a try. You may find that it meets your needs completely.

Setting Mail Preferences

Before attempting to use Netscape's mail facility, you must provide some basic information about yourself, your Internet provider, and your computer. Begin by choosing Options, and then select Mail and News Preferences. Netscape responds with a tabbed dialog box.

The best way to familiarize yourself with Netscape's mail settings is to step through each of the five tabs sequentially as you set up the program for the first time.

Appearance

The options on this tab, seen in Figure 7.1, affect the way Netscape displays message text. Under Messages and Articles Are Shown With, your choice tells Netscape whether to use a fixed-width or variable-width font when it displays the text of your mail. The default is Fixed Width Font; in most cases you'll want to stick to that setting because Variable Width Font can ruin the formatting of many Internet messages. The settings under Text Beginning With > (Quoted Text) Has the Following Characteristics affects the display of message excerpts included in a mailing to establish its subject and context. They're largely self-explanatory; change them to suit your taste.

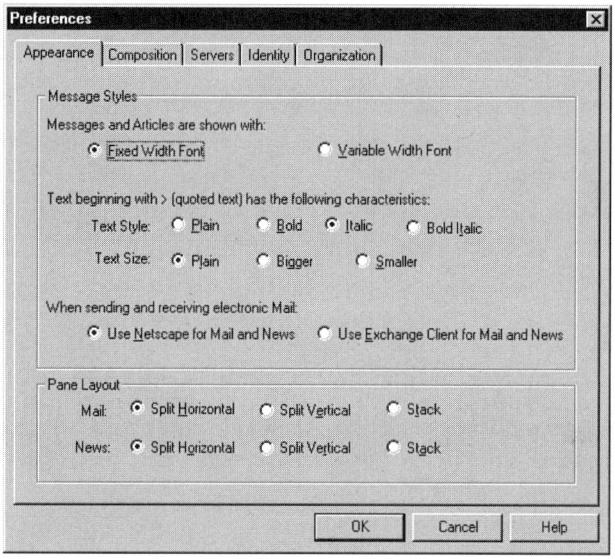

FIG. 7.1
The settings on the Appearance tab give the user control over the fonts Netscape uses to display the text of mail messages.

Preferences

Appearance | Composition | Servers | Identity | Organization

Message Styles
Messages and Articles are shown with:
Fixed Width Font   Variable Width Font

Text beginning with > (quoted text) has the following characteristics:
Text Style: Plain Bold Italic Bold Italic
Text Size: Plain Bigger Smaller

When sending and receiving electronic Mail:
Use Netscape for Mail and News   Use Exchange Client for Mail and News

Pane Layout
Mail: Split Horizontal Split Vertical Stack
News: Split Horizontal Split Vertical Stack

OK Cancel Help

The remaining buttons on this tab, found under the heading When Receiving Electronic Mail, tell Netscape whether to use its own built-in e-mail capabilities or those provided with every copy of Windows 95 by Microsoft Exchange. If you want to use Netscape's, click Use Netscape for Mail and News.

New to Netscape is the ability to configure the window layout of Netscape Mail. You can have Netscape Mail's window panes use one of three basic configurations. The default, Split Horizontal, lists your mail folders in the upper-left pane, the mail headers in the upper-right pane, and the letters themselves in the bottom pane. The Split Vertical option (see Figure 7.2) has the folders in the upper left, the headers in the lower left, and the messages on the right.

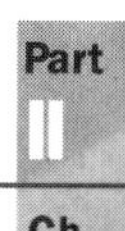

Finally, the Stack option puts the folders on top, the headers in the middle, and the mail body at the bottom. Just choose the window pane layout you want and click the OK button. The new layout won't be used until you quit out of Netscape Mail, and start it up again.

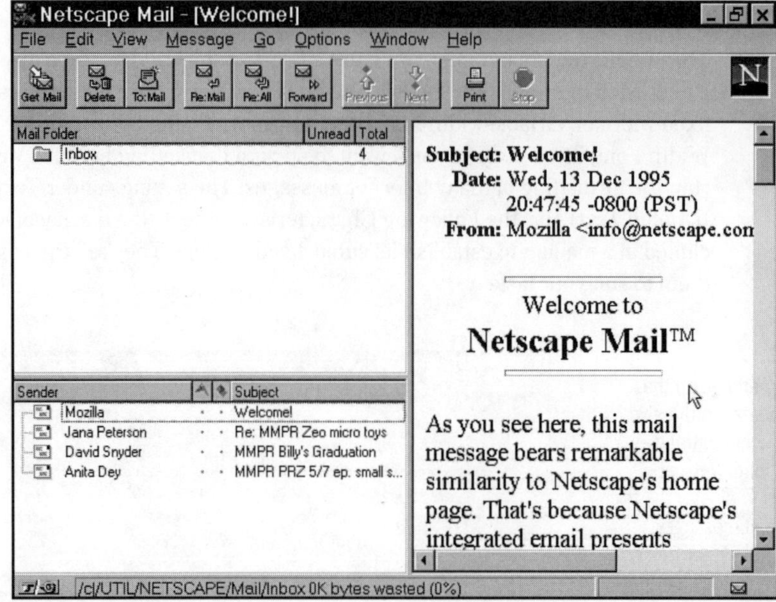

FIG. 7.2
This is one of the new Netscape Mail window pane layouts that's available with Netscape.

Composition

There are several key settings on this tab, seen in Figure 7.3:

- The Send and Post setting determines how file attachments are coded. Allow 8-bit is the default and is recognized by most mail programs.

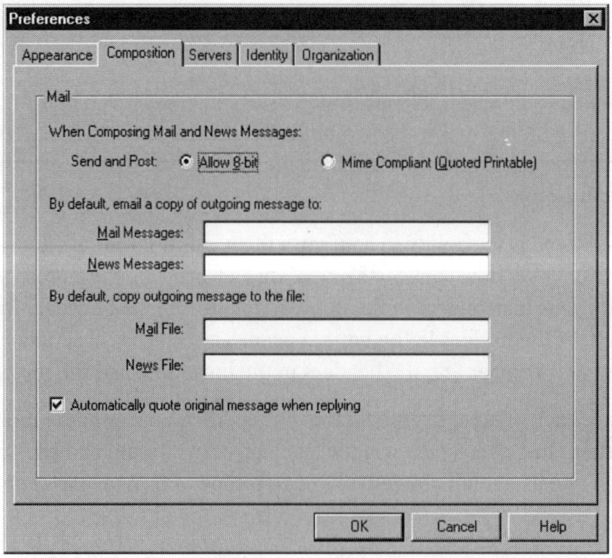

FIG. 7.3
The Composition tab controls key settings for file encoding and message queuing.

Preferences
Appearance | Composition | Servers | Identity | Organization
Mail
When Composing Mail and News Messages:
Send and Post: (•) Allow 8-bit ( ) Mime Compliant (Quoted Printable)
By default, email a copy of outgoing message to:
Mail Messages:
News Messages:
By default, copy outgoing message to the file:
Mail File:
News File:
[✓] Automatically quote original message when replying
OK Cancel Help

- The Deliver Mail setting tells Netscape whether you want to send each message when you're done writing it, or to hold it on disk. Choosing Automatically tells Netscape to send when you're done writing; Queue for Manual Delivery holds your message.

You'll probably want to queue your messages on disk if you do most of your work offline, as a dial-in Internet user. Send them by clicking File and choosing Deliver Mail Now.

- You can have Netscape send a copy of all your outgoing messages to a single address by entering that address in the Mail Messages field.
- The entry in the Mail File field tells Netscape where to store copies of your outgoing messages on disk. This is a key setting. In the following discussion of the Directories tab, we'll tell you how to avoid problems by reconciling it with that tab's Mail Directory field. If you don't care to keep copies of your outgoing traffic, you can avoid problems entirely by leaving this field blank.
- Checking Automatically Quote Original Message When Replying tells Netscape to insert the text of any message you answered with the Message menu's Reply option into the body of your answer.

Servers

This tab is probably the most important of the five on the Mail and News Preferences dialog box. On this tab, seen in Figure 7.4, you tell Netscape how to get to your mail.

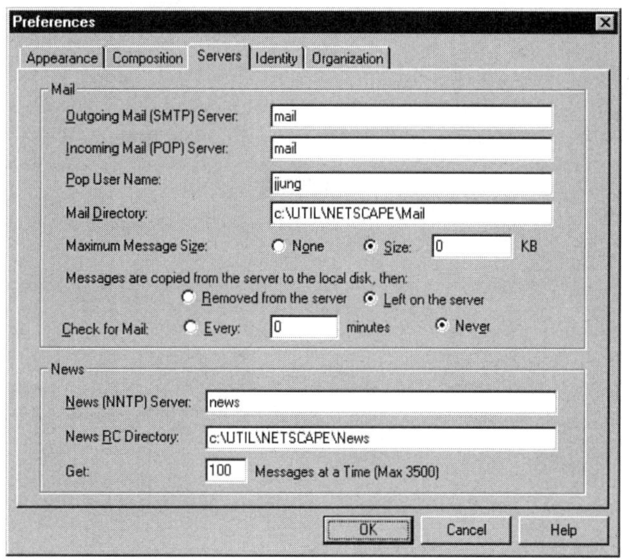

FIG. 7.4
Many of the controls that affect your use of Netscape's e-mail features are on the Mail and News Preferences dialog box. Here we're using it to enter information about our mail server.

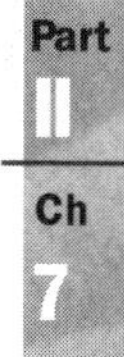

Do the following:

1. Type the Internet addresses for your service provider's SMTP (send mail) and POP3 (receive mail) clients in the Mail (SMTP) Server and Mail POP Server fields, which are

near the top of the tab. Get this information from your service provider if you don't already have it.

2. Type your e-mail name (in all likelihood, the one you use when you log into your Internet provider) in the Pop User Name box.
3. You should make sure Netscape's setup routine has provided access to the directory where your mail folders are stored by looking in the Mail Directory field. There should be some entry like C:\Program Files\ Netscape\Navigator\Mail, as seen in figure 7.3. The actual listing will vary depending on your Netscape setup.
4. If there's no path in the Mail Directory field, or you have reason to believe the path is incorrect, open Explorer, find the folder Netscape's installed in, and then find the Mail subfolder. Note the Windows 95 path, go back into Netscape, and type the path into the Mail Directory field.

You can use the Mail Directory field to tell Netscape to store your mail in any Windows 95 folder you want. Simply type its path in place of the one provided by Netscape.

5. Click the Composition tab. Look in the Mail File field, near the bottom of the tab. The Windows 95 path listed there should match that in the Mail Directory field, with the addition of the characters, \Sent (see Figure 7.5). Netscape stores a copy of your outgoing messages in this file.

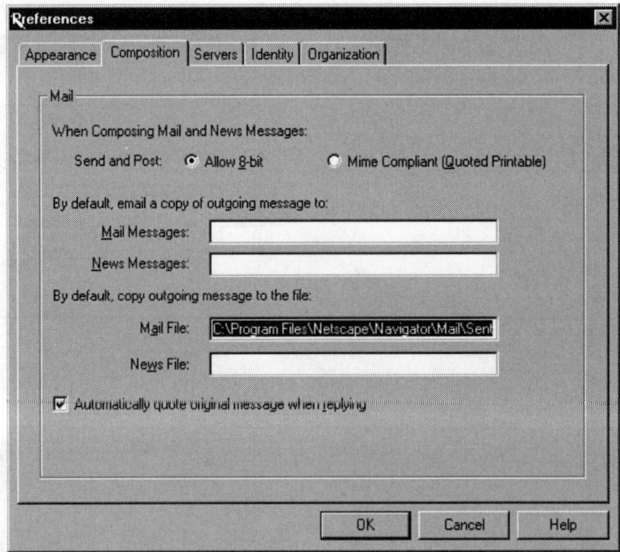

FIG. 7.5
Make sure the Composition tab's Mail File field refers to the same path as the Directories tab's Mail Directory field.

6. If it doesn't match, type the path in yourself. For example, if your Mail Directory is C:\Program Files\Netscape\Navigator\Mail, type C:\ Program Files\Netscape\ Navigator\Mail\Sent in the Mail File field.

TROUBLESHOOTING

When I try to send mail, Netscape responds with an error message that says Can't open FCC file. I've searched the Netscape directories and the rest of my hard drive and can't find an FCC file. Should I create one? No. This cryptic message is Netscape's way of telling you that the Composition tab's Mail File field isn't referring to the same Windows 95 path as your Mail Directory field. The Sent file has to be located in the same folder as the rest of your mail files.

This problem originally cropped up because the installation routines for the early betas of Netscape 3.0 wouldn't update the Mail File field when asked to install the program to any folder other than their default settings.

There are three ways to fix the resulting mess. Check the Mail Directory field, and then enter this path in the Mail File field, tagging the characters "\Sent" on the end. Alternatively, open Windows 95's Registry Editor and, using its search facility, find the phrase "Default FCC." It'll turn up among the HKEY_CURRENT_USER settings, as in Figure 7.6. Click Edit, choose Modify, and enter the proper path in the field provided.

Your remaining option, if you don't consider it important to keep copies of your outgoing messages, is to leave the Composition tab's Mail File field blank. If you do, Netscape won't save any copies, but it won't pop up an error message either.

7. After you're comfortable with Netscape's mail features, you'll likely want to click the Removed from the Server button so old mail doesn't clutter your Internet provider's disk.

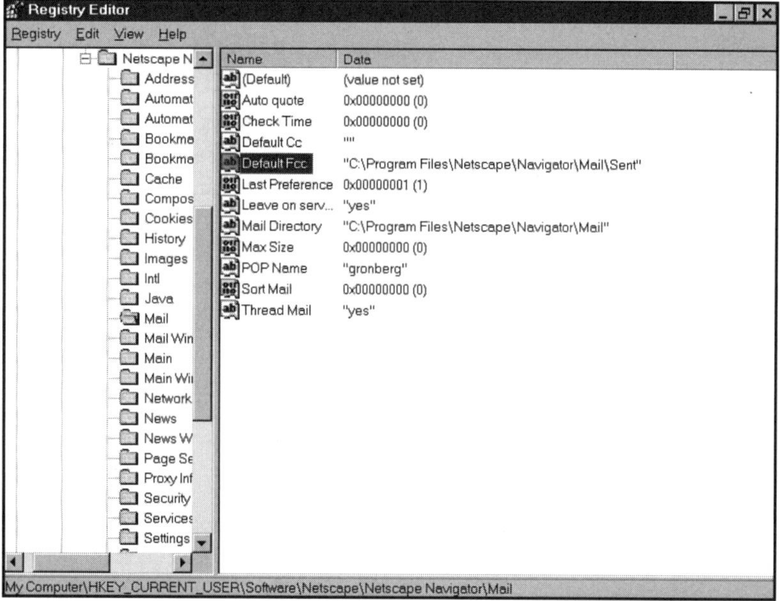

FIG. 7.6
You can use Windows 95's Registry Editor to reconcile the Mail Directory and Mail File fields. The path to the Sent file listed beside Default FCC should match the path beside Mail Directory.

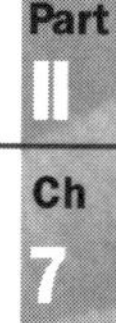

Identity

Netscape personalizes your outgoing messages by adding bits from the settings on this tab. You'll want to do the following:

1. Type your real name in the Your Name field.
2. Type your e-mail address in the Your Email field.
3. If you want replies to your outgoing messages sent to an address other than the one listed in Your Email, type it in the Reply-to Address field.
4. Fill in Your Organization if you want the name of your employer or the group you represent to appear on your mail.
5. If you want Netscape to append a signature file to your outgoing messages, use the Browse key next to Signature File on the Identity tab to search for and select a signature file from your hard drive. Your signature must be an ASCII text file. It should be hard-formatted and less than 80 characters wide. Internet etiquette would also suggest that you keep it short.
6. If you're concerned about retaining your privacy on the Internet, click either the Nothing: Anonymous User or A Unique ID Number button at the bottom of the tab. In most cases, however, you'll want your messages identified with Your Email Address.

Organization

The threading and sorting features of Netscape's mail manager are fully controllable from the mail window, but the program does allow you to designate their default settings. They're available on the Organization tab, seen in Figure 7.7.

- If you think you'll want your message traffic threaded (that is, with messages and replies on the same topic grouped together for easy reading), click the Organization tab and make sure the Thread Mail Messages box is checked.
- You may also want to change the default sort order for your incoming message traffic. If so, click the Organization tab and choose one of the Sort Mail By selections. The available sort options are by Date, Subject, and Sender.

For now at least, ignore the fields and buttons that control Netscape's newsreader functions. Read about them in Chapter 9, "Reading UseNet Newsgroups with Netscape."

When you're satisfied with the changes you've made to the various tabs on the Mail and News Preferences dialog box, click OK to save your work. Clicking Cancel abandons it.

Using the Mail Package

At first glance, Netscape 3.0 appears no more a sophisticated mail package than its predecessors. The picture begins to change, though, when you click the Window menu and select Netscape Mail.

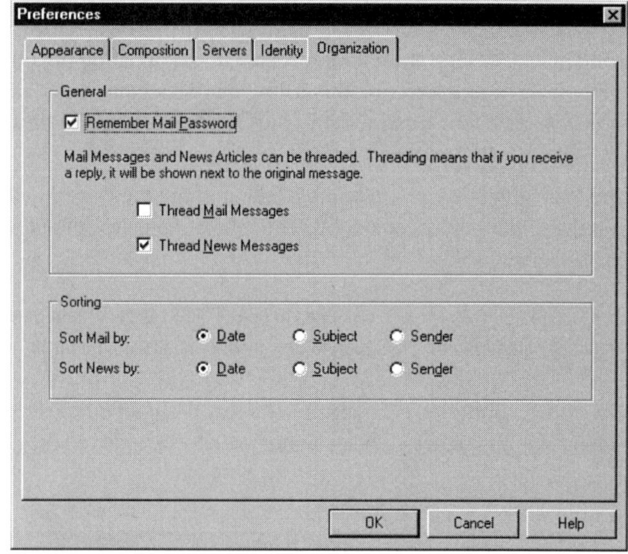

FIG. 7.7
The settings on the Organization tab tell Netscape how to sort and thread your message traffic.

The program responds first by asking you to enter a password. In the Password Entry dialog box, enter verbatim the phrase your Internet provider told you to use when logging on to your mail server (see Figure 7.8).

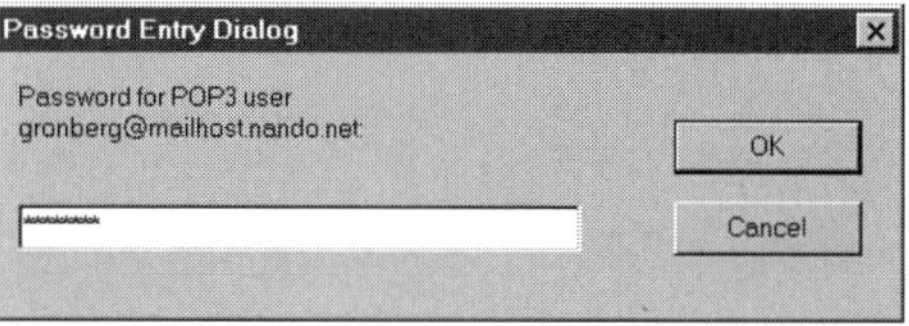

FIG. 7.8
Netscape demands that you enter the password for your Internet e-mail account every time you want to access its mail window.

If you click OK, Netscape immediately tries to log on to your mail server. If it finds that you're not online, or that it can't log on to your server, eventually it will give up and flash an error message. If you've opened a mail window to work offline, you can avoid this problem by clicking Cancel in the Password Entry dialog box.

Understanding the Screen

Once in the program, you're confronted by a screen that reminds some users of the Microsoft Exchange e-mail client that comes with every copy of Windows 95. Don't be fooled: Netscape's mail facility is nowhere near as sophisticated as Exchange and nowhere near as resource-hungry. In actual use Netscape's mail facility compares favorably with such light-footed freeware and shareware packages as Eudora and Pegasus.

Let's get oriented.

- On the top left of Netscape's mail screen, you see a listing of your personal mail folders (see Figure 7.9). At minimum, this listing contains your inbox and your trash folder. After you've sent your first message with Netscape, you should see a Sent folder that holds copies of your outgoing traffic.
- On the top right, you see a scrollable listing of the message headers for every piece of mail in the folder you're looking at. The inbox opens by default when you first open Netscape's mail facility.

NOTE Netscape highlights unread messages in bold. Folders that contain unread messages are also highlighted in bold. You open folders by double-clicking them.

- On the bottom of the screen, you see the text of the open message, along with headers indicating the message's subject, sender, sender's reply-to address, and the date it was sent.

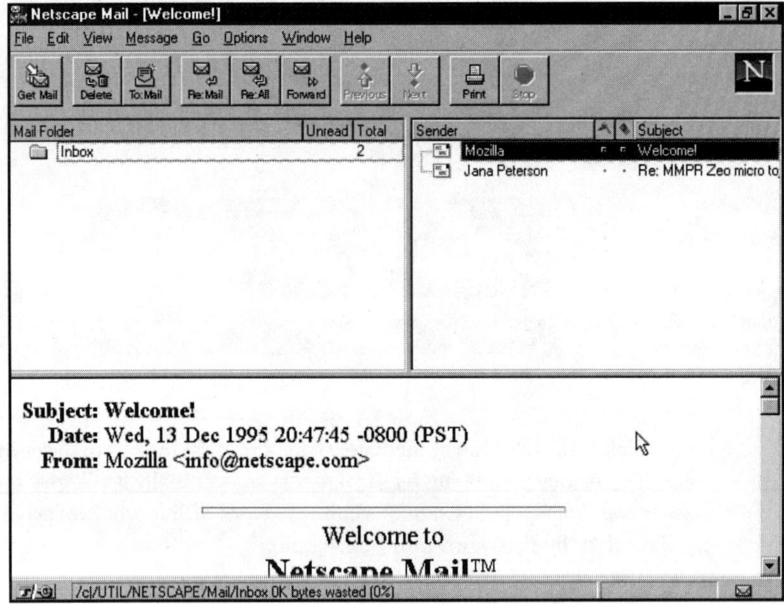

FIG. 7.9 Netscape's clean mail layout provides easy access to your message traffic and your personal mail folders.

One feature you'll learn to like may not be immediately obvious: If the message contains a URL, Netscape treats it as such, recognizing and highlighting it for immediate use. By clicking a URL, you can jump immediately to the Web page, FTP site, or other Internet service that it points to.

TIP Netscape gives you one-click access to any URL embedded in an e-mail message displayed on-screen.

NOTE You may notice at low screen resolutions that Netscape's mail display is a bit cramped. You can adjust the sizes of the various panes by clicking and dragging their frames. You'll find that the only real way to see what you're doing, video card permitting, is to use a higher screen resolution. Open Control Panel's Display properties, click the Settings tab, and set the Desktop Area slider to at least 800 × 600 pixels for a better look.

Netscape now has the ability to show you a variety of e-mail headers. Typically, all e-mail you send or receive has a lot of information stored in its headers. The information is often technical and not intended for most people to figure out. However, some mail headers can be useful to the casual person. Whether it's because of a cute quote that somebody put in, or a particular e-mail address, some header information is useful.

You can determine how much, or how little, of the e-mail header you want to see. Simply click on Options, Show Headers, and select between All, Normal, or Brief. The All option shows you every single bit of header information in the letter body. The Normal option only shows you the subject of the letter, the date it was sent, who it's from, and who it's to. The Brief option shows you pretty much the same information as the Normal option, but puts it into a compact, one-line format.

Composing and Sending Mail

Netscape 3.0's mail and news clients use the same front end for message composition. In the case of the mail client, you begin a message either by clicking the New Mail button on the toolbar or by clicking the File menu and selecting New Mail Message. A message form like the one shown in Figure 7.10 opens.

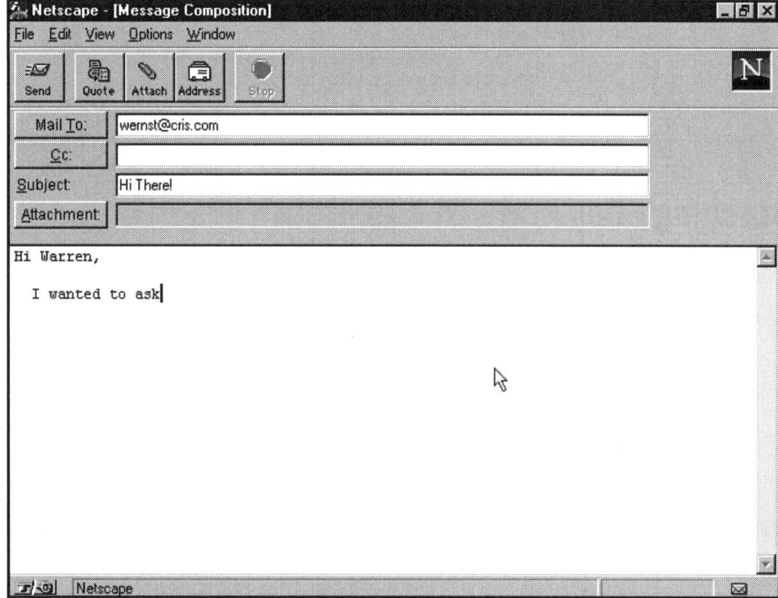

FIG. 7.10 Netscape uses a standard form for outgoing e-mail and UseNet articles. Here's an e-mail message ready to go.

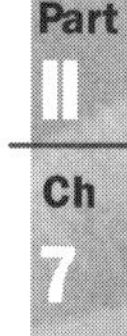

Netscape inserts the text of your signature file, if you use one, in the section of the screen reserved for message text. Fill out the rest of the message by following these steps:

1. Type the address of the person or organization you're writing to in the Send To field.
2. Type a short phrase in the Subject field describing the content of your message.

You don't have to open the Netscape Mail window to create a message. Click Netscape's File menu and choose New Mail Message to open a Composition window.

3. If you want to send copies of your message to third parties, click the View menu and select either Mail Cc or Mail Bcc. This adds a blank address field of the same name to your message header. Type the addresses of the additional recipients. Use Cc if you want to publicize the fact you've sent copies; use Bcc (blind copy) if you don't.
4. Click once in the main text box to set the cursor at the beginning of your message, and begin writing your text. Standard Windows 95 Cut, Copy, and Paste commands are available on the Edit menu.

NOTE If the recipient of your message is using Netscape's e-mail manager also, you can pass along interesting and useful URLs in one of two ways. First, you can simply type the URL into a message. Or, if you're viewing a Web page or some other resource in the browser, you can click the File menu and select Mail Document. When you do, Netscape opens a new message window with the URL listed in the body of the mailing. In either case, when the person viewing your message opens it in Netscape's mail manager, the URL will appear as a hotlink. You need do nothing more than type; Netscape detects the presence of the URL automatically.

5. When finished, make sure you're online and then click the Send button on the Composition window's toolbar.

Netscape sends a new message as soon as you click Send if its Composition preferences are set to deliver mail automatically. If they're set to queue messages, eventually you'll have to click the File menu and select Deliver Mail Now to send your outgoing traffic to your server.

Attaching Files and URLs to Mail

Most e-mail packages provide the capability to transmit binary files over the Internet by attaching ASCII-coded copies of them to your message traffic. Netscape is no exception. In fact, its attachment facility is one of the most versatile around.

You can attach files to a message any time before sending it. Open the Attachments dialog by clicking the Attachments button, which you'll see just below the Subject field. You may also click the Attach button on the message composition window's toolbar. Figure 7.11 shows the Attachments dialog box.

If the Attachment button is grayed out, you can enable it by clicking any of the message's header boxes.

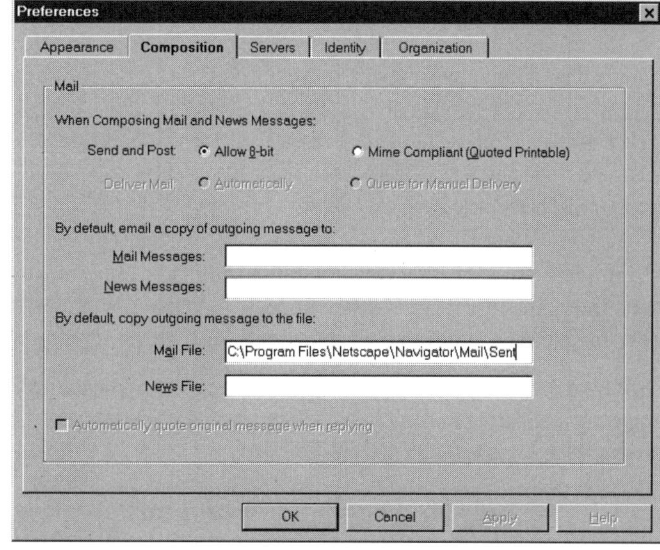

FIG. 7.11
You can attach a binary file to any outgoing message. Netscape will translate it using an ASCII coding scheme intelligible to most mail readers.

Once the Attachments dialog opens, you may add files to your message by clicking the Attach File button. Use the Enter File To Attach dialog box to select the file you want to transmit (see Figure 7.12).

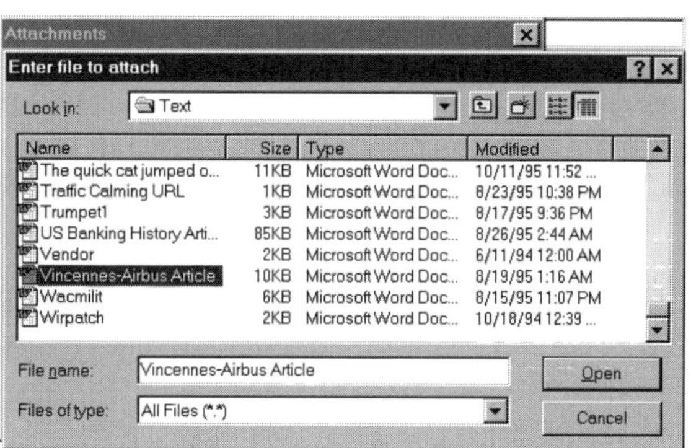

FIG. 7.12
The Enter File To Attach dialog box looks and works like any other Windows 95 file-handling dialog box.

Once you've actually selected the file, you have a decision to make:

- You'll want Netscape to code and transmit true binary files like a spreadsheet or a compressed archive using MIME rendering. Make sure it does so by highlighting the name of the file in the Attachments dialog and clicking the As Is button. Most e-mail software available automatically decodes and stores the attachment when it arrives on the receiving end.
- You may ask Netscape to incorporate ASCII text files, such as those created with Notepad, into the body of the message itself. You do this by clicking the Convert to Plain Text button. Netscape does not, however, let you control where this insertion takes

place. It always adds the new text to the bottom of the message. You will not see the text displayed in Netscape's message window, but as long as the file's visible in the Attachments dialog box it will appear in the finished message seen by your correspondent.

Bear in mind that you can always send an ASCII file As Is. If you do, Netscape will treat it as a binary file. This is perhaps the best way to handle heavily formatted plain-text files. Sending them in the body of a message could badly disrupt their formatting.

The Attachments dialog box also gives you the ability to e-mail a copy of an entire Web page—not just its Internet address. This new and exciting feature is unique to Netscape. If the recipients are using Netscape, they can view the Web page you're sending within a mail window.

Begin from the Attachments dialog box by clicking Attach Location (URL). Netscape opens the Please Specify a Location to Attach dialog box; type the full Internet address of the page you want to send (see Figure 7.13).

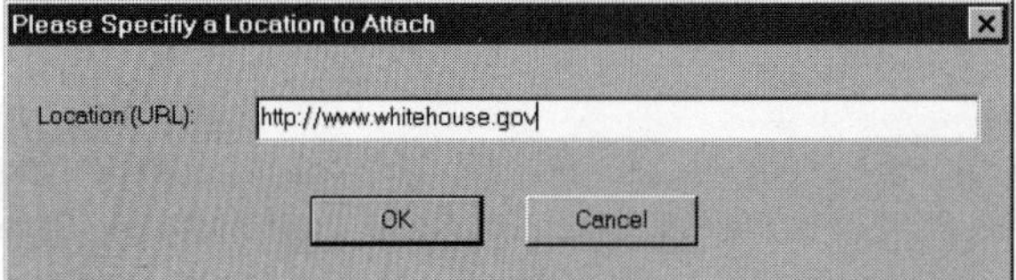

FIG. 7.13
Enter the URL of the Web page you want to send.

As with files, you have to decide whether to send the attachment as is or as plain text. If you know that the person to whom you're sending the URL is using Netscape 3.0 as a mail reader, click As Is. The result on the receiving end will be rather extraordinary (see Figure 7.14).

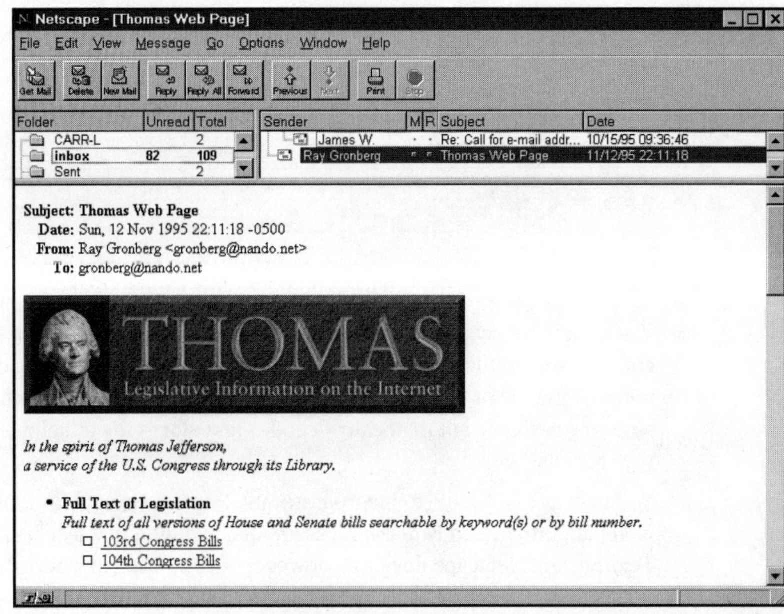

FIG. 7.14
Your friends don't have to seek out Web pages like this one from the Library of Congress. If they're using Netscape as a mail reader, you can send them a copy.

What you basically did is ask Netscape to mail the HTML source code of the URL to your correspondent. Because Netscape's mail facility treats every message as an HTML document, it is able to reconstruct a fully formatted and hotlinked Web page. Whatever you can do with that page from within a normal browser window, your friends can emulate within a Netscape mail window.

If your friends don't have Netscape, all is not lost. By clicking Convert to Plain Text, you instruct Netscape's mailer to strip the HTML codes out of the page and send the remaining text. You may send it As Is anyway; they'll see pure HTML, but after saving a copy to disk they can always open and view the page in any Web browser. Bear in mind that they won't get any of the artwork that gives a Web page its distinctive look and feel.

Receiving and Replying to Mail

As explained earlier, Netscape tries to log on and retrieve messages from your mail server the first time you open the Netscape Mail window.

TROUBLESHOOTING

When Netscape tries to deliver my mail, it responds with a message that it's unable to locate the server. What's wrong? One of four things—three of which you can do something about.

The first thing you want to do is note the name of the server Netscape's trying to access. It'll be listed in the error message. It should be the name of your Internet provider's mail server. If it isn't, open the Preferences dialog box, click the Directories tab, and correct the entry in the Mail (SMTP) Server field.

If Netscape has the right address but can't get through, you may be working offline or you may have another program open that's got the mail server tied up. Get on-line by dialing in or logging on. Close any other program that uses SMTP or POP service before you try to use Netscape's mail manager.

The remaining possibility is that your Internet provider's mail server is down. If that's the case, you can do little but wait. If your provider has a help desk, you may want to call to let them know there's a problem.

You can also retrieve messages any time while the Netscape Mail window is open either by clicking the File menu and selecting Get New Mail, or by clicking Get Mail button on the toolbar. If you haven't already entered your mail server's password, Netscape requests it.

Netscape dumps all new mail into the inbox. Unlike some mail software, it can't automate the sorting of messages into user-specified folders. That's a job you have to handle yourself.

Like most e-mail packages, Netscape lets you respond directly to a message without having to address a new one from scratch. You do this by using the Reply, Reply All, and Forward buttons on the mail screen's toolbar.

By clicking either Reply or Reply All, you can tell Netscape to create a preaddressed message. You can include the text of the message you received by clicking the mail window's File menu and selecting Include Original Text (see Figure 7.15). The Quote Icon on the Netscape Mail Composition Toolbar performs the same function. Trim the length of your quotation using the Edit menu's Cut, Copy, and Paste commands.

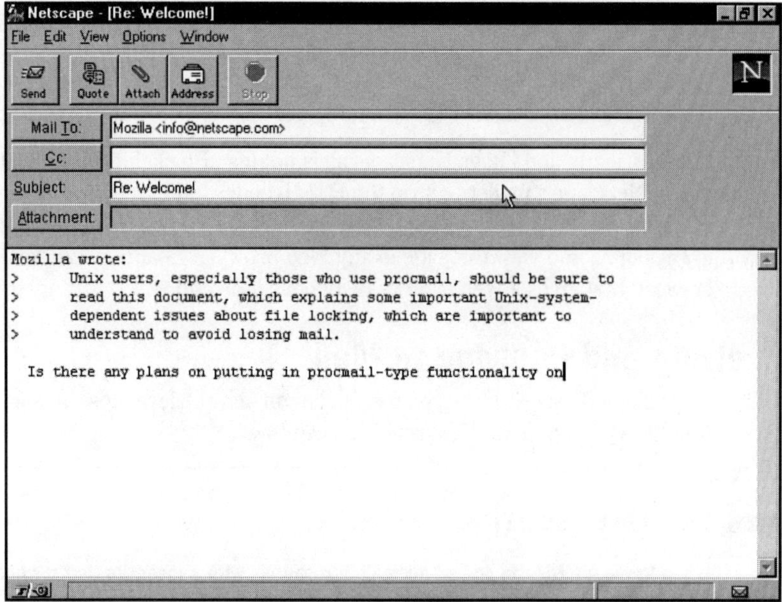

FIG. 7.15
By using the Reply and the Include Original Text commands located on the mail window's File menu, you can draft understandable answers to your mail quickly and easily.

The Forward button works a bit differently. As with Reply and Reply All, clicking it creates a new message. This time, however, you supply the address of your intended recipient. But you'll notice that Netscape has filled in the Attachment field for you. By doing so, it tacks a copy of the text open in Netscape Mail window to the bottom of the message you're creating, including it for the benefit of your correspondent.

Organizing Your Mail

Fortunately, Netscape doesn't make mail sorting hard. You can add and name an unlimited number of folders and shift messages between them at your discretion (see Figure 7.16).

FIG. 7.16
User-created message folders simplify the task of organizing your mail.

Create a folder by clicking the Netscape Mail window's File menu and selecting New Folder. A Netscape mail folder is nothing more than a Windows 95 file, so you can give it a name up to 255 characters long. You may want to keep your names shorter than that, though. As it displays your folders, Netscape truncates the names of any that are too long to fit in the available window.

NOTE Unlike many full-featured e-mail packages, Netscape does not offer any method of nesting folders within folders. High-volume mail users may find this a serious limitation that argues for keeping their current software. Low-volume users should be able to get along fine, but they may find it advisable to keep their filing system short and understandable.

Conversely, you kill an unused folder by clicking it once to highlight its name, and then selecting Delete Folder from the Edit menu.

The commands for shifting mail between folders—Move and Copy—are at the bottom of the Message menu (see Figure 7.17). Highlight either, and you'll find a list of your folders nested beneath them.

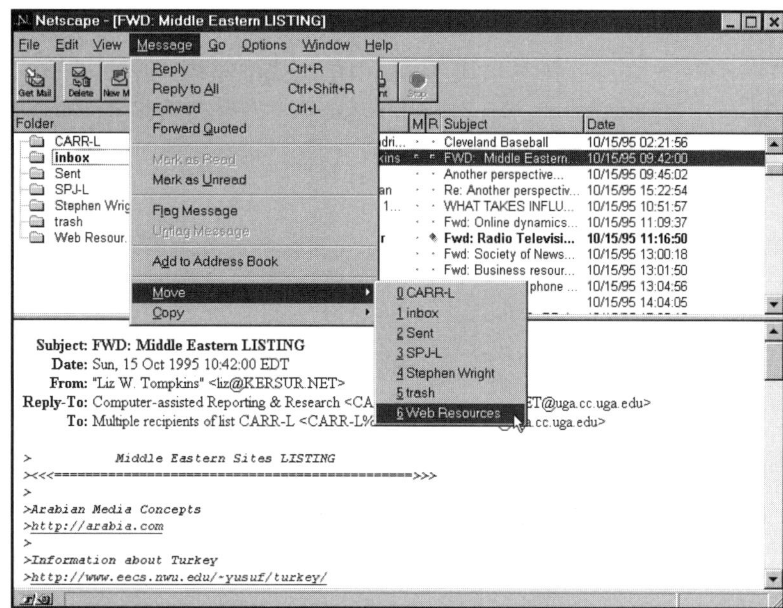

FIG. 7.17
The Move and Copy commands take only a single click. Highlight the directory you want to send the message to and release the mouse button.

The Move and Copy commands work the same way:

1. Highlight the message you want to move or copy in the Message Headers pane by clicking it.
2. Click the Message menu and select Move or Copy.
3. A list of your folders will pop up next to the Message menu. Select the folder you want the message transferred to.

Choosing Move places the selected message into the destination folder and deletes it from the source. Copy puts a copy in the destination folder while leaving the contents of the source folder unchanged.

Within folders, Netscape gives users several options for sorting messages. All are accessible by clicking the View menu and highlighting Sort.

The three major options—Sort by Date, Sender, and Subject—are largely self-explanatory. Toggling the Ascending command tells Netscape to arrange messages in ascending or descending order.

Netscape's capability to organize messages into threads is both unusual and powerful. By toggling Thread Messages, you're ordering the mail client to override normal sort order in cases where a single message has inspired at least one reply. It groups the original and any replies, making the conversation easy to follow as it develops over time (see Figure 7.18).

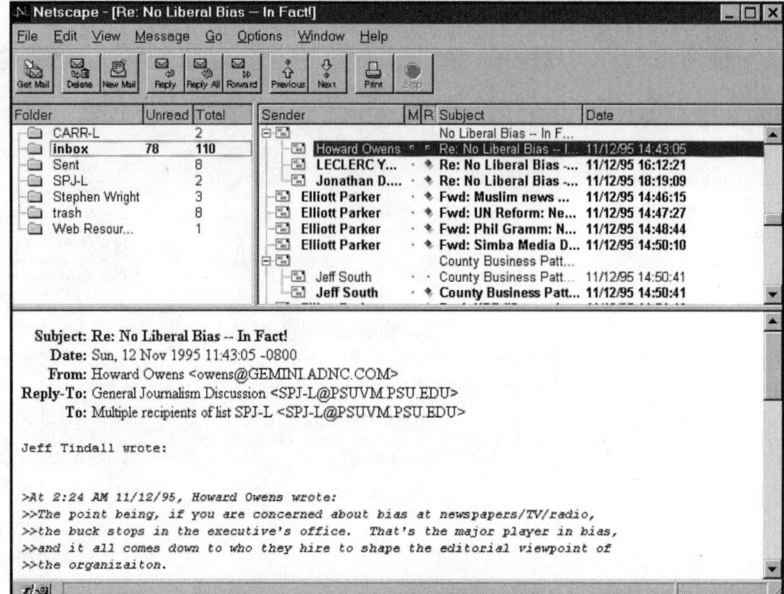

FIG. 7.18
The Windows Explorer-like tree structures indicate message threads.

You can send any highlighted message to the trash folder by clicking the Delete button on the toolbar, by clicking Edit and selecting Delete Message, or by transferring it there using the Message menu's Move command. Trash stays on your disk, however, until you click the File menu and select Empty Trash Folder. Unlike many mail packages, Netscape provides no way of automating deletions.

Using the Address Book

Any good e-mail software provides some quick and simple way of storing and retrieving the addresses of your most frequent correspondents. Most are very easy to use. See Figure 7.19.

Setting up an address book isn't difficult. In fact, Netscape gives you a couple of ways to do it. The easiest method is to open a message from someone you want to correspond with regularly, click the Message menu, and select Add to Address Book.

Netscape responds by opening a Windows 95 property sheet that has four fields (see Figure 7.20). If you're adding to your Address Book using the Message menu command, you'll find that two of them, Name and E-Mail Address, are already filled in.

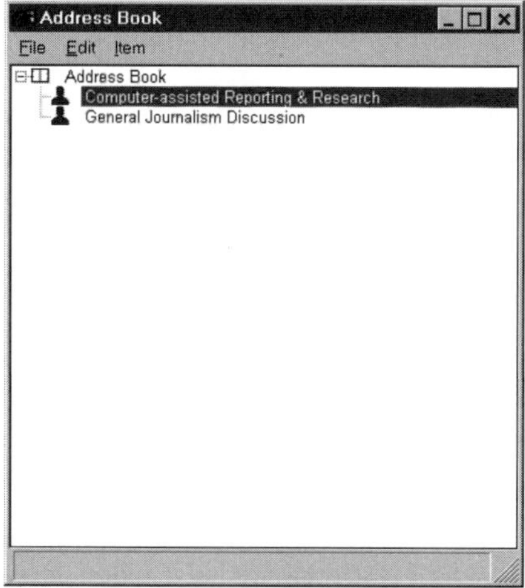

FIG. 7.19
Netscape's address book simplifies mailing chores by storing the names and addresses of the people you write to the most.

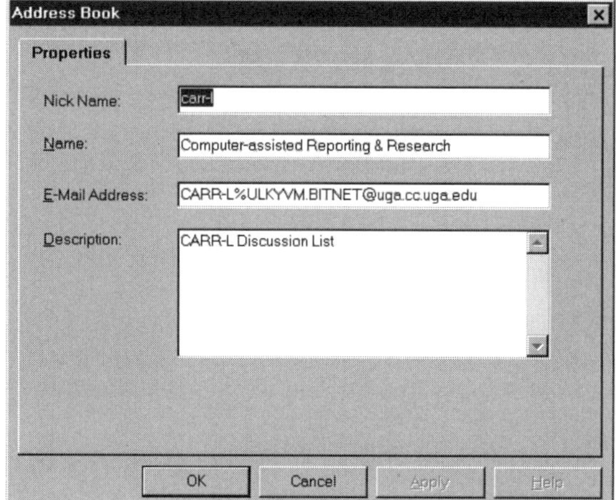

FIG. 7.20
Use the Address Book properties sheet to create and maintain your address list.

TROUBLESHOOTING

Netscape's Add to Address Book function filled out the properties sheet for the addition incorrectly. It didn't use the name and address of the person who wrote the original message. Why not? There's an entry in the message's Reply To field. When it's creating an Address Book entry, Netscape always takes the name and address listed in Reply To. This avoids problems with mailings to a list or to a person who takes return mail at a different address. But it means more work for you; you have to take the time to enter the correct name and address yourself. Always check the entries in these fields the first time you create an Address Book entry.

The Description field gives you a place to write a short note about your correspondent.

The remaining field, Nick Name, gives you a place to enter a short, one-word phrase that can serve as a shortcut to your Address Book entry. Be sure to use lowercase characters only; Netscape won't accept a Nick Name that contains uppercase characters.

You can also create Address Book entries from scratch. Click the Window menu and select Address book. Once the address book opens, click the Item menu and select Add User. Netscape will open a blank Address Book properties sheet. You can also modify any existing entry in the Address Book by right-clicking the entry and selecting Properties.

Once you've created your Address Book, Netscape gives you three ways to use it. They work with any of the available address fields, Mail To, Cc and Bcc:

- The simplest way, once you've placed the cursor in the Message Composition window's Mail To field, is to click the toolbar's Address button. Netscape opens a dialog box called Select Addresses (see Figure 7.21). Highlight the address you want to use, and then click the button that corresponds to the field you want it placed in. Click OK when you're done.

FIG. 7.21 Clicking either the toolbar's Address button or a message's Send To, Cc, or Blind Cc button opens the Select Addresses dialog box. Highlight your choice, click the button for the field you want it placed in, and click OK.

- You may also open the Select Addresses dialog box by clicking any of the labels next to your message's various address fields. Unfortunately, once you've highlighted the address you want to use, you still have to place it in the proper field by clicking the corresponding button on the dialog box. You can't just click OK and expect the address to pop up where you want it.
- If your memory is good, you can address a message quickly merely by typing an Address Book entry's Nick Name property in Mail To, Cc or Bcc. Netscape will automatically fill the box with the name and e-mail address associated with the Nick Name as soon as you move the cursor elsewhere.

You may notice that Netscape fills the message address boxes differently, depending on an Address Book entry's properties. If you've given the entry a Nick Name, it will use that until you close the Select Addresses dialog box. Once you do, it will fill a field with both the name and the address of your intended correspondent. This is nothing to be alarmed about. As long as the e-mail address itself is bracketed by the < and > symbols, your mail server will be able to find it.

If you haven't given an address book entry a Nick Name, Netscape will only list the e-mail address in the proper field. The recipient's name won't appear. Again, no harm is done.

Because an address book is an HTML document—just like your Bookmarks file—Netscape gives you one other way of getting at it quickly. Just as with your Bookmarks file, you can load your address book directly into your browser.

Close your mail window, and then open the File menu and select Open File. You should find address.htm somewhere in your Netscape folder structure, most likely in the Program subfolder. If it doesn't open readily, use Windows 95's Find Files or Folders utility to search for it. When you find it, double-click to load it in Netscape (see Figure 7.22).

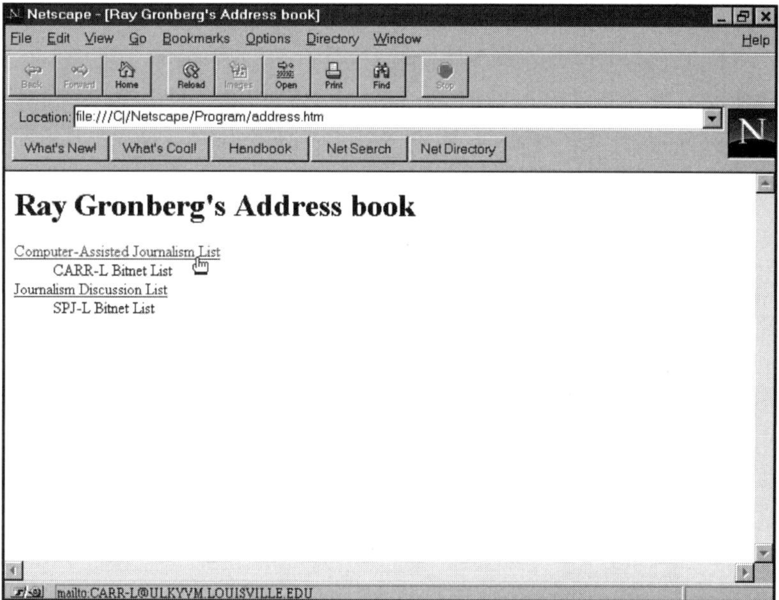

FIG. 7.22
Your address book is an HTML document you can see within Netscape. Load it, and you have the ability to address mail with a single click, just as you would from any Web page.

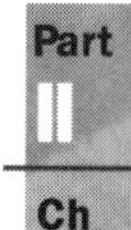

Once the file is there, you can create a new message, complete with precompleted address information, merely by clicking one of the highlighted links. Because it's HTML, clicking a link opens a message composition window, just as it would if you had clicked an e-mail link embedded on a Web page.

And, again because it's HTML, you can also add your Address Book to your Bookmarks menu, putting it one click away any time you're using your browser. ●

CHAPTER 8

E-Mail with Internet Explorer

Microsoft's first answer for an e-mail solution for their Internet Explorer Web browser, Microsoft Exchange, was overkill for many applications. While an excellent program for the heavy, corporate user, as a purely Internet e-mail client, Exchange was too big, too slow, and too hard to run.

With Internet Explorer 3, Microsoft has introduced an integrated Internet Mail Client designed to work with the Web browser to meet all of your Internet e-mail needs. The program is simple, easy to configure and use, and has many of the features you have come to expect from an e-mail program, such as encoded file attachment support, customizable folders for organizing e-mail, and an address book for frequently used e-mail addresses. ■

What is Microsoft's new Internet Mail Client?

In this chapter, you'll learn about the new Internet Mail Client Microsoft has released as a part of Internet Explorer 3.

How do I install and configure the Internet Mail Client?

Find out how to install and configure the program to work with your Internet service provider for incoming and outgoing e-mail.

How do I send and receive e-mail?

Learn how to compose and send e-mail, and read, reply to, and forward incoming e-mail.

Can I organize my incoming and outgoing e-mail?

Discover the Internet Mail Client's customizable folder structure and how you can use it to organize and archive both your incoming and outgoing e-mail.

How do I set up an Address Book?

Internet Mail Client has a system of organizing frequently used e-mail addresses.

Microsoft's New Internet Mail Client

Because Microsoft Exchange is not well suited to the average home user's Internet e-mail needs, Microsoft's Internet group—when they developed Internet Explorer 3—also created a new Internet e-mail client. Known as the Internet Mail Client, it is especially designed to interface with Internet Explorer 3 and to service all of your Internet e-mail needs. The new e-mail client provides most of the functionality that veteran Net users have come to expect from their software.

You can use the Microsoft Internet Mail Client for all of your Internet e-mail needs. Of course, you can use it to write and send messages—you can also reply to, forward, and carbon copy messages, just as users of third-party mail packages can. Message management is a snap because you have the ability to transfer your traffic to a set of custom, user-defined mail folders. Within those folders, you can sort your mail by subject, sender, or date. You can also keep and maintain a list of your most frequently used addresses.

If you're a casual e-mail user, you'll likely find that Internet Explorer 3's new mail capabilities, available through the Internet Mail Client, are all you need.

But if you're accustomed to using other mail packages—programs like Eudora and cc:Mail—you may find that Microsoft's package isn't quite complete. Power users will miss high-end features like automatic message filtering.

All in all, if you're happy with your current mail program, you'll have to make the call as to whether you want to switch to the Internet Explorer Mail Client just yet. You'd be well-advised, however, to watch carefully as it evolves in the future. It's quite clear that Microsoft is serious about making a complete set of products for accessing the Internet and the World Wide Web.

But if you're a new mail user, or if you haven't found a package quite to your liking just yet, you'll probably want to give Microsoft's Internet Mail Client a try. You may find that it meets your needs completely.

Installing the Internet Mail Client

Microsoft's Internet Mail and News Clients come bundled together in a self-extracting, self-installing file called `Mailnews95.exe`. To install either or both of these clients, follow these steps:

1. Execute `Mailnews95.exe`. The program will then self-extract the necessary files and automatically start the installation process. You will be shown an alert box giving you the option to start the installation, and asked to agree to the licensing agreement, after which the Internet Mail and News Setup Wizard will be started.
2. Fill in your name and organization and choose Next. The next dialog box that appears will ask you to confirm the name and organization.
3. You can elect to install either the Internet Mail or News clients, or both. Make your choice and choose Next.

4. That's it! The Internet Mail and/or News clients are now installed. The final step necessary to complete the installation process is to choose OK from the final dialog box to restart your computer.

After you have restarted your computer, you will be ready to run the Internet Mail Client. You can access the Internet Mail Client by clicking the Mail & News icon located on the toolbar (see Figure 8.1).

FIG. 8.1
Internet Explorer 3 provides easy access to your Internet Mail Client.

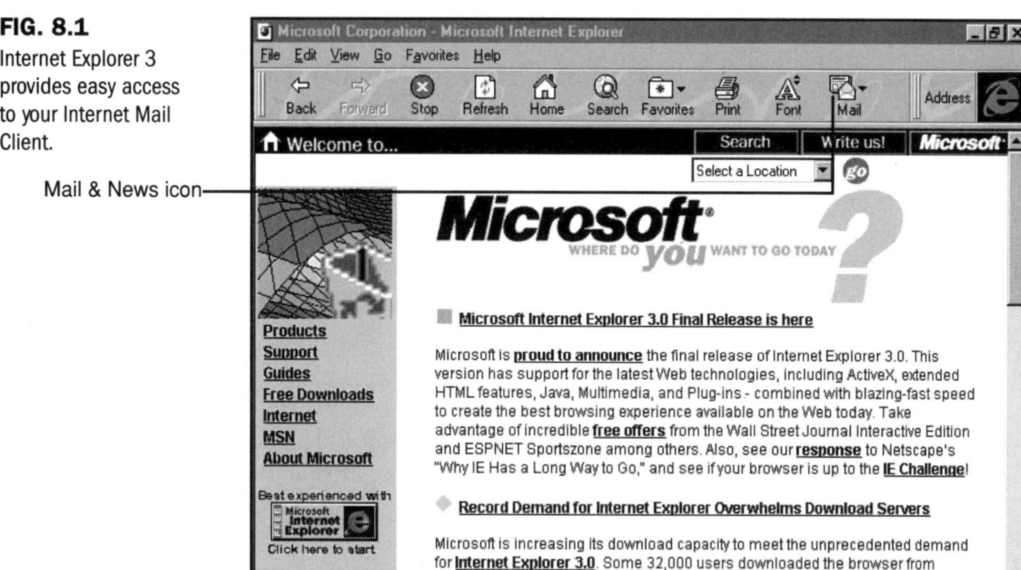

Setting Mail Preferences

The first time you run the Internet Mail Client, you will be asked to provide some basic information about yourself, your Internet provider, and your computer. The program will automatically ask you for this basic information, the minimum it needs in order to operate.

Initial Configuration

When you first run the Internet Mail Client, you will be greeted with the Internet Mail Configuration Wizard (see Figure 8.2). The purpose of this is to find out from you the minimum information needed to interface with your Internet service provider (ISP) to provide incoming and outgoing e-mail services.

NOTE Most of the information requested in this initial configuration process should have been provided to you by your ISP, so make sure you have everything from them in front of you when you begin. If you have any problems or questions with the configuration, they're probably your best source for help.

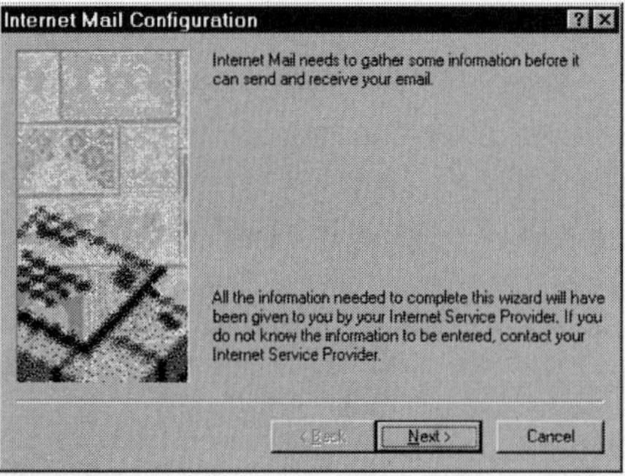

FIG. 8.2
The Internet Mail Configuration Wizard guides you through the process of the minimum configuration needed to send and receive Internet e-mail.

To run the initial configuration, follow these steps:

1. In the Internet Mail Configuration Wizard initial dialog box, press Next. You will then be prompted to enter the Internet addresses of the mail servers for incoming (POP3) and outgoing (SMTP) e-mail. Choose Next after you have done so.
2. Next, in order to access your e-mail account, you will be asked to enter your mail account ID and password—these are usually the same as your account ID and password.

   By default, the Internet Mail Client will remember your password and use it to connect automatically whenever you ask it to check your e-mail. However, if you consider this a security risk, you can leave the password entry blank. Then, whenever the Internet Mail Client checks for your e-mail, you will be asked to enter your password. As long as you leave the Remember Password box unchecked when entering your password, it will not be stored.
3. Next, you will be able to enter the information that the Internet Mail Client uses to "sign" your outgoing e-mail, your name and e-mail address. Normally, the e-mail address is the same as that used to send the e-mail, but there's no reason that you can't use a different one if you prefer to receive your e-mail in an account other than the one from which it is sent.
4. The final step in the initial configuration process gives you the opportunity to set the Internet Mail Client to be the default program to be used to send e-mail from your Web browser.

Configuration Options

To access all of the configuration options for the Internet Mail Client, you can select Mail, Options. Various options can be set under each of the tabs in the Options dialog box that appears.

The Read Tab The options on this tab, shown in Figure 8.3, affect the way the Microsoft Internet Mail Client checks for your e-mail, and how it informs you when you have some. You can set up the Internet Mail Client to periodically check for your e-mail whenever it is running.

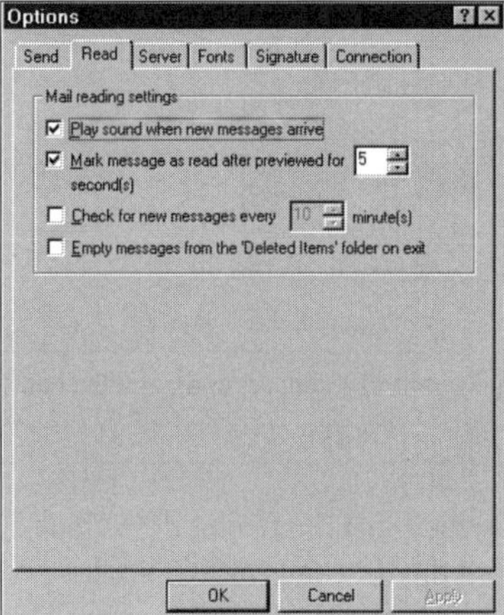

FIG. 8.3
The Read tab of the Options dialog controls how the Internet Mail Client reads and reacts to incoming e-mail.

The Send Tab The Send tab controls various aspects of the configuration for outgoing e-mail (see Figure 8.4). The options here are pretty self-explanatory, and you should feel free to experiment with them. If you press the HTML Settings or Plain Text Settings button on this tab, you are greeted with the Settings dialog box (see Figure 8.5). Here you can control the type of encoding used for file attachments, as well as control a few other options.

You'll probably want to queue your messages on disk if you do most of your work offline as a dial-in Internet user by not checking the Send messages immediately box. Send them by clicking the Send and Receive button or typing Ctrl+M.

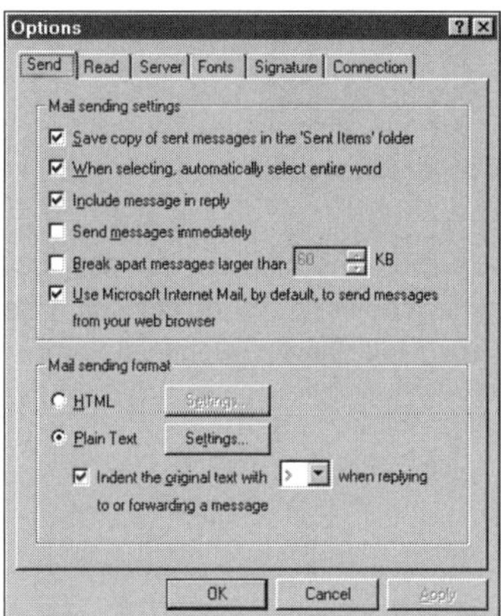

FIG. 8.4
Send options give you control over outgoing e-mail.

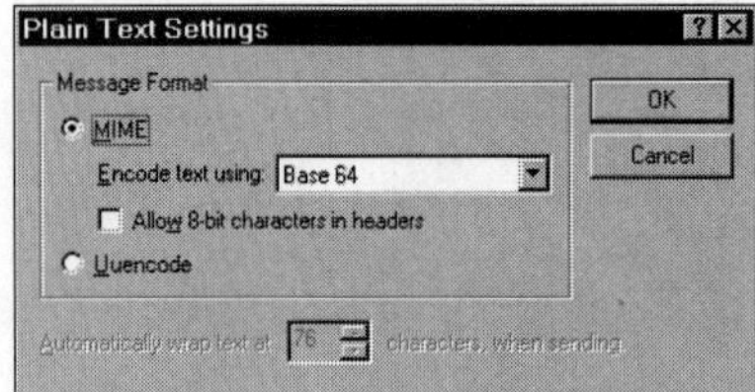

FIG. 8.5
The Settings of the Send options allow you to pick an encoding format for file attachments, and gives you more options.

For greatest compatibility, you will normally want to use Mime format, and Encode Text Using either Quoted Printable or Base 64.

The Server Tab This tab is probably the most important of the tabs on the Options dialog box. On this tab, seen in Figure 8.6, you tell the Internet Mail Client how to get and send your mail. This information is necessary for correct operation of the Internet Mail Client, and so was read in when you performed the initial configuration.

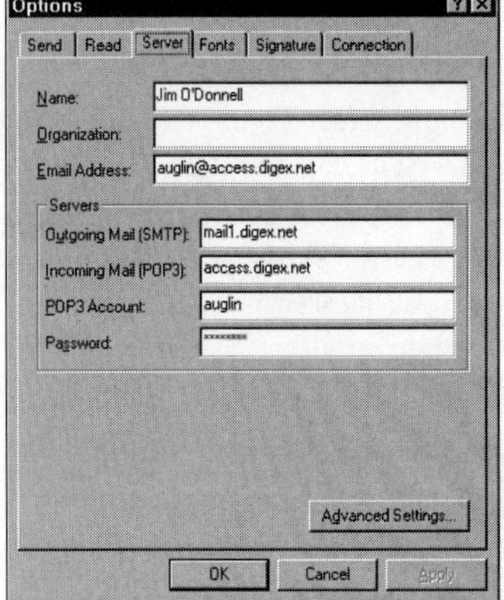

FIG. 8.6
The Servers options are the heart and soul of the Internet Mail Client, as these are what allows you to send and receive Internet e-mail.

If there is anything out of the ordinary about the mail servers provided to you by your Internet service provider, you can configure your copy of the Internet Mail Client by pressing the Advanced Settings button. This causes the Mail Server Advanced Settings dialog box to appear (see Figure 8.7).

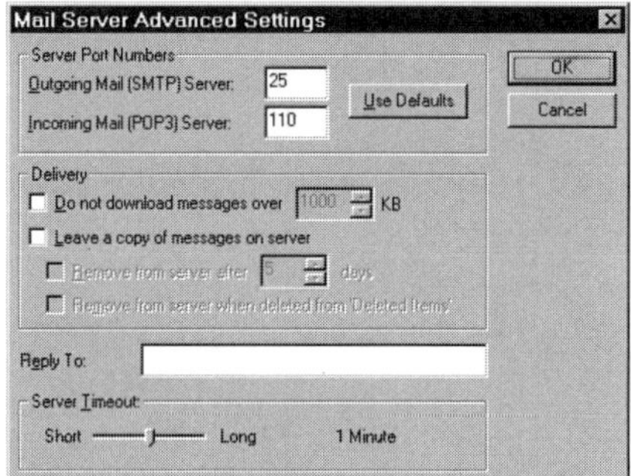

FIG. 8.7
The Mail Server Advanced Settings dialog box allows you to configure the Internet Mail Client for out-of-the-ordinary mail servers, and gives you further control over its behavior.

The Fonts Tab The Fonts tab allows you to choose what fonts are used for the display of e-mail messages in the Internet Mail Client (see Figure 8. 8). You can pick the font to be used to display all e-mail, the color for outgoing e-mail, and the language encoding to use.

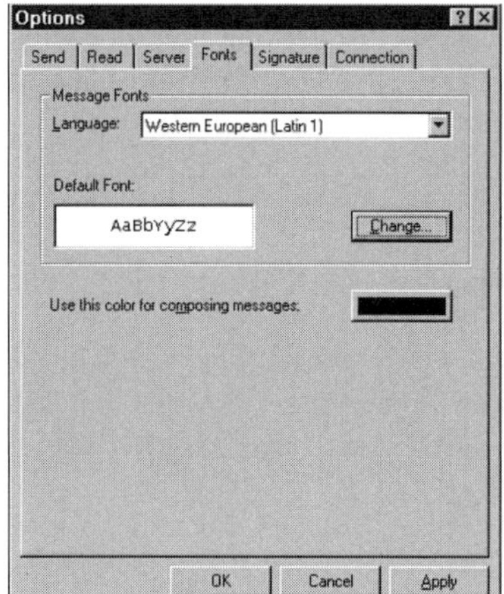

FIG. 8.8
The Fonts tab allows you to set the display fonts for incoming and outgoing e-mail.

E-mail messages are often formatted with monospaced fonts in mind, such as Courier, so you should probably pick a monospaced display font. (I like Lucida Console.)

The Signature Tab The Signature tab, shown in Figure 8.9, allows you to select whether or not you want to include a signature text block at the end of each of your outgoing e-mail messages. If you want to, you can either specify the text directly in the area shown, or specify a file, called a *sigfile*, with the information in it.

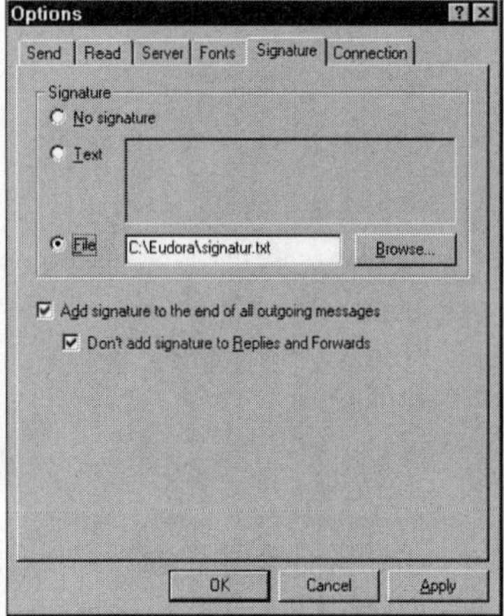

FIG. 8.9
You can set up your signature block information using this tab.

The Connection Tab The final configuration tab is the Connection tab. This allows you to tell the Internet Mail Client how you connect to the Internet. In addition, if you use a dial-up connection, you can specify which Windows 95 Dial-Up Networking connection to use. This information will allow the Mail Client to automatically establish an Internet connection to periodically check your mail, and then to disconnect immediately afterwards.

Using the Mail Package

Now that you have your Internet Explorer 3 Internet Mail Client installed and configured, you're ready to use it to send and receive your Internet e-mail. It has many features that you can use to effectively send, receive, and organize your e-mail.

Understanding the Screen

When you run the Internet Mail Client, the window that you get is divided into several different areas. In addition to the familiar title, menu, and toolbars, there are other distinct areas. The default window setup is shown in Figure 8.10.

There are many different parts to this screen. Let's get oriented with the following parts:

- At the top of the screen, just underneath the menu bar, is the Mail Client toolbar. The buttons on this toolbar perform the normal Windows 95 cut/copy/paste operations, as well as print and delete messages, check for new mail, and search mail messages.
- Underneath the toolbar is the icon bar which gives a list of Mail Client actions that you can perform.
- Also near the top of the mail screen is a drop-down menu giving you access to a list of the mail folders, currently showing the Inbox of incoming e-mail. At minimum, this listing contains your Inbox, Outbox, Deleted Items, and Sent Items—it will also contain any new folders that you create. This is also known as the status bar.

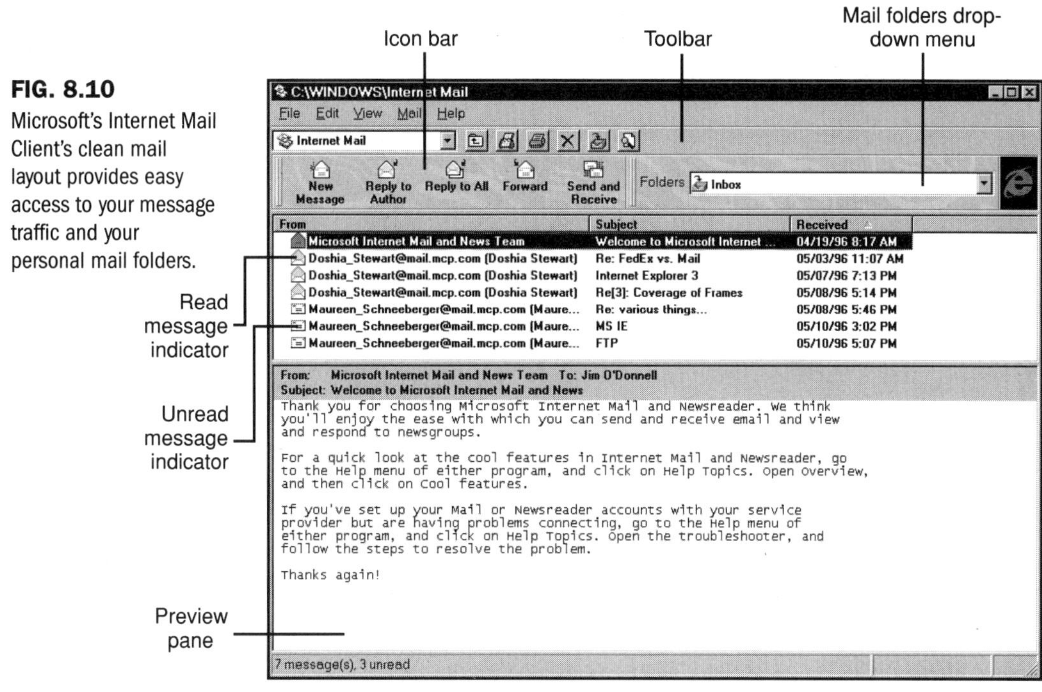

FIG. 8.10
Microsoft's Internet Mail Client's clean mail layout provides easy access to your message traffic and your personal mail folders.

TIP You can adjust the amount of space taken up by these three items be grabbing them with the mouse and moving them around or dragging them up and down to conceal their text descriptions. Also, the toolbar, icon bar, and status bar can all be individually turned off or on under the View menu.

- Underneath the mail folders drop-down menu is a scrollable list of message headers for every piece of mail in the folder you're looking at. The Inbox opens by default when you first open the Internet Mail Client. The icon shown to the left of each message header indicates whether the message has been read or not.
- On the bottom of the screen, you see the text of the open message, along with headers indicating the message's subject, sender, and recipient. This is the Internet Mail Client's preview pane—if you want, you can view a given message in a full screen of its own by double-clicking its header in the message header pane.

NOTE You may notice at low screen resolutions that the Internet Mail Client's mail display is a bit cramped. You can adjust the sizes of the various panes by clicking and dragging their frames. You'll find that the only real way to see what you're doing, video card permitting, is to use a higher screen resolution. Open Control Panel's Display Properties, click the Settings tab, and set the Desktop Area slider to at least 800×600 pixels for a better look.

Checking for Mail

Whenever the Internet Mail Client is running and your Internet connection is up, the mail client will check for incoming e-mail messages in a couple of different circumstances. If you click the Send and Receive button, choose Mail, Send and Receive Mail, or press Ctrl+M, (or at fixed intervals, if you set up the Internet Mail Client to periodically check for your e-mail under the Read tab of the Mail, Options dialog), the alert box shown in Figure 8.11 will be displayed. The Internet Mail Client will then contact your mail server to check for your e-mail. If you have any outgoing e-mail queued, it will also be sent at this time. Any new messages will have their headers displayed in your Inbox, and you will be able to read them.

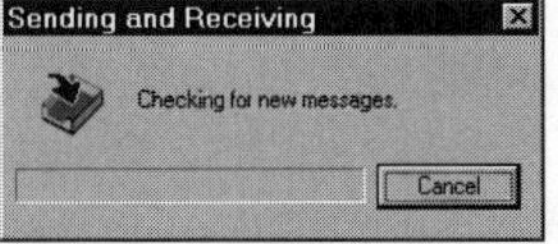

FIG. 8.11
The Internet Mail Client is querying your POP3 mail server to see if you have any new e-mail.

Composing and Sending Mail

Microsoft's Internet Mail and News Clients use a similar front end for message composition. In the case of the Mail Client, you begin a new message either by clicking the New Message button on the icon bar; by selecting Mail, New Message; or by pressing Ctrl+N. A message form like the one shown in Figure 8.12 opens.

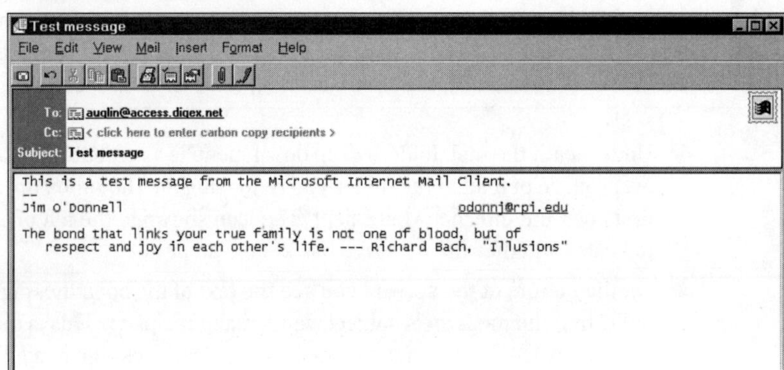

FIG. 8.12
Internet Mail Client uses a standard form for outgoing e-mail and UseNet article. Here's an e-mail message ready to go.

Fill out the message by following these steps:

1. Type the address of the person or organization you're writing to in the To field.
2. Type a short phrase in the Subject field describing the content of your message.
3. If you want to send copies of your message to third parties, add one or more e-mail addresses in the Cc field.

Once you have entered e-mail addresses into the To and Cc fields, you can ask the Mail Client to check them by clicking the Check Names button on the toolbar, selecting Mail, Check Names, or pressing Ctrl+K. If you do this, the Mail Client will see if the name is one from your Address Book, or verify that it is a well-formed Internet e-mail address (in other words, of the form **username@host.domain**).

Once you have checked the names and the Mail Client has verified that they all seem to be proper, they will be underlined, as shown in Figure 8.13. (For more information about the Mail Client's Address Book, see "Using the Address Book" later in this chapter.)

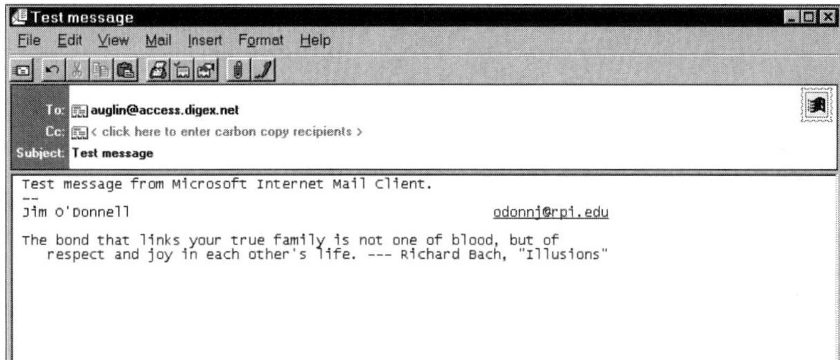

FIG. 8.13
Once you have asked the Internet Mail Client to check the names and e-mail addresses in the To and Cc fields, they will be displayed underlined.

4. Click once in the main text box to set the cursor at the beginning of your message, and begin writing your text. Standard Windows 95 Cut, Copy, and Paste commands are available on the Edit menu.

5. When finished, click the Send button on the far left side of the Composition window's toolbar. Unless you have chosen the send messages immediately, this will queue the message to be sent the next time the Internet Mail Client connects to your mail server to send and receive e-mail.

Attaching Files to Mail

Most e-mail packages provide the capability to transmit binary files over the Internet by attaching ASCII-coded copies of them to your message traffic. Microsoft's Internet Mail Client is no exception. In fact, its file attachment facility is one of the most versatile around.

You can attach files to a message any time before sending it. Click the Insert File toolbar button to open the Insert Attachment dialog box (see Figure 8.14). You may also do this by selecting Insert, File Attachment.

Once the Insert Attachment dialog opens, you may add files to your message by selecting the file and choosing the Attach button. Once a file has been attached, it will appear in the message composition screen as shown in Figure 8.15.

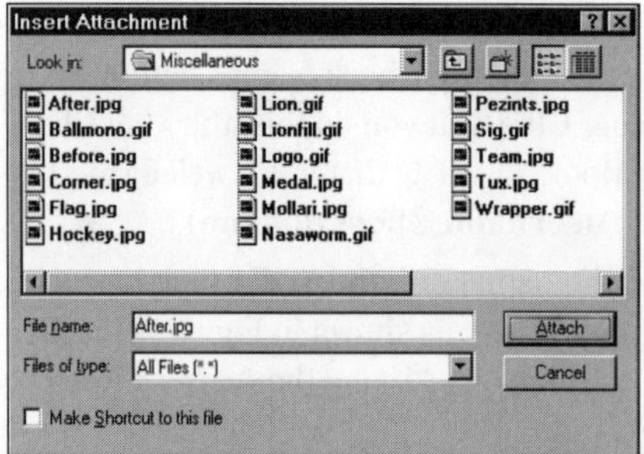

FIG. 8.14
The Insert Attachment dialog box looks and works like any other Windows 95 file-handling dialog box.

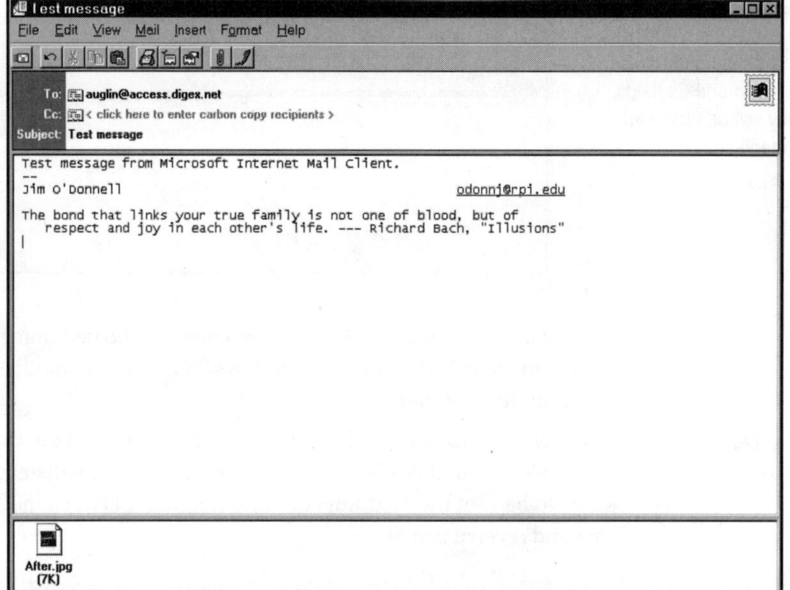

FIG. 8.15
File attachments to Internet Mail Client's outgoing messages are denoted by icons in the bottom pane on the composition screen.

Receiving and Replying to Mail

As explained earlier, the Internet Mail Client will try to log on and retrieve messages from your mail server whenever you ask it to, or at fixed intervals.

TROUBLESHOOTING

When the Internet Mail Client tries to deliver my mail, it responds with a message that it's unable to locate the server. What's wrong? There could be one of four things wrong—three of which you can do something about. The first thing you want to do is note the name of the server the Internet Mail Client is trying to access. It'll be listed in the error message. It should be the name of your ISP's mail server. If it isn't, choose Mail, Options to open the Options dialog box. Click the Servers tab and correct the entry in the Mail (SMTP) Server field.

If the Internet Mail Client has the right mail server address but can't get through, you may be working offline or you may have another program open that's got the mail server tied up. Get online by dialing in or logging on. Close any other program that uses SMTP or POP service before you try to use the Internet Mail Client.

The remaining possibility is that your Internet provider's mail server is down. If that's the case, you can do little but wait. If your provider has a help desk, you may want to call to let them know there's a problem.

The Internet Mail Client dumps all new mail into the Inbox, unless you have configured its Inbox Assistant. This is available under the Mail, Inbox Assistant menu option, and allows you to look for words in any of the To, Cc, From, or Subject fields. If there is a match, the incoming message can be automatically routed to one of your mail folders (including the Deleted Items folder, if its from someone you really don't want to hear from).

Like most e-mail packages, the Internet Mail Client lets you respond directly to a message without having to address a new one from scratch. You do this by using the Reply to Author, Reply to All, and Forward buttons on the mail screen's icon bar.

By clicking either Reply to Author or Reply to All, you can tell the Internet Mail Client to create a pre-addressed message. The text of the message you received will be included if you checked the Include message in reply check box in the Send tab of the Options dialog box (see Figure 8.16). Trim the length of the included text to only what is necessary using standard editing cut, copy, and paste commands.

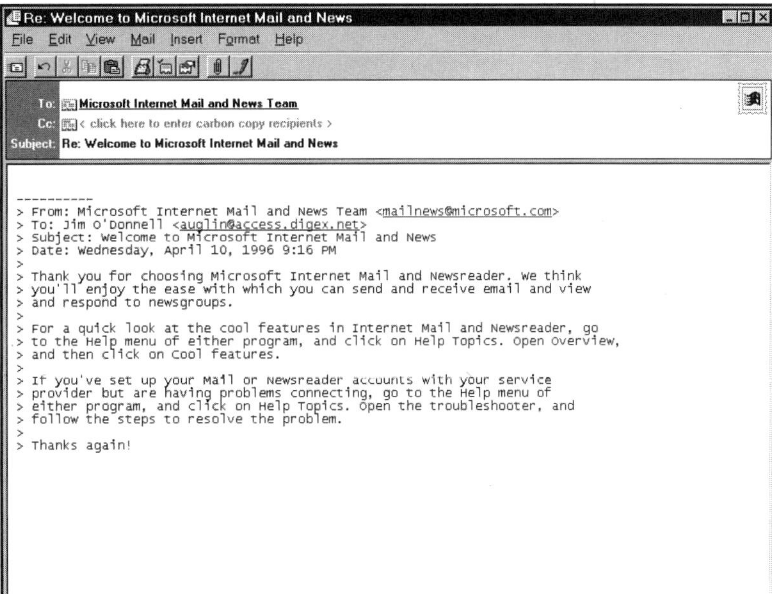

FIG. 8.16
By using the Reply command, you can draft understandable answers to your e-mail quickly and easily.

The Forward button works a bit differently. As with Reply to Author and Reply to All, clicking it creates a new message. This time, however, you supply the address of your intended recipient.

Organizing Your Mail

Fortunately, Microsoft doesn't make mail sorting hard with its Internet Mail Client. You can add and name an unlimited number of folders and shift messages between them at your discretion.

Create a folder by selecting File, Folder, Create. The Create New Folder dialog box appears (see Figure 8.17). An Internet Mail Client mail folder is nothing more than a Windows 95 file, so you can give it a name up to 255 characters long. You may want to keep your names shorter than that, though. As it displays your folders, the Internet Mail Client truncates the names of any that are too long to fit in the available window.

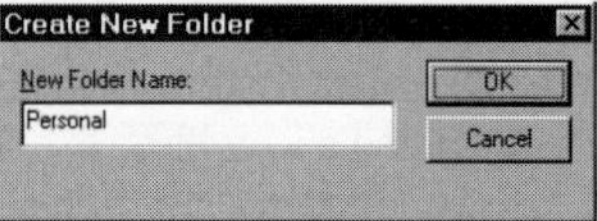

FIG. 8.17
User-created message folders simplify the task of organizing your e-mail.

NOTE Unlike many full-featured e-mail packages, the Internet Mail Client does not offer any method of nesting folders within folders. High-volume mail users may find this a serious limitation that argues for keeping their current software. Low-volume users should be able to get along fine, but they may find it advisable to keep their filing system short and understandable.

Conversely, you can kill an unused folder by choosing File, Folder, Delete, and selecting the name of the folder you want to delete.

The commands for shifting mail between folders—Move to and Copy to—are under the Mail menu (see Figure 8.18). Highlight either, and you'll find a list of your folders nested beneath them.

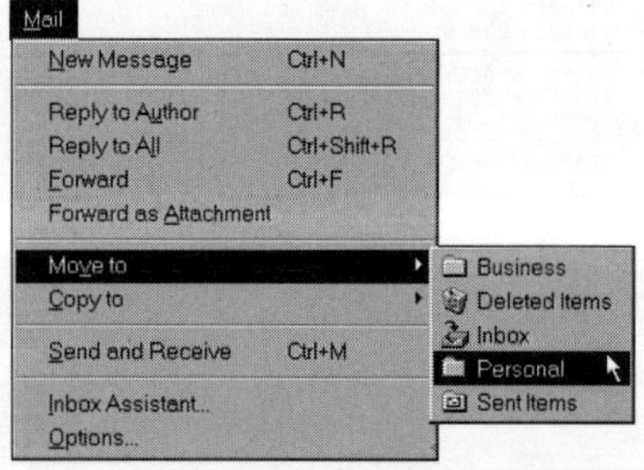

FIG. 8.18
The commands to move and copy messages into folders take only a single click. Highlight the folder you want to send the message to, and release the mouse button.

The Move and Copy commands work the same way:

1. Highlight the message(s) you want to move or copy in the Message headers pane by clicking them.
2. Click the Mail menu and select Move to or Copy to.
3. A list of your folders will pop up next to the Mail menu. Select the folder you want the message transferred to.

Choosing Move to places the selected message into the destination folder and deletes it from the source. Copy to puts a copy in the destination folder while leaving the contents of the source folder unchanged.

Within folders, the Internet Mail Client gives users several options for sorting messages. All are accessible by clicking the View menu and highlighting Sort By. The three options—Sort By From, Subject, and Received—are largely self-explanatory. Toggling the Ascending command tells the Internet Mail Client to arrange messages in ascending or descending order.

You can send any highlighted message to the Deleted Items folder by clicking the Delete button on the toolbar; by selecting File, Delete; pressing Ctrl+D; or by transferring it there using the Message menu's Move to command. Deleted Items stay on your disk, however, until you delete the item from the Deleted Items folder, unless you have selected the Empty messages from the Deleted Items folder on exit option under the Read tab of the Mail, Options menu. This is done by deleting the item from the Deleted Items folder using any of the methods given at the beginning of this paragraph.

In addition to deleting unwanted messages, you can further reduce the disk space needs of the Internet Mail Client by compacting mail folders by choosing File, Folder, Compact, and selecting the desired folder (see Figure 8.19).

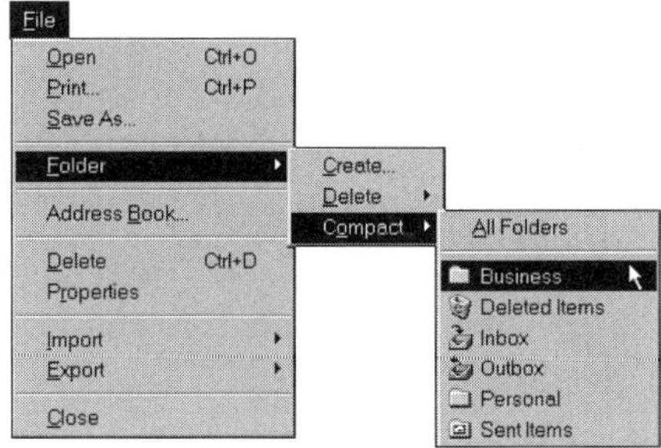

FIG. 8.19
You can ask the Internet Mail Client to compact some or all of your mail folders–this slows down retrieval of these messages a little, but saves space on your hard drive.

Using the Address Book

Because typing in the full e-mail address for someone every time you want to send them a message can get pretty tiresome, almost all e-mail programs include some way to assign names, nicknames, or aliases to frequently used e-mail addresses. Microsoft's Internet Mail Client is no exception.

The Internet Mail Client maintains an Address Book that you can use to store names and e-mail addresses for your correspondents. The Address Book is accessed by choosing File, Address Book—it looks like Figure 8.20.

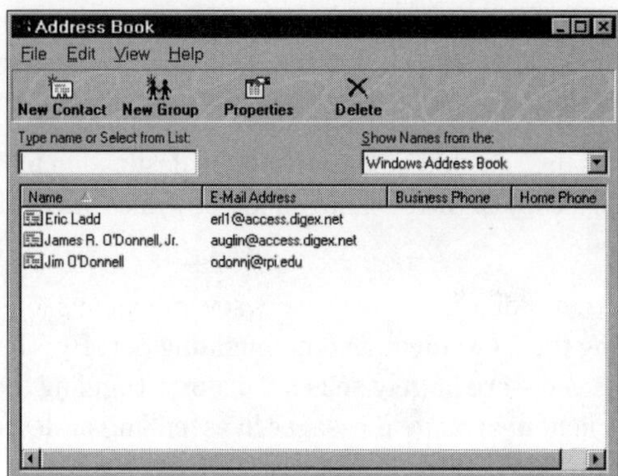

FIG. 8.20
The Mail Client's Address Book gives you an easy way to keep track of frequently used e-mail addresses, and the names of the folks they belong to.

You can add someone to your Address Book—or edit the name or e-mail address of someone already in it—by clicking the New Entry or Properties buttons, respectively. In either case, you will get the Properties dialog box which will allow you to add information about the person you want to put in your Address Book under its Personal, Home, Business, and Notes tabs (see Figure 8.21).

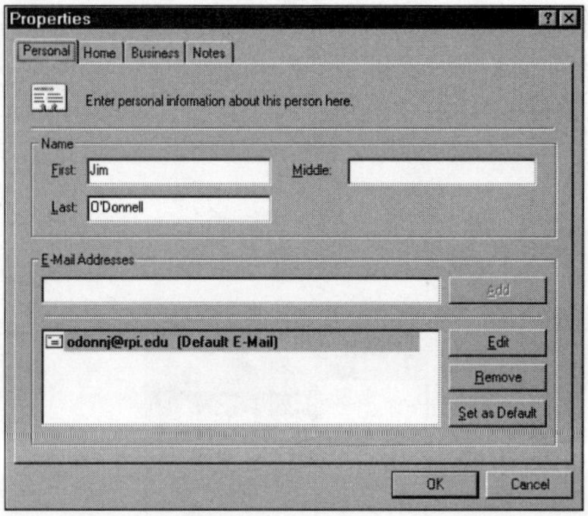

FIG. 8.21
Entries in the Address Book, consisting of a name and e-mail address, make it easier to send e-mail.

Another way to add addresses to your Address Book is right from the mail composition screen. Once you have entered an e-mail address into the To or Cc field and had the Internet Mail Client check it for validity (so that it is underlined), you can right-click it, and select Add To Address Book (see Figure 8.22). Selecting Properties from this pop-up menu also allows you to enter a name into the Address Book for the e-mail address.

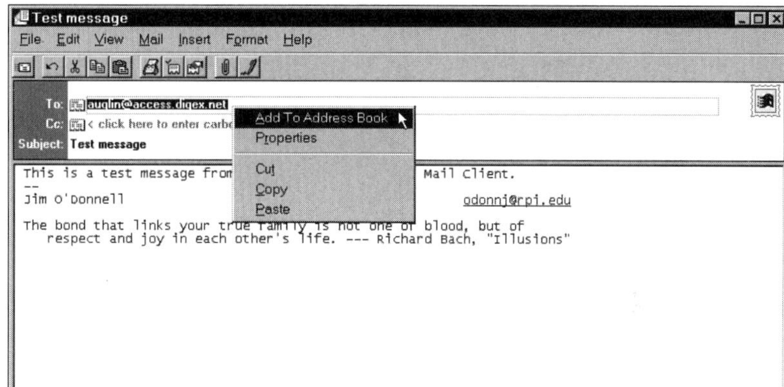

FIG. 8.22 You can also add entries to your Address Book directly from a message window.

Once you have defined names in your Address Book, it is easy to include them in the To or Cc fields of messages that you are composing. You can do this by choosing Mail, Choose Recipients from the message composition window, or by clicking the small icon immediately to the right of the words To or Cc. The Select Recipients dialog appears (see Figure. 8.23). You can select names from the window at left, and click the To or Cc buttons, and this adds the appropriate names to the recipients lists of your e-mail message (see Figure 8.24).

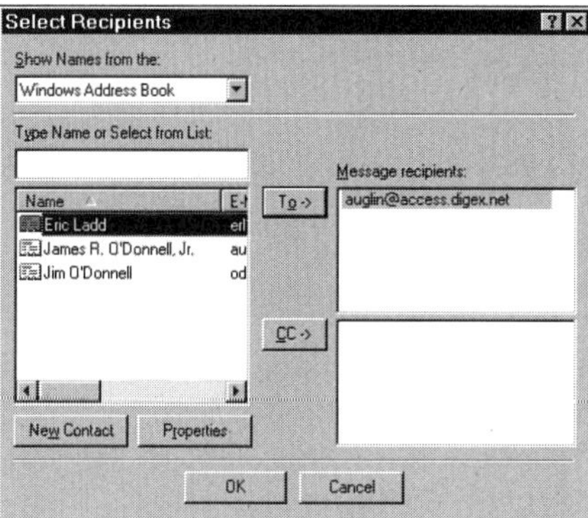

FIG. 8.23 The Select Recipients dialog box gives you an easy way to send messages to people in your Address Book.

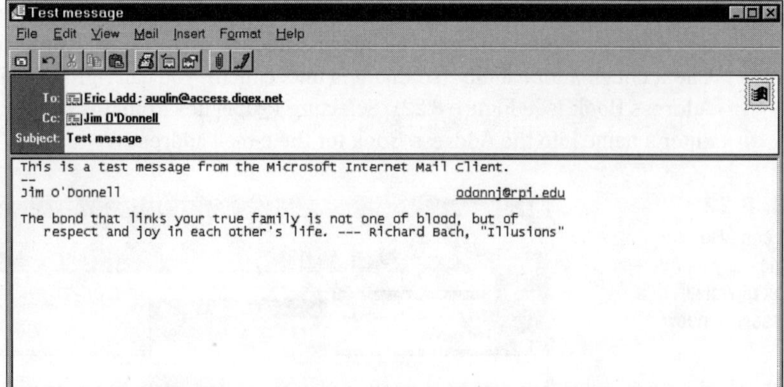

FIG. 8.24
Mail recipients identified in your Address Book by name are listed by name in your mail messages.

Another option you can use under the Mail Client Address Book is to set up group names. This is done by clicking the New Group button from the Address Book icon bar (or by selecting an existing group and clicking the Properties button). You can then specify a group name and a list of people in that group. Once a group has been established, you can then use that group name in the To or Cc field of an outgoing message—that message will then go to all members of that group. ●

CHAPTER 9

Reading UseNet Newsgroups with Netscape

- How newsgroups work
- The different types of newsgroups on UseNet
- The organization of UseNet newsgroups
- Using Netscape's newsreader to access newsgroups
- Accessing newsgroups without using the newsreader

CompuServe calls them forums. The Microsoft Network calls them BBSs (bulletin board systems). At your office, they're possibly known as cork boards. They are all places where people come together to exchange ideas and opinions, post public notices, or look for help. The Internet has such a place, too. On the Internet, it's called UseNet newsgroups, or just newsgroups for short. ■

A UseNet Primer

Newsgroups are a bit more complicated than forums, BBSs, and cork boards—not in a technical sense, but in a cultural sense. Newsgroups don't have official rules that are enforced by anyone in particular. They have unofficial rules that newsgroup peers enforce. Newsgroups concentrate cultures, from all over the world, in one place—a source of a lot of conflict as you can imagine.

So, take a few moments to study this section before you dive into newsgroups head first. Make sure that you understand how newsgroups and the UseNet culture works. Then, you'll learn how to use Netscape's newsreader to access one of the most dynamic parts of the Internet—newsgroups—later in this chapter.

CAUTION

If you're particularly sensitive or easily offended, newsgroups may not be right for you. Unlike the forums and BBSs on commercial online systems, no one is watching over the content on newsgroups. The material is often very offensive to some folks. You'll find plenty of nasty language and abusive remarks in some newsgroups, just like you'd expect to find in some pubs.

The Basics of Using Newsgroups

If you've ever used a forum or BBS on a commercial online service, you're already familiar with the concept of a newsgroup. Readers post messages, or articles, to newsgroups for other people to read. They can also reply to articles that they read on a newsgroup. It's one way for people like yourself to communicate with millions of people around the world.

Newsgroups are a bit looser, however. A newsgroup doesn't necessarily have a watchdog—other than the readers themselves. As a result, the organization is a bit looser, and the content of the messages is often way out of focus. The seemingly chaotic nature of newsgroups, however, produces some of the most interesting information you'll find anywhere.

Newsgroup Variety Is Good The variety of content is exactly what makes newsgroups so appealing. There are newsgroups for expressing opinions—no matter how benign or how radical. There are other newsgroups for asking questions or getting help. And, best of all, there are newsgroups for those seeking companionship—whether they're looking for a soul mate or longing to find someone with a similar interest in whittling. The following is a sample of the types of newsgroups you'll find:

- alt.tv.simpsons contains a lot of mindless chatter about *The Simpsons.*
- comp.os.ms-windows.advocacy is one of the hottest Windows newsgroups around. You'll find heated discussions about both Windows 3.1 and Windows 95.
- rec.games.trading-cards.marketplace is the place to be if you're into sports trading cards.
- rec.humor.funny is where to go to lighten up your day. You'll find a wide variety of humor, including contemporary jokes, old standards, and bogus news flashes.

Alternative and Regional Newsgroups Not all the newsgroups available are true UseNet newsgroups. Some newsgroups are created to serve a particular region or are so obscure that they wouldn't make it through the rigorous UseNet approval process. If something looks like a newsgroup and acts like a newsgroup, however, it can find its way onto your news server.

Here are some examples:

- Regional—Many localities, such as Dallas or San Francisco, have their own newsgroups where people exchange dining tips, consumer advice, and other regional bits of information.
- Alternative—The alt newsgroups are responsible for most of the variety on UseNet. Some of these groups have a reputation for being downright nasty (for example, pornography), but also have groups dedicated to your favorite TV shows, books, or politicians.

NOTE If you have a child who will be using newsgroups, you might consider finding a service provider that makes the pornographic newsgroups, such as alt.sex.pictures and alt.binaries.pictures.erotica, unavailable.

Moderated Newsgroups Moderated newsgroups are a bit more civil, and the articles are typically more focused than unmoderated newsgroups. Moderators look at every article posted to their newsgroup before making it available for everyone to read. If they judge it to be inappropriate, they nuke it.

So what are the advantages of a moderated newsgroup? You don't have to wade through ten pounds of garbage to find one ounce of treasure. Check out some of the alternative newsgroups and you'll get the picture. Most the alternative newsgroups are unmoderated. As such, they're a free-for-all—profanity, abusiveness, and childish bickering. The value and quality of the information that you'll find in moderated newsgroups is much higher than their unmoderated cousins.

The disadvantages, on the other hand, are just as clear. Some people believe that moderating a newsgroup is the equivalent of censorship. Instead of the group as a whole determining the content of a newsgroups, the judgment of a single individual determines the content of the newsgroups. Another significant disadvantage is timeliness. Articles posted to moderated newsgroups can be delayed days or weeks.

Participating in a Newsgroup Every Internet resource that you want to use requires a client program on your computer. Newsgroups are no exception. The program that you use to read newsgroups is called a newsreader.

A newsreader lets you browse the newsgroups that are available, reading and posting articles along the way. Most newsreaders also have more advanced features that make using newsgroups a bit more productive. Later in this chapter, you'll learn how to use Netscape's newsreader to access the news. You'll also find other ways to read the newsgroups without using a newsreader.

So How Do Newsgroups Work, Anyway?

NNTP (Network News Transport Protocol) is used to move the news from one server to another. It's very similar to e-mail in a lot of respects. Instead of all the messages sitting on your machine, however, they are stored on an NNTP news server that many other people can access. Therefore, the news only has to be sent to the server, instead of each user. Each user is then responsible for retrieving the articles she's interested in.

UseNet news makes its way to your news server using a process called flooding. That is, all the news servers are networked together. A particular news server may be fed by one news server, while it feeds three other news servers in turn. Periodically, it's flooded with news from the server that's feeding it, and in turn floods all of its news to the servers that it feeds.

Wading Through UseNet

Sometimes, you'll feel like you're knee-deep in newsgroups. There are over 10,000 newsgroups available. Wading through them all to find what you want can be a daunting task. What's a new user to do?

It's all right there in front of you. There's a lot of logic to the way newsgroups are named. Once you learn it, you'll be able to pluck out a newsgroup just by how it's named. You'll also find tools to help you locate just the right newsgroup, as well as a few newsgroups that provide helpful advice and pointers to new users.

Newsgroup Organization Newsgroups are organized into a hierarchy of categories and subcategories. Take a look at the alt.tv.simpsons newsgroup discussed earlier. The top-level category is alt. The subcategory is tv. The subcategory under that is simpsons. The name goes from general to specific, left to right. You'll also find other newsgroups under alt.tv, such as alt.tv.friends and alt.tv.home-imprvment.

alt.tv.* is a notational convention that means all the newsgroups available under the alt.tv category.

There are many different top-level categories available. Table 9.1 shows some that you probably have available on your news server.

These categories help you nail down exactly which newsgroup you're looking for. A bit of practice helps, as well. If you're looking for information about Windows 95, for example, start looking at the comp top-level category. You'll find an os category, which probably represents operating systems. Under that category, you'll find an ms-windows category.

NOTE Exactly which newsgroups are available on your news server is largely under the control of the administrator. Some administrators filter out regional newsgroups that don't apply to your area. Some also filter out the alt newsgroups because of their potentially offensive content.

Table 9.1 Internet Top-Level Newsgroup Categories

Category	Description
alt	Alternative newsgroups
bit	BitNet LISTSERV mailing lists
biz	Advertisements for businesses
clarinet	News clipping service by subscription only
comp	Computer-related topics; hardware and software
k12	Educational, kindergarten through grade 12
misc	Topics that don't fit the other categories
news	News and information about UseNet
rec	Recreational, sports, hobbies, music, games
sci	Applied sciences
soc	Social and cultural topics
talk	Discussion of more controversial topics

Searching for Newsgroups on the Web Scouring the categories for a particular newsgroup may not be the most efficient way to find what you want. Here are a couple of tools that help you find newsgroups based upon keywords that you type:

- Point Netscape at **www.cen.uiuc.edu/cgi-bin/find-news**. This tool searches all the newsgroup names and newsgroup descriptions for a single keyword that you specify.
- Another very similar tool is at **www.nova.edu/Inter-Links/cgi-bin/news.pl**. This tool allows you to give more than one keyword, however.

Newsgroups for New Users Whenever I go someplace new, I first try to locate a source of information about it. Likewise, the first few places that you need to visit when you get to UseNet are all the newsgroups that are there to welcome you. It's not just a warm and fuzzy welcome, either. They provide useful information about what to do, what not to do, and how to get the most out of the newsgroups. Table 9.2 shows you the newsgroups that you need to check out.

NOTE Don't post test articles to these newsgroups. Don't post articles asking for someone to send you an e-mail, either. This is a terrible waste of newsgroups that are intended to help new users learn the ropes. See the section "Practice Posting in the Right Place" later in this chapter to learn about a better place to post test articles.

Table 9.2 Newsgroups for the Newbie

Newsgroup	Description
alt.answers	A good source of FAQs and information about alt newsgroups
alt.internet.services	This is the place to ask about Internet programs and resources
news.announce.newsgroups	Announcements about new newsgroups are made here
news.announce.newusers	Articles and FAQs for the new newsgroups user
news.newusers.questions	This is the place to ask your questions about using newsgroups

news.announce.newusers

The news.announce.newusers newsgroup contains a lot of great articles for new newsgroup users. In particular, look for the articles with the following subject lines:

- What is UseNet?
- What is UseNet? A second opinion
- Rules for posting to UseNet
- Hints on writing style for UseNet
- A Primer on How to Work with the UseNet Community
- Emily Postnews Answers Your Questions on Netiquette
- How to find the right place to post (FAQ)
- Answers to Frequently Asked Questions about UseNet

Getting Real News on UseNet

UseNet is good for a lot more than just blathering and downloading questionable art. There's a lot of news and great information coming from a variety of sources. You'll find "real" news, current Internet events, organizational newsgroups, and regional newsgroups as well—all of which make newsgroups worth every bit of trouble.

ClariNet You can be the first kid on the block with the current news. ClariNet is a news service that clips articles from sources such as the AP and Reuters news wires. They post these services to the clari.* newsgroups. These newsgroups aren't free, though. They sell these newsgroups on a subscription basis. You wouldn't want to pay for them, either, because they can be expensive. Many independent service providers do subscribe, however, as a part of their service.

ClariNet has more than 300 newsgroups from which to choose. My favorite ClariNet newsgroups are shown in Table 9.3. You'll come up with your own favorites in short order. One

ClariNet newsgroup that you definitely need to check out is clari.net.newusers. It's a good introduction to all the newsgroups that ClariNet offers.

Table 9.3 Popular Clarinet Newsgroups

Newsgroup	Description
clari.biz.briefs	Regular business updates
clari.local.State	Your own local news
clari.nb.online	News about the online community
clari.nb.windows	News about Windows products and issues
clari.news.briefs	Regular national and world news updates

For your convenience, Table 9.4 describes each ClariNet news category. You'll find individual newsgroups under each category. Under the clari.living category, for example, you'll find arts, books, music, and movies.

Table 9.4 ClariNet News Categories at a Glance

Category	Description
clari.news	General and national news
clari.biz	Business and financial news
clari.sports	Sports and athletic news
clari.living	Lifestyle and human interest stories
clari.world	News about other countries
clari.local	States and local areas
clari.feature	Special syndicated features
clari.tw	Technical and scientific news
clari.matrix_news	A networking newsletter
clari.nb	Newsbytes, computer industry news
clari.sfbay	San Francisco Bay Area news
clari.net	Information about ClariNet
clari.apbl	Special groups for the AP BulletinLine

Net-happenings If it seems that the Internet is moving too fast to keep up with, you're right—without help, anyway. The comp.internet.net-happenings newsgroup helps you keep track of new events on the Internet, including the World Wide Web, mailing lists, UseNet, and so on.

The subject line of each article tells you a lot about the announcement. Take, for example, the following announcement:

> WWW>Free Internet service for first 100 visitors

The first part tells you that the announcement is about a World Wide Web site. You'll find many other categories such as FAQ, EMAG, LISTS, and MISC. The second part is a brief description about the announcement. Most of the time, the description is enough to tell you whether you want to see more information by opening the article. The article itself is a few paragraphs about the announcement, with the address or subscription information near the top.

Regional Newsgroups Is your geographical region represented on UseNet? A lot are. The Dallas/Fort Worth area has a couple of newsgroups, such as dfw.eats, dfw.forsale, and dfw.personals. Virtually every state has similar newsgroups. Other states might have special needs. For example, California users might be interested in the ca.environment.earthquakes newsgroup.

Using Netscape to Read the News

All that news is out there, just sloshing around on the news server, and you need a program to get it. There are a lot of newsreaders out there, but you already have Netscape's newsreader. It's one of the cleanest and easiest to use newsreaders available.

Starting the Netscape newsreader is easy. Choose Window, Netscape News from the Netscape main menu. Figure 8.1 shows the Netscape newsreader, and Table 9.5 shows what each of the buttons on the toolbar do.

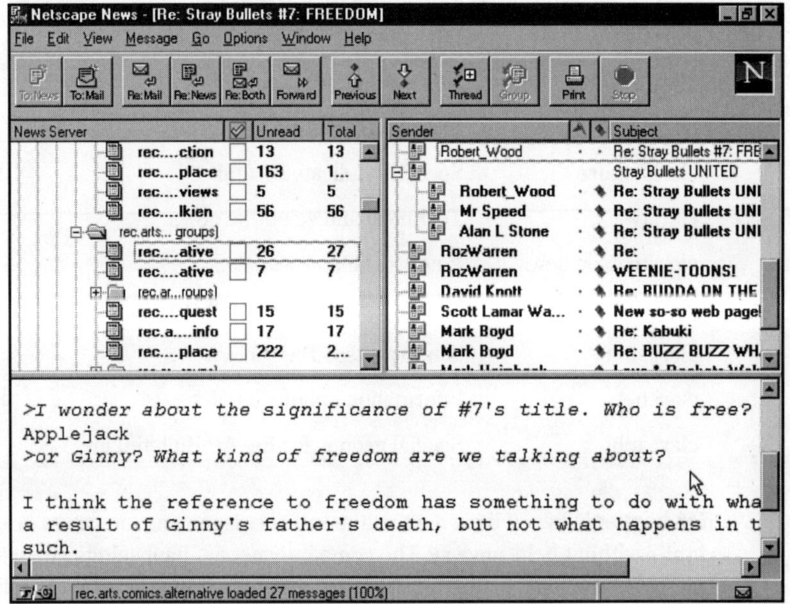

FIG. 9.1
The Netscape newsreader window is divided into three panes: groups list, article list, and article body.

Table 9.5 Buttons on the Netscape Newsreader Toolbar

Button	Name	Description
	Post new	Post new article to newsgroup
	New message	Create a new e-mail message
	Reply	Reply using an e-mail message
	Post reply	Post reply to newsgroup article
	Post and reply	Post and e-mail a reply
	Forward	Forward article to e-mail address
	Previous Unread	Previous article in a newsgroup
	Next Unread	Next article in a newsgroup
	Mark thread read	Mark entire conversation as read
	Mark all read	Mark entire newsgroup as read
	Print	Print the current article
	Stop	Stop transferring from news server

Configuring Netscape to Read the News

To configure Netscape for your service provider, use the following steps:

1. Choose Options, Mail and News Preferences from the Netscape newsreader main menu, and click the Servers tab. Netscape displays the dialog box shown in Figure 9.2.
2. Fill in your NNTP (Network News Transfer Protocol) and SMTP (Simple Mail Transfer Protocol) servers as shown in Figure 9.2, and click the Identity tab. Netscape displays the dialog box shown in Figure 9.3. You can also control how many UseNet messages Netscape will retrieve using the Get test field. If you're paying toll charges to access your UseNet server, or your computer is a bit on the slow side, you'll want to set this to a low number.

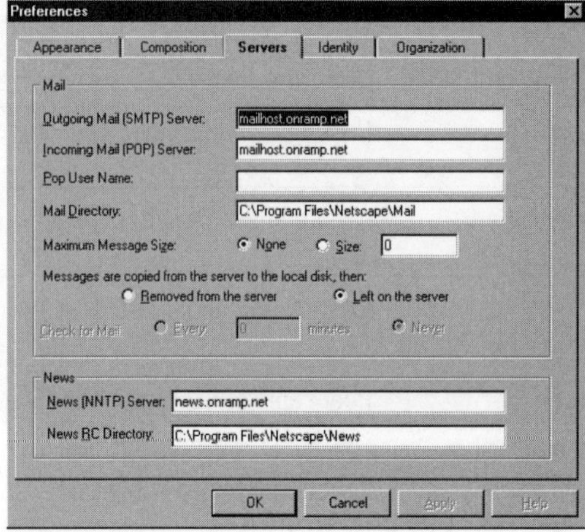

FIG. 9.2
Your service provider should have given you the NNTP news server and SMTP mail server.

3. Fill in Your Name, Your Email, and Reply-to Address as shown in Figure 9.3. If you want to attach a signature file to the end of your postings, select a text file by clicking Browse. Click OK to save your changes.

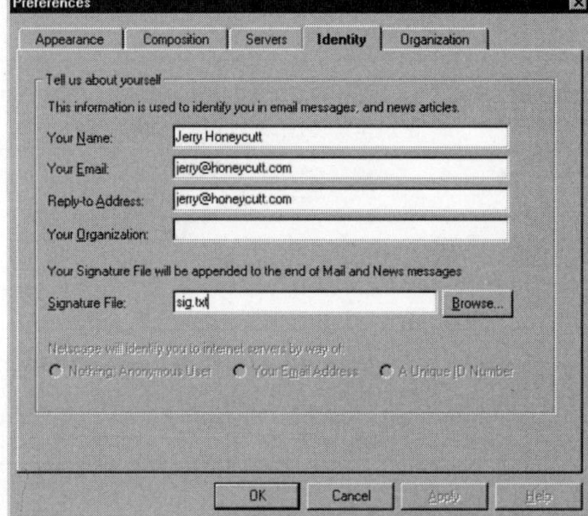

FIG. 9.3
You need to provide a name and e-mail address so that other people can respond to your postings.

TROUBLESHOOTING

Why do I get an error message that says Netscape couldn't find the news server? First, make sure that you have a connection to your service provider. If you're definitely connected, make sure that you correctly configured your NNTP news server. Don't remember the exact address your provider gave you? Try this: If your domain name is provider.net, then add news to the front of it like this: news.provider.net.

Can I use Netscape to access UseNet through CompuServe? Yes. The CompuServe news server is news.compuserve.com and the SMTP mail server is mail.compuserve.com.

A Note about Signatures

You can easily personalize your postings with a signature. Save about three lines that say something about yourself, such as your address and hobbies, into a text file. Then, in step 3 of "Configuring Netscape to Read the News," select the text file you created. Here's an example of a signature file:

Jerry Honeycutt | jerry@honeycutt.com
| (800) 555-1212
| Buy Using the Internet, Now!

Your signature can communicate anything that you want about yourself including your name, mailing address, phone number, address, or a particular phrase that reflects your outlook on life. It is considered good form, however, to limit your signatures to three lines.

Subscribing to Newsgroups

After you've configured the Netscape newsreader for your service provider, you need to download a complete list of the newsgroups available on your news server. Highlight your news server in the groups pane, and choose Show All Newsgroups from the Options menu. Netscape displays a dialog box warning you that this process can take a few minutes on a slow connection. Click OK to continue.

Before you can read the articles in a newsgroup, you have to subscribe to it. When you subscribe to a newsgroup, you're telling Netscape that you want to read the articles in that newsgroup. Normally, Netscape only displays the newsgroups to which you've subscribed. Thus, subscribing to a handful of newsgroups keeps you from having to slog through a list of 15,000 newsgroups to find what you want.

Categories are indicated with a file folder icon; newsgroups are indicated with a newspaper icon.

Earlier you learned that newsgroups are named in a hierarchical fashion. Netscape takes advantage of this by organizing newsgroups the same way, using folders in the groups pane. Initially, all you see under a news server is the top-level categories. If you click one of the top-level categories, you see the subcategories underneath it. Continue clicking categories until you see a newsgroup to which you can subscribe.

If you want to subscribe to alt.tv.simpsons, for example, follow these steps:

1. Click the alt top-level newsgroup.
2. Find alt.tv in the list under alt, and click it.
3. Find alt.tv.simpsons in the list under alt.tv, and check the box that is to the right of the name to indicate that you want to subscribe to that newsgroup.

After you subscribe to all the newsgroups you want, you can tell Netscape to display only those newsgroups to which you've subscribed. Choose Options, Show Subscribed Groups from the main menu.

NOTE You can sample the articles in a newsgroup before subscribing. If you click a newsgroup to which you haven't subscribed, Netscape displays that newsgroup's articles in the article pane. If you like what you see, subscribe to the group by checking the box next to the name of the newsgroup.

Browsing and Reading Articles

Select a newsgroup in the groups Pane and Netscape displays all the current articles for that group in the articles pane. You can scroll up and down the list of articles looking for an interesting article. When you click an article in the article pane, Netscape displays the contents of that article in the body pane.

Articles that you haven't read have a green diamond in the R column.

Notice that some of the articles are indented under other articles. These are replies to the articles under which they are indented. All the messages indented under an article, including the original message, are called a thread. Netscape indents articles this way so you can visually follow the thread. Figure 9.4 shows what a thread looks like in Netscape.

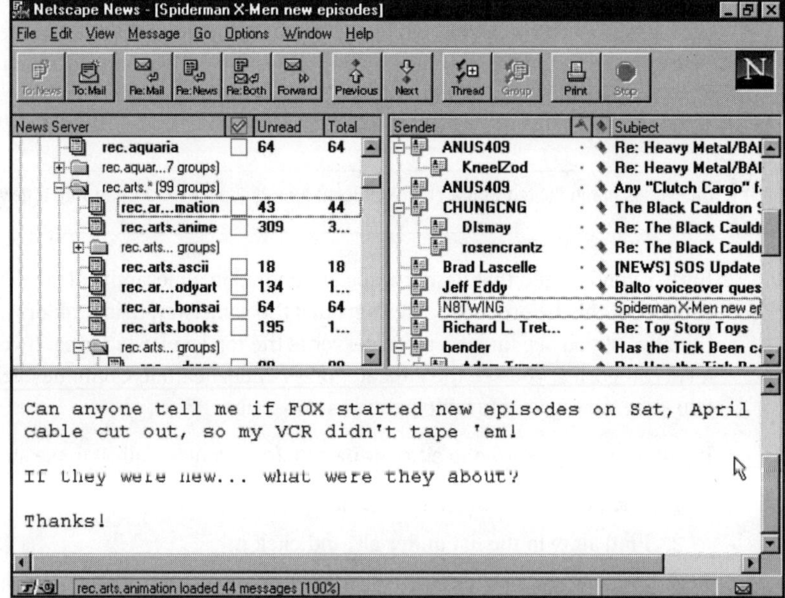

FIG. 9.4
The top portion of the message's body tells you who posted the message and what other groups they posted the message to.

TROUBLESHOOTING

What happened to the articles that were here a few days ago? It's not practical to keep every article posted to every newsgroup indefinitely. Your service provider deletes the older articles to make room for the newer articles. Another way of saying this is that a message scrolled off. The length of time that an article hangs around varies from provider to provider, but is usually between three days and a week.

Moving Around the Article Pane When you click an article header in the article pane, the article's contents are automatically displayed in the body pane. After you read the article, you can click another article, or you can use the following options from Netscape's toolbar and menu to move around:

- Choose Go, Next Unread from the main menu to read the next message you haven't read.
- Choose Go, Previous Unread from the main menu to read the previous message you haven't read.
- Click the Next button to read the next article in the newsgroup—whether you've read it already or not.
- Click the Previous button to read the previous article in the newsgroup—whether you've read it already or not.
- Choose Go, First Unread to read the first message in the newsgroup that you haven't yet read.

TROUBLESHOOTING

I opened an article, but its contents were all garbled. You've probably opened an article that is ROT13-encoded. ROT13 is an encoding method that has little to do with security. It allows a person who is posting a potentially offensive message to place the responsibility for its contents on you–the reader. It essentially says that if you decode and read this message, you won't hold me responsible for its contents. To decode the article, right-click in the body pane, and choose Unscramble (ROT-13).

Downloading Files from Newsgroups Posting and downloading files from a newsgroup is a bit more complicated than your experience with online services. Binary files can't be posted directly to UseNet. Many methods have evolved, however, to encode files into text so that they can be sent.

The downloading process works as follows:

1. A file is encoded, using UUEncode, to a newsgroup as one or more articles.
2. While you're browsing a newsgroup, you notice a few articles with subject lines that look like this (headings are provided for your convenience):

Lines	File name	Part	Description
5	HOMER.GIF	[00/02]	Portrait of Homer Simpson
800	HOMER.GIF	[01/02]	Portrait of Homer Simpson
540	HOMER.GIF	[02/02]	Portrait of Homer Simpson

These articles are three parts of the same file. The first article is probably a description of the file because it is part zero, and because there are only five lines in it. The next two articles are the actual file.

3. To download a file from a newsgroup, you retrieve all the articles belonging to that file. Then, you UUDecode the articles back into a binary file.

Replying to an Article You'll eventually want to post a reply to an article you read in a newsgroup. You might want to be helpful and answer someone's question. You're just as likely to find an interesting discussion to which you want to contribute. Either way, the following are two different ways you can reply to an article you have read:

- Follow up—If you want your reply to be read by everyone who frequents the newsgroup, post a follow-up article. Your reply is added to the thread. To reply to an article, click the Post Reply button on the toolbar. Fill in the window shown in Figure 9.5, and click the Send button.

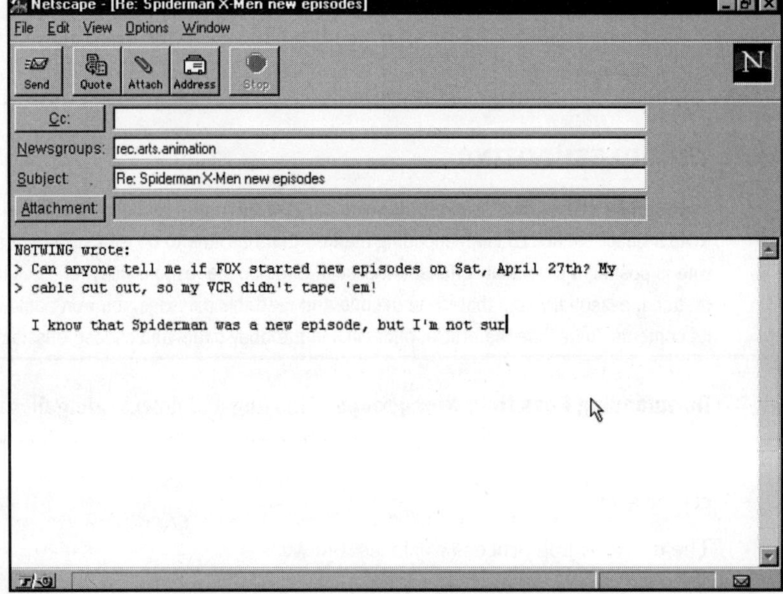

FIG. 9.5 The text that starts with the greater-than sign (>) is the original article. Delete everything that you don't need to remind the reader of what he posted.

- E-mail—If your reply would benefit only the person to whom you're replying, respond with an e-mail message instead. That person gets the message faster, and the other newsgroup readers aren't annoyed. To reply by e-mail, click the Reply button on the toolbar. Fill out the window shown in Figure 9.6 and click the Send button.

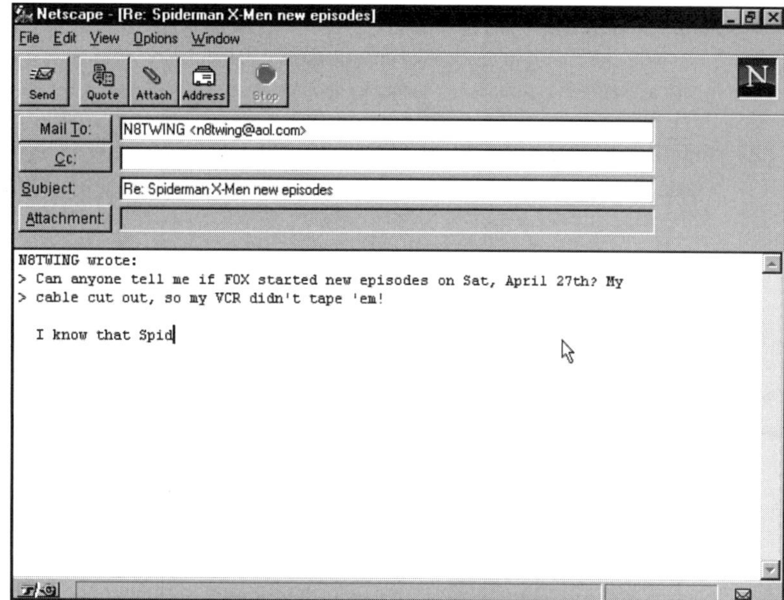

FIG. 9.6
Look carefully–the only difference between this window and the window in Figure 8.5 is this window has the Mail To field and the previous window has the Newsgroups field.

Stay out of Trouble; Follow the Rules

Etiquette, as Miss Manners will tell you, was created so that everyone would get along better. Etiquette's rules are not official rules, however; they're community standards for how everyone should behave. Likewise, netiquette is a community standard for how to behave on the Internet. It's important for two reasons. First, it helps keep the frustration level down. Second, it helps prevent the terrible waste of Internet resources by limiting the amount of noise.

- Post your articles in the right place. Don't post questions about Windows 95, for example, to the alt.tv.simpsons newsgroup.
- NEWSGROUP READERS REALLY HATE IT WHEN YOU SHOUT BY USING ALL CAPS. It doesn't make your message seem any more important.
- Don't test, and don't beg for e-mail. There are a few places where that is appropriate, but this behavior generally gets you flamed (a flame is a mean or abusive message).
- Don't spam. Spamming is posting an advertisement to several, if not hundreds, of newsgroups. Don't do it. It's a waste of Internet resources.
- Don't cross-post your article. This is a waste of Internet resources, and readers quickly tire of seeing the same article posted to many newsgroups.

Posting a New Article

It's no fun being a spectator. You'll eventually want to start a discussion of your own. To post a new article, click the Post New button on the toolbar. Fill in the window shown previously in Figure 9.5, and click the Send button.

NOTE Lurk before you leap. Lurking is when you just hang out, reading the articles and learning the ropes without posting an article. You'll avoid making a fool of yourself by learning what's acceptable and what's not before it's too late.

Practice Posting in the Right Place You'll find a special newsgroup, called alt.test, that exists just for test posting. You can post a test article to that newsgroup all day long and no one will care.

In fact, you should go ahead and post a test article just to make sure that everything works. You'll get a good idea of how long it takes your article to show up, and you'll also learn the mechanics of posting and replying to articles.

Test your file uploads in the alt.test newsgroup, too, instead of testing them in productive newsgroups.

Posting a File Netscape makes posting a file easy. Post a new article as described earlier in the section "Posting a New Article." Before you click the Send button, however, follow these instructions:

1. Click Attachment. Netscape displays the Attachments dialog box as shown in Figure 9.7.

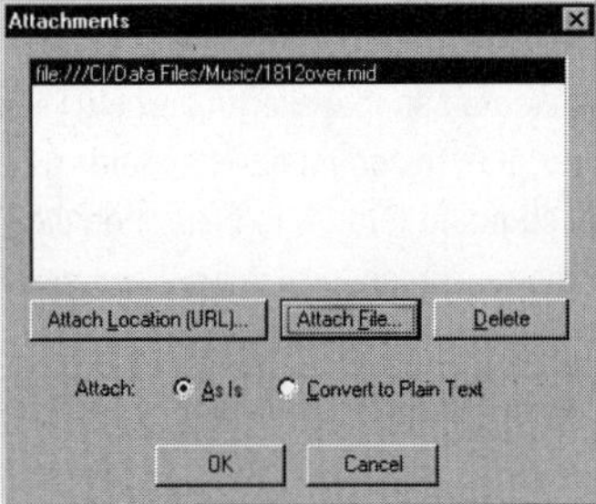

FIG. 9.7 You can attach more than one file to an article.

2. Click Attach File, choose the file you want to attach in the Enter File to Attach dialog box, and click Open.
3. Repeat step 2 for each file you want to attach to your article. Then, click OK to save your attachments.

After you've selected the files you want to attach to your posting, you can continue editing it normally. Click the Send button when you're finished.

Other Ways to Read the News

If browsing newsgroups with a newsreader seems like too much trouble, the tools described in this section might be just what you need. You'll learn to use DejaView, which lets you search UseNet for specific articles. You'll also learn how to use SIFT, a tool that filters all the newsgroup postings and saves them for you to read later.

Searching UseNet with DejaNews

DejaNews is a Web tool that searches all the newsgroup articles, past and present, for terms that you specify. Point your Web browser at **http://www.dejanews.com/forms/dnq.html**. Figure 9.8 shows you the DejaNews search Web page. To search UseNet, fill in the form as shown in Figure 9.8, and click Search.

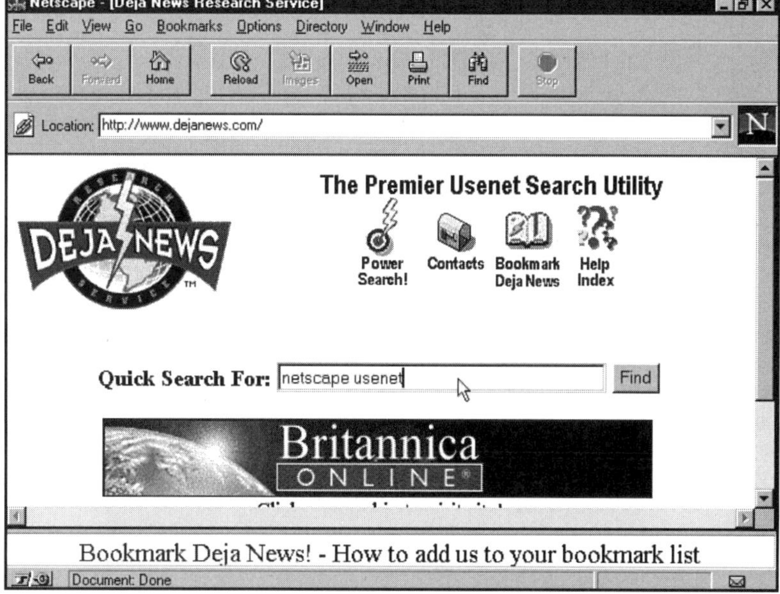

FIG. 9.8
Click the Create a Query Filter link to specify exactly which newsgroup, author, or date range to search.

DejaNews displays another Web page that contains a list of the newsgroup articles it found. You can click any of these articles to read them, or click Get Next 30 Hits to display the next page full of articles. The following are a couple of other things you should know:

- The author's name is the last item on each line. You can click it to see what other newsgroups they typically post to.
- You can click the subject line of an article to display the complete thread that contains that article.

Filtering UseNet with SIFT

SIFT is a tool provided by Stanford that filters all the articles posted to UseNet. As an added bonus, it filters a lot of public mailing lists and new Web pages, too. You tell SIFT the keywords in which you're interested, and it keeps track of all the new documents on the Internet that match those keywords. Like DejaNews, this is a Web tool, so point your browser at **http://sift.stanford.edu**.

The first time you access SIFT, it asks you for an e-mail address and password. You don't have one, yet. That's OK. Type your e-mail address and make up a password. You'll need to use the same password the next time that you access SIFT. Click Enter to go to the search form.

The most effective way to use SIFT is as follows:

1. Figure 9.9 shows the SIFT search form. Select the Search option button, and type the topics you're looking for. If you want to make sure that some topics are not included, type them in Avoid.
2. Click Submit. SIFT displays a page containing all of today's new articles that match your keywords. The most relevant line is at the top; the least relevant is at the bottom. Read some of the articles, Web pages, and mailing list messages by clicking them.
3. If you're happy with these test results, click Subscribe at the bottom of the Web page. Then, click Submit. The next time you log on to SIFT, you'll see additional lines at the bottom of the Web page, as shown in Figure 9.9, that let you delete subscriptions or review the current day's hits.

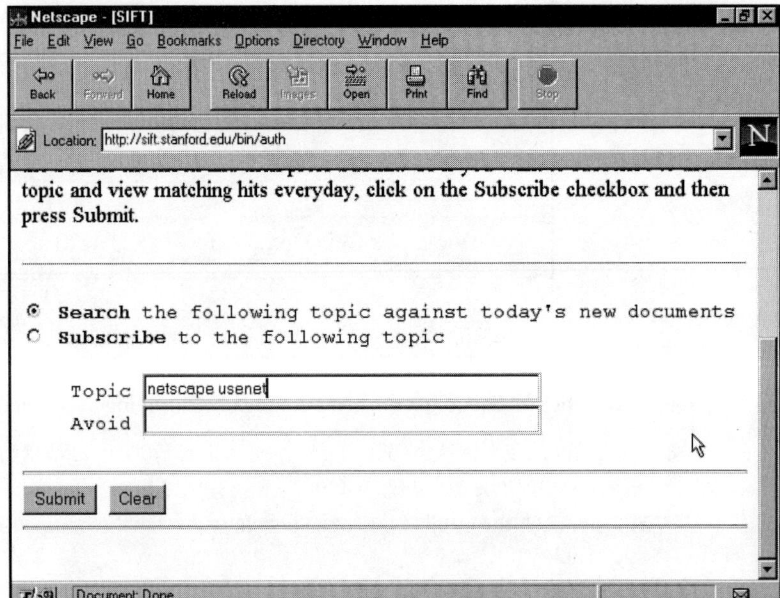

FIG. 9.9
You won't see the Read and Delete Topic choices until you've submitted at least one subscription.

4. If you're not happy with the results, click Search at the bottom of the Web page. Then, adjust the keywords in Topic and Avoid, and click Submit. SIFT displays a similar Web page using your new search keywords.

The Pros and Cons of Netscape's Newsreader

There's a wide variety of newsreaders available on the Internet. They range from the most basic (Qnews) to complex (Free Agent). Netscape's newsreader is at the basic end of this spectrum. It doesn't have the features that an avid UseNet junkie needs to be productive. Netscape doesn't let you choose a UUEncoded file, for example, then download and UUDecode it automatically. If you need more advanced features such as this, you should consider some of the freeware and shareware newsreaders available. Free Agent is available on the Web at **www.forteinc.com/forte/agent/dlmain.htm**.

Netscape's newsreader does have everything that a casual user needs, however. You can easily post, reply, and view articles—possibly easier than with the other newsreaders available. You can also view UUEncoded images on UseNet just by selecting the article in the list. This is about all most people use UseNet for anyway. Incidentally, the most important feature of Netscape's newsreader is how solid and well thought out it appears to be. For example, Newsgroups are organized using an outline metaphor, and the article list is easy to navigate. ●

CHAPTER 10

Reading UseNet Newsgroups with Internet Explorer

What is UseNet?

Get a brief primer on UseNet, which is necessary if this is the first time you'll be connecting to it.

What is Microsoft's new Internet News Client?

Learn about the new Internet News Client Microsoft has released as a part of Internet Explorer 3.

How do I install and configure the Internet News Client?

Find out how to install and configure the program to work with your Internet service provider for accessing and responding to UseNet news.

How do I read and respond to UseNet news?

Learn how to browse through and access UseNet newsgroups, read articles, reply to them, and post original articles of your own.

How do I send and receive binary files?

Discover Internet News Client's capabilities to automatically encode and decode file attachments to UseNet news articles.

With Internet Explorer 2, Microsoft added the capability to access UseNet newsgroups through its Web browser. However, this capability was rudimentary at best and a far cry from the newsgroup support available in many freeware and shareware newsreaders, such as News Xpress and Free Agent.

With Internet Explorer 3, however, Microsoft has added an Internet News Client that brings its news reading capabilities a long way. While still not possessing all of the capabilities of dedicated news readers, the Internet News Client has more than enough functionality for most of your UseNet news needs. ■

A UseNet Primer

Newsgroups are a bit more complicated than forums, BBSes, and cork boards. Not in a technical sense, but in a cultural sense. Newsgroups don't have official rules that are enforced by anyone in particular. They have unofficial rules that newsgroup peers enforce. Newsgroups concentrate cultures, from all over the world, in one place—a source of a lot of conflict as you can imagine.

So, take a few moments to study this section before you dive into newsgroups head first. Make sure that you understand how newsgroups and the UseNet culture works. Then, you'll learn how to use Microsoft's Internet News Client to access one of the most dynamic parts of the Internet, newsgroups, later in this chapter.

> **CAUTION**
>
> If you're particularly sensitive or easily offended, newsgroups may not be right for you. Unlike the forums and BBSes on commercial online systems, no one is watching over the content on newsgroups. The material is often very offensive to some folks. You'll find plenty of nasty language and abusive remarks in some newsgroups, just like you'd expect to find in some pubs.

The Basics of Using Newsgroups

If you've ever used a forum or BBS on a commercial online service, you're already familiar with the concept of a newsgroup. Readers post messages, or articles, to newsgroups for other people to read. They can also reply to articles that they read on a newsgroup. It's one way for people like yourself to communicate with millions of people around the world.

Newsgroups are a bit loose, however. A newsgroup doesn't necessarily have a watchdog—other than the readers themselves. As a result, the organization is a bit loose, and the content of the messages is often way out of focus. The seemingly chaotic nature of newsgroups, however, produces some of the most interesting information you'll find anywhere.

Newsgroup Variety Is Good The variety of content is exactly what makes newsgroups so appealing. There are newsgroups for expressing opinions—no matter how benign or how radical. There are other newsgroups for asking questions or getting help. And, best of all, there are newsgroups for those seeking companionship—whether they're looking for a soul mate or longing to find someone with a similar interest in whittling. The following is a sample of the types of newsgroups you'll find:

- **alt.tv.simpsons** contains a lot of mindless chatter about the Simpsons.
- **comp.os.ms-windows.advocacy** is one of the hottest Window's newsgroups around. You'll find heated discussions about both Windows 3.1 and Windows 95.
- **rec.games.trading-cards.marketplace** is the place to be if you're into collecting and trading cards.
- **rec.humor.funny** is where to go to lighten up your day. You'll find a wide variety of humor, including contemporary jokes, old standards, and bogus news flashes.

Alternative and Regional Newsgroups Not all the newsgroups available are true UseNet newsgroups. Some newsgroups are created to serve a particular region or are so obscure that they wouldn't make it through the rigorous UseNet approval process. If something looks like a newsgroup and acts like a newsgroup, however, it can find its way onto your news server.

Here are some examples:

- Regional—Many localities, such as Dallas or San Francisco, have their own newsgroups where people exchange dining tips, consumer advice, and other regional bits of information.
- Alternative—The alternative newsgroups are responsible for most of the variety on UseNet. Some of these groups have a reputation for being downright nasty (for example, pornography), but also have groups dedicated to your favorite TV shows, books, or politicians.

NOTE If you have a child who will be using newsgroups, you might consider finding a service provider that makes the pornographic newsgroups, such as **alt.sex.pictures** and **alt.binaries.pictures.erotica**, unavailable. ■

Moderated Newsgroups Moderated newsgroups are a bit more civil, and the articles are typically more focused than unmoderated newsgroups. Moderators look at every article posted to their newsgroup before making it available for everyone to read. If they judge it to be inappropriate, they nuke it.

So what are the advantages of a moderated newsgroup? You don't have to wade through ten pounds of garbage to find one ounce of treasure. Check out some of the alternative newsgroups and you'll get the picture. Most of the alternative newsgroups are unmoderated. As such, they can be a free-for-all of profanity, abusiveness, and childish bickering. The value and quality of the information that you'll find in moderated newsgroups is much higher than their unmoderated cousins.

The disadvantages, on the other hand, are just as clear. Some people believe that moderating a newsgroup is the equivalent of censorship. Instead of the group as a whole determining the content of newsgroups, the judgment of a single individual determines the content of the newsgroups. Another significant disadvantage is timeliness. Articles posted to moderated newsgroups can be delayed days or weeks.

Participating in a Newsgroup Every Internet resource that you want to use requires a client program on your computer. Newsgroups are no exception. The program that you use to read newsgroups is called a *newsreader*.

A newsreader lets you browse the newsgroups that are available, reading and posting articles along the way. Most newsreaders also have more advanced features that make using newsgroups a bit more productive. Later in this chapter, you'll learn how to use Microsoft's Internet News Client to access the news. You'll also find other ways to read the newsgroups without using a newsreader.

So How Do Newsgroups Work, Anyway?

NNTP (Network News Transport Protocol) is used to move the news from one server to another. It's very similar to e-mail in a lot of respects. Instead of all the messages sitting on your machine, however, they are stored on an NNTP news server that many other people can access. Therefore, the news only has to be sent to the server, instead of each user. Each user is then responsible for retrieving the articles he or she is interested in.

UseNet news makes its way to your news server using a process called *flooding*. That is, all the news servers are networked together. A particular news server may be fed by one news server, while it feeds three other news servers in turn. Periodically, it's flooded with news from the news server that's feeding it, and it floods all of its news to the news servers that it feeds.

Wading Through UseNet

Sometimes, you'll feel like you're knee deep in newsgroups. There are over 10,000 newsgroups available. Wading through them all to find what you want can be a daunting task. What's a new user to do?

It's all right there in front of you. There's a lot of logic to the way newsgroups are named. Once you learn it, you'll be able to pluck out a newsgroup just by how it's named. You'll also find tools to help you locate just the right newsgroup, as well as a few newsgroups that provide helpful advice and pointers to new users.

Newsgroup Organization Newsgroups are organized into a hierarchy of categories and subcategories. Take a look at the **alt.tv.simpsons** newsgroup discussed earlier. The top-level category is **alt**. The subcategory is **tv**. The subcategory under that is **simpsons**. The name goes from general to specific, left to right. You'll also find other newsgroups under **alt.tv**, such as **alt.tv.friends** and **alt.tv.home-imprvment**.

alt.tv.* is a notational convention that means all the newsgroups available under the **alt.tv** category.

There are many different top-level categories available. Table 10.1 shows some that you probably have available on your news server.

Table 10.1 Internet Top-Level Newsgroup Categories

Category	Description
alt	Alternative newsgroups
bit	BitNet LISTSERV mailing lists
biz	Advertisements for businesses

Category	Description
clarinet	News clipping service by subscription only
comp	Computer-related topics like hardware and software
k12	Educational, kindergarten through grade 12
misc	Topics that don't fit the other categories
news	News and information about UseNet
rec	Recreational, sports, hobbies, music, and games
sci	Applied sciences
soc	Social and cultural topics
talk	Discussion of more controversial topics

These categories help you nail down exactly which newsgroup you're looking for. A bit of practice helps as well. If you're looking for information about Windows 95, for example, start looking at the **comp** top-level category. You'll find an **os** category, which probably represents operating systems. Under that category, you'll find an **ms-windows** category.

NOTE Exactly which newsgroups are available on your news server is largely under the control of the administrator. Some administrators filter out regional newsgroups that don't apply to your area. Some also filter out the alternative newsgroups because of their potentially offensive content. ■

Searching for Newsgroups on the Web Scouring the categories for a particular newsgroup may not be the most efficient way to find what you want. Here are a couple of tools that help you find newsgroups based upon keywords that you type:

- Point Internet Explorer 3 to **http://www.cen.uiuc.edu/cgi-bin/find-news**. This tool searches all the newsgroup names and newsgroup descriptions for a single keyword that you specify.
- Another very similar tool is at **http://www.nova.edu/Inter-Links/cgi-bin/news.pl**. This tool allows you to give more than one keyword, however.

Newsgroups for New Users Whenever you go someplace new, you usually try to locate a source of information about it. Likewise, the first few places that you need to visit when you get to UseNet are all the newsgroups that are there to welcome you. It's not just a warm and fuzzy welcome, either. They provide useful information about what to do, what not to do, and how to get the most out of the newsgroups. Table 10.2 shows you the newsgroups that you might want to check out.

Table 10.2 Newsgroups for the Newbie

Newsgroup	Description
alt.answers	A good source of FAQs and information about alt newsgroups
alt.internet.services	This is the place to ask about Internet programs and resources
news.announce.newsgroups	Announcements about new newsgroups are made here
news.announce.newusers	Articles and FAQs for the new newsgroups user
news.newusers.questions	This is the place to ask your questions about using newsgroups

NOTE Don't post test articles to these newsgroups. Don't post articles asking for someone to send you an e-mail, either. This is a terrible waste of newsgroups that are intended to help new users learn the ropes. See the section "Practice Posting in the Right Place" later in this chapter to learn about a better place to post test articles. ■

news.announce.newusers

The **news.announce.newusers** newsgroup contains a lot of great articles for new newsgroup users. In particular, look for the articles with the following subject lines:

- What is UseNet?
- What is UseNet? A second opinion
- Rules for posting to UseNet
- Hints on writing style for UseNet
- A Primer on How to Work with the UseNet Community
- Emily Postnews Answers Your Questions on Netiquette
- How to find the right place to post (FAQ)
- Answers to Frequently Asked Questions about UseNet

Getting Real News on UseNet

UseNet is good for a lot more than just blathering and downloading questionable art. There's a lot of news and great information coming from a variety of sources. You'll find "real" news, current Internet events, organizational newsgroups, and regional newsgroups as well—all of which make newsgroups worth every bit of trouble.

ClariNet You can be the first kid on the block with the current news. ClariNet is a news service that clips articles from sources such as the AP and Reuters news wires. They post these services to the **clari.*** newsgroups. These newsgroups aren't free, though. They sell these newsgroups on a subscription basis. You wouldn't want to pay for them, either, because they can be expensive. Many independent service providers do subscribe, however, as a part of their service.

ClariNet has more than 300 newsgroups from which to choose. My favorite ClariNet newsgroups are shown in Table 10.3. You'll come up with your own favorites in short order. One ClariNet newsgroup that you definitely need to check out is **clari.net.newusers**. It's a good introduction to all the newsgroups that ClariNet offers.

Table 10.3 Popular Clarinet Newsgroups

Newsgroup	Description
clari.biz.briefs	Regular business updates
clari.local.*state*	Your own local news (insert your state in place of ***state***)
clari.nb.online	News about the online community
clari.nb.windows	News about Windows products and issues
clari.living.columns.miss_manners	How can you live without it?
clari.news.briefs	Regular national and world news updates

For your convenience, Table 10.4 describes each ClariNet news category. You'll find individual newsgroups under each category. Under the **clari.living** category, for example, you'll find arts, books, music, and movies.

Table 10.4 ClariNet News Categories at a Glance

Category	Description
clari.news	General and national news
clari.biz	Business and financial news
clari.sports	Sports and athletic news
clari.living	Lifestyle and human interest stories
clari.world	News about other countries
clari.local	States and local areas
clari.feature	Special syndicated features
clari.tw	Technical and scientific news
clari.matrix_news	A networking newsletter

continues

Table 10.4 Continued

Category	Description
clari.nb	Newsbytes, computer industry news
clari.sfbay	San Francisco Bay Area news
clari.net	Information about ClariNet
clari.apbl	Special groups for the AP BulletinLine

Net Happenings If it seems that the Internet is moving too fast to keep up with, you're right—without help, anyway. The **comp.internet.net-happenings** newsgroup helps you keep track of new events on the Internet, including the World Wide Web, mailing lists, UseNet, and so on.

The subject line of each article tells you a lot about the announcement. Take, for example, the following announcement:

WWW>Free Internet service for first 100 visitors

The first part tells you that the announcement is about a World Wide Web site. You'll find many other categories such as FAQ, EMAG, LISTS, and MISC. The second part is a brief description about the announcement. Most of the time, the description is enough to tell you whether you want to see more information by opening the article. The article itself is a few paragraphs about the announcement, with the address or subscription information near the top.

Regional Newsgroups Is your geographical region represented on UseNet? A lot are. The Dallas/Fort Worth area has a couple of newsgroups, such as **dfw.eats**, **dfw.forsale**, and **dfw.personals**. Virtually every state has similar newsgroups. Other states might have special needs. For example, California users might be interested in the **ca.environment.earthquakes** newsgroup.

Using the Microsoft Internet News Client to Read the News

All that news is out there, just sloshing around on the news server, and you need a program to get at it. There are a lot of newsreaders out there, but you already have Microsoft's Internet News Client along with the Internet Explorer 3 Web browser. It's one of the cleanest and easiest to use newsreaders available.

Installing the Internet News Client

Microsoft's Internet Mail and News Clients come bundled together in a self-extracting, self-installing file called `Mailnews95.exe`. To install either or both of these clients, follow these steps:

1. Execute `Mailnews95.exe`. The program will then self-extract the necessary files and automatically start the installation process. You will be shown an alert box giving you the option to start the installation, and asked to agree to the licensing agreement, after which the Internet Mail and News Setup Wizard appears.
2. Fill in your Name and Organization and choose Next. The next dialog box will ask you to confirm the name and organization.
3. You can elect to install either the Internet Mail or News clients, or both. Make your choice and choose Next.
4. That's it! The Internet Mail and/or News clients are now installed. The final step necessary to complete the installation process is to choose OK from the last dialog to restart your computer.

After you have restarted your computer, you will be ready to run the Internet News Client. You can access the Internet News Client by clicking the Mail & News icon located on the toolbar (see Figure 10.1).

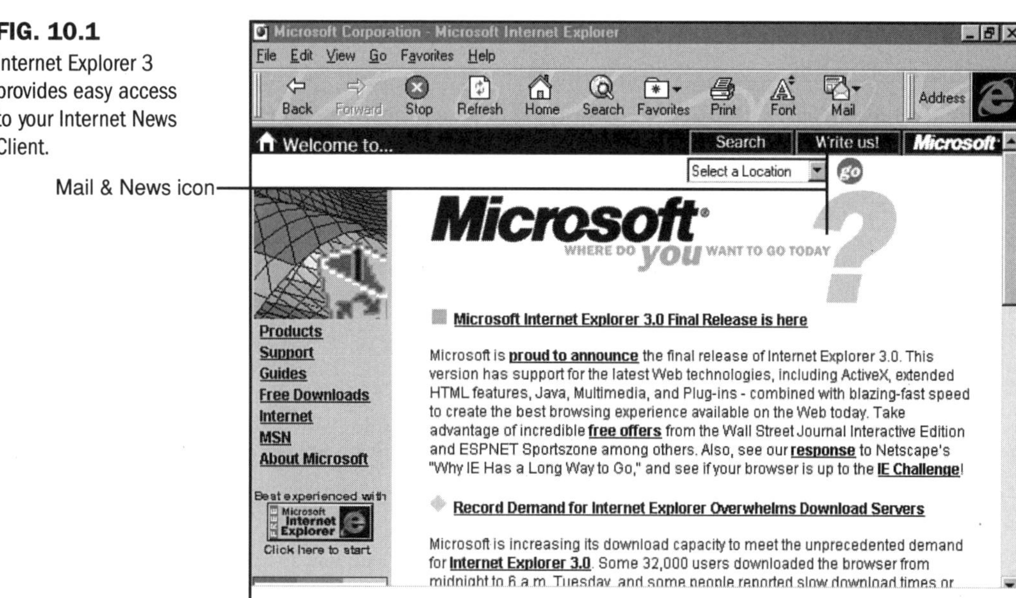

FIG. 10.1
Internet Explorer 3 provides easy access to your Internet News Client.

Initial Configuration of the Internet News Client

When you first run the Internet News Client, you will be greeted with the Internet News Configuration Wizard (see Figure 10.2). The purpose of this is to find out from you the minimum information needed to interface with your Internet service provider (ISP) to provide access to UseNet news.

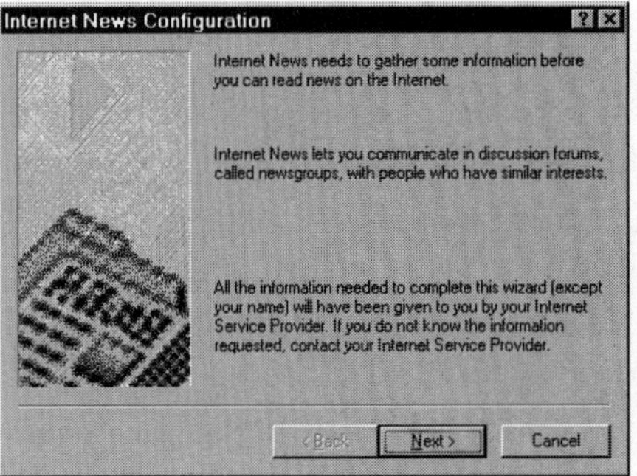

FIG. 10.2
The Internet News Configuration Wizard will guide you through the process of the minimum configuration needed to use it to access UseNet news.

NOTE Most of the information requested in this initial configuration process should have been provided to you by your ISP, so make sure you have everything from them in front of you when you begin. If you have any problems or questions with the configuration, they're probably your best source for help. ■

To perform the initial configuration process, follow these steps:

1. In the Internet News Configuration Wizard, press Next. The most important information needed is the News Server to be used to access UseNet news. Enter this into this dialog box. If the news server provided by your ISP requires you to log on (most do not require a separate news server logon), enter the logon information as well. When you are done, choose Next.

NOTE The Internet News Client is able to access more than one news server. You will find out how to do this later in the chapter, when you connect to Microsoft's news server and access its newsgroups. ■

2. Next, enter your Name and E-mail Address, which is the information that the Internet News Client uses to "sign" your outgoing news article.
3. The final step in the initial configuration process gives you the opportunity to set the Internet News Client to be the default program to be used to read news from your Web browser.

TROUBLESHOOTING

Why do I get an error message that says the Internet News Client couldn't find the news server? First, make sure that you have a connection to your service provider. If you're definitely connected, make sure that you correctly configured your NNTP news server. Don't remember the exact address your provider gave you? Try this: If your domain name is **provider.net**, then add news to the front of it like this: **news.provider.net**.

Can I use the Internet News Client to access UseNet through CompuServe? Yes. The CompuServe news server is **news.compuserve.com** and the SMTP mail server is **mail.compuserve.com**.

Making the Initial Connection

Once you have configured the Internet News Client through the Internet News Configuration Wizard, it will start up. At this point, you're just about ready to access UseNet news.

Finding Newsgroups of Interest

After you've configured the Microsoft Internet News Client for your service provider and made your first connection, it will download a complete list of the newsgroups and group descriptions available on your news server (see Figure 10.3). The Internet News Client displays a dialog box warning you that this process can take a few minutes on a slow connection.

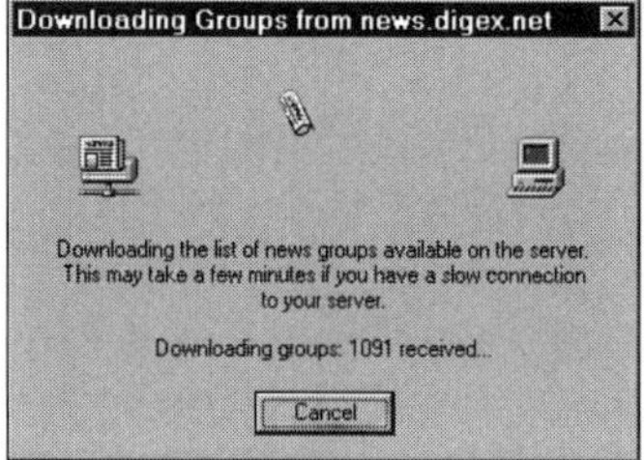

FIG. 10.3
Upon its initial connection to a news server, the Internet News Client downloads the list of news groups available on the server.

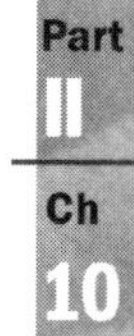

Before you can read articles in a newsgroup, you need to find newsgroups that you are interested in. After the initial download of newsgroup names and descriptions, the Internet News Client automatically pops up the Newsgroups dialog box, shown in Figure 10.4 (this dialog box is also available by selecting News, Newsgroups or pressing Ctrl+W).

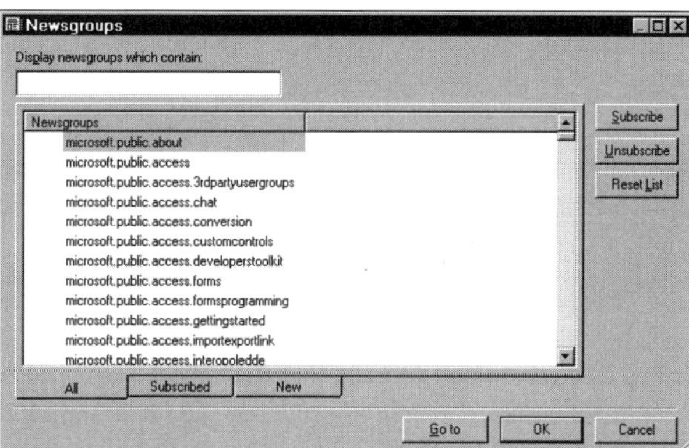

FIG. 10.4
The Newsgroups dialog box allows you to browse through the newsgroups available on a news server.

It would still be kind of difficult to find newsgroups of interest in this list if the Internet News Client didn't give you some means of narrowing down your search. And it does. By typing text into the Display Newsgroups Which Contain text area, you narrow the displayed list of newsgroups to only those that contain that text, as shown in Figure 10.5.

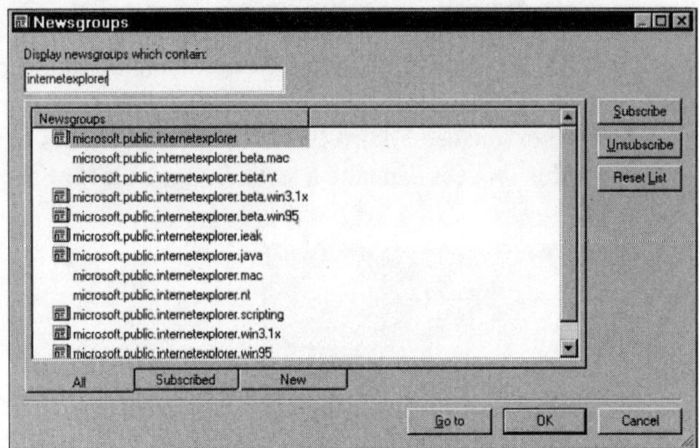

FIG. 10.5
The Internet News Client allows you to narrow your search for newsgroups of interest, and can also include the group's description, as well as its name, in the search criteria.

Once you have found newsgroups of interest, you can start browsing through them for articles that you'd like to read. Unlike many other news readers, the Internet News Client doesn't require you to subscribe to a newsgroup in order to read articles from it. It does allow you to subscribe to a group, which makes it easier to access. You'll learn how to do that a little later in the chapter.

Further Configuration Options

To access all of the configuration options for the Internet News Client, you can select News, Options which brings up the Options dialog box. Various options can be set under each of the tabs in this dialog box.

The Read Tab The options on the Read tab affect the way the Microsoft Internet News Client checks for news articles (see Figure 10.6). You can set up the Internet News Client to periodically check for new articles whenever it is running.

The Send Tab The Send tab controls various aspects of the configuration for outgoing news articles (see Figure 10.7). The options here are pretty self-explanatory, and you should feel free to experiment with them. If you select the HTML or Plain Text radio buttons on this tab, you are greeted with the Settings dialog box (see Figure 10.8). Here you can control the type of encoding used for file attachments, as well as control a few other options.

While MIME encoding is the up-and-coming standard, UseNet has historically used UUEncode for binary file attachments.

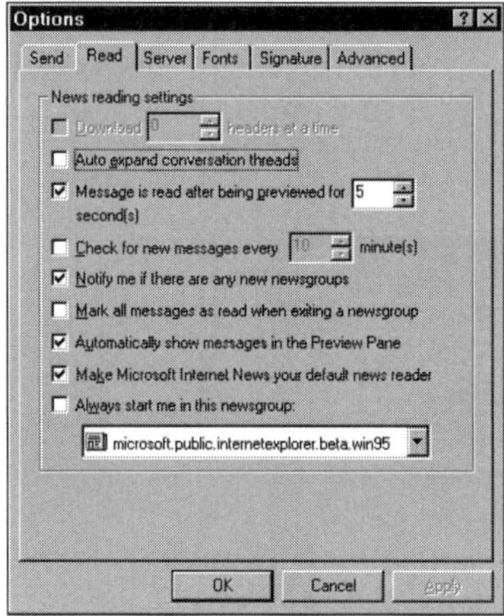

FIG. 10.6
The Read tab controls how the Internet News Client reads and reacts to new news articles.

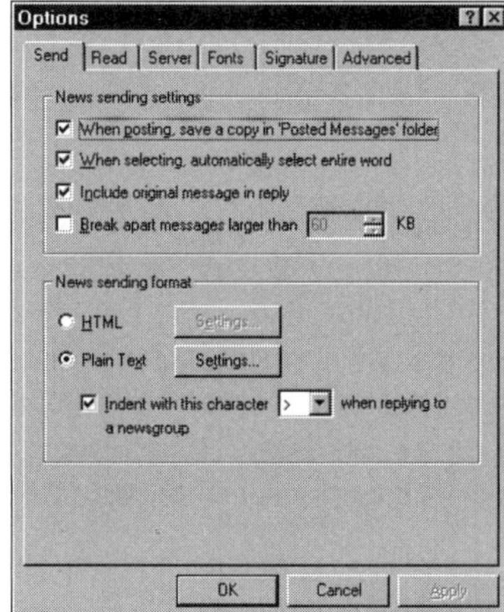

FIG. 10.7
Send options give you control over outgoing e-mail.

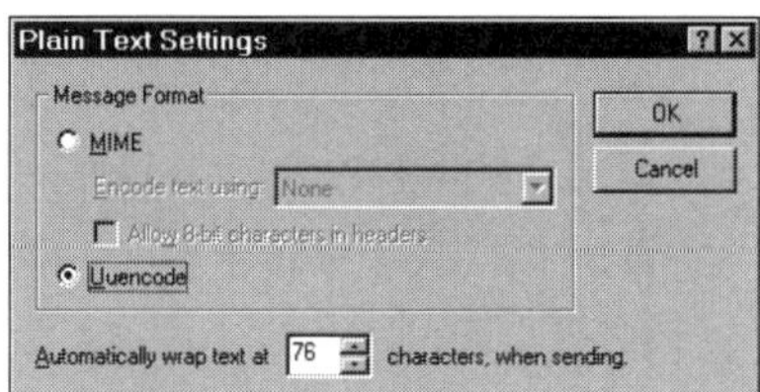

FIG. 10.8
The Plain Text Settings dialog box allows you to pick an encoding format for file attachments and gives you a few more options.

The Server Tab This tab is probably the most important of the five on the Options dialog box. On the Server tab, seen in Figure 10.9, you tell the Internet News Client where to get your news. This information is necessary for correct operation of the Internet News Client, and so was read in when you performed the initial configuration.

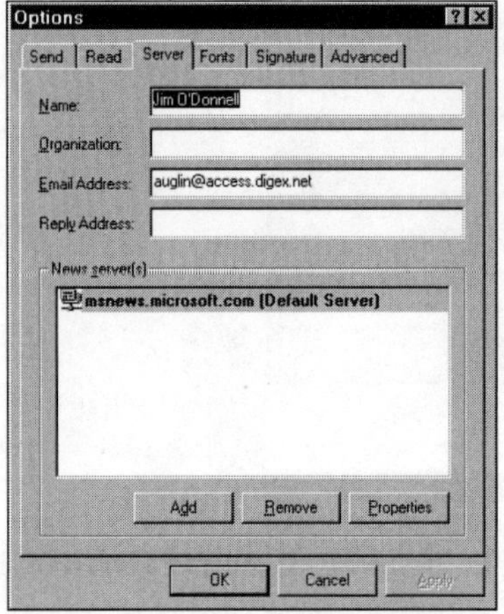

FIG. 10.9
The Server options are the heart and soul of the Internet Mail Client, as these are what allow you to send and receive Internet e-mail.

The important thing to note about this tab is that you can use more than one news server. Normally, your Internet service provider will supply you with a news server that should meet most of your needs. You may, however, find a need to connect to another server, either to get access to regular UseNet newsgroups that your provider's news server doesn't carry or to get access to a provider's news server. For instance, if you want to access Microsoft's many products, click the Add button in the Server tab. The News Server Properties dialog box appears, enabling you to enter the information to connect to a new server (see Figure 10.10).

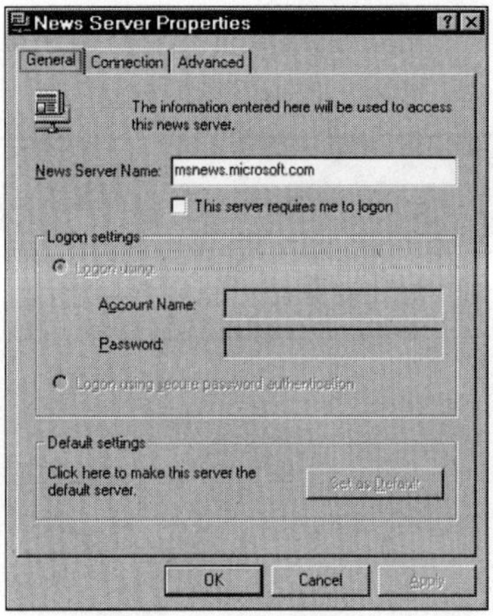

FIG. 10.10
Use the News Server Properties dialog box to connect to more than one news server.

The Fonts Tab The Fonts tab allows you to choose what fonts are used for the display of news articles in the Internet News Client (see Figure 10.11). You can individually pick the font, the color for outgoing articles, and the language encoding to be used.

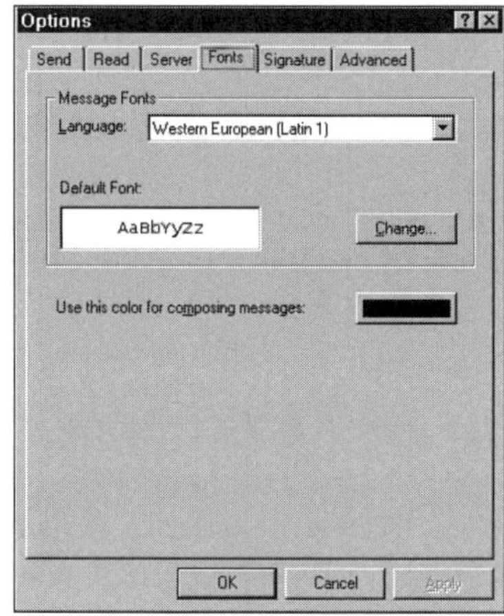

FIG. 10.11
The Internet News Client allows you to select which fonts you would like it to display.

UseNet articles are often formatted with monospaced fonts in mind, such as Courier, so you should probably pick a monospaced display font.

Signature Tab This Options tab, shown in Figure 10.12, allows you to select whether or not you want to include a signature text block at the end of each of your outgoing news articles. If you want to, you can either specify the text directly in the area shown or specify a file, called a *sigfile*, with the information in it.

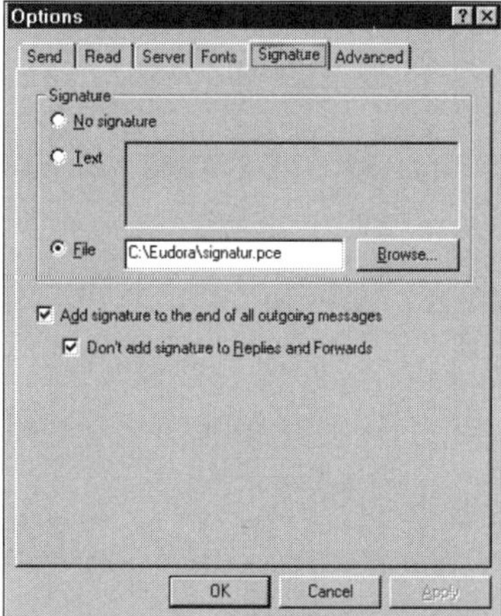

FIG. 10.12
You can set up your signature block information using this Options tab.

NOTE If you've read Chapter 8, "E-Mail with Internet Explorer," you may notice that the configuration menus are very similar. As it turns out, they're more than just similar, some of them are shared between the two.

Similar settings in the Options dialog box's Send, Fonts, and Signature tabs in either the Internet Mail or News Client also appear in the other.

A Note about Signatures

You can easily personalize your postings with a signature. Save about three lines that say something about yourself, such as your address and hobbies, into a text file. Here's an example of a signature file:

```
Jim O'Donnell                    |               odonnj@rpi.edu
                                 |                 800-555-1212
                                 |      Buy SE Using HTML, Now!
```

Your signature can communicate anything about yourself including your name, mailing address, phone number, address, or a particular phrase that reflects your outlook on life. It is considered good form, however, to limit your signatures to three or four lines.

Browsing and Reading Articles

Now that you've configured your copy of the Internet News Client and added the Microsoft news server, let's take a look at some of the newsgroups it has to offer. You'll find out how to subscribe to newsgroups, what it means to do that, and how to browse through and read UseNet news articles.

Subscribing to Newsgroups

Select News, Newsgroups or press Ctrl+W to get the Newsgroups dialog box (see Figure 10.13). This dialog box looks a little different than the one first shown in Figure 10.5. This is because there is now more than one news server configured.

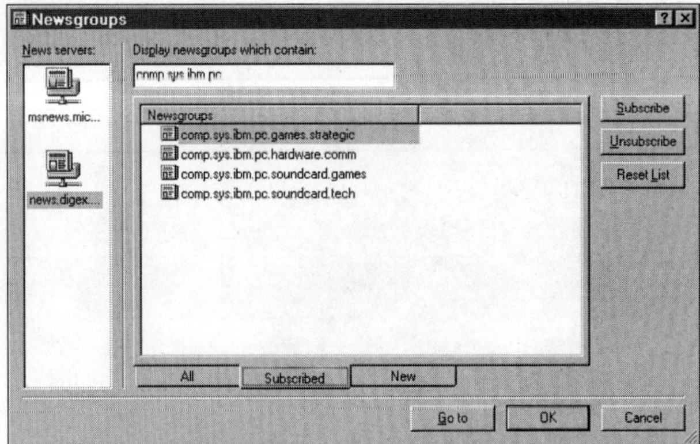

FIG. 10.13
The Newsgroups dialog box changes to accommodate multiple mail servers.

If you were interested in those Microsoft newsgroups that discussed the Internet, you would type **internet** into the Display Newsgroups Which Contain text area. To subscribe to newsgroups, either click them and then click the Subscribe button, or just double-click them. By clicking the Subscribed tab, only the current subscribed newsgroups for that news server are listed. Clicking the New tab results in a list of those newsgroups on the current news server that are new since the last time you were on. Once you have finished subscribing to newsgroups, choose OK to save your selections.

The News Client Screen

If you have used Microsoft's Internet Mail Client, you will immediately notice that its Internet News Client window is set up very similarly (see Figure 10.14). The common interface between the two makes going back and forth between them very easy.

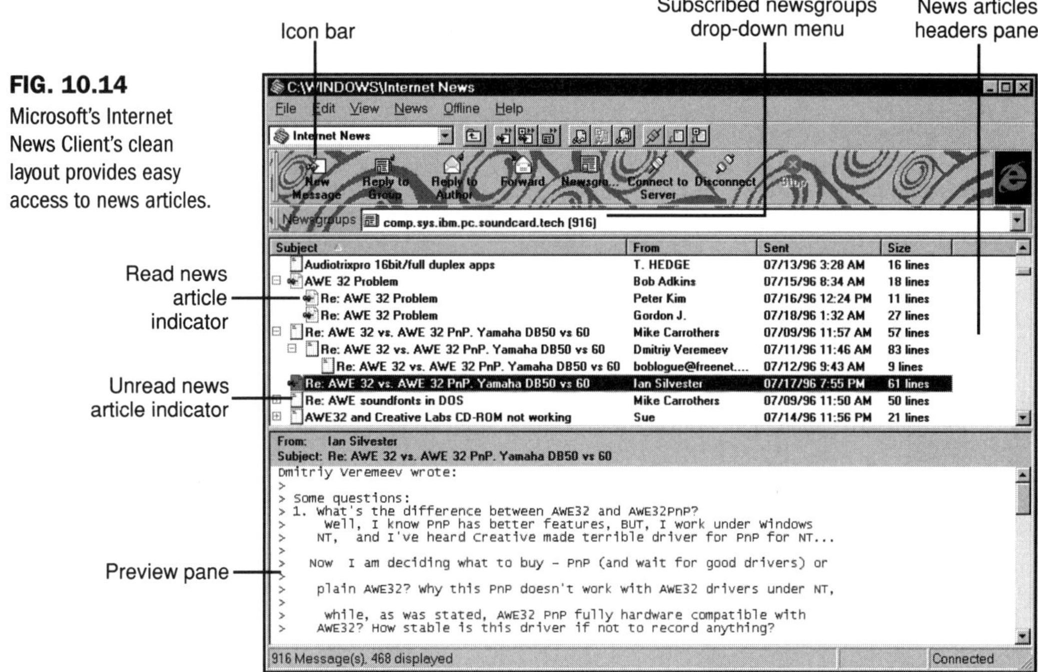

FIG. 10.14
Microsoft's Internet News Client's clean layout provides easy access to news articles.

There are many different parts to this screen. Let's get oriented with the following parts:

- At the top of the window is the icon bar, which gives a list of actions that you can perform. You can use the mouse to grab this icon bar and change its size.

If you think the icon bar takes up too much of the screen, you can turn it off by deselecting View, Icon Bar. This will remove the icon bar and replace the icon with much smaller buttons on the toolbar (as long as it is enabled).

- Underneath the icon bar is a drop-down menu giving you access to a list of your subscribed newsgroups for the current news server, as well as a list of news servers.
- Underneath the subscribed newsgroups drop-down menu is a scrollable list of message headers for every news article in the newsgroup you're looking at. The icon shown to the left of each news article header indicates whether the message has been read or not.
- On the bottom of the screen, you see the text of the open news article, along with headers indicating the article's subject and sender. This is the Internet Mail Client's preview pane—if you want, you can view a given message in a full screen of its own by double-clicking its header in the message header pane.

Notice that some of the articles are indented under other articles. These are replies to the articles under which they are indented. All the messages indented under an article, including the original message, are called a *thread*. The Internet News Client indents articles this way so you can visually follow the thread.

TROUBLESHOOTING

What happened to the articles that were here a few days ago? It's not practical to keep every article posted to every newsgroup indefinitely. Your service provider deletes the older articles to make room for the newer articles. Another way of saying this is that a message scrolled off. The length of time that an article hangs around varies from provider to provider, but is usually between three days and a week.

Downloading Files from Newsgroups Posting and downloading files from a newsgroup is a bit more complicated than your experience with online services. Binary files can't be posted directly to UseNet. Many methods have evolved, however, to encode files into text so that they can be sent. The Internet News Client has the ability to automatically download and decode files that are attached to UseNet news articles. Sometimes, however, the files are encoded and attached in a way that the News Client doesn't recognize.

The downloading process works as follows:

1. A file is encoded, using UUEncode, to a newsgroup as one or more articles.
2. While you're browsing a newsgroup, you may notice a few articles with subject lines that look like this (headings are provided for your convenience):

Lines	Filename	Part	Description
5	`HOMER.GIF`	[00/02]	Portrait of Homer Simpson
800	`HOMER.GIF`	[01/02]	Portrait of Homer Simpson
540	`HOMER.GIF`	[02/02]	Portrait of Homer Simpson

These articles are three parts of the same file. The first article is probably a description of the file because it is part zero, and because there are only five lines in it. The next two articles are the actual file.

3. To download a file from a newsgroup, you retrieve all the articles belonging to that file. Then, you UUDecode the articles back into a binary file.

Replying to an Article You'll eventually want to post a reply to an article you read in a newsgroup. You might want to be helpful and answer someone's question. You're just as likely to find an interesting discussion to which you want to contribute. Either way, the following are two different ways you can reply to an article you have read:

- **Follow up**—If you want your reply to be read by everyone who frequents the newsgroup, post a follow-up article. Your reply is added to the thread. To reply to an article, click the Reply to Group icon on the icon bar. Fill in the window shown in Figure 10.15, and click the Post Message toolbar button.

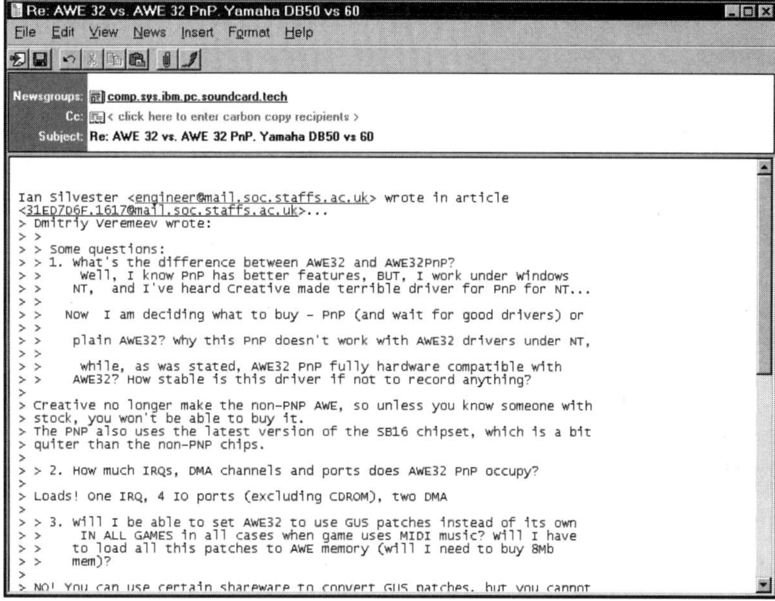

FIG. 10.15
The text that starts with the greater-than sign (>) is the original article. Delete everything you don't need to remind the reader of what was posted.

- **E-mail**—If your reply would benefit only the person to whom you're replying, respond with an e-mail message instead. That person gets the message faster, and the other newsgroup readers aren't annoyed. To reply by e-mail, click the Reply to Author icon on the icon bar. Fill out the window shown in Figure 10.16, and click the Send button.

Stay out of Trouble; Follow the Rules

Etiquette, as Miss Manners will tell you, was created so that everyone would get along better. Etiquette rules are not official rules, however; they're community standards for how everyone should behave. Likewise, *netiquette* is a community standard for how to behave on the Internet. It's important for two reasons. First, it helps keep the frustration level down. Second, it helps prevent the terrible waste of Internet resources by limiting the amount of noise. For good netiquette, follow these simple rules:

- Post your articles in the right place. Don't post questions about Windows 95, for example, to the **alt.tv.simpsons** newsgroup.
- NEWSGROUP READERS REALLY HATE IT WHEN YOU SHOUT BY USING ALL CAPS. It doesn't make your message seem any more important.
- Don't test, and don't beg for e-mail. There are a few places where that is appropriate, but this behavior generally gets you flamed (a flame is a mean or abusive message).
- Don't spam. Spamming is posting an advertisement to several, if not hundreds, of newsgroups. Don't do it. It's a waste of Internet resources.
- Don't cross-post your article to too many newsgroups. This is a waste of Internet resources, and readers quickly tire of seeing the same article posted to many newsgroups.

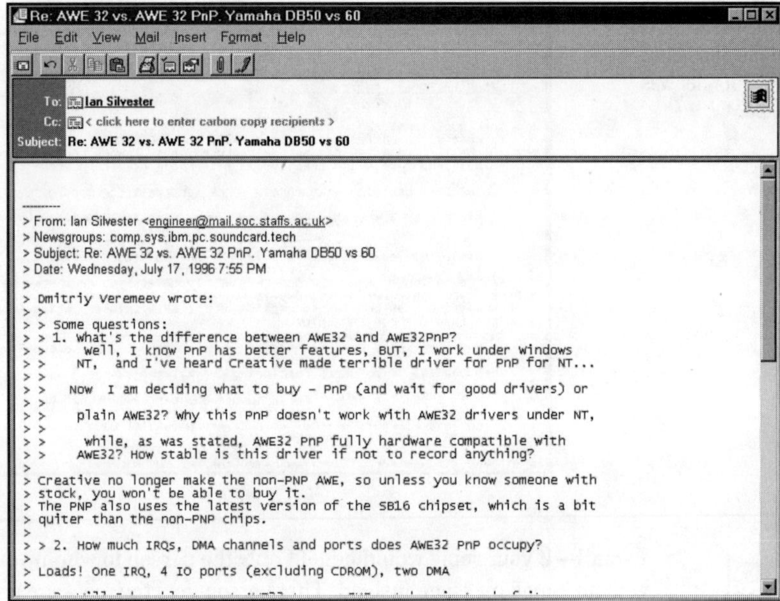

FIG. 10.16
Look carefully—the only difference between this window and the window in Figure 10.15 is this window has the To: field and the previous one has the Newsgroups: field.

Posting a New Article

It's no fun being a spectator. You'll eventually want to start a discussion of your own. To post a new article, click the New Message icon on the icon bar. Fill in your message and click the Send button.

NOTE Lurk before you leap. Lurking is when you just hang out, reading the articles and learning the ropes without posting an article. You'll avoid making a fool of yourself by learning what's acceptable and what's not before it's too late.

Practice Posting in the Right Place You'll find a special newsgroup, called alt.test, that exists just for test posting. You can post a test article to that newsgroup all day long and no one will care.

In fact, you should go ahead and post a test article just to make sure that everything works. You'll get a good idea of how long it takes your article to show up, and you'll also learn the mechanics of posting and replying to articles.

Test your file uploads in the **alt.test** newsgroup, too, instead of testing them in productive newsgroups.

Posting a File The Internet News Client makes posting a file easy. Post a new article as described in the section, "Posting a New Article." Before you click the Send button, however, follow these instructions:

1. Click the Insert File toolbar button or select Insert, File Attachment. The Internet News Client displays the Insert Attachment dialog box.
2. Find the desired file, click it, and then click Attach.
3. Repeat steps 1 and 2 for each file you want to attach to your article (see Figure 10.17).

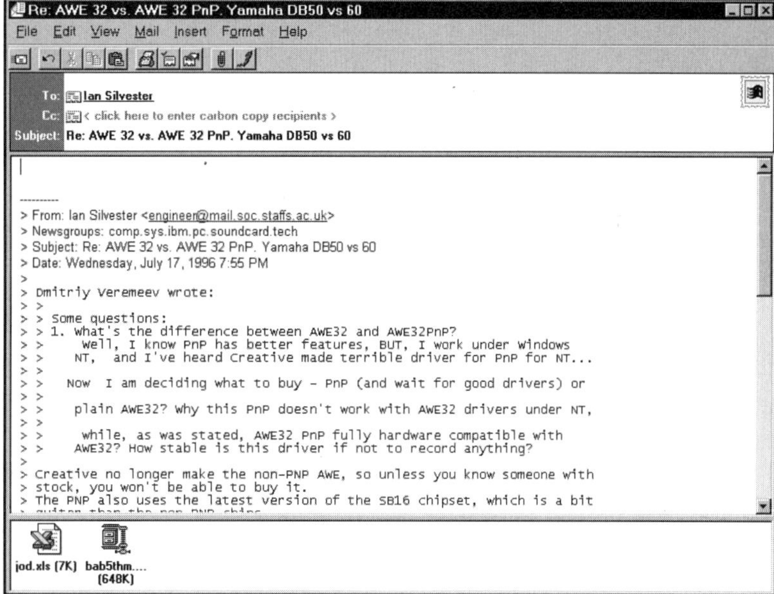

FIG. 10.17
Attached files are indicated by the icons in the bottom pane of the news article composition window.

After you've selected the files you want to attach to your posting, you can continue editing it normally. Click the Send button when you're finished.

Other Ways to Read the News

If browsing newsgroups with a newsreader seems like too much trouble, the tools described in this section might be just what you need. You'll learn to use Deja News Research Service, which lets you search UseNet for specific articles. You'll also learn how to use SIFT, a tool that filters all the newsgroup postings and saves them for you to read later.

Searching UseNet with Deja News

Deja News is a Web tool that searches all the newsgroup articles, past and present, for terms that you specify. Point your Web browser to **http://www.dejanews.com/**.

Filtering UseNet with SIFT

SIFT is a tool provided by Stanford that filters all the articles posted to UseNet. As an added bonus, it filters a lot of public mailing lists and new Web pages, too. You tell SIFT the keywords in which you're interested, and it keeps track of all the new documents on the Internet that match those keywords. Like Deja News, this is a Web tool, so point your browser at **http://sift.stanford.edu**.

The first time you access SIFT, it asks you for an e-mail address and password. You don't have one, yet. That's OK. Type your e-mail address and make up a password. You'll need to use the same password the next time that you access SIFT. Click Enter to go to the search form.

The most effective way to use SIFT is as follows:

1. Make sure the SIFT search form is open. Select the Search radio button, and type the topics for which you're looking in the Topic box. If you want to make sure that some topics are not included, type them in the Avoid box.
2. Click Submit. SIFT displays a page, containing all of today's new articles that match your keywords, on each line. The most relevant line is at the top; the least relevant is at the bottom. Read some of the articles, Web pages, and mailing list messages by clicking them.
3. If you're happy with these test results, click Subscribe at the bottom of the Web page. Then, click Submit. The next time you log on to SIFT, you'll see additional lines at the bottom of the Web page that let you delete subscriptions or review the current day's hits.
4. If you're not happy with the results, click Search at the bottom of the Web page. Then, adjust the keywords in Topic and Avoid, and click Submit. SIFT displays a similar Web page using your new search keywords.

CHAPTER 11

Getting Up-to-the-Minute News with PointCast

- Installing and configuring PointCast
- Personalize channels
- Automatically update channels
- Copying and printing articles

The PointCast Networkis an Internet news service that delivers up-to-the-minute information to your computer 24 hours a day. It's the information you care about—right on your desktop. No need to surf the Web looking for the latest national and international news, sports news and scores, weather forecasts, or stock quotes. The PointCast Network delivers.

With PointCast Network, you select the types of information you want to receive—including national and international news, business and industry updates, current sports scores, weather forecasts for cities around the world, and even horoscopes and lottery results. It's like having a personalized TV news network right on your desktop.

PointCast also replaces old-fashioned screen savers with SmartScreens that display the latest news, weather, sports, and more while your computer is idle. See something of interest? Just click it, and PointCast Network gives you the full text of the story.

With PointCast, staying up-to-date doesn't mean staying connected to the Internet all day (and racking up connection charges with your Internet service provider). Instead, you can connect to the Internet when it's convenient, update PointCast Network with the latest information, and then disconnect and find out what's new—all at your leisure.

You can use PointCast's built-in Web browser—or install AT&T's custom Internet Explorer or Earthlink's Netscape Navigator so that the Internet is always available. ■

System Requirements

This is the minimum hardware and software you need in order to use PointCast Network:

- An IBM-compatible personal computer with a 486-33 processor or better with at least 8M of RAM and at least 10M of free hard disk space
- A 14.4Kbps (28.8Kbps is preferred) internal or external modem or a direct Internet local area network (LAN) connection
- Microsoft Windows 3.1 or Windows 95

Getting Ready to Install

In addition to a computer and a modem, you must have a connection to the Internet in order to use PointCast Network. Before you install:

1. Check your modem.

   Is your modem turned on and connected to both your computer and a telephone jack? Is the telephone line available (no one is using it)?

2. Decide on an Internet connection.

   There are two types of Internet connections you can use: direct connections or dial-up connections through an Internet service provider.

   An Internet service provider, such as AT&T WorldNet or Earthlink, is a company that acts as a gateway, giving you access to the Internet. Like a telephone company, an Internet service provider charges a monthly fee for this service.

   - If you already have an account with a service provider or an online service that gives you access to the Internet (for sending and receiving e-mail, for example), you can use that account.
   - If you're installing PointCast Network on your office computer, you may already have direct access to the Internet. Check with your system administrator.
   - If you want to set up an AT&T WorldNet or Earthlink account, you can install and set up the account when you install PointCast Network.

Installing PointCast Network

To install PointCast Network:

1. Insert the CD-ROM in the back of this book in your CD-ROM drive.

2. **For Windows 3.1 users:** In the Program Manager, choose Run from the File menu.

   For Windows 95 users: From the desktop, click the Start button and choose Run from the Start menu.
3. In the Run dialog box, type **d:setup** and click OK.
4. Follow the instructions on your screen to install PointCast Network.

What Happens Next?

After installing all the software you selected, the installer asks if you want to personalize PointCast. Your selection depends on how you like to work with new programs.

To launch PointCast Network:

1. Click Launch PointCast.
2. In the Internet dialog box, choose the way you want to connect to the Internet.

   If you are using your modem to dial an Internet service provider, choose Windows 95 Dialer or Other Modem Service (Windows 3.1).

   If your computer is connected to a network, choose Direct Connection (non-modem).
3. Click Configure Connection and select your Internet service provider connection.
4. If you plan to use your own version of Netscape Navigator, click Find Navigator and specify the path.

   After you finish installing, a message welcomes you to PointCast and lets you know that you're ready to download your first batch of news (see Figure 11.1).

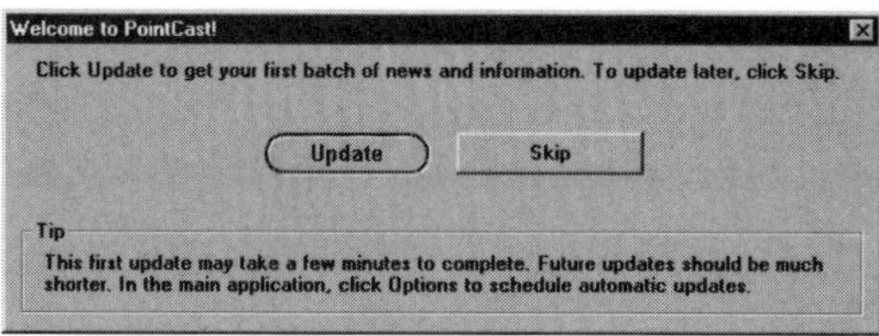

FIG. 11.1
Welcome message.

5. Click Update to begin downloading your first batch of news.

   After PointCast Network downloads the news, it disconnects from your Internet service provider, and you're ready to start exploring.

Exploring PointCast Network

PointCast Network organizes the information that it retrieves in channels and displays it on your screen. Let's start with a tour of a typical PointCast Network window (see Figure 11.2).

While you're viewing information in a channel (except for the Weather channel), you can

- Copy the current article to the Windows Clipboard.
- Save the article in a separate text file.
- Print the current article or business chart.

And at any time, you can connect to the PointCast Network to retrieve the latest information available for all of your channels.

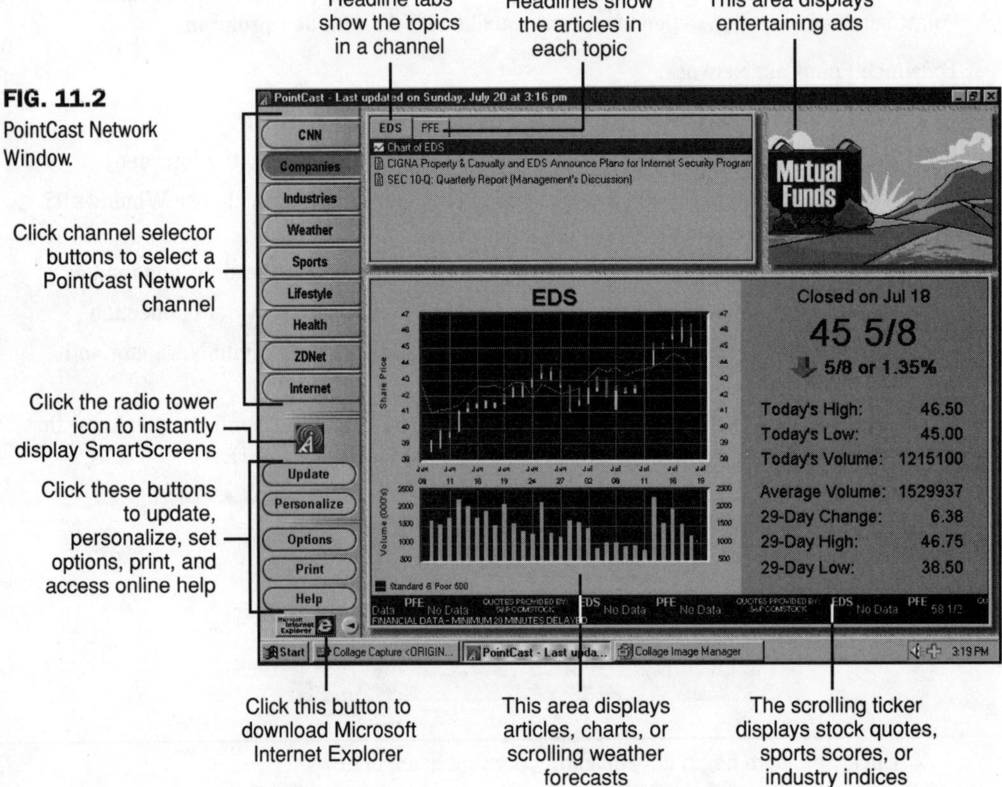

FIG. 11.2
PointCast Network Window.

Getting Personal

Because you can personalize PointCast Network, you can expect your PointCast Network to look different from the illustrations in this book. For example, you may see different channels, and even the same channels may be in a different order (see Figure 11.3).

Clicking Around

Next, let's see how PointCast Network and its contents change when you click around in it (see Figure 11.4). Note that your PointCast Network window probably looks a little different from this one.

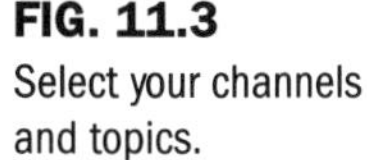
FIG. 11.3
Select your channels and topics.

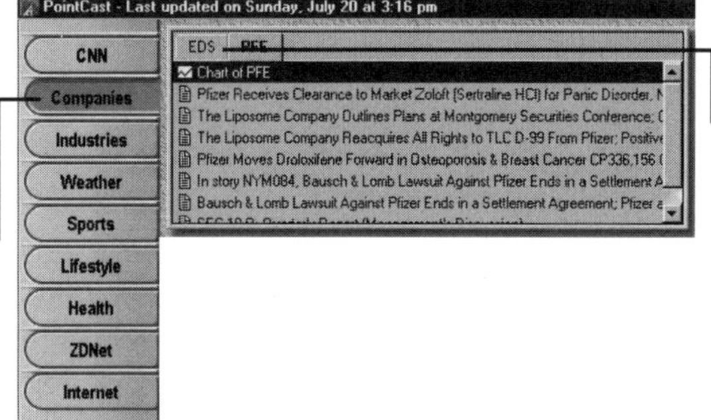

You select the topics that appear in each channel, so you may see different tabs here

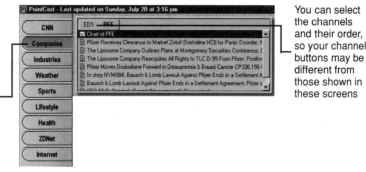

You can select the channels and their order, so your channel buttons may be different from those shown in these screens

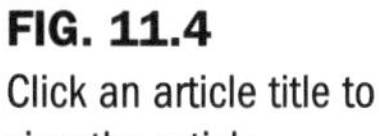
FIG. 11.4
Click an article title to view the article.

Click a tab to view a topic in a channel. You choose which topics appear

Click an article title to view the article

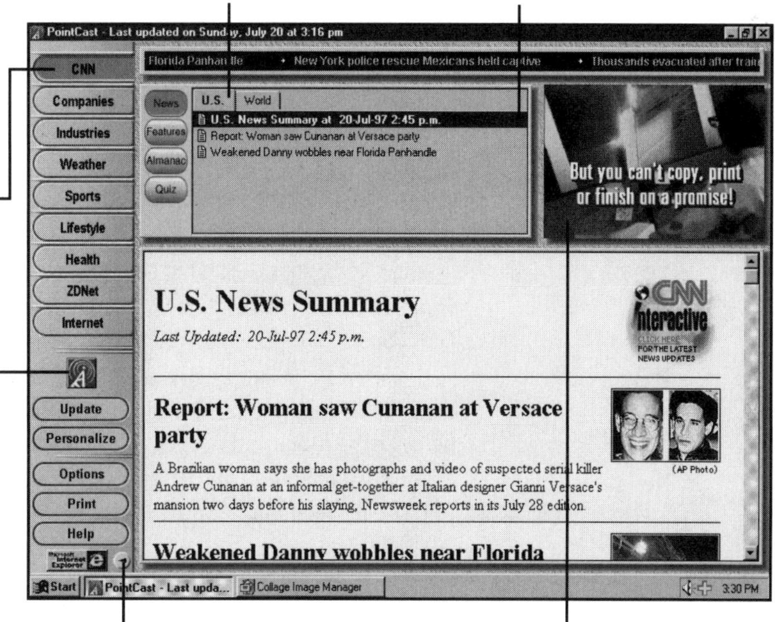

Click a button to view a channel. You personalize which channels appear and set their order

If the radio tower icon says Upgrade Now, a new version of PointCast Network is available. Click the icon to download it

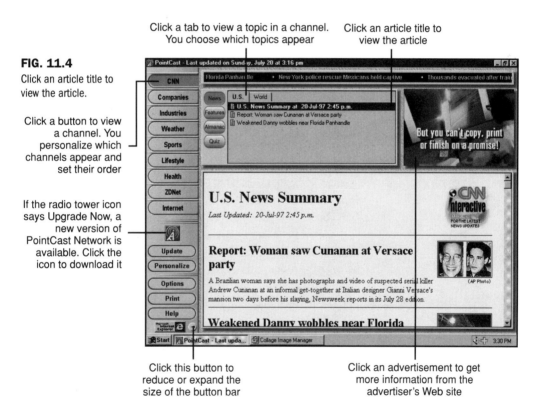

Click this button to reduce or expand the size of the button bar

Click an advertisement to get more information from the advertiser's Web site

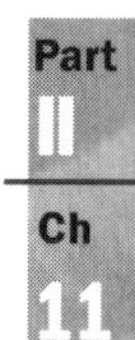

About PointCast Network Channels

Each PointCast Network channel is devoted to a specific type of information. The following table shows you what kinds of information some of the PointCast Network channels display. Additional channels will be available in the future; your PointCast Network may include these additional channels.

This Channel	Displays
CNN	Up-to-the-minute news articles in four categories and their subtopics: News, Features, Almanac, and Quiz.
Companies	The latest news and stock reports for the companies you select. It also tracks the current net asset value for the mutual funds you select.
Industries	The latest news and market valuations for industries as a whole, such as advertising, insurance, or real estate. It also tracks the most recent indices for major stock markets, such as the Dow Jones Industrials, Standard & Poor's 500, and the like.
Weather	Weather summaries and forecasts for cities around the world as well as weather maps and satellite images for the United States, Europe, and Asia.
Sports	The latest stories, team standings, schedules, and scores for a wide variety of sports.
Lifestyle	Articles about movies, theater, musical events, and other arts and entertainment. It displays daily horoscopes and lottery results.
Health	Articles concerning health and fitness. It tracks topics such as General, Men & Women's Health, Fitness, and Air Quality. It also displays Maps and localized Air Quality information.
ZDNet	Articles from Ziff-Davis publications. Tracked topics include News, Products, Whole Web Catalog, Mac, Software Library, and GameSpot.
Boston Globe	Articles from the online version of *The Boston Globe*. Topics include Page One, Nation/World, Metro/Region, Editorials, Business, Living/Arts, and Sports.
News	Up-to-the-minute news articles in four categories: Top Stories, Politics, International, and Business.
CNNfn	Current financial-oriented news, including Hot Stories, Market News, Market Data, Your Money, and Digital Jam.
LA Times	Articles from the online version of the *Los Angeles Times*. Topics are Daily Photo, Front Page, Nation & World, State & Local, Sports, Business & Technology, Life & Style, Calendar, and Commentary.
Pathfinder	Articles from Time-Warner's daily online versions of *Time*, *Money*, *Fortune Business Report*, and *People* magazines. The Netly News is also a topic from the Pathfinder service.
TechWeb	Articles from CMP Media on topics in high technology, including personal computing, networking, and new products.

This Channel	Displays
Chicago Tribune	Articles from the online version of the *Chicago Tribune.* Topics tracked are Front Page, Sports, Columnists, Local News, Tempo, and Homes/Jobs/Cars.
Philadephia Online	Localized Philadelphia articles from the following topics: City/Region, Sports, Nation/World, and Business.
Miami Herald	Articles from the online version of *The Miami Herald.* Topics are Front Page, Dade, Broward, Florida, Americas, Sports, Business, Living, Gran Miami, America Latina, and Deportes.
Wired	Articles from Wired Magazine Group on topics in high technology, including personal computing, networking, and new products.
Mercury Center	Articles from the online version of the *San Jose Mercury News,* Topics tracked are: Front Page, Silicon Valley, Breaking News, Business, Sports, and Bay Area.
Star Tribune	Articles from the online version of the *Star Tribune* of Minneapolis/St. Paul. Topics include Metro, Nation/World, Business, Sports, and Variety.
New York Times	Articles from the online version of *The New York Times.* Topics covered are World, Business, Politics, Cyber Times, Metro/Region, and Sports.
Tampa Tribune	Articles from the online version of *The Tampa Tribune.* Top Stories, Florida Metro, Sports, Business, Entertainment, Baylife, Hillsborough, Pinellas, Pasco, and Polk are the topics tracked.
Seattle Times	Articles from the online version of *The Seattle Times.* Topics are Local News, Nation/World, Business, Technology, Seattle Sports, Seattle Scene, and For and About Schools.
Hot CoCo	Articles from the San Francisco East Bay *Contra Costa Times.* Topics tracked are Breaking News, East Bay, Sports, Entertainment, and Business.
Wall St. Journal	Articles from the online version of *The Wall Street Journal.* Categories covered are Top News, Europe, Asia, and Editor's Picks.

Personalizing Your PointCast Network

You can personalize PointCast Network to include only the channels that interest you and define the order in which their buttons appear in the channel selector. You can also personalize each channel to retrieve only the types of information that interest you, such as world stories in the CNN News channel or NBA basketball in the Sports channel.

Quick Steps

In a hurry? Here's how you personalize the PointCast Network:

1. Click Personalize in the button bar to get started.
2. Click the Channels tab in the Personalize dialog box to select channels.
3. Click the individual channel tabs to personalize each channel.
4. Make your selections and click OK.

Selecting Channels

You can specify which channels to include in your PointCast Network and the order in which their buttons appear. You can select a total of ten channels, including the CNN and Internet channels.

To select channels:

1. Click Personalize in the button bar, and then click the Channels tab in the Personalize dialog box. You may see other channels in addition to the ones that appear in Figure 11.5.

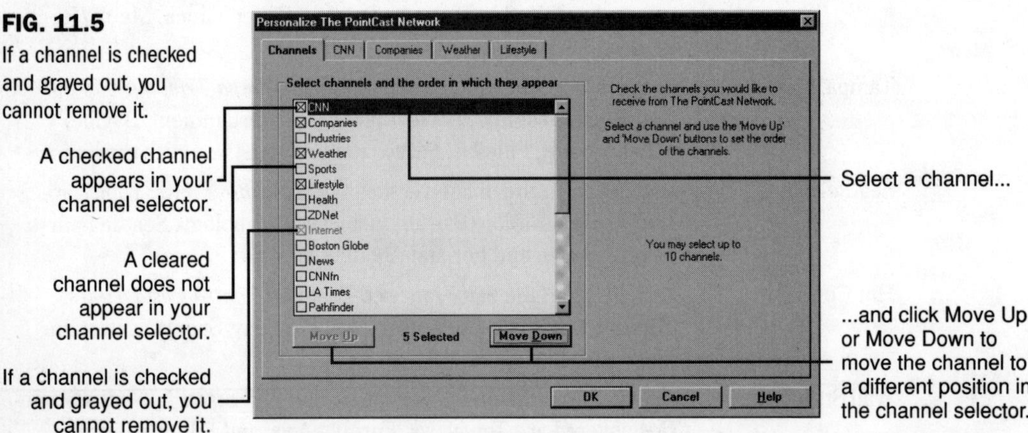

FIG. 11.5 If a channel is checked and grayed out, you cannot remove it.

2. Select a check box to include a channel. Clear a check box to remove a channel.
3. To move a channel to a different position, select the channel and click either the Move Up or Move Down button.

Personalizing Channels

You can personalize each PointCast Network channel so that it displays the information in which you're most interested.

The following table shows how you can personalize some of the PointCast Network channels.

For This Channel	You Can Select
CNN	Types of news (national, international, and so forth), features, and a quiz
Companies	Companies Funds
Industries	Industries Market indices
Weather	Forecasts for cities Weather maps
Sports	Specific sports or leagues
Lifestyle	Astrological signs A state lottery
Health	General Men & women's health Fitness Air quality
ZDNet	News Products Whole web catalog Mac Software library GameSpot
Boston Globe	Boston newspaper sections
News	Types of news (national, international, and so forth)
CNNfn	Financial news
LA Times	Los Angeles newspaper sections
Pathfinder	Magazines
TechWeb	Topics
Chicago Tribune	Chicago newspaper sections
Philadelphia Online	Philadelphia newspaper sections
Miami Herald	Miami newspaper sections
Wired	Various topics; not user-modifiable at this time
Mercury Center	San Jose newspaper sections
Star Tribune	Minneapolis/St. Paul newspaper sections
New York Times	New York newspaper sections

continues

continued

For This Channel	You Can Select
Tampa Tribune	Tampa newspaper sections
Seattle Times	Seattle newspaper sections
Hot CoCo	San Francisco East Bay newspaper sections
Wall St. Journal	Business newspaper sections

Quick Steps

In a hurry? Here's how you personalize a channel:

1. Click Personalize in the button bar.
2. Click a Channels tab to personalize a channel.
3. Make your selections and click OK.

Personalizing the CNN Channel

You can set the CNN channel to display news articles in any of these categories: U.S., World, and Politics.

To personalize the CNN channel:

- Click Personalize in the button bar, and then click the CNN tab in the Personalize dialog box (see Figure 11.6).

FIG. 11.6
Select a check box to include a news category.

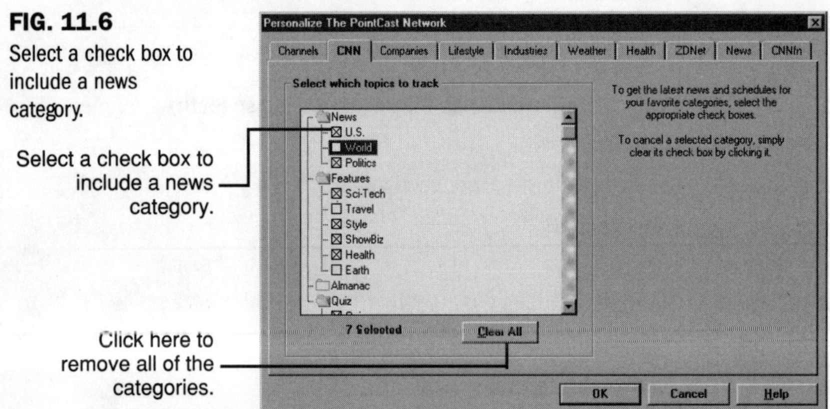

Personalizing the Companies Channel

You can set the Companies channel to display news and stock reports for particular companies and the current net asset value for mutual funds. The companies are any of those that are traded on the AMEX, NASDAQ, or NYSE exchange. If you don't know the symbol for a company or fund, you can use the online PointCast Ticker Search to look it up.

To personalize the Companies channel:

- Click Personalize in the button bar, and then click the Companies tab in the Personalize dialog box (see Figure 11.7).

FIG. 11.7
Companies channel.

To add a company or mutual fund, type its ticker symbol here and click Add.

To remove a company or mutual fund, select its ticker symbol here and click Remove.

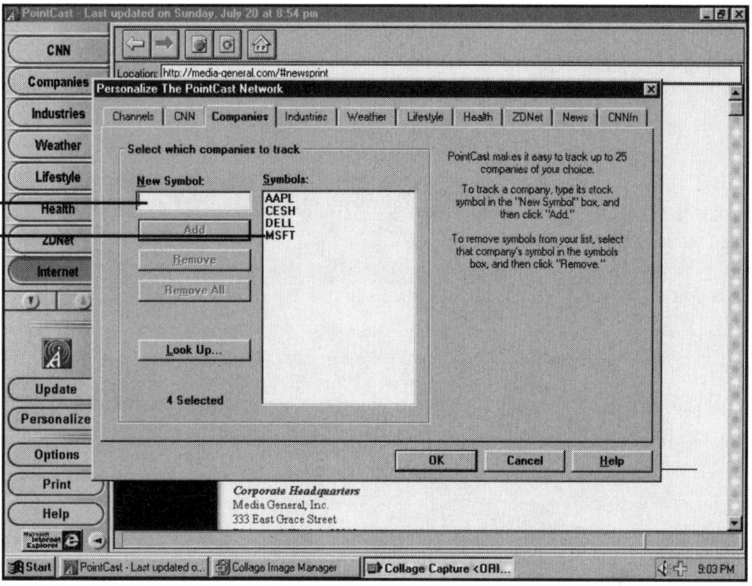

To look up the ticker symbol for a company or fund:

1. Click Look Up.

   If you're not already connected to the Internet, PointCast Network dials your service provider. The Ticker Search window appears (see Figure 11.8).

FIG. 11.8
Ticker search window.

Type at least part of the name here and click Find.

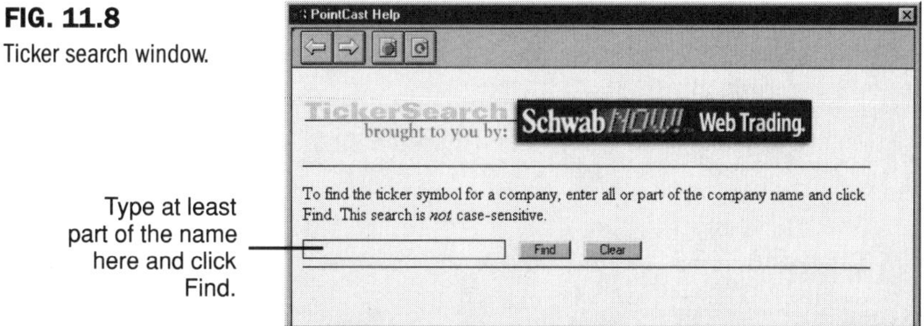

2. Enter at least part of the company or fund name and click Find. When you've found the symbol, click Close to return to the Personalize dialog box, and then enter the ticker symbol.

Personalizing the Industries Channel

You can set the Industries channel to display news and market valuations for particular industries.

To personalize the Industries channel:

- Click Personalize in the button bar, and then click the Industries tab in the Personalize dialog box (see Figure 11.9).

FIG. 11.9
Select a check box to include an industry.

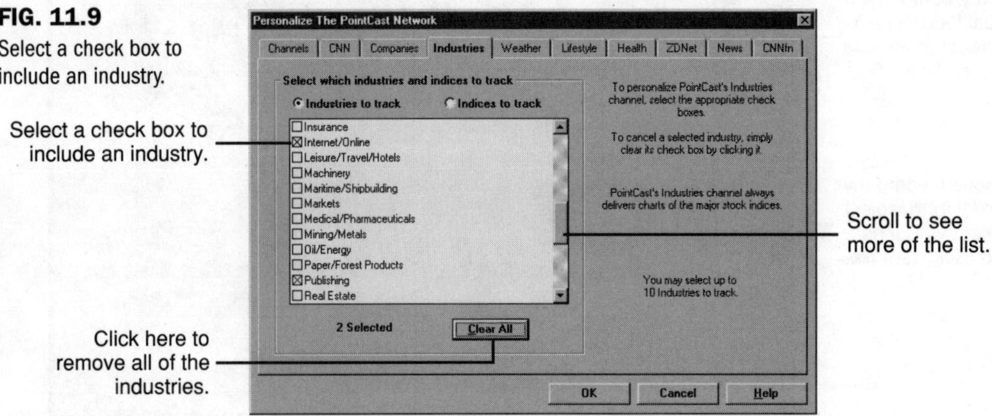

Personalizing the Weather Channel

You can set the Weather channel to show weather information for up to 50 cities around the world and several types of weather maps and satellite images for the continental United States, Europe, and Asia.

To personalize the Weather channel:

- Click Personalize in the button bar, and then click the Weather tab. Click Forecasts to select cities (see Figure 11.10).
- Click Maps to select the maps that appear (see Figure 11.11).

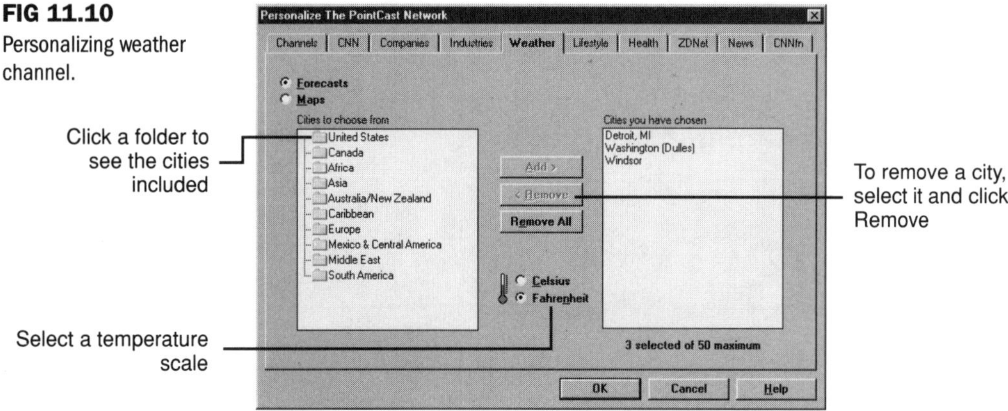

FIG 11.10 Personalizing weather channel.

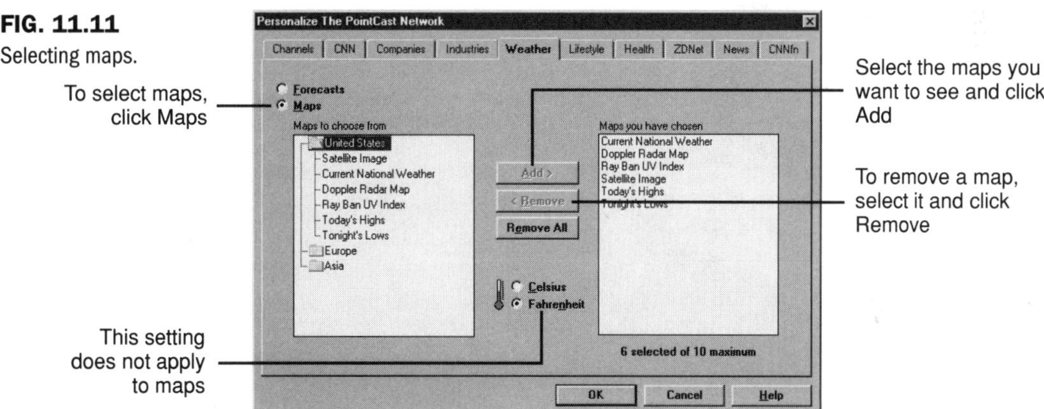

FIG. 11.11 Selecting maps.

Personalizing the Sports Channel

You can set the Sports channel to display news articles, scores, and game times for the sports you select.

To personalize the Sports channel:

- Click Personalize in the button bar, and then click the Sports tab (see Figure 11.12).

Personalizing the Lifestyle Channel

You can set the Lifestyle channel to display daily horoscopes and a state's lottery results.

To personalize the Lifestyle channel:

- Click Personalize in the button bar, and then click the Lifestyle tab (see Figure 11.13).

FIG 11.12
Sports channel window.

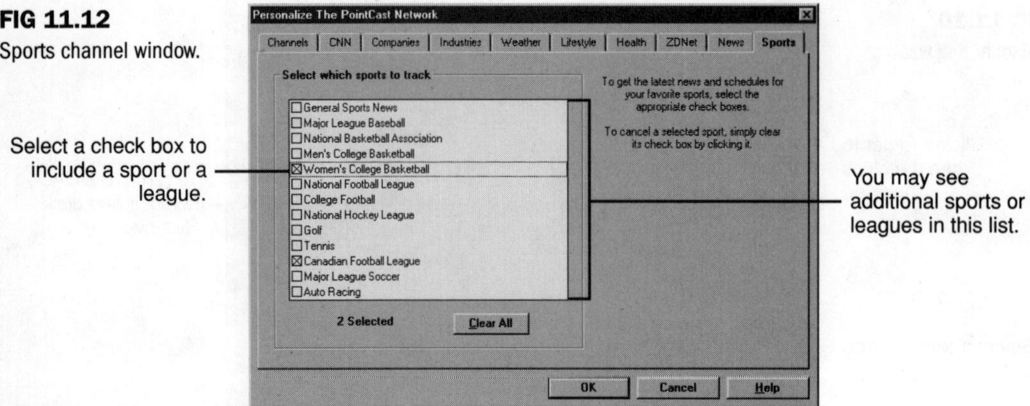

FIG. 11.13
Lifestyle channel window.

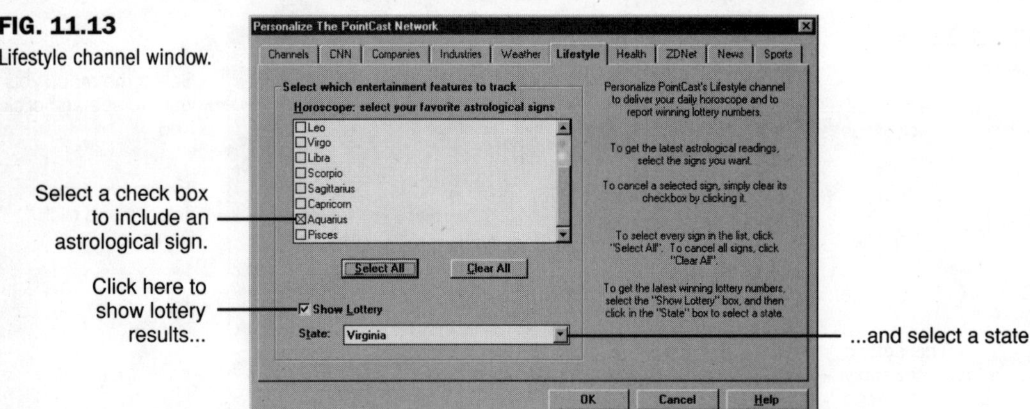

Personalizing the Health Channel

You can set the Health channel to display news from General, Men's Health, Women's Health, Fitness, and Air Quality.

To personalize the Health channel:

- Click Personalize in the button bar, and then click the Health tab (see Figure 11.14).

Personalizing the ZDNet Channel

You can set the ZDNet channel to display news articles from the Ziff-Davis publication family.

To personalize the ZDNet channel:

- Click Personalize in the button bar, and then click the ZDNet tab (see Figure 11.15).

FIG. 11.14
Health Channel window.

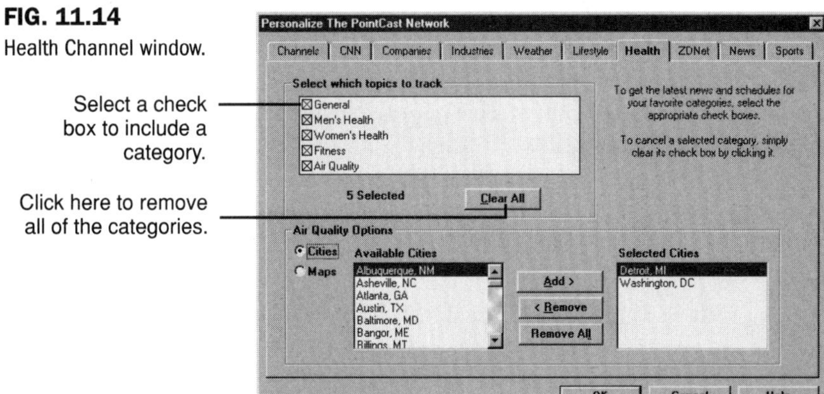

FIG. 11.15
ZDNet channel window.

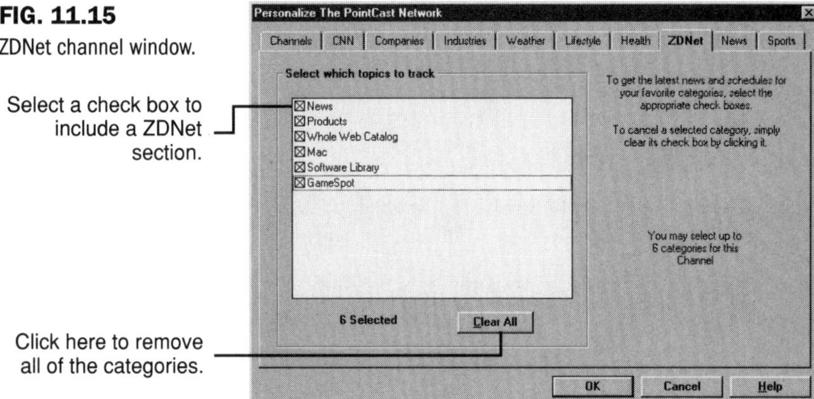

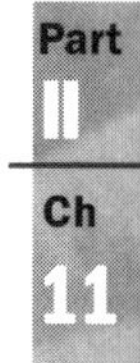

You cannot personalize the Wired Channel at this time.

Getting the Latest Information

After you select the information you want to view, the next step is to connect to the PointCast Network and download the latest information.

To update the PointCast Network:

- Click Update in the button bar. PointCast Network launches the dial-up connection to your Internet service provider.

- After the connection is established, PointCast Network downloads the latest information. You can change channels while the update is in progress, but the Personalize, Options, Print, and Help buttons are not available. The title bar in the PointCast Network window shows you the progress of the update (see Figure 11.16) and lets you know when the update completes (see Figure 11.17).

FIG. 11.16
This message tells you an update is in progress.

PointCast - Getting PointCast upgrade files ...

FIG. 11.17
This message tells you the update is finished.

PointCast - Last updated on Sunday, July 20 at 9:31 pm

- When the update is complete, PointCast Network disconnects from your Internet service provider, and you're ready to view the latest information.

Upgrading PointCast Network

Halfway down the button bar is the radio tower icon. Occasionally, this icon changes to say Upgrade Now, which means that a new version of PointCast Network is available.

When this happens, you can click the icon to begin downloading. A message tells you how long the download will take and how much space you'll need, and it gives you a chance to cancel the download. After you upgrade, you may want to check out the new channels and personalize them.

Viewing a Channel

After you download from the PointCast Network, you can take a look at what's new. Figure 11.18 shows some of the ways in which you can view information in a channel.

Quick Steps

In a hurry? Here's how to view a channel:

1. Click the channel's button in the channel selector.
2. To read an article or view a chart, click the tab for the topic you want, and then select the article's headline or the chart's title.
3. To see more of the current article or chart at once, click anywhere in the article or chart. Click in the article or chart again to reduce it to its original size.
4. If the channel has a ticker (for stock quotes or sports scores, for example), drag the ticker faster, slower, or in a different direction to change its speed or direction.

FIG. 11.18
Click a channel button to display a channel.

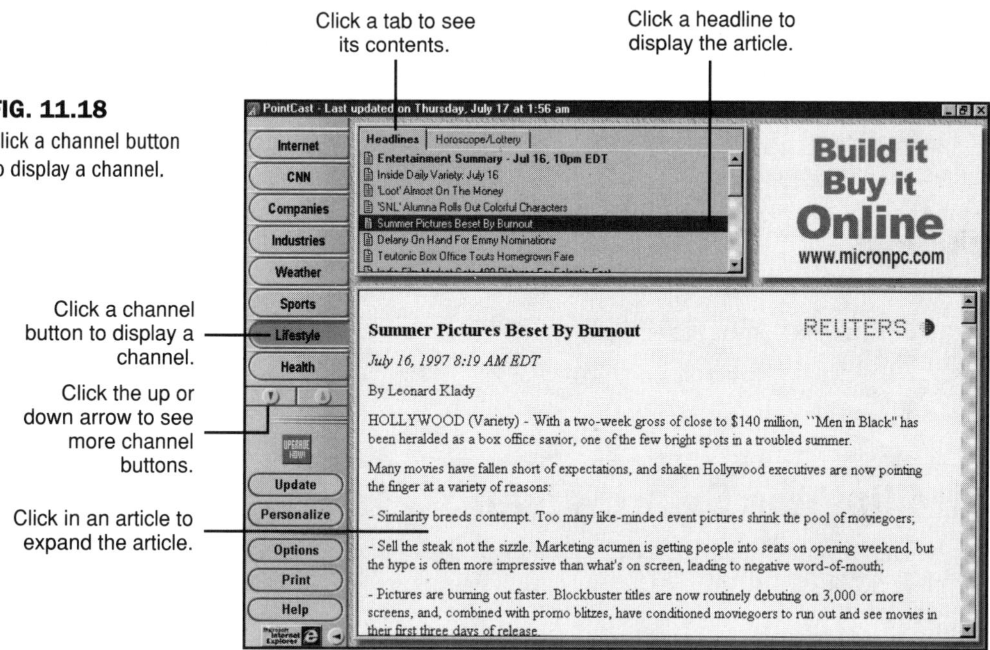

Using the Internet Channel

The Internet channel gives you full access to the World Wide Web without leaving PointCast Network. You can set up your Internet connection to use either the PointCast Browser or any other browser when you go to this channel.

If you're using the PointCast Browser, you can navigate the Web in these ways:

- To go to a specific Web site, enter the site's URL in the Location box.
- To move backward or forward through your history of already-viewed pages, click the left or right arrow button.
- To stop the retrieval of pages or a search in progress, click the Stop button (the button's icon shows a stop sign on a page).
- To reload the current page, click the Reload button (the icon shows a curved arrow on a page).
- To return to the PointCast home page, click the Home button.

If you're using another browser, see the respective home page for it (usually **http://home.netscape.com** or **http://www.microsoft.com/iesupport/**) for information on how to use it.

Setting PointCast Options

Using the PointCast Network options, you can control how the SmartScreens turn on and off, determine when PointCast should update automatically, define your connection to the Internet, and establish a proxy for access to the World Wide Web from within a firewall (if you're connected to a network).

Quick Steps

In a hurry? Here's how to set PointCast Network options:

1. Click the Options button.
2. Click a tab for the options you want to set.
3. Set your options and click OK.

Controlling the SmartScreen

Whenever your computer is idle, PointCast can display SmartScreens that show constantly changing headlines. You can control how the screens are activated and how you close the screens.

To control the SmartScreen:

- Click the Options button. The options always open (see Figure 11.19) first to the SmartScreen options page (see Figure 11.19).

FIG. 11.19
SmartScreen window.

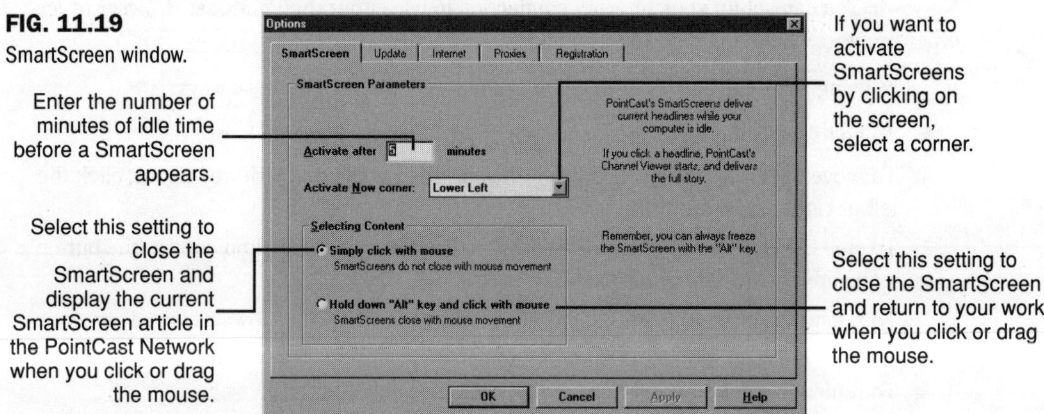

Specifying When to Update

PointCast Network can periodically retrieve the latest news and other information for you. You can define when PointCast should update—either automatically on a regular schedule or only when you click Update. If you use a dial-up connection to an Internet service provider, updating only when you want is the best alternative.

To specify when to update, click the Options button, and then click the Update tab (see Figure 11.20).

FIG. 11.20
Setting update times.

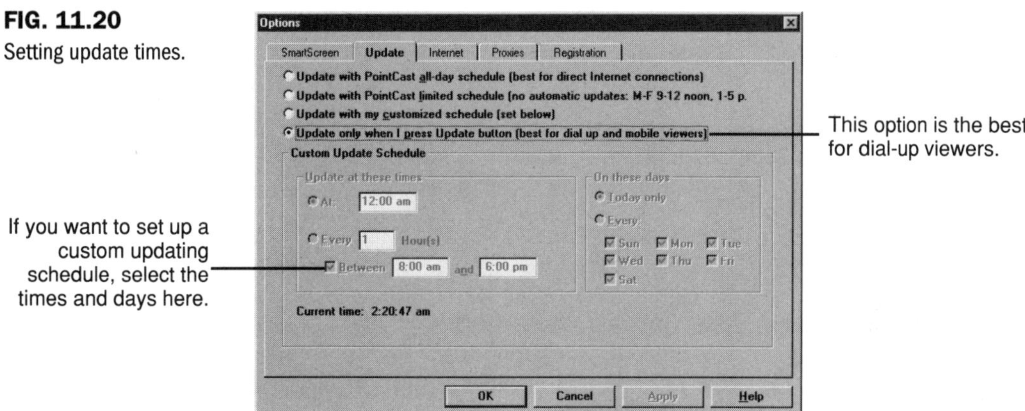

Setting Up an Internet Connection

You can specify your connection to the Internet and select either the PointCast Browser or Netscape Navigator for the Internet channel. If you're using the PointCast Browser, you can also define options such as an e-mail address and a method for checking cache files (the place where the browser stores Web pages that you've already viewed for faster return access).

When you first set up PointCast Network, you had to select a connection setting. The only time you need to change the Connect Using setting is when you change Internet service providers or change the way you access the Internet.

To set up an Internet connection click the Options button, and then click the Internet tab (see Figure 11.21).

If you change connection settings, you may need to configure a dialer connection.

To set up the PointCast Browser:

- Enter e-mail information if you want to use the PointCast Browser for sending and receiving e-mail, and change the Verify Documents setting if necessary. Check with your Internet service provider or system administrator for any information you're missing.

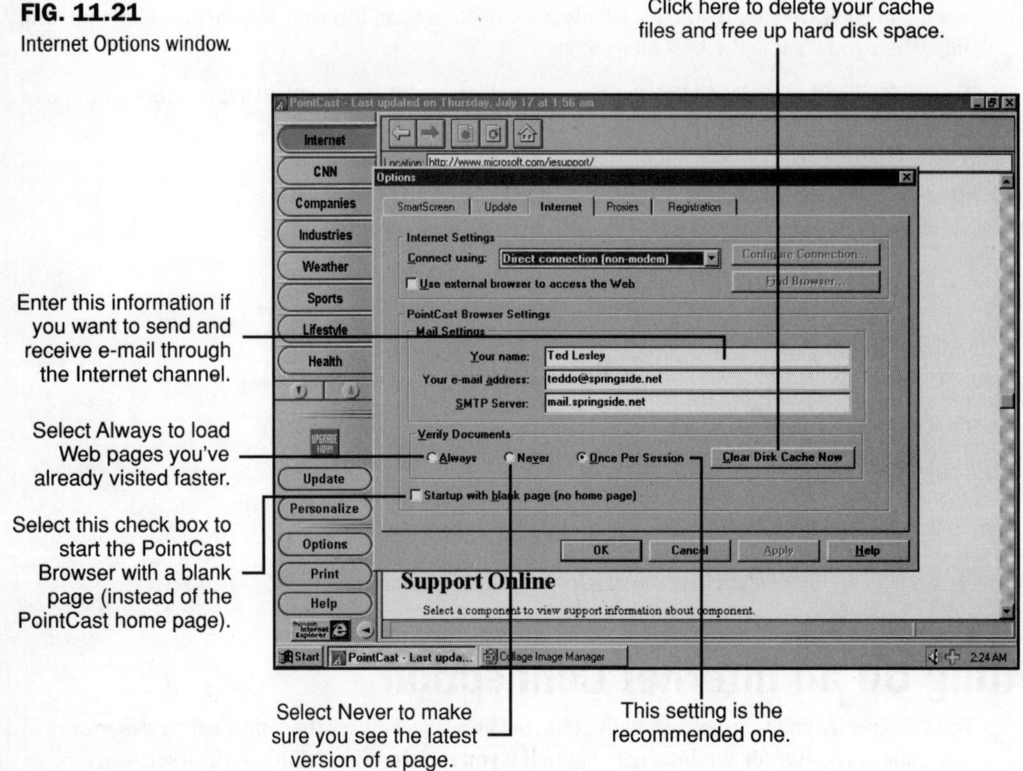

FIG. 11.21
Internet Options window.

Copying, Saving, and Printing Articles

You can copy, save, or print the article that currently appears in the PointCast network. You can print from every channel except for Weather.

To place a copy of the current article on the Windows Clipboard:

- Press the right mouse button over the article and choose Copy from the pop-up menu. You can use the Paste command in another application to paste the item into a document.

To save the current article in a text file:

- Press the right mouse button over the article and choose Save from the pop-up menu. Use the dialog box that appears to give the new file a name and location.

To print a copy of the current article:

- Click Print in the button bar.

Solving Problems

For most people, using PointCast Network is a trouble-free experience. Problems and questions do sometimes crop up, however. The pages that follow offer descriptions and solutions for the most common problems and questions that other PointCast Network users have experienced. And the end of this section includes a list of numbers you can call for technical support.

You Get the Message, "Winsock Could Not Be Loaded"

Situation: You see this message, "Winsock could not be loaded. Communications functions are disabled" when you try to get the latest news from the PointCast Network.

What it means: This problem can arise when PointCast Network cannot locate the WINSOCK.DLL file required for connecting to your Internet service provider. When you install PointCast Network, the installation program looks for a WINSOCK.DLL somewhere in your system, usually in your \WINDOWS or \WINDOWS\SYSTEM directory. However, your Internet browser or dialer may use a WINSOCK.DLL that is located in a different directory. You also can get this problem when you have a direct Internet connection and use proxies.

Setting the Active WINSOCK.DLL

To set the active WINSOCK.DLL correctly:

1. Click the PointCast Network Help button to display the Help window, and check the Winsock information at the bottom of the window.

   The WINSOCK.DLL location should be the directory \WINDOWS or \WINDOWS\SYSTEM.
2. If the path is incorrect, or if you're not sure of the path, exit from PointCast Network. Start a different application that successfully connects to the Internet (such as your Internet browser or mail program), and make sure that it is running OK.
3. Start PointCast Network while the other application is still running. The PointCast Viewer automatically finds and sets itself to the active WINSOCK.DLL.

Checking Your Proxy Settings

If you have a direct Internet connection, the problem may be in your proxy settings. To check whether this is the case, look at the proxy setup for another working Internet application. Copy the HTTP address to the PointCast Network Http Proxy setting.

▶ **See** "Checking Your Proxy Settings," **p. 193** for information about proxy settings.

If you continue to have problems, check with your network administrator to see if you are using a firewall and need special settings.

You Get the Message, "Invalid Dynamic Link"

Situation: You see his message, "Your program is making an invalid dynamic link to a .DLL file" when you try to run PointCast Network.

Explanation: Most likely, an invalid version of MFC250.DLL (a Microsoft file that normally resides in your \WINDOWS\SYSTEM directory) is the cause of the problem. Although this file is not installed during the normal Windows installation, various applications, including PointCast Network, require it and install it on your computer if you use them.

You may have a version of this file that has been modified in some way or is different from the one that Microsoft authorizes for distribution. If you have that version of MFC250.DLL when PointCast Network is installed, you get this error message, "Call To Undefined Dynalink."

Replacing MFC250.DLL (Windows 3.1 Users)

To replace the MFC250.DLL file for Windows 3.1:

1. Exit Windows.
2. At the DOS prompt, type **cd \windows\system**, and then press Enter.
3. Type **ren mfc250.dll mfc250.pcn**, and then press Enter.
4. Type **win** to restart Windows.
5. Install PointCast Network again. Reinstalling PointCast Network adds the correct, authorized MFC250.DLL file to your \WINDOWS\SYSTEM directory.

Replacing MFC250.DLL (Windows 95 Users)

To replace the MFC250.DLL file for Windows 95:

1. Close all open applications (including Microsoft Office, if you have it running).
2. Open Windows Explorer, open the Windows folder, and then open the System folder.
3. Select the MFC250.DLL file and change its name to MFC250.PCN.
4. Install PointCast Network again. Reinstalling PointCast Network adds the correct, authorized MFC250.DLL file to your \WINDOWS\SYSTEM directory.

Renaming MFC250.DLL (Windows 95 Users)

Even though you have no applications running, Windows 95 may still think that MFC250.DLL is in use and prevent you from renaming it. If so, you need to go out to DOS and rename the file there.

To rename the MFC250.DLL file:

1. Click Start, choose Shut Down, and select Restart the Computer in MS-DOS Mode.
2. At the DOS prompt, type **cd \windows\system**, and then press Enter.

3. Type **ren mfc250.dll mfc250.old**, and then press Enter.
4. Type **win** to restart Windows, and then restart PointCast Network. When you restart PointCast Network, it looks for the correct MFC250.DLL file, which may have been in use elsewhere.

Using PointCast Network with Netscape

Situation: You want to run PointCast Network within Netscape Navigator as a plug-in.

Explanation: You can use the Start Netscape Plug-in button located on the PointCast home page to run PointCast Network as a Netscape Navigator plug-in. Then, if you set the PointCast Network as your home page, PointCast Network runs as an application within Netscape Navigator whenever you launch the Navigator.

Starting the PointCast Netscape Plug-In

To run the PointCast Network as a Netscape Navigator plug-in:

1. Click the Internet button to access the Internet channel or to start Netscape Navigator.
2. In the location field, type this URL: **http://www.pointcast.com/viewpoint**.
3. Click the Start Netscape Plug-In! button to load PointCast Network inside Netscape Navigator.

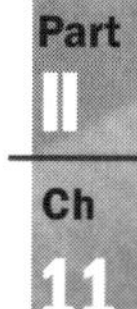

Setting PointCast as Your Home Page

To set the PointCast Network as your home page:

1. Using Netscape Navigator 2.0 or later, choose General Preferences from the Options menu.
2. Click the Appearance tab. In the Startup area, type this URL in the Home Page Location field: **http://www.pointcast.com/viewpoint/run.pcn**.

I Don't See Many Advertisements

Situation: You see the same few advertisements over and over, and you'd like a bit more variety.

Explanation: In order to keep its installation efficient and manageable, PointCast Network initially downloads only a few advertisements. PointCast Network downloads the remaining advertisements during the next dozen subsequent updates. As a result, you should start seeing new advertisements after about 8 to 12 updates.

Checking Your Ad Sequence File

The file ADQS.DAT controls the sequence in which the advertisements are shown. In some cases, the file could be damaged. To check the ADQS.DAT file:

1. Open File Manager (Windows 3.1) or Windows Explorer (Windows 95).
2. Go to the PCN directory and look at the modified date for the ADQS.DAT file.
3. If the date for the ADQS.DAT file hasn't been modified during the current month, delete the ADQS.DAT file, and then close File Manager or Windows Explorer.
4. Return to PointCast Network and click Update.

My System Locks Up

Situation: Occasionally, users experience a system lockup while using PointCast Network.

Explanation: System lockups often result from insufficient system resources (that is, because you have too much going on). As a rule of thumb, you should have at least 50 percent system resources free before trying to run any application (including PointCast Network). If you need to free up additional resources, try quitting unused applications.

Checking System Resources (Windows 3.1 Users)

To check system resources:

- Choose About Program Manager from the Program Manager Help menu.

Checking System Resources (Windows 95 Users)

To check system resources:

1. Double-click the My Computer icon on your Desktop. Double-click the Control Panel folder to open it.
2. Double-click the System icon and click the Performance tab.

Password Protection for SmartScreens

Situation: You want to set up password protection for PointCast Network SmartScreens.

Setting Up Password Protection (Windows 3.1 Users)

To enable password protection on PointCast SmartScreens:

1. In Program Manager, open the Main program group and double-click the Control Panel icon.
2. Double-click the Desktop icon.
3. In the Screen Saver area, click the Setup button.
4. Select the Password Protected check box and click the Set Password button.
5. If you already have a password, type it in the Old Password field.
6. Type a new password in the New Password field. Type the same password again in the Retype New Password field. Click OK.
7. Click OK until you return to the main control panel, and then close it.

Setting Up Password Protection (Windows 95 Users)

To enable password protection on PointCast SmartScreens:

1. Right-click an empty area of your desktop, and then choose Properties from the pop-up menu.
2. Click the Screen Saver tab. In the Screen Saver area, select the Password Protection check box. Click the Settings button.
3. Type a password in the New Password field. Type the same password again in the Confirm New Password field. Click OK.

Connecting with America Online

Situation: Your Internet connection is through America Online and you can't update PointCast Network.

Explanation: Although PointCast Network does not yet have full dial-up Internet support with America Online, you can still update PointCast Network manually through AOL. First, make sure that you have the correct version of a file called WINSOCK.DLL. Then connect to AOL and update PointCast Network.

NOTE When you update PointCast Network using AOL for your Internet connection, you must manually connect to AOL before you update and then disconnect after you update. PointCast Network cannot connect or disconnect for you.

Getting the AOL Winsock DLL File

To verify that you have the AOL Winsock:

1. Open the AOL GOTO menu.
2. Choose Search and type **winsock**.
3. Download the AOL WINSOCK.DLL file and use File Manager or Windows Explorer to place a copy of it in the \PCN directory.
4. Start PointCast Network, click the Options button, click the Proxies tab, and make sure that the proxy fields are blank. Close PointCast Network.

Updating PointCast Network Information

To update PointCast Network manually:

1. If you aren't already connected, use your dialer to connect to AOL as usual and go to any Web page.
2. Start PointCast Network.
3. With PointCast Network running, click the Update button.
4. When PointCast Network finishes updating, disconnect from AOL.

PointCast provides technical support. If you have questions about installing PointCast Network, using the PointCast Network, getting the latest information from the PointCast Network, or upgrading to a new version of the PointCast Network, you can get Web-based support from PointCast at **http://www.pointcast.com/support/pcn**. At this site, you can also:

- Search the PointCast support knowledge-base.
- Mail questions to PointCast support.
- Review the PointCast support Frequently Asked Questions (FAQs).
- Review the PointCast support technical notes.

CHAPTER 12

Speed Up the Web with WebWhacker

- The benefits of surfing offline
- How WebWhacker captures a site
- The basic operation of WebWhacker
- WebWhacker's advanced features

The CD-ROM that accompanies this book includes a trial copy of WebWhacker, a program designed to shorten the amount of time you spend online surfing the World Wide Web. WebWhacker allows you to download Web sites of your choice so that you can view them later, after you have disconnected from the Internet. Pages from the sites you choose are stored on the hard drive of your computer, and viewed within your browser window. This easy-to-use program helps you negotiate the jungle of the Web with greater efficiency and enjoyment! ■

Surfing Offline

Why surf offline? Perhaps you pay only a single monthly fee for unlimited Internet access; if so, surfing offline certainly won't save you any money. But that's not the only reason to surf offline. A program like WebWhacker can save you a great deal of time and effort.

WebWhacker visits your favorite Web sites for you. While you're off working or doing something really critical, WebWhacker checks all of your favorite sites, downloading and organizing the most recent pages at these sites. You don't have to sit by the computer, waiting for pages to trickle through your modem. By the time you view the pages offline, all the information you need has already been stored on your computer, and the pages appear immediately.

How WebWhacker Works

First of all, you need to realize that Web pages are actually *compiled* in your browser window. Your browser connects with a description of the page, written in HTML (the programming language of the Web). This HTML description tells your browser such things as what text to display, where to position images and video files, and what elements on the page are active links.

When WebWhacker downloads (or "whacks") a Web page of your choice, it downloads all of the constituent parts of that page, and stores the HTML description, along with all the necessary image, video, and audio files, on your hard drive. As a result, you can completely re-create these pages on your computer when you browse offline.

When you give WebWhacker the addresses of the Web sites that you want it to visit, you also tell the program how may *levels* you want it to capture at each site. What is a level? Web sites usually are organized in a pyramid structure. When you connect with a Web site, you access the top of the pyramid, the site's first level: namely, its homepage. The home page is then linked to other pages on the site; these linked pages constitute the second level of the site. All of the pages linked to the second-level pages constitute the third level of the site, and so on.

Now, you may want to capture all of the pages of some Web sites but examine just the first few levels of others. Fortunately, WebWhacker allows you to customize your surfing. That's right, you can set a different "whack level" for each individual site that you want the program to capture.

Operating WebWhacker's Basic Features

Installing WebWhacker is easy. Just go to the WebWhacker folder on the CD-ROM that comes with this book, open the WebWhacker install file, and follow the on-screen instructions.

NOTE The version of WebWhacker on the CD-ROM is a trial version. If you like the program, you can purchase a permanent version from ForeFront, the company that created the program, by going to ForeFront's Web site at **http://www.ffg.com/**.

Programming WebWhacker

Click the Start button and launch the program. The WebWhacker Desktop window appears. This window is the heart of the program; WebWhacker records the progress of each whack here, as well as a list of all pages it captures. The menu bar at the top of the same window allows you to access the program's functions easily. You can also open these same functions through commands available on the program's various pull-down menus.

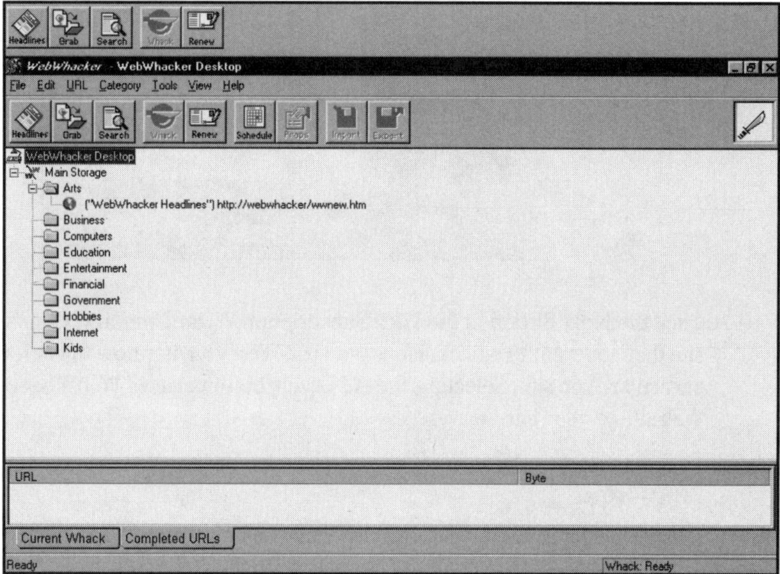

FIG. 12.1 The WebWhacker Desktop window, with its menu bar.

First, you must tell WebWhacker how to find your Web browser. Choose Tools, Preferences. A collection of tabbed pages appears. Select the Browser/Mail page. Use the Browse button on this page to find your Web browser. This makes it possible for WebWhacker to interact automatically with your browser. If you ever want to use a different browser to view your WebWhacker pages, you must select that browser here before the program can interact with it. If you like, you can also type your e-mail address in the appropriate box on this page.

Choose Add… in the URL pull-down menu, and the Add URL Subscription Wizard window appears. In the URL to Add field, type the URL you want to whack. If you prefer, you can also enter URLs directly from Web pages as you surf the Net. If you discover a site you want to add to your whack list, make sure that the page is displayed in your browser window, open the WebWhacker program, and select Grab from the URL pull-down menu, or click the Grab button on the menu bar in the WebWhacker List window. The URL Subscription Wizard appears, with the address for the grabbed site already entered.

Does the Web site you want to add usually require you to enter a username or password to gain entrance? If you want, you can type them into the appropriate spaces in the URL Subscription

Wizard's second window, and the next time you access the site, WebWhacker adds this information for you automatically.

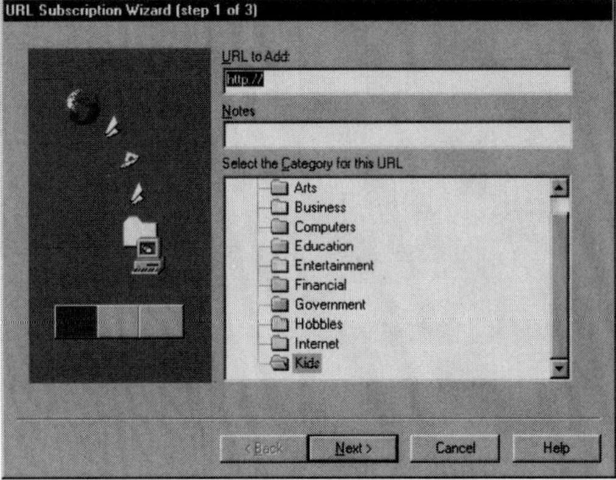

FIG. 12.2 The First URL Subcription Wizard window.

Click the Next Button of the URL Subscription Wizard window. Choose the Levels of the Web site that you want to whack. Here, you tell WebWhacker how many levels to capture from this particular Web site. Selecting the All Levels button causes WebWhacker to download the entire Web site to your hard drive.

CAUTION

Be careful when you select the All Levels button. WebWhacker could end up downloading a dangerously enormous amount of information! Downloading too many levels of a large site could very well deplete all the storage space on your hard disk.

If you want to tell the program to travel less deeply into a Web site, select the Levels button and enter the number of levels you want the site to access. Unsure of how many levels you should indicate? Play it safe—keep the number low and see what you get the next couple of times you download the site. Then increase the number of levels until you are satisfied with the amount of information you want from the site.

Keep the Remain on site check box selected. Many Web sites include many links to other sites on their pages. If you allow the program to follow all these links to other sites, it could download Web pages forever! So make sure that this box remains selected. The program still lists the URLs for these links in the WebWhacker List window, without downloading their pages.

All finished? Don't worry about the other parts of the URL Subscription Wizard window just yet. Go ahead and click Next. The Last URL Subscription Wizard window opens, and your WebWhacker gives you the option of determining when you want to update and whack the URL/site. Follow the process described above for every URL you want to add to your list. Be sure to choose a Whack level for each site.

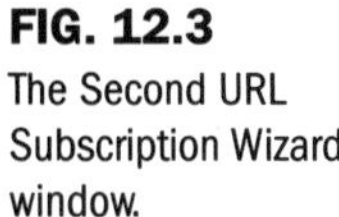

FIG. 12.3
The Second URL Subscription Wizard window.

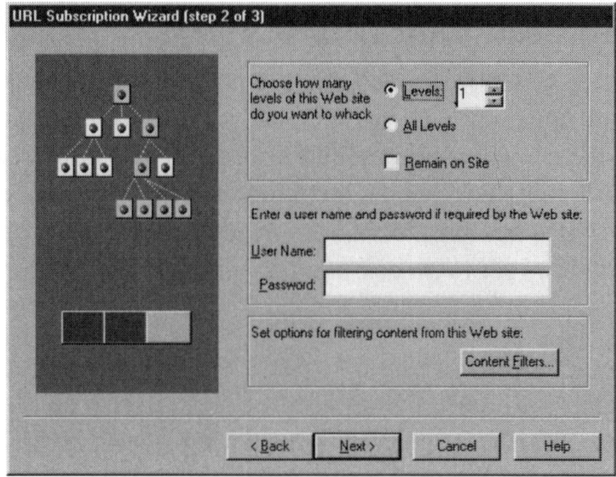

Capturing Your Sites

So, now that you have programmed a full list of sites into WebWhacker, it's time to whack your sites—the moment that you've been waiting for! Make sure that you're connected to the Internet, and then choose File, Whack, or click the Whack button on the menu bar of the WebWhacker List window. The program kicks into action!

The Whacker status bar at the bottom of the WebWhacker List window keeps you informed of the progress of the whack. WebWhacker lists every file that it downloads by name. The Current Download section of the status bar describes the activities of the program and your modem, and the Total Whacked section counts up the pages, images, and bits that you receive.

When you first add an address to the WebWhacker List window, the program marks it with a sword icon to indicate that the URL is ready for whacking. After you whack the site, the sword icon changes to a page icon. You probably also will notice a plus sign (+) in a small box to the left-hand side of the URL. Click on this plus sign to display the Web pages and URLs collected from that Web site. Page icons indicate the pages from the site that WW has saved to your hard disk, and globe icons represent links that it has listed on these pages but not yet downloaded to your computer.

Although WebWhacker is designed to run unsupervised, leaving you free to do other things, there are times when you may want to oversee the program's work downloading Web sites. This is particularly true when you are downloading a potentially large site for the first time. During a whack, the Whack button changes to a Stop button. If a download proves too large or time-consuming, you can put an end to it by clicking this Stop button. In your WebWhacker List window, the site's icon turns red to remind you that you did not complete the whack.

The WebWhacker menu bar is usually displayed at the top of every window on the desktop, apart from the WebWhacker List window. It can be "autohidden" to give you more of your desktop until you move the mouse up to the top, much like you can configure the Start menu. That way, the toolbar is always around, making it easy to grab to your list any Web sites you encounter while surfing.

Viewing Your Downloaded Web Sites

To view the full pages you've downloaded, disconnect from the Internet, open both the WebWhacker program and your Web browser, and click the pages from your WebWhacker List that you want to view. Each page appears in its entirety in your browser window. If you want to view any of the globe icon links listed in your window, you must reconnect to the Internet. Because WebWhacker has not downloaded the pages from these globe URLs to your computer, it instructs your browser to access them directly.

Renewing Your Web Sites

When your favorite sites have been entered, WebWhacker can visit them again and again, keeping you informed of the latest changes—"renewing" them, in the language of the program. To check your sites, just open the program and choose File, Renew, or click the Renew button on the menu bar in the WebWhacker List window. (Would you like to check just a single site from your list? Highlight it first, then choose Renew.) WebWhacker automatically revisits your sites, downloading to your hard disk any pages that have been added or changed. Then, to view the new pages, just click the new listings in your WebWhacker List window.

Want to see a summary of everything that has been changed or added? Choose Tools, View Modified. The View Modified window opens. Establish a time period in the Modified in field by typing in the number of past days you want to review. Then click the Query button, and all changes recorded by WebWhacker are listed. Click on any listing to view the modified file.

If you ever want to remove a URL from your list, just highlight it in the WebWhacker Desktop window, go to the Edit pull-down menu, and select Clear. All of the pages and URLs connected to this URL are eliminated from the window.

Automatic Renewal of Your Web Sites

You also can tell WebWhacker to renew your sites automatically. It can even do this while you are away from your computer!

To enable this feature, you must enter information in two separate places within the program. First, you must establish an "update frequency" for each of your Web sites. This can be done when you first add, or grab, a URL to WebWhacker. In the Third URL Subscription Wizard window, click in the top box how often you would like to 'renew' or update this web site. You can choose to have WebWhacker check this site "Just This Once," "Daily," "Weekly," or "Monthly," Make a selection, and click OK.

To set the update frequency for a Web site that you have already entered into the program, highlight the address of the site in your WebWhacker Desktop window, and then choose File, Properties, or click the Props button on the menu bar. The URL Properties window opens. This window records much of the information found in the URL Subscription Wizard window, along with some additional site data that the program has recorded. Just select the Whack tab, make your selection in the Update Frequency popup, and click OK.

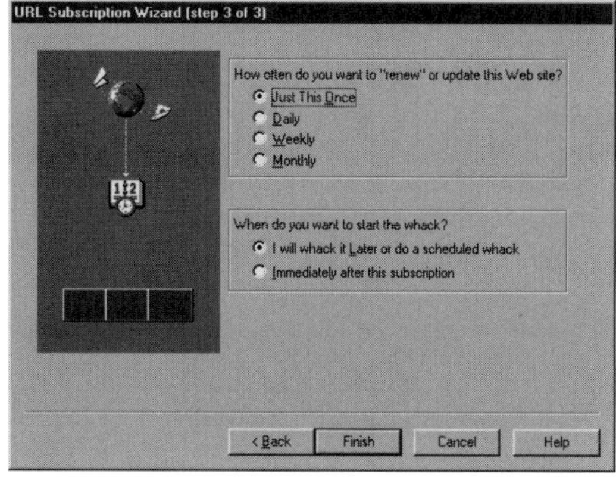

FIG. 12.4
The Third URL Subscription Wizard window.

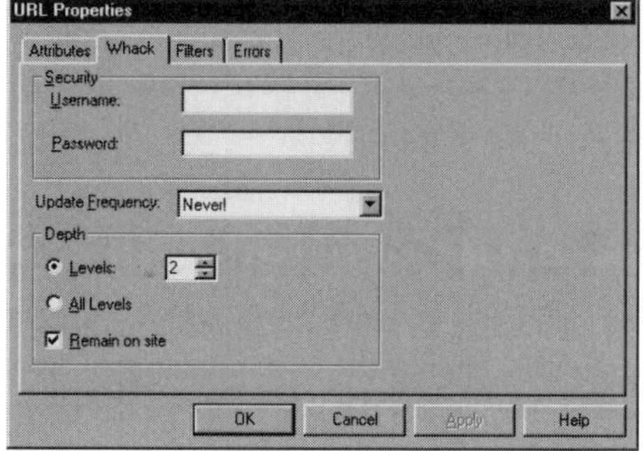

FIG. 12.5
The URL Properties window with the Whack tab displayed.

After you have set the update frequency for all the Web sites that you want the program to visit, you must tell WebWhacker when you want it to perform the automatic updates. To do this, click the Scheduling button on the menu bar.

The Scheduling window opens. Here, you tell WebWhacker to check your sites "Daily" (seven days a week), "Weekdays Only," or on a "Specific Day" of the week.

Keep in mind that if you choose to have WebWhacker renew your sites on a specific day, the program automatically checks your sites only once a week, even if you have selected "Daily" in the Update Frequency windows that belong to individual sites.

You also must select a specific time of the day for the program to update your sites. Many people have WebWhacker check their sites in the evening, or in the middle of the night, when the Net is less crowded.

Next, you need to tell the program to perform either a whack (the program checks only new sites that you have not yet whacked) or a renewal (the program checks only old sites that have already been whacked). You can also select both check box options here, and WebWhacker checks all of your sites, old and new.

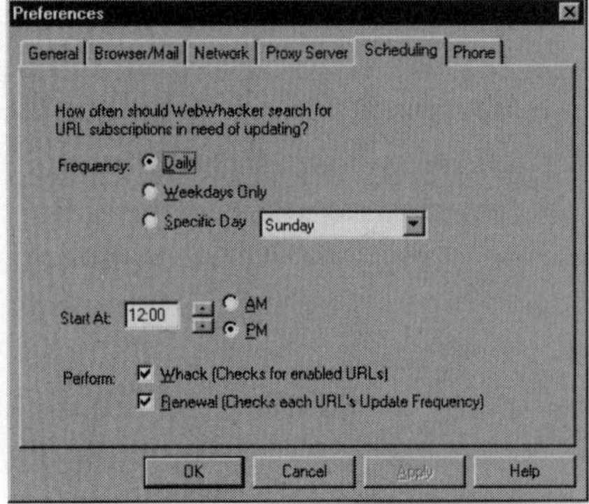

FIG. 12.6
The Scheduling window.

Finally, let's state the obvious: For the program to update your site automatically, you must leave your computer and modem turned on, and you must leave WebWhacker running. You do not need to have your computer connected to the Internet, however. When the scheduled update time arrives, WebWhacker opens your Internet connection and completes its check of your sites.

Searching Through Your Downloaded Web Pages

One of WebWhacker's great features is its capability to search through the pages that you have downloaded. Choose Tools, Search, or click the Search button on the menu bar. The Search window appears. In the Look for field, enter the keywords for the information or topics you want to find. At the Look in pull-down box, tell the program whether to search "title" (the search engine looks only at the titles of your whacked URLs) or "title and body" (the search engine looks through the text as well as checking the title of each Web page).

The keywords that you use are not case-sensitive—the search engine does not care whether you use capital letters. Keep in mind, though, that if you use any advanced Boolean search terms (like AND, OR, and NOT), these terms must be typed in capital letters.

Using WebWhacker Desktop

If you are familiar with Web browsers, you know that you can save and organize the URLs that you have visited, turning them into bookmarks (in Netscape Navigator) or favorites (in Internet Explorer). WebWhacker also lets you save and organize your favorite URLs by using the program's WebWhacker Desktop.

URLs can be entered into the WebWhacker Desktop in two ways. When you add or grab new URLs, you can use the Add URL window to add the URL to the WebWhacker Desktop. This window displays all of the WebWhacker Desktop's topic folders, along with an instruction to "Select the category for this URL." Highlight the folder in which you want to store the URL, and when you finally close the URL Subscription Wizard window, the URL is added to the WebWhacker Desktop.

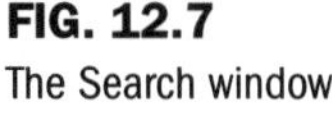

FIG. 12.7
The Search window.

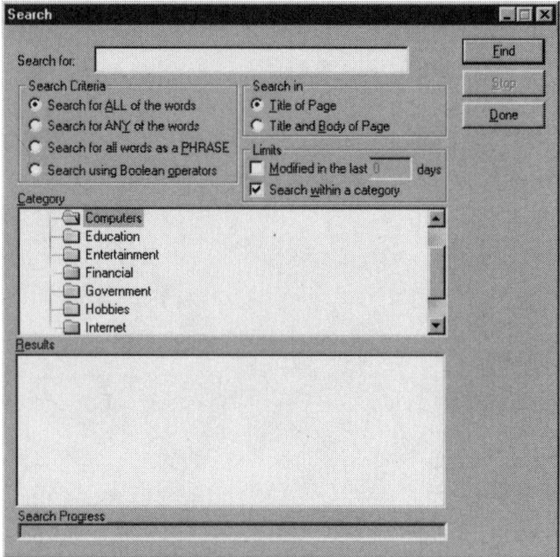

Maintaining the Database

The biggest problem with WebWhacker lies in the program's clumsy database. You can't limit the amount of space that the program can use on your hard disk. Every time you whack your sites, the program just adds pages and images to the WebWhacker Database folder.

Additional Preferences

There are a few other WebWhacker preferences that you might find useful. Choose Tools, Preferences, and a collection of tabbed pages appears.

Click the General tab. On this page, you can tell WebWhacker to download just the text on your chosen sites. To do so, check Ignore Inline Images.

We set the Browser/Mail preferences earlier in this chapter.

On the Network page, you can set the number of times you want WebWhacker to attempt to connect with a site when it can't do so on its first attempt. Just enter a number from 1 to 9 in the Number of Retries box. You can also tell the program how may seconds it should wait between tries. Just enter a number from 0 to 1000 in the Reconnect Delay box.

You use the Proxy Server page if you are running WebWhacker on a computer that lies behind a firewall. If you're like most readers, you don't need to worry about this box. If you are behind a firewall, however, the administrator of your computer network will know what information to enter here. ●

CHAPTER 13

Printing Web Booklets with WebPrinter

- Setting up WebPrinter on your computer
- Creating a Web booklet with WebPrinter
- Setting additional preferences in WebPrinter
- Using WebPrinter with other applications

As you become familiar with the Web, you become more adept at dealing with information in electronic form. But no matter how familiar bits and bytes become to you, you will still have times when you need a good, old-fashioned printed document—paper that you can hold in your hand, carry around, and share with other people.

That's why Web browsers have Print buttons!

Sometimes, though, you don't really need a full 8 1/2" x 11" printout of a Web page. Perhaps your needs would be satisfied by something smaller. Perhaps you just don't like wasting paper.

Whatever the reason, WebPrinter may be the program for you. WebPrinter gives you a way to print out miniversions of the Web pages you enjoy. Using this program, you can print four Web pages onto a single sheet of 8 1/2" x 11" paper—two on the front of the paper sheet and two on the back. These smaller images of your Web pages are still quite readable, giving you a very compact record of your favorite sites.

This simple change in your printer's output raises all kinds of possibilities. WebPrinter arranges the printout of each page so you can fold the sheet of paper in half, creating a four-page 5 1/2" x 8 1/2" booklet. If you have more than four pages in your Web document, WebPrinter arranges the printout to create a booklet of whatever length you want; you just have to take the final sheets from your printer, fold them in half, staple them in the middle, and... Voilà!

WebPrinter's booklet format allows you to create a booklet version of an entire Web site, arranging the site's various pages in whatever order you want. You can put together a booklet composed of pages from several different Web sites, if you prefer. And you can also use WebPrinter to print pages created in applications besides your Web browser. For example, you can takes stories you've created in a word processing program and run them through WebPrinter to turn them out in booklet form. You can even, within a single WebPrinter booklet, combine a variety of documents, even if each document has been created using a different application. ■

Setting Up WebPrinter on Your Computer

Before beginning this lesson, make sure that you have installed and registered your copy of WebPrinter. WebPrinter is located on the CD accompanying this book. You must also have already installed your printer on your system—WebPrinter doesn't work unless your printer drivers are in place. (WebPrinter is available only for the Windows operating system.)

In essence, WebPrinter interacts with the printer software in your computer. It works as an intermediary between your Web browser and your printer. You display the page you want to print, choose the Print command in your browser, and the page is sent, not to your printer, but to WebPrinter, which reformats the page so that it prints in booklet form. (It does not alter any of the rest of the document's format—the margins, image positions, line breaks, and so on in the original document stay the same.) You then need to choose the Print command in WebPrinter to send the page to the printer.

So, for WebPrinter to work properly, you must first configure the program to work with your printer. This must be done with the program in "stand-alone" mode; that is, with your browser closed, and with WebPrinter as the only application open on your computer (see Figure 13.1).

To configure WebPrinter, open the program and click the Printer Setup tab in the program window.

From the Printer to set up list, choose the name of your printer model, and then click the Easy Printer Setup button as shown in Figure 13.2.

Make sure that the correct printer is displayed in the Easy Printer Setup window (see Figure 13.3). The printer displayed in the window here should start with "CB," followed by the name of your printer. When you have the right printer name displayed here, click Accept.

If the name of your printer does not appear for some reason (this occurs only rarely), click Cancel and then return to the Printer Setup screen. Click Custom Printer Setup, and follow the directions given there.

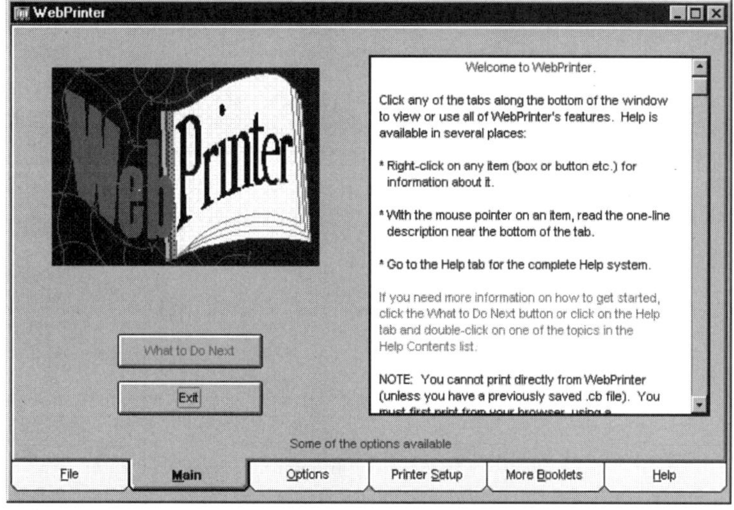

FIG. 13.1
WebPrinter's introductory window, which opens automatically to the Main tab. Note the Printer Setup tab.

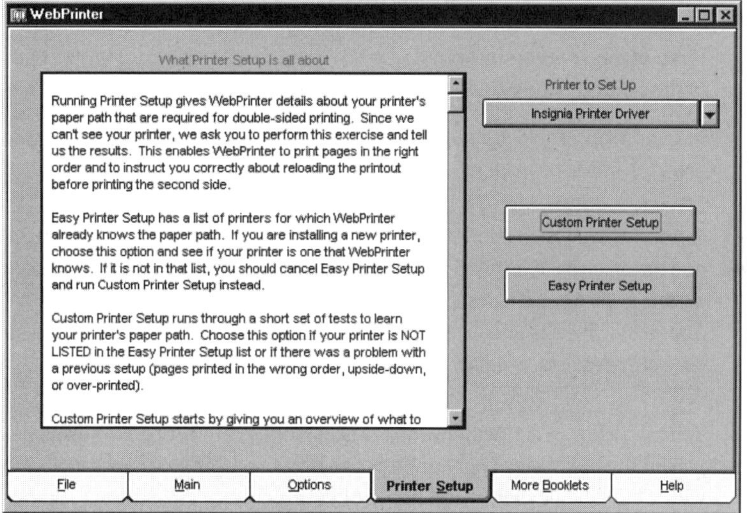

FIG. 13.2
The Printer Setup page.

Stumped already? Anytime you need help with WebPrinter, just go to WebPrinter's main page and click the Help tab. The Help Contents list and the Help Index list, both displayed on the Help tab, point you in the right direction.

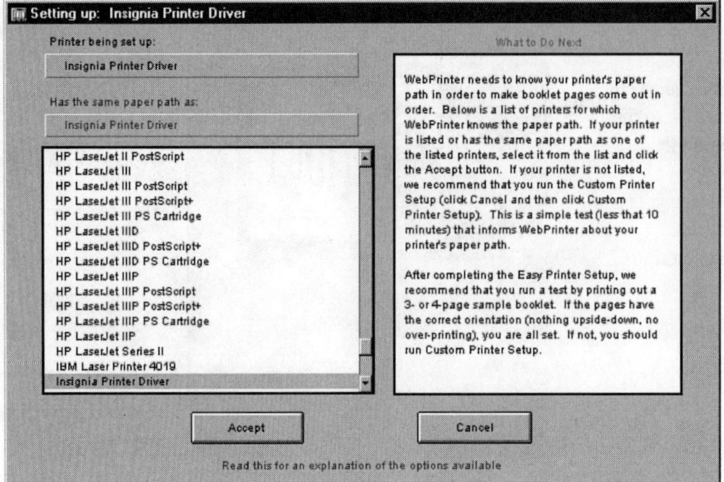

FIG. 13.3
The Easy Printer Setup page.

Printing a Booklet of Web Sites

First, of course, you have to find a Web site worth printing. We've chosen Thomas, the Web site of the United States Congress, found at **http://thomas.loc.gov/** (see Figure 13.4).

In your Web browser window, open the Web page that you want to print, and then choose your browser's Print command.

As we have discussed, WebPrinter reduces the size of the Web pages you select. To make it easier to read the printouts of your Web pages, you may want to enlarge the text displayed in your browser window. To change the font size that your browser uses, do the following: In Internet Explorer, click the Font button on the toolbar, or choose View, Fonts. In Navigator, go to the Options menu, choose General Preferences, and then choose the Fonts tab.

Your Windows Print window appears as shown in Figure 13.5. Make sure that the printer displayed in the Printer Name field is the driver for WebPrinter on your system. (It should begin with a "CB," followed by the name of your printer.) If you don't see this printer driver, scroll down the list in the window until you find the correct name.

After you have properly selected the printer driver required to run WebPrinter, click OK. WebPrinter opens automatically, to a new version of its Main tab page (see Figure 13.6). You see it creating a schematic diagram of the booklet, displaying pages 4 and 1 of the booklet. You also see a status report that informs you of WebPrinter's progress in reformatting the Web page you selected for printing. You also see a box listing the name of the Web site that you selected.

After WebPrinter finishes reformatting your page, the status box says `All pages received.` Click the Print Preview button. The Print Preview window opens (see Figure 13.7), presenting you with a rough version of the booklet layout, a two-page layout, showing pages 4 and 1. (Remember, you fold the final printout in half, making the right side of the page the first page in the booklet, and the left side of the page the last page in the booklet. We don't have enough information to stretch over four pages yet, so our page 4 is blank here.)

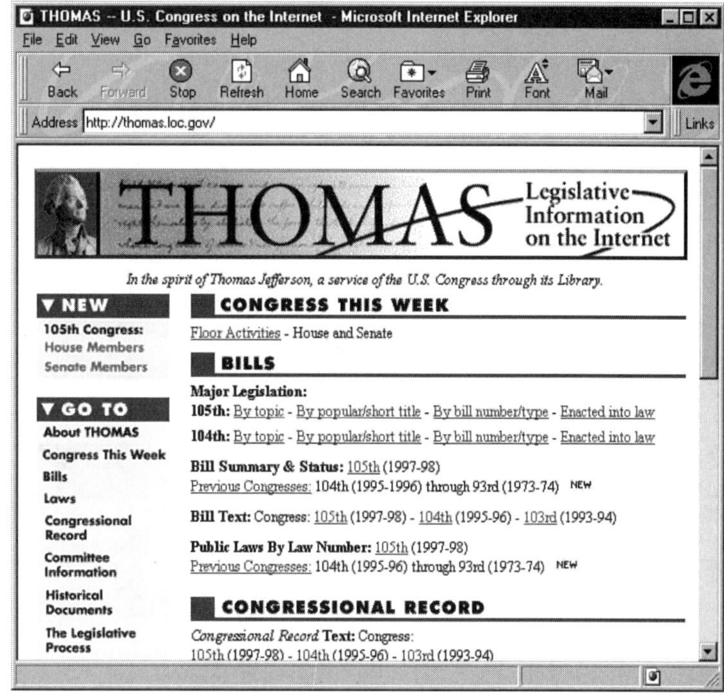

FIG. 13.4
The Thomas Web site, displayed within Internet Explorer.

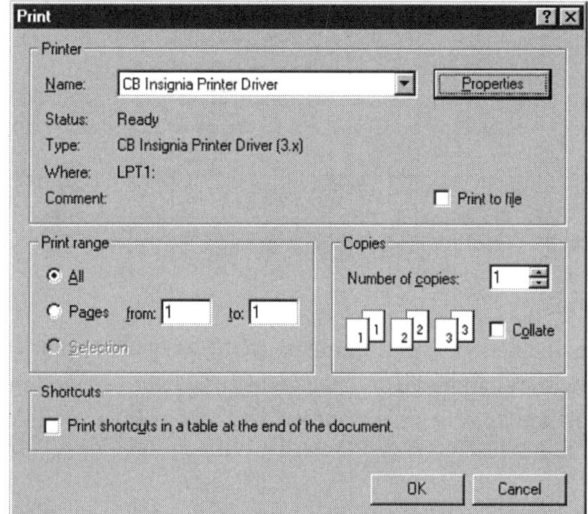

FIG. 13.5
The Windows Print window, displaying the WebPrinter CB driver for our printer.

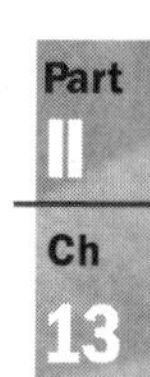

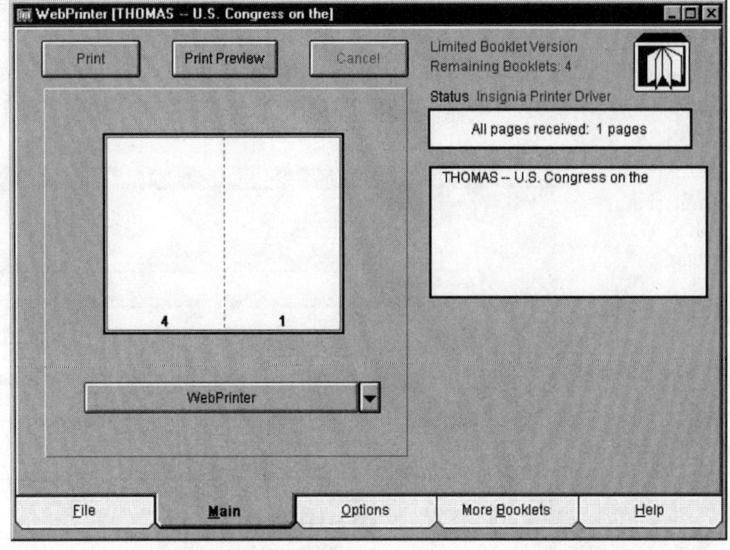

FIG. 13.6
The new WebPrinter Main tab page, showing information about the booklet you are creating with the Thomas site.

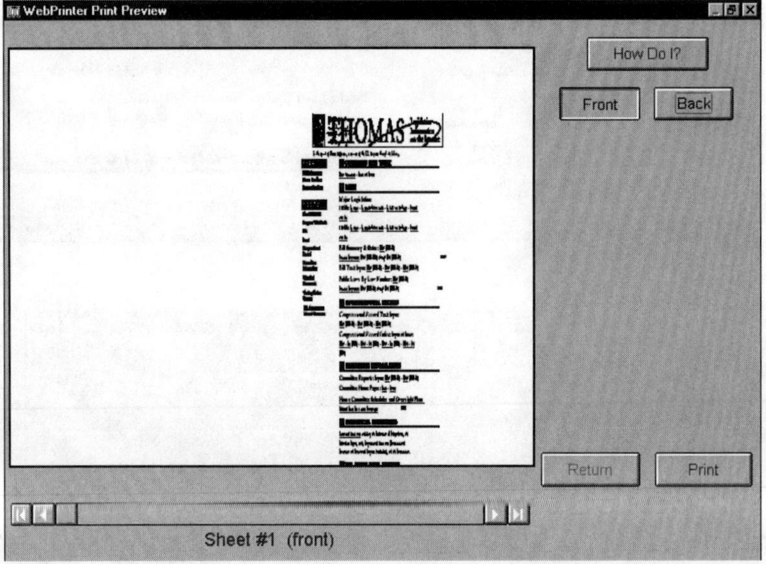

FIG. 13.7
The two-page Print Preview, with the Thomas site on page 1.

Want to see a more detailed view of a single page? Move your cursor onto page 1, and then click. The Print Preview changes to an enlarged single-page view as shown in Figure 13.8. This view still isn't as detailed as your final printout, but it does give you a better look.

FIG. 13.8
The single-page Print Preview of the Thomas site.

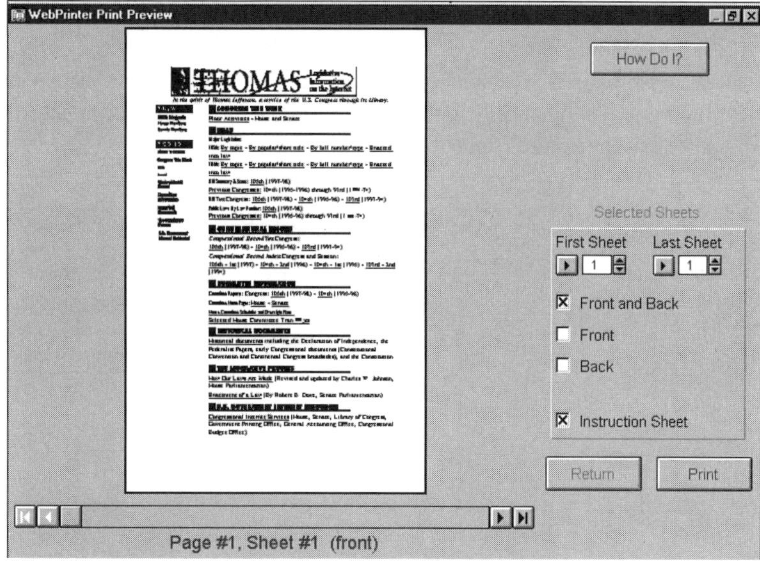

Now, let's go back to our Web browser and select another Web site to add to our booklet. As you can see, we've chosen the White House Web site—a logical choice to accompany the US Congress (see Figure 13.9). The White House site is located at **http://www.whitehouse.gov/WH/Welcome.html**, although entering **http://www.whitehouse.gov** gets you there as well.

FIG. 13.9
The White House Web site, displayed within Internet Explorer.

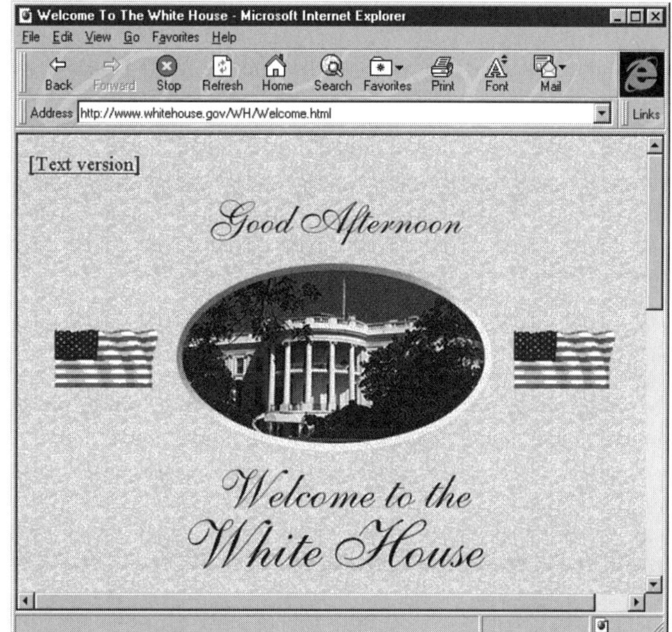

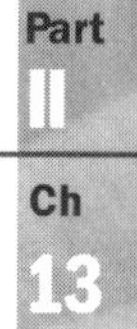

Once again, after displaying the site, choose your browser's Print command. The Window's Print window again appears, and it should still be displaying the correct printer driver for WebPrinter. Click OK, and once again, the Web page you are displaying is sent to WebPrinter. It is added automatically to the booklet you are creating, placed after the Web site you have already sent to WebPrinter (see Figure 13.10).

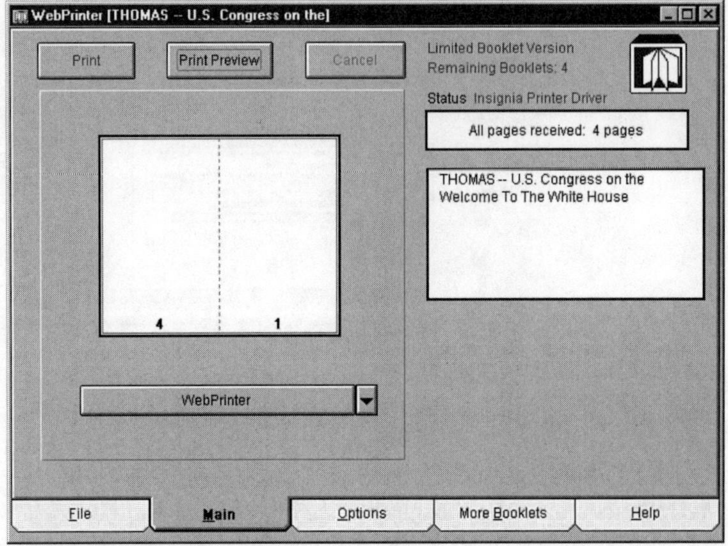

FIG. 13.10
The Main tab page, listing the addition of the White House site to your booklet.

WebPrinter has now configured a total of four pages for our booklet, with the Thomas site displayed on pages 1 and 2 of your booklet, and the White House site displayed on pages 3 and 4.

Click the Print Preview button once again, and you get a new preview. On the left, you see page 4, the second part of the White House site, and on the right, you find page 1, the first part of the Thomas site. Click the Back button to the right of the preview display, or on the appropriate slider button below the display, to view pages 2 and 3; namely, the second part of the Thomas site, followed by the first part of the White House site.

As before, you can click any page within the preview display to obtain an enlarged single-page view of that page.

Finally, click the Print button on the Main tab page to print your booklet. Two pages of your booklet print onto the front side of a single page. You must then reinsert the page back into the printer so that WebPrinter can print the remaining two pages of the booklet onto the back side of the page. So that you don't get confused, along with your first printout, WebPrinter also prints out a separate page that gives you exact instructions for reinserting the page back into the printer. Follow these instructions to the letter.

After you print the front of the page and reinsert the page back into the printer, come back to your computer screen. A print prompt awaits you as shown in Figure 13.11. Click the Print Second Side button in this prompt window, and your printer finishes the job.

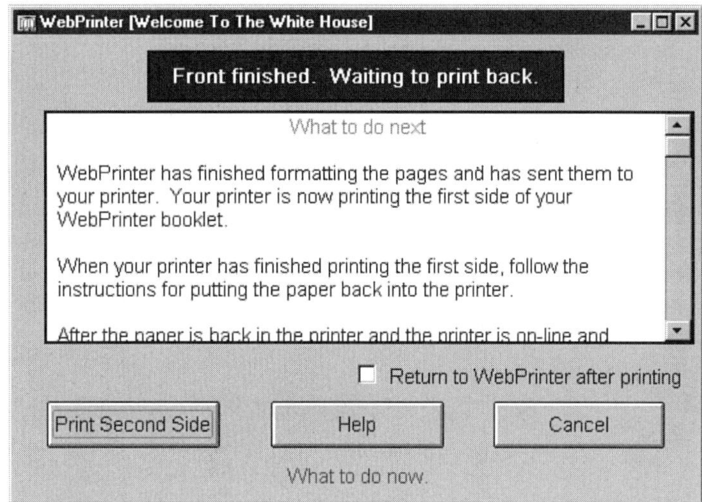

FIG. 13.11
The Print Prompt. Note the Print Second Side button.

Finally, remove the finished page from your printer, fold it in half, and… you have your first Web booklet in hand.

Follow the basic procedures delineated in this chapter to create Web booklets of any length. As you did here, open each Web site in your browser and use your browser's print command to load the site into WebPrinter. The program stores the pages in the order in which you send them. When you have collected all the pages you want in your booklet, print them in WebPrinter as described earlier. WebPrinter automatically organizes your pages into booklet structure, regardless of the number of pages involved, printing them out in the correct order. All you have to do is reinsert the pages back into the printer according to directions, and then fold the final printout in half—adding a staple to the center of the booklet if you wish.

Additional Preferences in WebPrinter

You have control over a few more options in WebPrinter. In the main window, click the Options tab. The Options page lists some of these additional choices as shown in Figure 13.12. Select the check box beside each option you want to use:

- **Print second side instructions.** This option instructs the program to print out an additional page with instructions for reinserting booklet pages into your printer.
- **Print assembly instruction.** This option instructs the program to also print out an additional page instructing you on the proper way to assemble the finished booklet.

- **Use printer's duplexing.** Some printers create both sides of the page automatically without forcing you to reinsert pages manually. If you have this kind of printer, select this option, and read the detailed information in the Help window on using duplexing printers.
- **Round font size down.** Use of this option is not recommended. It causes the program to slightly reduce the size of the type on your pages; the text often ends up clipped when you use this option.

Return to WebPrinter after printing: Normally, the WebPrinter window closes after the print job is complete. Click this box if you want to keep it open.

Note that there are a few other choices available to you. In the Number of Copies field, you can choose to print any number of copies of your current booklet. You can also use other paper sizes besides letter size—just change the setting under Default Paper Size. And, using the Sheet Selection button, you can choose to print out specific pages of your booklet instead of the entire document.

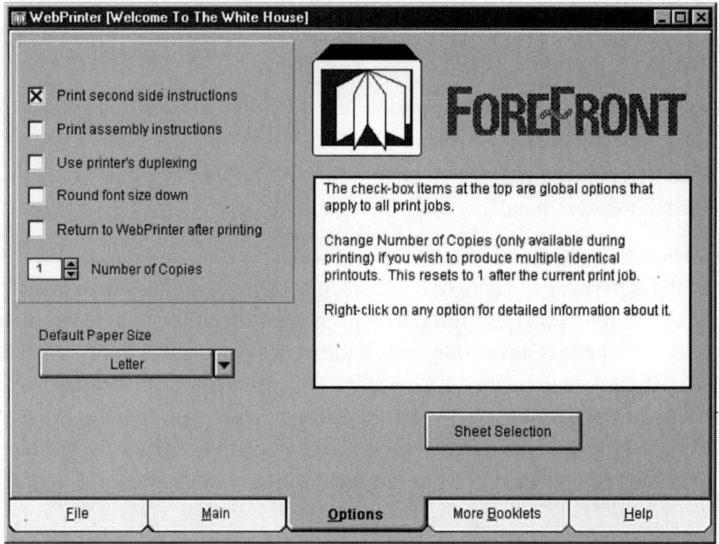

FIG. 13.12
The Options tab page.

Even after WebPrinter formats all of your pages, you can still alter the form of the booklet before you print it. Click the File tab, and you will see still another set of options available to you.

In the Documents being printed window, you see a list of all of the documents you have sent to WebPrinter during the creation of your present booklet. You can change the position of a document in the booklet simply by dragging its name to a different place in the list. You can also choose to delete a document entirely from the booklet, simply by highlighting the document in this list and clicking the Delete button. Change your mind? Highlight the name again and click Undelete.

You can save your booklet and its configuration so you can open it again and print it later. Click the Save As button (see Figure 13.13) and give the file any name you want, along with a .CD extension. When you want to print the file again, just open it up, and click Print.

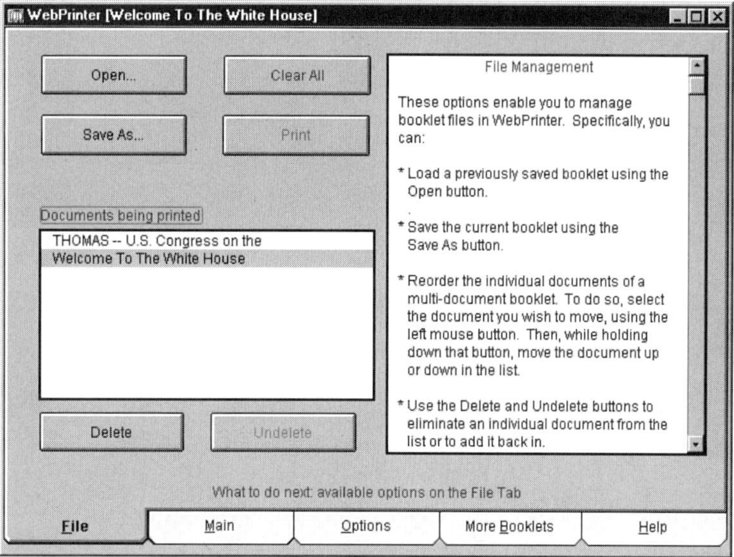

FIG. 13.13
The File tab page.

TIP Keep in mind, too, that, you can resize the WebPrinter window, making it smaller on your desktop, by dragging the edges of the window.

Using WebPrinter with Other Applications

In this lesson, we have emphasized the way in which you can use WebPrinter to create booklets of pages viewed in your Web browser. You can, however, turn any document created in a Windows application into a WebPrinter booklet. For example, you can reformat a story you have written in your word processing program, creating a small published book of your writing. Just open this document in the program in which you created it, choose Print, select the WebPrinter printer in the Print window, and WebPrinter takes over from there.

Because WebPrinter reformats documents at the printing stage, you can send documents from many different applications to WebPrinter and print them all in the same booklet. For example, you may want to create a booklet that displays your favorite Web site, along with your comments about the site. Create a document in your word processing program with your comments. Open your browser to your favorite site and send it to WebPrinter. Next, send the document that contains your comments to WebPrinter. The program creates a single booklet that contains both of these files.

Using WebPrinter with Other Applications

PART III

Part III Web Tools and Utilities

CHAPTER 14

Making Free Phone Calls with Internet Phone

- Installing Internet Phone
- Making phone calls using the Internet
- Communicating better with written text and pictures
- Transferring files to people you're chatting with

Long distance phone calls can be extremely expensive—even at a dime a minute, it's $6 an hour, and it's even worse when you try to talk to someone overseas. The long distance companies all talk like they're giving you a bargain, but there's an even bigger bargain…

Free phone calls using the Internet.

Okay. These calls are not exactly free—you had to pay for a computer, and your Internet service provider sends you a bill every month—but you're going to make those payments anyway. So what it really boils down to is that you can make long distance (or local) telephone calls for no *extra* money. And it gets even better, because you can do things with an Internet telephone connection that you just can't do with your basically-hasn't-changed-since-1876 Bell issue telephone.

So how do you take advantage of the Internet as a substitute to Ma Bell and save tons of money? That's what I tell you about in this chapter, which is all about one of the most versatile Internet telephone programs, Internet Phone. ■

Internet Phone from VocalTec

The full, registered version of *Internet Phone* costs less than a one-hour overseas phone call, has an easy-to-use interface, and provides an awful lot of powerful accessories. It's the best of both worlds.

The CD-ROM that comes with this book contains a trial-ware version of *Internet Phone* that lets you talk for one week over the Internet—free. If you find you like the program, you can either register the software online at the VocalTec Web site (**www.vocaltec.com**) or purchase a copy at your local computer store.

Installing Internet Phone

Before you begin making all those free phone calls to Aunt Freeda in Germany, you need to install *Internet Phone* from the CD-ROM and configure it for your system.

Before You Start

You need to know a few things before you begin the installation process—you don't want to get halfway through before realizing that you just don't have what it takes and you have to quit, get the information (or hardware) and start all over again.

Internet Phone's hardware and software requirements are fairly modest. Pretty much any computer purchased within the last year or two is capable of running *Internet Phone.*

Computer:

- 486 class processor
- 66 MHz minimum speed
- 8M RAM (although a more realistic minimum is 12M)
- 3.5M free hard drive space
- A Windows 95 compatible sound card
- A microphone
- Speakers

Software:

- Windows 95
- A 32-bit connection to the Internet (for instance, through an ISP such as AT&T World Link, America Online for Windows 95, or CompuServe)

You also need to know the name of your service provider's SMPT (or mail) server. If you have set up an Internet mail program, such as Microsoft Internet Mail, you've already had to determine this information. If you're not sure, check with your service provider's technical support department. America Online's mail server is just named "mail."

Installing the Software

To install *Internet Phone*:

1. Insert the *Using the Internet Starter Kit* CD in your CD-ROM drive.
2. Click the Chapter 14 icon to access Internet Phone.
3. Click the OK button. The Install Shield system begins.
4. Click the Next button twice to get past the License Agreement and Welcome pages.
5. At the Choose Destination Location page, either press the Next button to proceed, or press the Browse button to select a new location to store the *Internet Phone* files and then press Next.
6. Click Next to accept the program folder. The *program folder* is the folder in the Start/Programs menu from which you start *Internet Phone*.
7. In the User Information dialog box, fill in the text boxes, and then click the Next button. Note that only a nickname is required. (See Figure 14.1.)

The only information required in the User Information dialog box is a nickname. If you want to maintain your anonymity, enter a false name and false e-mail address.

FIG. 14.1
Your personal information helps other people who try to find you online.

TIP If you use America Online, leave the SMPT Server as "mail."

8. In the System Information page, enter the name of your SMPT Server (also known as your mail server) and modem speed. Unless you are sure that your IP (Internet Protocol) address always remains the same, do not enable the "I have a fixed IP address" check box.
9. Click Next to close the dialog box. *Internet Phone* begins to load on your system.
10. Follow the rest of the instructions to complete the installation.

Unless you have a full-time connection to the Internet (such as a network or ISDN connection) leave the checkbox asking if you want Internet Phone in your Startup folder deselected.

Setting Up Your Hardware

The first time that you run Internet Phone, you have to configure the system for the noise level in your office space (is it quiet or noisy) and possibly adjust your microphone volume.

To start Internet Phone and set your environment:

1. Open the Start menu, choose Programs, Internet Phone4, and then select the program item Internet Phone Release 4. When Internet Phone starts, the Audio Test dialog box opens (see Figure 14.2).

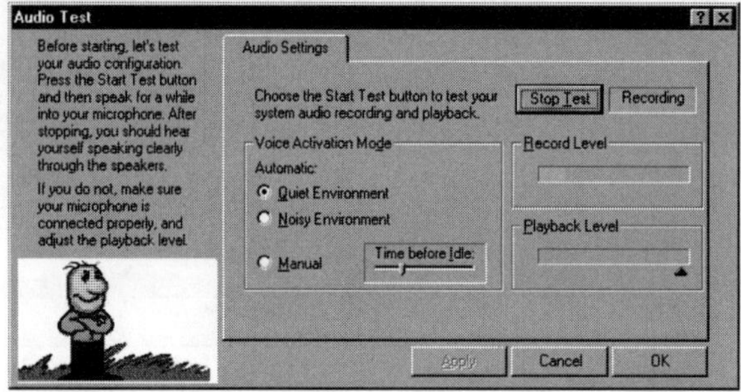

FIG. 14.2 The Audio Test dialog box lets you specify information about the ambient noise level where you use Internet Phone.

2. Position your microphone at a comfortable distance for talking, then click the Start Test button. The indicator next to the button changes from "Not Active" to "Idle."
3. Speak for a few moments in a normal tone of voice. The "Active" indicator now says "Recording" and the Record Level volume meter rises and falls in response to your voice. You want the VU meter to read about mid-level (halfway across) for most of your talking.
4. Stop speaking and let Audio Test play back your voice for you.

   If your voice plays back at a good volume, click the OK button to enter Internet Phone.

   If a lot of background noise was recorded before or after you spoke, select the Noisy Environment check box and repeat the test. If the problem disappears, press OK to enter Internet Phone.

If your voice did not record, or sounds extremely quiet or very loud and crackly, you need to adjust the recording volume of your system's microphone. To do that, click OK to enter Internet Phone, and then follow the next set of instructions.

Follow these instructions to adjust the volume of your microphone:

1. Choose Audio, Audio Mixer. The Master Volume dialog box opens. (You also could double-click the speaker icon in the system tray to open this dialog box.)
2. Choose Options, Properties.
3. In the Properties dialog box, select the Recording radio button to display your available recording devices.
4. Make sure that the Microphone check box has an X in it, and then press OK. The Master Volume dialog box changes to the Recording Control dialog box.
5. If you couldn't record your voice, make sure that the Select check box in the Microphone column is enabled, and then retry the audio test.

   If your voice is too soft or too loud in the playback, adjust the volume slider in the Microphone column up or down, respectively, and then retry the audio test.
6. If your recording and playback are okay now, click the Options button and select Exit. You now are ready to make your first call.

   If you are still having trouble, check your microphone connection or adjust your speaker volume. If neither of these solutions works, contact your sound board manufacturer for other possible remedies.

When you return to the Internet Phone window, you need to tell the system to let both parties in a phone call talk at the same time (if your hardware will allow it). Open the Audio menu and select the Full Duplex check box. If the Full Duplex check box is already enabled, your system is already set.

Making Your First Call

You have many options and utilities that you can use when you use Internet Phone to make a call, but you want to get up and running right away and try to talk to someone. In this section, I lead you through your first call.

Connecting to Someone Online

If you plan to use Internet Phone a lot, you might want to place a shortcut to it on your desktop.

To start Internet Phone:

1. Start your connection to the Internet.
2. Open the Start menu, choose Programs, Internet Phone4, and then select the program item Internet Phone Release 4. The VocalTec Internet Phone window opens (see Figure 14.3).

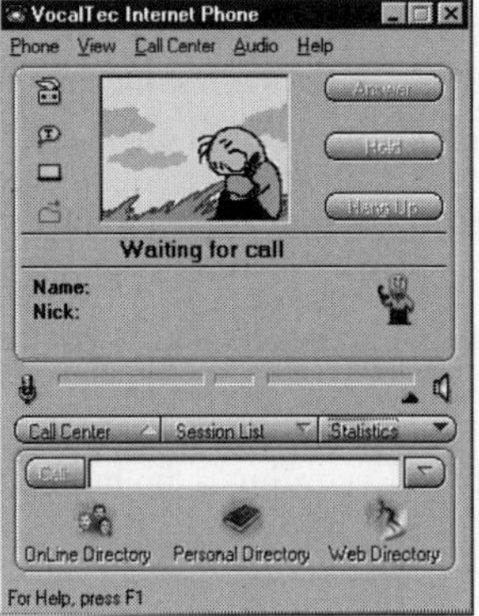

FIG. 14.3 The Internet Phone window lets you place and receive calls—all with a handy animated assistant to show you what's happening.

3. Because this version of Internet Phone is unregistered trialware, you can connect only to someone who is using the Global OnLine Directory (GOLD). If the GOLD window did not start automatically, choose Call Center, OnLine Directory. The Internet Phone Global OnLine Directory window opens (see Figure 14.4).

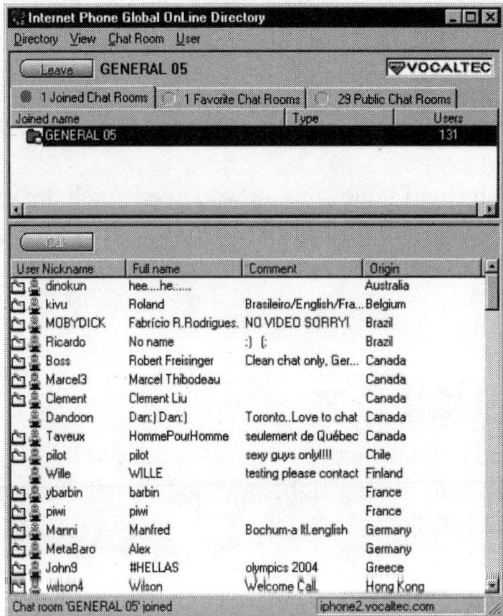

FIG. 14.4 You can select someone to talk to from any of the chat rooms in GOLD.

4. If you don't see any chat rooms listed under the Joined Chat Rooms tab, click the Public Chat Rooms tab, then double-click a chat room to join it.

5. Find someone on the list at the bottom of the window who looks interesting (either from an interesting nickname, comment, or place of origin), highlight their name, and click the Call button. (You also could just double-click the person's name.)
6. If the person accepts your call, he or she answers the "phone" and you can begin talking. You can tell the phone has been answered when the animated assistant in the middle of the screen splits and shows two people (notice how the one in the upper-left corner moves when you speak).

   If no one answers, press the Hang Up button in the Internet Phone screen, and then try someone new from the GOLD directory.

NOTE There is a delay between when you speak and when the other person hears you (and vice versa). If you don't hear anyone speak right when they pick up the phone, say "Hello" and wait a moment or two to see if it's just a delay problem. It may take some practice to talk over the Internet without becoming confused by the delay.

Hanging Up Your "Phone" and Exiting

After you finish your call, simply click the Hang Up button (after saying "good bye," of course). If want to make another call, you can do it now, or if you want to leave Internet Phone now, just choose Phone, Exit. Don't forget to close your connection to the Internet.

The Internet Phone Screens

Now that you've made your first call, you'll want to explore all of the power available in Internet Phone. One of the great things about this program is that, while it *is* extremely powerful, it is also very easy to use.

These options are much easier to understand if you are online and talking to someone. If you have a friend who also has Internet Phone, give him or her a call. If not, try to find a helpful soul in one of the "Testing" chat rooms that you can find in the Public Chat Rooms area of the GOLD directory.

The Internet Phone Window

The Internet Phone window is divided into up to four different areas: the Main Section, the Call Center, the Session List, and Call Statistics (see Figure 14.5). The next sections describe each of these areas.

Main Section The Main Section gives you direct control over how you speak to the other person and what utilities you use (see Figure 14.6).

FIG. 14.5
Each of the four Internet Phone window sections provides a different control for your phone calls.

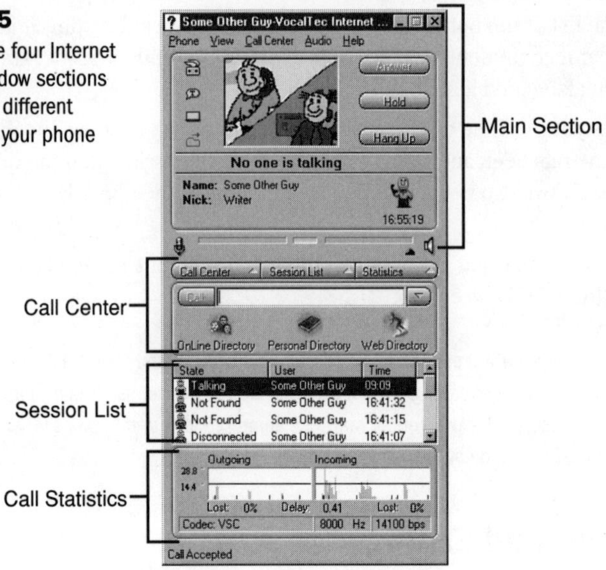

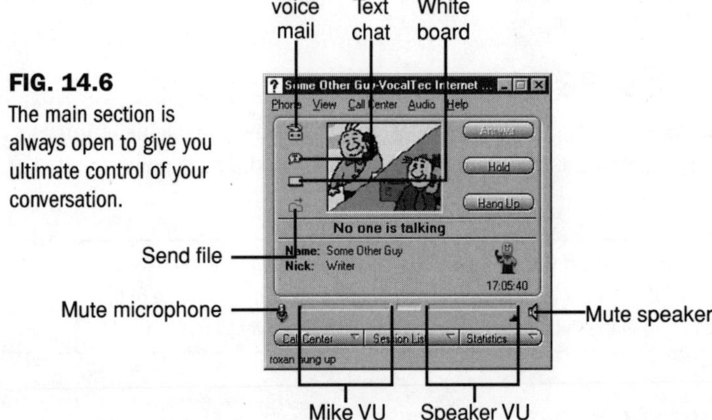

FIG. 14.6
The main section is always open to give you ultimate control of your conversation.

Along the right side of screen are the three buttons that you use to control the length of the conversation: the Answer, Hold, and Hang Up buttons. These buttons operate just like the equivalent functions on a regular phone.

Along the left side of the screen are the four utility buttons: Send Voice Mail, Text Chat, Whiteboard, and Send File. These buttons enable you to perform feats that are impossible using a regular telephone:

- **Send Voice Mail.** If the person you want to speak with is not online, you can send a voice mail message to him or her. Internet Phone sends these messages as attachments to regular e-mail. You also can send voice messages to people who don't have Internet Phone, although they need to have a program before they can play back your messages.

- **Text Chat.** Maybe you don't want to speak, or maybe you need to write down what you need to say.
- **Whiteboard.** A picture is worth a thousand words. The whiteboard lets both people in a conversation *draw* what they need to communicate.
- **File Transfer.** Rather than attaching a file to an e-mail message, you can use the file transfer system to instantly send any type of file to someone you're talking to.

The two VU meters—one for the microphone and one for the speakers—give you a running display of the volume of each person in the conversation. You also can mute either your microphone or the speaker independently.

The Call Center You access the Call Center by pressing the Call Center button of the Main section (see Figure 14.7). Note that only the OnLine Directory button of the Call Center is useful to people who have not yet registered Internet Phone. The other options, Personal Directory, Web Directory, and the history drop down are not active until after you register.

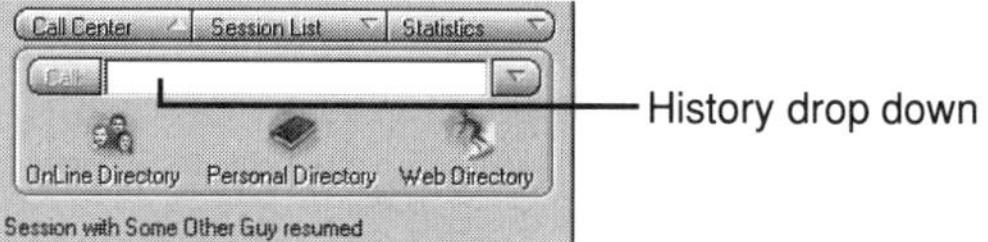

FIG. 14.7 The Call Center becomes *more* useful after you register Internet Phone.

The Session List The Session List provides a quick listing of everyone you've talked to, including how long you talked, during this session of *Internet Phone* (see Figure 14.8).

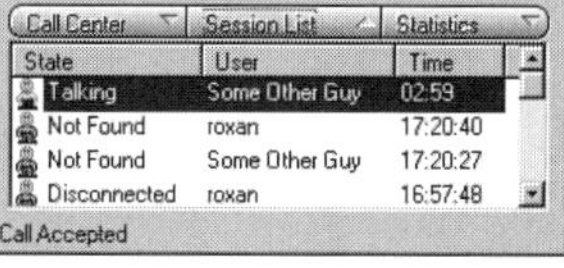

FIG. 14.8 The Session List is useful if you want to become depressed with how much time you spend online.

Call Statistics The Call Statistics area (see Figure 14.9) provides a graphic representation of how your connection is doing. The graph moves from right to left, depicting how the conversation is travelling from your computer to the other, and vice versa. The green vertical lines indicate speech (the taller the line, the more talking) and the blue lines represent lost information (the taller the line, the more lost information).

If you are having trouble understanding the other person in a conversation, open the statistics area and check the height of the blue lines. If they are fairly tall, or if the percentage after the word "lost" is above about 10 percent, you should consider ending the conversation, restarting your Internet connections, and hope for a better connection.

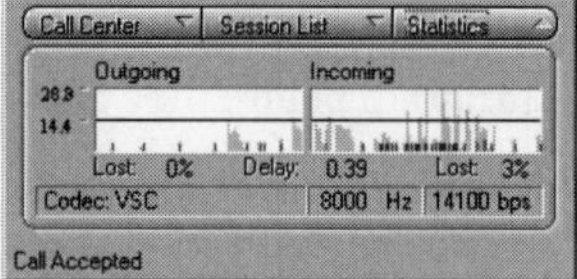

FIG. 14.9
The Statistics are useful for tracking down problems with a conversation (contact, *not* content).

The Global OnLine Directory (GOLD)

Although the registered version of Internet Phone allows you to make calls using the Personal and Web directories, the unregistered version that comes with this book restricts you to working through the chat rooms located in the GOLD directory (see Figure 14.10). This restriction is not an obstacle, as long as you know which chat room to enter.

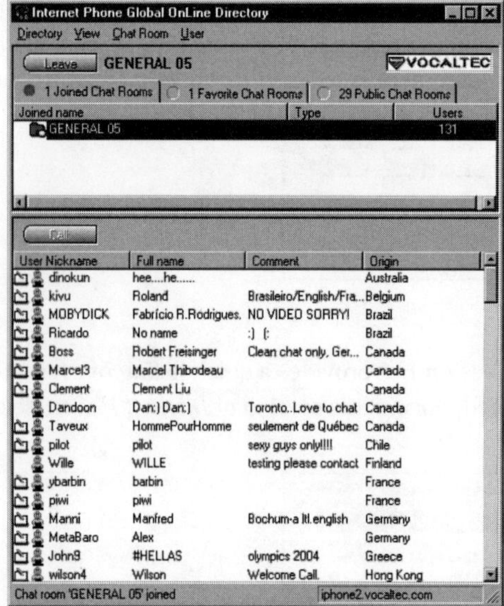

FIG. 14.10
The GOLD Directory helps you find people to talk to in different, named chat rooms.

The GOLD Directory consists of hundreds of different chat rooms. It would get terribly confusing if you didn't have a number of ways to work with them.

Joining Chat Rooms

You can't talk to anyone (nor can anyone find you to talk to you) unless you join a chat room. You can join up to 10 chat rooms at one time to make yourself available to many, many different people. To join a chat room:

1. Click the Public Chat Rooms tab to list the available public chat rooms.

To organize the chat rooms by name, click the Name column header.

2. Highlight a chat room that has a title that interests you. If you're just starting out, one of the General... or Testing... chat rooms would be a good choice.
3. Open the Chat Room menu and select Join. The chat room appears under your Joined Chat Rooms tab and a list of possible people to talk to appears at the bottom of your screen.

To organize the users in alphabetical order, click the User Nickname or Full Name column header. (You also can alphabetize the lists based on the Comment and Origin columns.)

Setting Default Chat Rooms

If you log in to some chat rooms every time you enter the GOLD directory, you can save yourself a lot of trouble by telling GOLD to join you to them automatically as soon as you log on.

To set a chat room as one to which you want to join automatically when you connect:

1. Highlight the name of the chat room you're interested in.
2. Open the Chat Room menu and select Auto Join On Connect.

If you want to talk to someone in this chat room now, you'll have to join it; you only automatically join it when you start the GOLD Directory.

Creating Your Own Chat Rooms

Creating your own chat room is easy—and very useful. If you're trying to meet someone online, there are so many chat rooms that you may never find one another. By creating your own chat room, with a name with which the person trying to find you is familiar, you can make short work of getting connected.

To create a new chat room:

1. Open the Chat Room menu and select New/Private.
2. Enter a name for your new room and click OK.

The new chat room appears in your Joined Chat Rooms list and you become available for anyone else to call.

Favorite Chat Rooms

Favorite chat rooms are another real time-saver. If you find that people you really want to talk with are generally in a couple of chat rooms, you can add these rooms to your favorites list and save yourself the time of trying to find them every time you log in to the GOLD directory.

To add a chat room to your favorites list:

1. Highlight the chat room by clicking on it once.
2. Open the Chat Room menu and select Add to Favorites.

Hiding Chat Rooms

The names and themes of chat rooms are entirely unregulated by VocalTec. This is a great boon for the cause of free speech, but the downside is that much of this free speech is rather crude. One way to make sure that you are not assaulted by vulgar chat room titles (and to help make the rooms you're interested in easier to find) is to hide chat rooms you don't care about.

Although hiding the chat rooms that you'd rather not have to wade through can take a while, what with several hundred public chat rooms available and more being created all the time, the few minutes spent weeding out offensive chat rooms can be time well-spent.

While you could go through all the public chat rooms and indicate certain ones as favorites, new chat rooms are always opening and it would be a shame for you to miss any potentially good ones just because you won't enter the public chat rooms area.

To hide a chat room, simply click it once to highlight it, and then open the Chat Room menu and select Hide. The chat room is removed from the public chat rooms area.

If you find that you've hidden a chat room by mistake, open the View menu and select Hidden Chat Rooms. Then highlight the chat room you want to "unhide" and click the Remove button. The chat room becomes available in the public chat rooms area again.

Receiving Calls and Declining Calls

You aren't always the person making calls. As often as not, you're the one on the receiving end of an invitation to talk.

Internet Phone announces an incoming call just like a regular phone—it starts ringing. It even furnishes a Caller ID type service; when the phone rings, the name and nickname of the person calling appear in the Internet Phone main screen.

If you want to accept the call, just press the Answer button. If you don't want to take the call, either ignore the ringing until the other person gets bored and "hangs up" or press the Hang Up button.

The Cool Tools

As I mentioned earlier, four terribly useful tools come with Internet Phone that just aren't available when you use a regular telephone. Although you may have loaded up Internet Phone just for the really cheap phone rates on long distance calls, these extras may get you using Internet Phone for local calls, too!

Text Chat

The Text Chat tool (see Figure 14.11) lets you send and receive written messages as easily as you speak (as long as you're a good typist). You may sit there and wonder "Why do I want a text chat window in the middle of a voice chat program?" Well, that's a valid question. The answer is, you've just got to have it. Text chat is amazingly useful if the boss is in the next cubicle and you need to discuss the latest management snafu, or if the dog ate your microphone and you aren't done discussing last night's game. You may not think you need text chat, but the first time you need it, you'll be hooked.

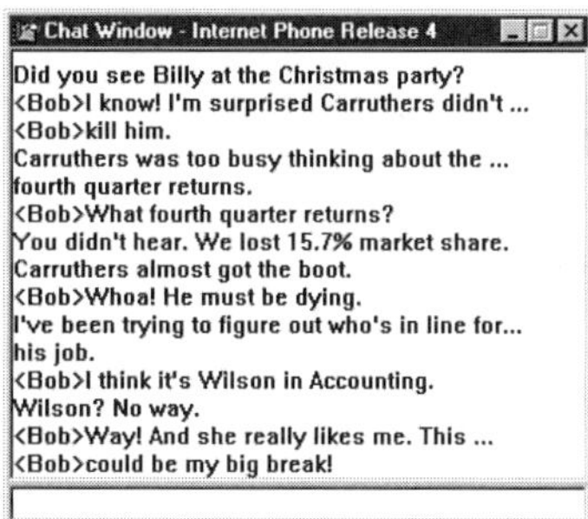

FIG. 14.11
Text Chat makes it easy to "speak" quietly.

To use text chat, just click the text chat button, and then place the cursor in the small box at the bottom of the window and type your message. Every time you press the Enter key, Internet Phone transmits your message to everyone in your conversation.

Whiteboard

Sometimes words, spoken or written, just can't take the place of a simple picture. Being able to draw something out is often the easiest way to get your point across.

Internet Phone's whiteboard makes dealing with pictures a breeze (see Figure 14.12). All you do is start the whiteboard (by pressing the whiteboard button on the Internet Phone main screen), and then draw on it just as you would in the Windows paint program.

The Whiteboard Tools The Whiteboard tools are pretty self-explanatory and tend to work the same way: click the given tool button, move the cursor into the "canvas," and then click and drag the cursor. You also can select tools by choosing them from the Tools menu.

The Whiteboard doesn't have an undo option. After you draw something on the whiteboard, you can get rid of it only by erasing it or deleting it. And if you erase something by accident, you just have to redraw it.

The main tools are

- **Stroke.** Use this tool to draw on the canvas.
- **Erase.** Drag over the canvas to erase.
- **Highlighter.** Use the highlighter to draw attention to certain parts of the canvas.

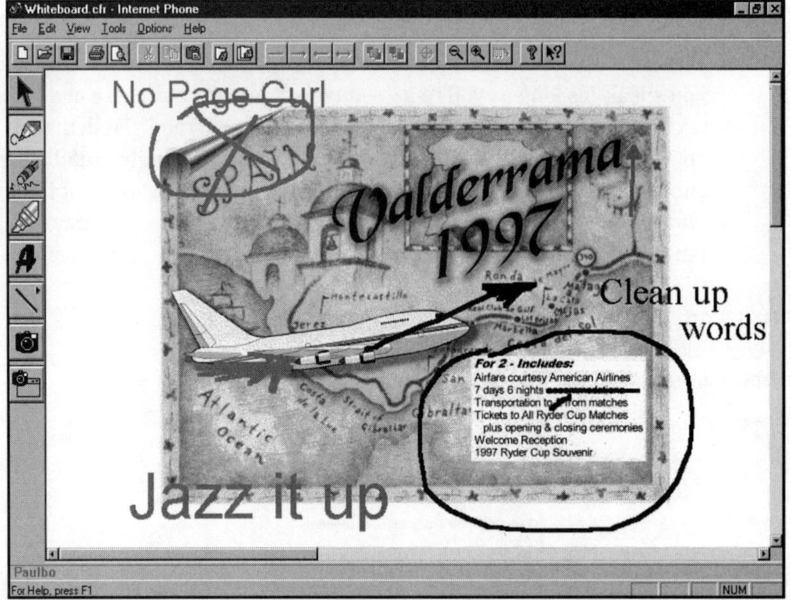

FIG. 14.12
Use the Whiteboard to make short work of often complicated discussions.

- **Text.** Add neat, typewritten text to the canvas. This tool works slightly differently than other tools; instead of clicking and dragging, just click once where you want the text to start, then enter your information.
- **Shapes.** Internet Phone provides four built-in shape tools: line, rectangle, ellipse, and diamond. The current tool is shown in the toolbar; to select a different shape, right-click the shape tool and choose the new shape from the pop-up menu. All the shape tools work by clicking and dragging.

You can draw arrows at the beginning or end (or both) of a line by selecting the line tool, and then selecting one of the arrow options from the top toolbar.

- **Capture Region.** This tool lets you capture portions of the screen and place them on the Whiteboard. To use this tool, click its button (the Whiteboard minimizes so that you can see the desktop or any other running program), click and drag the cursor to highlight a rectangle that you want to capture, and then release the mouse button. The Whiteboard reopens, containing a ghosted rectangle that indicates where Internet Phone will place the captured area when you decide to click the mouse. Move the cursor until you have the rectangle in the right place, then click the mouse button. A copy of what you captured now appears on the canvas.
- **Capture Window.** This tool works similarly to the Capture Region tool, except that instead of clicking and dragging to define the area to be captured, you move the cursor until the area you want to capture is highlighted, then simply click the mouse button.

To change the typeface and other text attributes, choose Options, Font to open a standard Windows font dialog box. Pick the font, style, and size from the three lists, and then press the OK button to return to the Whiteboard. Everything you type from now on has the formatting that you specified.

To change the color that you draw or type in, choose Options, Color, and then select the color you want from the menu.

Change the color before using the highlighter tool. If you don't, the highlighter paints over everything you've already done and then you can't read it.

Internet Phone gives you four optional line widths for use with the stroke and shape tools. To change the line width, choose Options, Line Width, and then pick the width you want to use. (Note: There is only one width available for the highlighter and the eraser.)

Adding Other Information to the Whiteboard In addition to just capturing pictures of the computer screen for display on the Whiteboard, you can import pictures from other programs or from your hard drive.

To copy pictures from other, currently running programs, highlight what you want (how to do this depends on the program) and press Ctrl+C to copy it to the Clipboard. Next, move back to the Whiteboard and press Ctrl+V to paste it on the canvas. You can move the picture around by using the mouse, then click the left mouse button to drop it in place. (Note: You can't copy text from a word processor into the Whiteboard.)

To import a picture:

1. Choose File, Import. The Import Graphic Files dialog box opens.
2. Navigate your hard drive to find the picture you want to import, and then highlight it.
3. Click the Open button. You return to the Whiteboard and your picture is placed at the upper-left corner of the canvas.

NOTE The only type of images that you can import into the Whiteboard are JPEG images. If you want to import a picture that's in another format, either convert the image to JPEG format and then import it, or open the picture and copy and paste it into the Whiteboard.

If you want to move an imported picture, select the select objects tool (the arrow), and then click on the picture. Now you can drag the picture anywhere around the canvas.

Printing and Saving the Whiteboard After you finish working with the Whiteboard, you may want to print or save what you've done; for example, you have been working on an advertisement and want to be able to refer to your markups while you're editing the actual piece.

To print the contents of the Whiteboard, choose File, Print. The Print dialog box opens. Click OK to print the Whiteboard.

To save the Whiteboard, choose File, Save. You can open a Whiteboard later to review it.

Voice Mail

If the person you want to talk to isn't available, you can send him or her a voice mail message, just as you can with a regular phone. Unlike an answering machine, however, this isn't automatic and therefore requires a little more work. Fortunately, though, the Record and Playback buttons work just like those on a VCR or cassette recorder.

You can send a voice mail message to anyone who has an e-mail account. Just address the message to their address (`bob@whatever.com`). If the recipient doesn't have Internet Phone, he or she needs to download a small program from VocalTec before the message can be played (the text message that accompanies the voice mail lets the person know of this requirement).

To send a voice mail message:

1. Click the Voice Mail button on the Internet Phone screen. The Internet Phone Voice Mail window opens (see Figure 14.13).

FIG. 14.13
Send recorded messages to anyone who has an e-mail address using Internet Phone Voice Mail.

2. Enter the person's e-mail address in the To: text box.
3. Press the Record button and begin speaking into your microphone.

You may find it necessary to mute the microphone in Internet Phone before you can record a voice mail message.

4. After you finish recording, press the Stop button.
5. Click the Send button to send your message.
6. Click the Close button to return to Internet Phone.

Troubleshooting

Troubleshooting is straightforward with Internet Phone. The automated Support Wizard gathers information about your computer system and its connection to the Internet and transmits it to VocalTec technical support, where technicians analyze your problem and e-mail back a message. What could be easier?

To use the Support Wizard:

1. Choose Help, Support Wizard. The Internet Phone Support Wizard dialog box opens (see Figure 14.14). This dialog box collects information about your system.

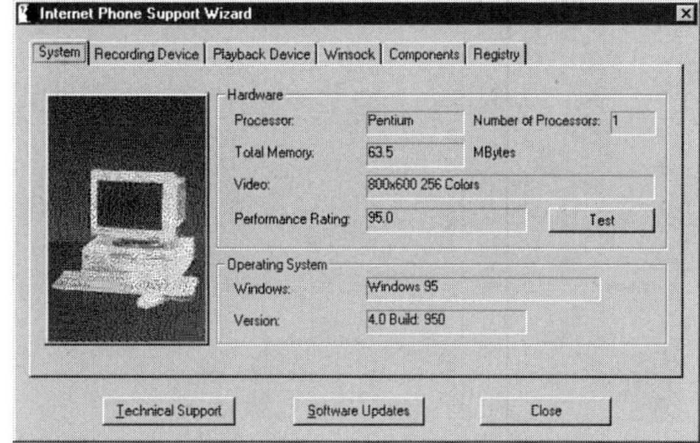

FIG. 14.14
The Support Wizard saves you from hours of manually digging up system information and trying to relate it to the tech support person.

2. Click the Technical Support button. A limited Web browser opens and connects to the VocalTec support site.
3. Answer a few short questions about yourself and your problem, and then press the Submit button. Your information and problem description transmit to technical support, who in turn send you an e-mail offering suggestions on how to solve your problem.

If the Support Wizard can't get through to the VocalTec site, you have to manually save and e-mail your support request. A dialog box opens and walks you through the procedure.

If you don't get a reply from technical support, or you need a faster answer, you can reach VocalTec Monday through Friday during normal business hours at (201) 768-9400, or by fax at (201) 768-8893. ●

Troubleshooting

CHAPTER 15

Chatting with mIRC

- **Getting and installing mIRC**
- **Chatting on IRC with mIRC**
- **Setting mIRC options to maximize your chat sessions**

Traditionally, many of the IRC clients (programs for accessing IRC) available on Internet access systems tend to reflect their UNIX heritage—shell accounts running the UNIX operating system. They're usually very powerful but based on command-line prompts and command codes, and therefore, are extremely difficult to master.

For many PC-based systems, a new generation of IRC clients is being developed with a much more intuitive, graphical interface. The mIRC program for Windows 95 is just such a program. ■

Why Use mIRC?

Internet Relay Chat has been around for a long time and is a popular way for people on the Internet to hang out. At any given time, as many as eight or nine thousand people from all over the world may be connected via IRC.

UNIX system IRC clients have been around for a long time, too. So, why do you need mIRC, a relative newcomer that allows you to connect to IRC from Windows 95?

The answer to that question is the same as the answer to the question, "Why use Windows 95 when you can use MS-DOS, which has been around for a long time as well?" Both MS-DOS and UNIX IRC clients can provide you with powerful tools for doing their respective function…but they're not easy or much fun to use. Sure, everything you might want to do is somewhere in there, but learning how to do it all could take the rest of your life…or longer.

mIRC takes all of the command-line drudgery out of accessing IRC, providing an easy, intuitive Windows interface for joining discussions, having private conversations, and exchanging files over IRC.

Installing mIRC

The version of mIRC used in this book is mIRC version 5.02. This version of mIRC comes with automated installation.

To install mIRC, follow these steps:

1. You'll find the file mirc502t(1).exe on the ftp site at

   `ftp.onramp.net/pub/win95/IRC`

2. After you download the file to a temporary directory on your computer, double-click the file name to begin the installation program.
3. Double-clicking the file name brings up the Installation dialog box (see Figure 15.1).

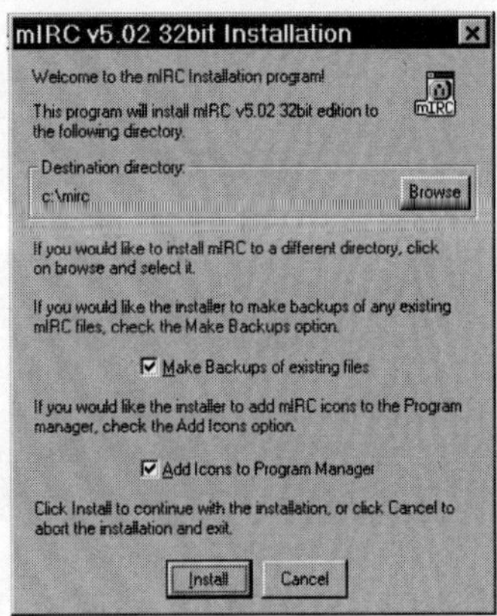

FIG. 15.1
Select Install to put mirc5.02 on your system.

As the program installs on your computer, a graphical progress indicator tells you how far along the installation is. And when the installation is complete, a message appears, telling you so. That's it! Your installation is complete! You might want to take this opportunity to take a quick look at the Readme.txt and Versions.txt files, which give some history for the program and other information.

Setting Up mIRC

When you first start mIRC, you need to fill in some setup information before you can use it to connect. To access this screen, click the Setup Information toolbar button or choose File, Setup. The Setup screen appears (see Figure 15.2).

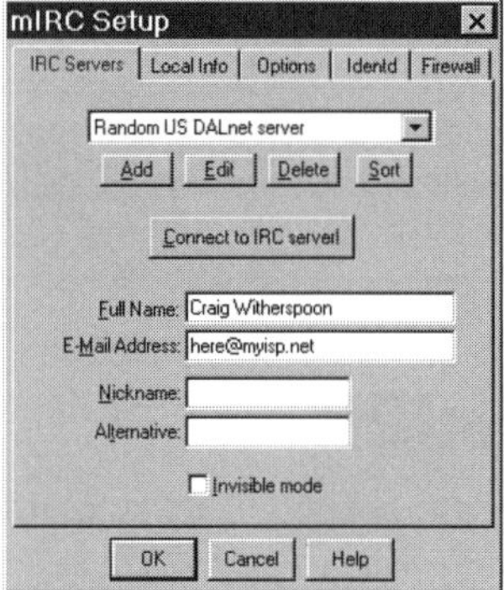

FIG. 15.2
This is the setup screen after I have filled in all of the necessary information.

On this screen, you fill in the real name that you want to appear in IRC, along with your e-mail address, and main and alternative choices for nickname. The nickname identifies you on IRC. If you have a dedicated local host name and IP number, click the Local Info tab and fill in that information (see Figure 15.3).

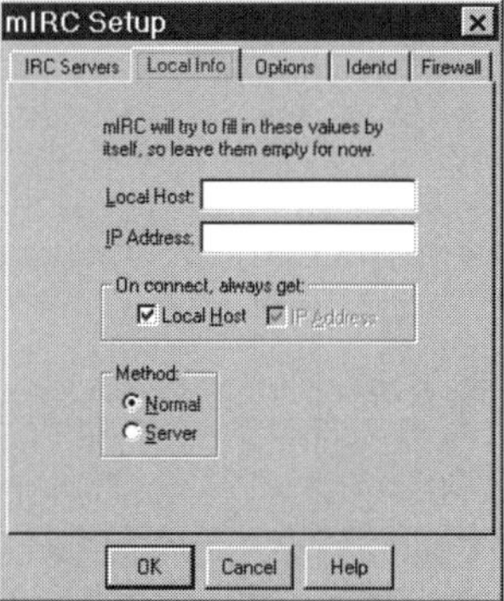

FIG. 15.3
You can enter your local info in this dialog box.

If your Internet service provider furnishes you an IP number upon connection, click one of the choices in On Connect, always get:. You access the list of IRC servers by clicking Add Server from the IRC Servers tab, which opens the Add Server dialog box (as shown in Figure 15.4). You can choose one of the servers shown or you can choose one supplied by your Internet service provider.

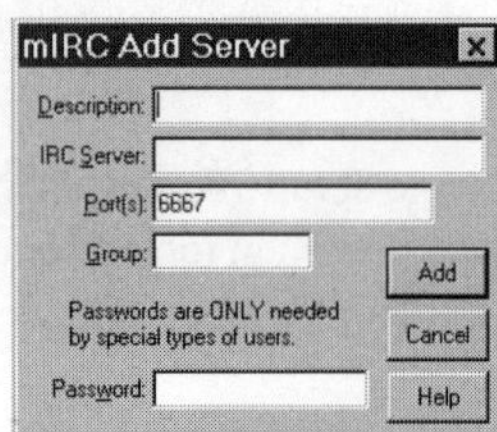

FIG. 15.4
If your Internet service provider has its own IRC server, be sure to add it to the list!

The IRC servers shown in the Add Servers dialog box are publicly available servers and tend to be pretty busy. If your Internet service provider has an IRC server of its own, you should add it to the mIRC server list and use it.

Accessing the IRC Using mIRC

When you have set up mIRC, you are ready to connect. After you close the Setup window (and any time you start mIRC), you see the mIRC Status window, which remains empty until you connect to IRC.

Connecting to IRC

To connect to IRC, click the Connect to IRC Server toolbar button or choose File, Connect. If you fill out the setup information correctly, mIRC connects you to IRC. You see the mIRC Status window; yours should look similar to that shown in Figure 15.5. This is the IRC server's Message Of The Day (MOTD).

Joining the Discussion

Once you have connected to an IRC server, you are ready to join the conversation. But which one? IRC often has thousands of *channels*—the IRC term for discussion groups. How can you find out which ones you want to join?

If you are completely new to IRC (and mIRC), there are a few places you can start. If you click the Channels Folder toolbar button, you get the window shown in Figure 15.6. By default, mIRC includes a list of channels in this window that are good places for new IRC users to join to get a feel for the system. After you find other channels to join, you can add them to this list for easy access in the future.

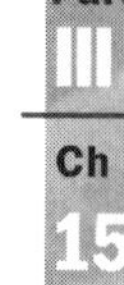

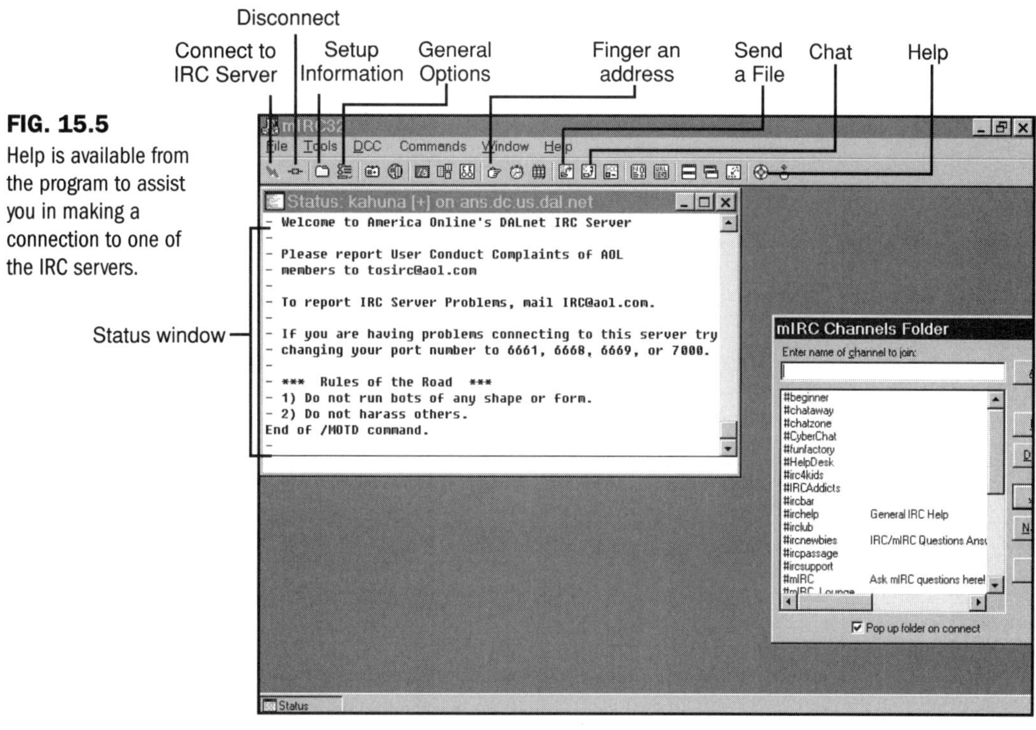

FIG. 15.5
Help is available from the program to assist you in making a connection to one of the IRC servers.

FIG. 15.6
Clicking the Channels folder toolbar button gives you this list of IRC channels to choose from.

But how do you find other groups to join? mIRC allows you to get a list of the names of all of the available public channels by clicking the List Channels toolbar button. Because up to thousands of channels might be available, it might take a few minutes for mIRC to list them all in the list window that pops up.

You should wait until all of them are listed before trying to browse through this list—mIRC continuously sorts the groups alphabetically as it adds them to the list, so it's impossible to scroll through the list until they are all there.

N O T E To narrow down your list of groups, you can type a phrase in the window, as shown in Figure 15.7. For example, if you type **irc** in that window, mIRC lists only those channels that contain irc in their names. If you want to narrow your search to the more (or less) popular groups, you can specify a minimum and/or maximum number of users for the listed groups.

FIG. 15.7
If you click the List Channels toolbar button, mIRC gives you a list of the channels that are available.

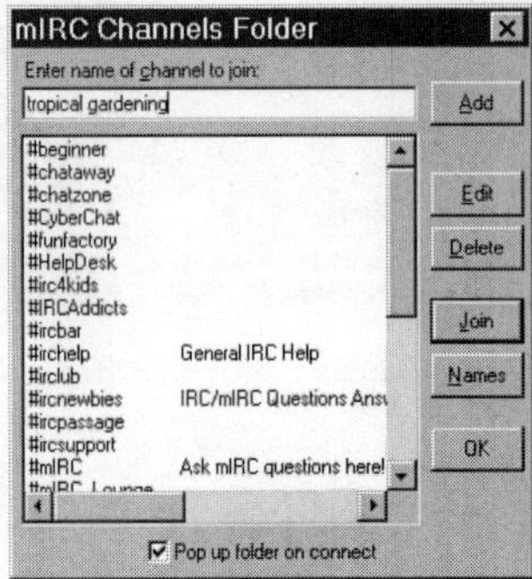

You can join a channel by double-clicking its name in the Channel List window.

What if you can't find a channel for what you want to discuss? You can just start your own channel! The procedure for starting your own channel is the same as for joining an existing channel. If you join a channel that doesn't exist, IRC creates the channel with you as its only member. If your topic is pretty obscure, you might have to wait a while before anyone else joins your channel.

When you join a channel through any of these methods, you see a window for that channel similar to that shown in Figure 15.8. The left side of the window is the main part where everything that everyone in the channel says (including you) appears.

FIG. 15.8
Once you're in a channel, you can join the conversation!

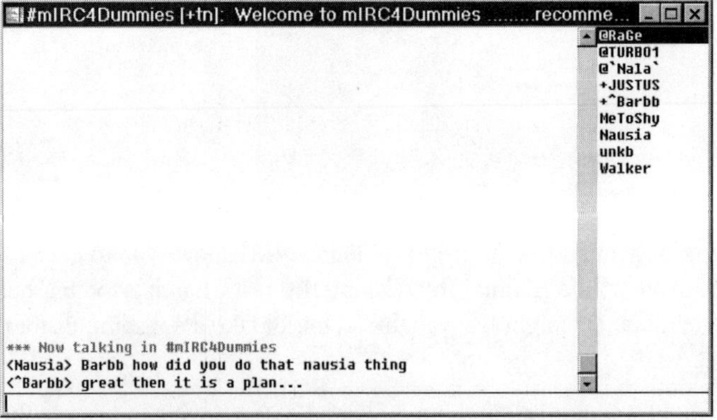

The right side shows a list of the nicknames for everyone in the channel. The input line on the bottom of this (and most mIRC) windows is the area where you type what you want to send.

Private Conversations

When you have joined a channel and entered a discussion, or after you have been on IRC for a while and have gotten to know other folks, you might want to have a one-on-one discussion with someone. There are two ways to do that in IRC, and mIRC allows you to access them both.

The first is to use private messages via the IRC /msg or /query commands. The second is to use the Direct Client-to-Client protocol (described in the next section).

If you want to send a message to your friend Rochlem, instead of just typing a message, you preface it with **/msg Rochlem** in the input line of any window. mIRC then sends a message only to the IRC user whose nickname is Rochlem. You also can type the command **/query Rochlem** without a message, to open an mIRC Query window (see Figure 15.9). Everything you type in this window is sent to Rochlem only.

FIG. 15.9
If you want to have a private conversation with someone, mIRC allows you to do that by using a Query window.

NOTE If you send a message using **/msg Rochlem <message>**, mIRC does not create a query window but it does send the message only to Rochlem. If Rochlem replies to your message by sending a private message back, mIRC then automatically creates a Query window.

CAUTION

Be careful about having private conversations on IRC. Normally, when having a one-on-one conversation with someone on IRC, you can assume that it is *private*—just between the two of you. Because of the nature of IRC, however, there is no guarantee. Using DCC Chat (see next section) is more secure, but it also does not guarantee privacy. Don't say anything you might regret—particularly if you expect to be a Supreme Court nominee someday!

A Little More Privacy Using DCC

As mentioned in the preceding section, IRC offers a way to have a one-on-one conversation with someone else using something called a Direct Client-to-Client (DCC) connection. To have a conversation with someone, you can use DCC Chat. You can also send and receive files from someone over IRC by using DCC Send and DCC Receive.

To initiate a DCC Chat with someone, either click the DCC Chat toolbar button or select the Chat item in the DCC menu. mIRC presents a dialog box (similar to that shown in Figure 15.10) in which you can select the nickname of the person you want to talk to.

FIG. 15.10 A Direct Client-to-Client (DCC) Chat with someone is usually a faster, more private way to communicate one-on-one.

Once the DCC Chat is accepted, the Chat window behaves the same way as the Query window (discussed in the preceding section). mIRC sends everything you type in the input line only to the other person. Because this is a direct connection between your IRC client (mIRC) and theirs, though, bypassing any IRC servers, it should be quicker and more secure—but don't get careless, it's still not completely secure!

You also can use a DCC connection to send and receive files from another user on IRC. To send a file to someone, click the DCC Send a File to Someone toolbar button, or select the Send item in the DCC menu. A DCC Send dialog box opens (similar to that shown in Figure 15.11), allowing you to select the IRC user and the file (or files) that you want to send. After you select the files, a mIRC pop-up window informs you of the progress of your DCC send.

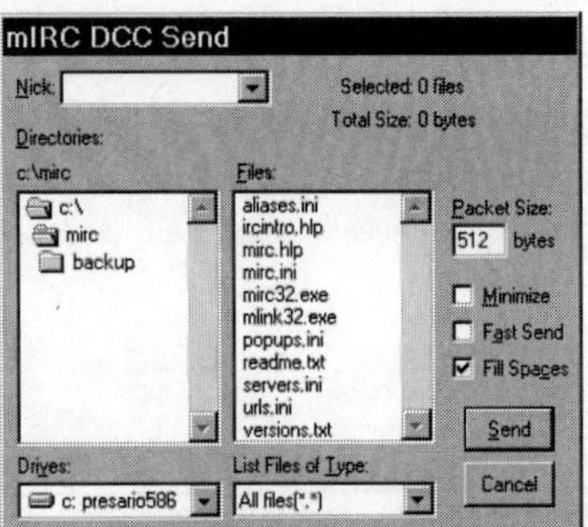

FIG. 15.11 You can send a file to someone else on IRC by using DCC Send.

NOTE When you receive a file via DCC Get, the file has the name that it had on the sending computer, and it downloads to the mIRC directory (for example, C:\Mirc). You can change this default location (along with other aspects of mIRC's DCC behavior) by clicking the DCC Options toolbar button or by selecting the Options item in the DCC menu.

Setting mIRC Options

You can customize the behavior and look of mIRC by setting the different IRC options. You do this by clicking the General Options toolbar button (see Figure 15.12).

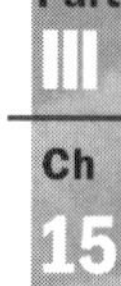

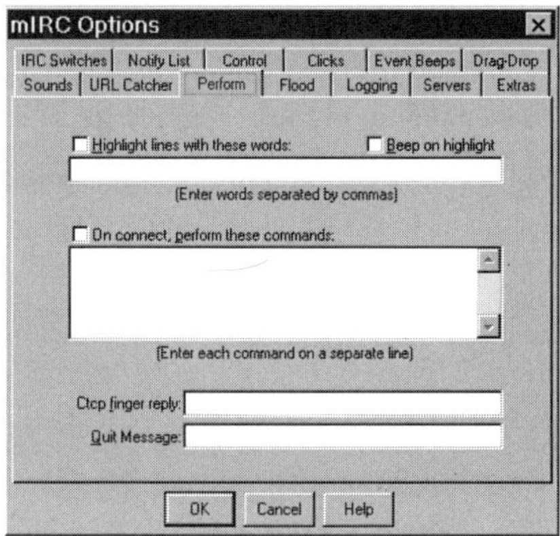

FIG. 15.12
You can access and change mIRC options by using General Options toolbar buttons or choosing File, Options from the Misc menu.

General Options

The bulk of the options you can use to customize mIRC's settings are accessed by clicking the general options toolbar button or by selecting the Options item from the File menu. The general options window includes several categories of options that you can access and change by selecting the appropriate tab.

IRC Switches The first mIRC general options window is called IRC Switches (see Figure 15.13). The default settings for most of these options are good, and you can experiment with them to see what you like. There are a few in particular that you might want to change.

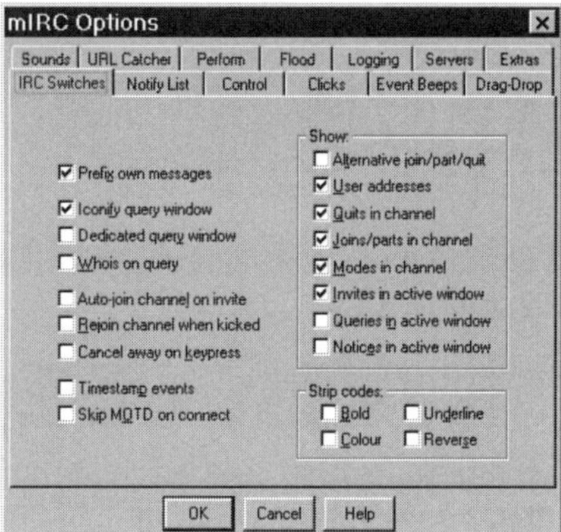

FIG. 15.13
IRC options allow you to change some of mIRC's general settings.

The two options in the upper left relate to mIRC's connection with an IRC server. Selecting the top box causes mIRC to connect automatically with its default IRC server upon startup of the program. If you always use the same server, you might want to check this box. If you have or are using an IRC server that frequently disconnects you, check the second box, which tells mIRC to attempt to reconnect with the server if you get disconnected.

Two other options that you might want to change, also found on the left side, relate to mIRC's response to private messages from other users. Selecting the Iconify query window in this group of options tells mIRC to start a private message window as an icon in mIRC.

I usually like to see these messages right away, so I disable this option. The last option in this group, Whois on query, displays the nickname, address, and server in the Status window of any user who sends you a private message.

Feel free to experiment with the other options in this window to see if you like the way they change mIRC's behavior.

Perform The Perform general option window (see Figure 15.14) allows you to define IRC commands that execute when you connect to an IRC server. If you type a series of words in this window, separated by commas, these words are highlighted when they appear in any mIRC window. This is a good way to highlight messages from certain people or about certain topics.

FIG. 15.14
Perform allows you to specify words that you want mIRC to highlight.

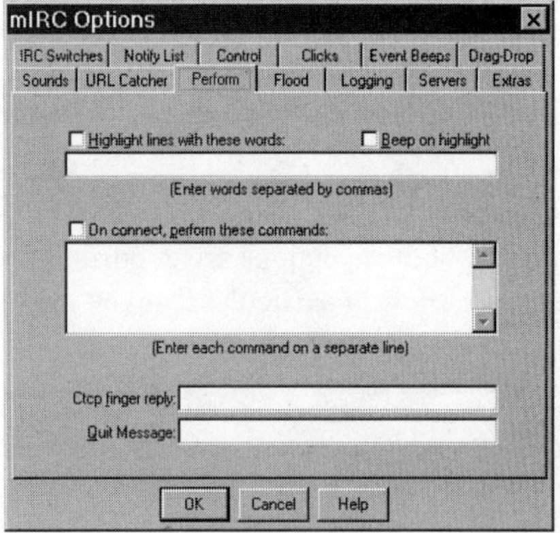

Control The Control general option window (see Figure 15.15) lets you define how you want mIRC to handle certain user nicknames.

- **Auto-Op—Any**. Entering IRC user nicknames in this box tells mIRC to automatically make those users an operator in any IRC channel in which you are an operator.
- **Ignore**. Entering IRC user nicknames in this box tells mIRC to ignore anything those users say—you will not even see messages from them.

Notify List A list of IRC nicknames entered in a Notify list (shown in Figure 15.16), separated by spaces, causes mIRC to notify you, by displaying a message in the Status window, whenever one of the users named is on IRC. This is a great way to keep an eye out for friends on IRC with whom you want to chat (or not-so-good-friends whom you want to avoid).

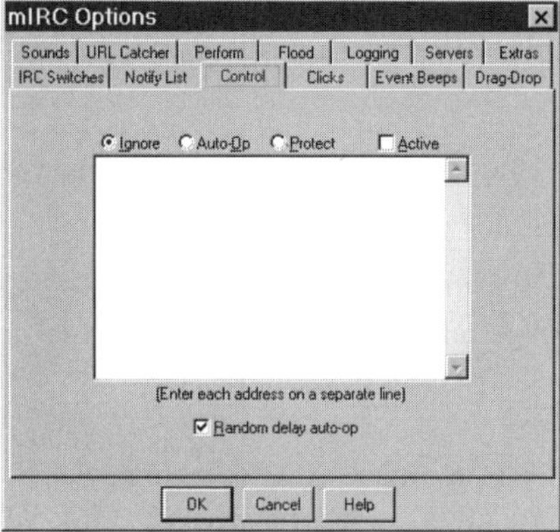

FIG. 15.15 Make sure that Active is selected to enable Auto-Op and Ignore.

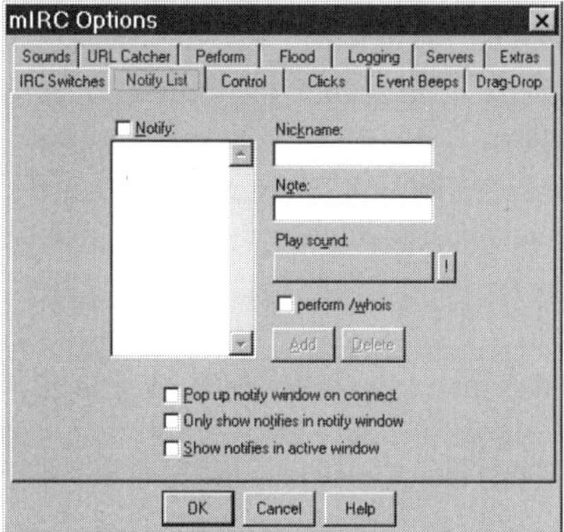

FIG. 15.16 Use this list to keep an eye out for close friends and problem IRC users.

URL Catcher A handy feature of mIRC is its URL Catcher (see Figure 15.17). If you select the Enable URL catcher box, mIRC scans all incoming messages to see if they contain World Wide Web (WWW) URLs, and Internet FTP and Gopher addresses.

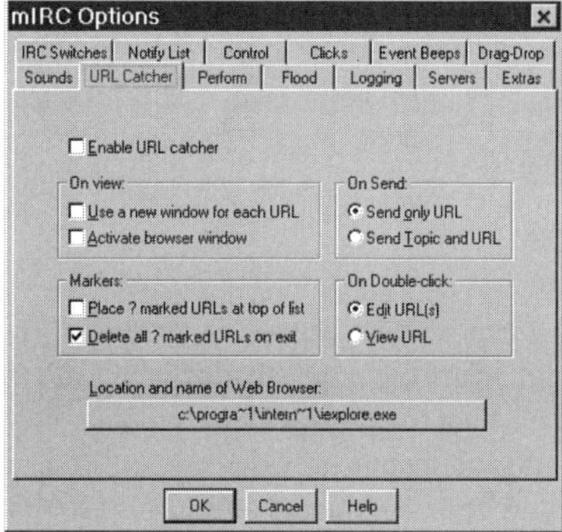

FIG. 15.17 The URL Catcher scans all incoming text for Internet and WWW addresses, and saves them to your URL list.

For instance, if someone sends you the URL of Microsoft's home page, as shown in Figure 15.18, mIRC grabs the URL and puts it in its URL list. You access mIRC's URL list by clicking the URL List toolbar button.

Other General Options The other general option windows allow you to control the following aspects of mIRC's operation:

- **Event Beeps**. Controls what events mIRC notifies you of using audible beeps.
- **Logging**. Allows you to have mIRC automatically log channel or one-on-one (Query or DCC Chat) discussions to files on your computer, as well as specify the path where the log files are put.
- **Sound Requests**. Specifies how mIRC handles incoming and outgoing sound requests—basically allowing mIRC to send, receive, and play .WAV sound files.
- **Servers**. Allows mIRC to act as an ident server and to send the specified User ID and System as identification. The default values that mIRC puts in this box usually are fine, and you should never need to look at it.
- **Double-click**. Allows you to set up actions you want mIRC to take when you double-click in its different windows.
- **Extras**. Miscellaneous extra mIRC options. Most of these options are pretty self-explanatory—go ahead and experiment with them if you'd like.

Fonts

By default, mIRC uses the fixed system font for displaying text in all of its windows. Clicking any window's control menu, as shown in Figure 15.18, allows you to specify a different font for that window. Choose Font from this menu to display the Font Selection dialog box.

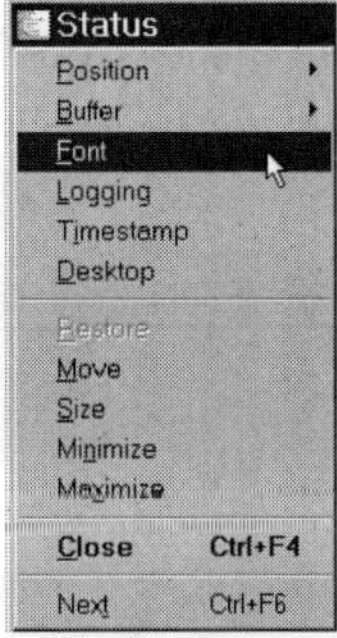

FIG. 15.18 mIRC allows you to select what font to use for the different types of windows.

Pop-up Menus

mIRC has a very powerful and useful feature, called *pop-up menus*. These are user-defined menus that appear when you right-click the mouse in different mIRC windows. While you can define each of these menus by clicking the pop-up menu's toolbar button or selecting the pop-up item in the Tools menu, the default menus provided with mIRC are very useful. The best way to modify these menus would be to use the defaults as a starting point.

Figure 15.19 shows a sampling of how one of the pop-up menus is defined. The one shown appears when you right-click in either the main part of a channel or in the Status window. Although this definition looks kind of complicated, it is pretty easy to figure out by comparing the definition with the actual menus (see Figure 15.20).

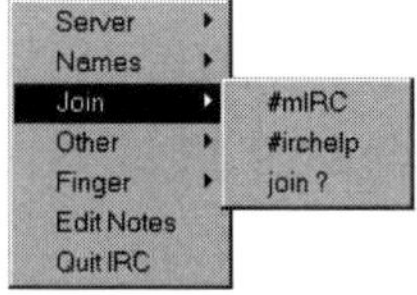

FIG. 15.19
mIRC allows you to define pop-up menus with a right-click in the different windows. These pop-up menus allow you to perform mIRC actions easily.

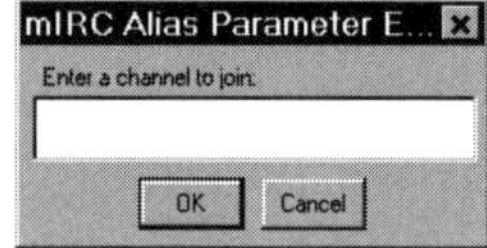

FIG. 15.20
After you define the pop-up menus, you can access them in mIRC. The default pop-up menu for the main window is shown here.

CHAPTER 16

Protect Your PC from Viruses

- Keep people from snooping while you're online
- Protect yourself from viruses
- Shopping online is safe at secured sites
- Control the content that your browser downloads

You can send your credit card number over a plain Internet connection a hundred times, and, in all likelihood, no one will ever nab it. You can download all sorts of shareware software to your computer, and you'll rarely, if ever, get a virus. The odds are in your favor.

Don't play those odds. You need to protect yourself from the idiots on the Internet who would like to do you harm. This chapter shows you how. ■

Keeping the Contents Files on Your Computer Private

Networking and *file sharing* (a service that enables you to share files and printers on a peer-to-peer network) can expose your hard drive to unauthorized access if it's configured incorrectly. You can keep people off your computer, though, by updating your network configuration. By removing the association between file sharing and the Dial-Up Adapter, your computer ceases to expose your file system to the Internet. (Note: By following these instructions, you won't be able to share files on any peer-to-peer network on which you connect via a Dial-Up Networking connection.) Use these steps:

1. Right-click the Network Neighborhood icon and choose Properties to open the Network properties dialog box. You should see a dialog box that appears in Figure 16.1.

FIG. 16.1
The Network property sheet is where you configure all of your network settings.

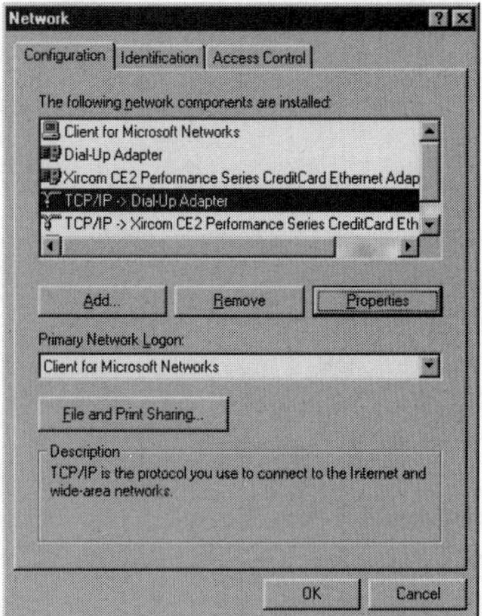

2. Select TCP/IP -> Dial-Up Adapter (or TCP/IP if you don't have a network card installed) from the list of networking components, and then click Properties.
3. Click the Bindings tab. Do you see an item in the list that says `File and printer sharing for Microsoft Networks`? If not, click Cancel a few times to get rid of the Networking properties dialog box. If the list item is present, move on to the next step.
4. If there is a check mark next to `File and printer sharing for Microsoft Networks`, click the box until the check mark disappears. The Bindings tab you see on your screen should look exactly like the one shown in Figure 16.2.
5. Click OK to save your changes to the TCP/IP Properties dialog box. If you see a message that says `You have not selected any drivers to bind with. Would you like to select one now?`, click No. Click OK again to save your Network properties dialog box; and restart your computer.

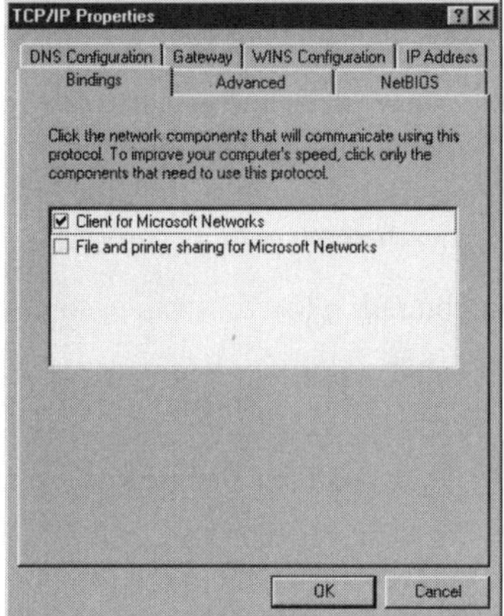

FIG. 16.2
Don't tamper with any of the other settings in this dialog box; otherwise, you may break your connection.

Downloading Programs Only from Known Sources

The only *guaranteed* way to avoid viruses is to refuse to download freeware and shareware programs onto your computer.

But your best *realistic* solution is to download files only from reputable sites. Be wary of downloading shareware files from newsgroups, for example, since everyone has unregulated access to them.

CAUTION

Remember that some companies have strict policies regarding the use of downloaded software on a networked computer. Check to see what your company's policy is before you download or install any software from the Internet.

Debunking Myths about Viruses

Viruses can't spread via Internet mail messages or data files such as pictures. A virus is a program, like any other program. It has to execute in order to spread.

TROUBLESHOOTING

My Windows 95 computer has suddenly ground to a halt. It was working fine, but the next time I started my computer, everything suddenly slowed down. My animated cursors don't work anymore, either. What's wrong?

You have probably caught a virus. If Windows 95 thinks that the system areas on your boot drive have been tampered with, it starts your computer in something called DOS Compatibility Mode the next time you log on. It's much slower, because it uses DOS-compatible disk drivers. Use one of the virus scanners and see if your hard drive is infected.

Using Norton AntiVirus to Scan for Viruses

Norton AntiVirus scans your computer for viruses and protects your computer from getting new infections. You can download an evaluation version of Norton AntiVirus from **http://www.symantec.com/nav**. Click Free Downloads; then, click the link that corresponds to the operating system that you use, and follow the instructions you see on the screen.

After you download the file onto your computer, use these steps to install Norton AntiVirus:

1. Double-click the file you downloaded, and then click Setup to start the installation program.
2. Type your name, and optionally, your company name in the spaces provided. Click Next.
3. Click Next to scan your system for viruses before Setup finishes installing Norton AntiVirus. Do not interrupt this process by clicking the Stop button; you can't be completely sure that your computer doesn't have a virus.
4. You should see a dialog box telling you that your system is virus free. Click Next to continue.
5. Click Next to accept Symantec's license agreement.
6. Click Next to accept the Setup program's default installation path.
7. Click Next to let the Setup program do a complete install of Norton AntiVirus.
8. If you have Netscape Navigator installed, you see a dialog box telling you that Norton AntiVirus can be installed as a helper application. Click Next to do so.
9. Click Next to accept Norton AntiVirus' default settings, which protect your computer automatically.
10. Click Next to create a Rescue Disk that you can use to repair your computer if it becomes infected with a virus. Follow the instructions you see on the screen to create this disk.
11. Review your setup information, and click Next to finish installing the files on your computer. If you see any dialog boxes titled Add Netscape Helper Application, click OK to install Norton AntiVirus as a Netscape helper application for those files.
12. Click Next, to allow Setup to change your AUTOEXEC.BAT file.
13. Click Next after reading about Norton AntiVirus' LiveUpdate feature.
14. Click Next after reading about Symantec's support options.
15. Click Next after reading about Symantec's online presence.
16. Click Next after reading about Symantec's other products.
17. Choose the country in which you live from the list, and click Next to register your copy of Norton AntiVirus.
18. Type your name, address, city, state, and zip code. Optionally, provide your company, title, telephone number, and fax number. Click Next.
19. Fill in the survey you see on the screen, and click Next.

20. Select Modem to register online, and type the digits required to access an outside line in the space provided. Click Next. Setup goes online and transmits your registration information.
21. Select Restart my computer now, and click Finish.

The trial version lasts 30 days. If you want to purchase Norton AntiVirus, you can do so online or at your local software retailer.

Scanning Your Computer for Existing Viruses

When you installed Norton AntiVirus, it scanned your computer for existing viruses. You can scan your computer at time, however, by following these steps:

1. Choose Programs, Norton AntiVirus, Norton AntiVirus from the main menu.
2. If you use the trial version, you see a window showing you how much time you have left on your trial run. You can click Buy Now to purchase the software, or click Try First to open Norton AntiVirus. You see the window shown in Figure 16.3.

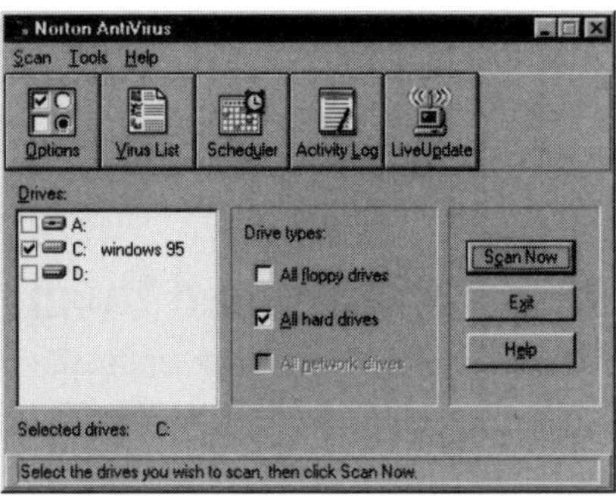

FIG. 16.3
Select all of the hard disks that you want to scan in the Drives list.

3. Click Scan Now, and Norton AntiVirus scans your computer for existing viruses. It updates its status in the window shown in Figure 16.4.
4. If your computer is infected by a virus, you see the Norton AntiVirus Repair Wizard shown in Figure 16.5. Select Automatic, and click Next to remove the virus.
5. You see a window that shows you the name of each file that's infected. Click Next to continue, and Norton AntiVirus removes the virus.
6. Click Finish to close the Norton AntiVirus Repair Wizard.

FIG. 16.4
If you see anything other than zeros under the Infected column, your computer might have a virus.

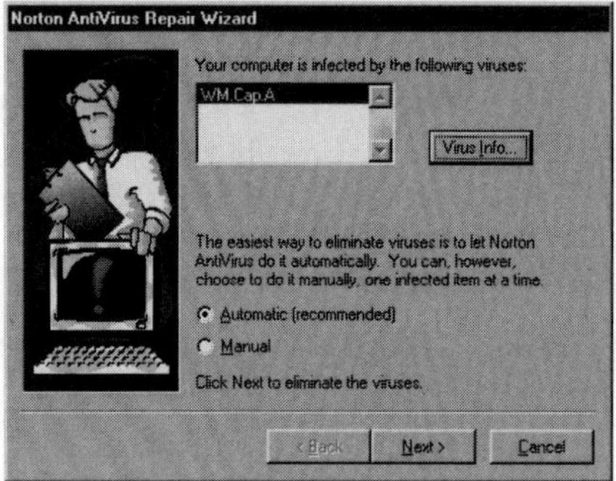

FIG. 16.5
Select a virus from the list, and click Virus Info to learn more about it.

Checking Files for Viruses as You Download Them

Norton AntiVirus will scan a file for viruses as you download the file in Netscape Navigator:

1. Click the link to the file that you want to download.
2. You see a dialog box that gives you the choice between opening the file or saving it to disk. Select Save it to disk, and click OK.
3. Select the path to which you want to save the file, and type the file's name. Click Save.
4. After Netscape saves the file to your computer's disk, Norton AntiVirus immediately scans it for viruses.
5. If Norton AntiVirus does find a virus, you see a blue DOS screen that notifies you. Press **S** if you don't want to save the file on your computer, press **R** if you want to remove the virus from the file, or press **D** to delete the file.

Protecting Your Computer from New Viruses Infections

Norton AntiVirus automatically scans any file you run, open, or create for viruses:

1. When Norton AntiVirus detects a virus, you see a blue and red screen that says `The file` *`Filename`* `is infected with the` *`VirusName`* `Virus. What would you like to do?`.
2. Press **S** to stop running or opening the file, press **R** to fix the file, or press **D** to delete the file from your computer.

If you don't see Norton AntiVirus' icon in the taskbar's system tray (next to the clock in the lower right-hand corner), you need to enable Auto-Protect. Choose Tools, Options from the main menu, then select Load Auto-Protect at startup, click OK, and restart your computer.

Downloading Current Information about Recent Viruses

According to Symantec, three new viruses are created every day. You need to frequently update Norton AntiVirus to take into account the latest virus definitions:

1. Connect to the Internet.
2. Start Norton AntiVirus, and choose Tools, LiveUpdate from the main menu.
3. You see a window that lets you choose to preview the phone number that LiveUpdate uses. Click OK.
4. Select Internet from the list, and click Next.
5. Norton AntiVirus automatically connects to Symantec's FTP site, downloads the latest data about viruses, and installs them on your computer.
6. Select Restart my computer now, and click Finish.

Scanning for Viruses with Anyware Antivirus for Windows

The award-winning Anyware Antivirus utility is an extremely thorough, yet flexible virus protection package. Combining ease of use with a pleasant and compact interface, this powerful tool makes virus protection virtually pain free.

Pass the cursor over each button displayed at the top of the Scan tab if you want to view its function. From left to right, they are Scan memory, Scan start-up process, Scan DOS system files, Scan Windows system files, Scan Only/Automatic removal, Scan compressed files, Scan files with extension VIR, Select objects to scan, Select exceptions, Use Anyware SmartScan, Use Anyware FastScan, Use heuristic scan, Delete ANYCHECK.VAL files, and Delete *.VIR files.

NOTE Anyware Antivirus is located on the CD-ROM of this disk.

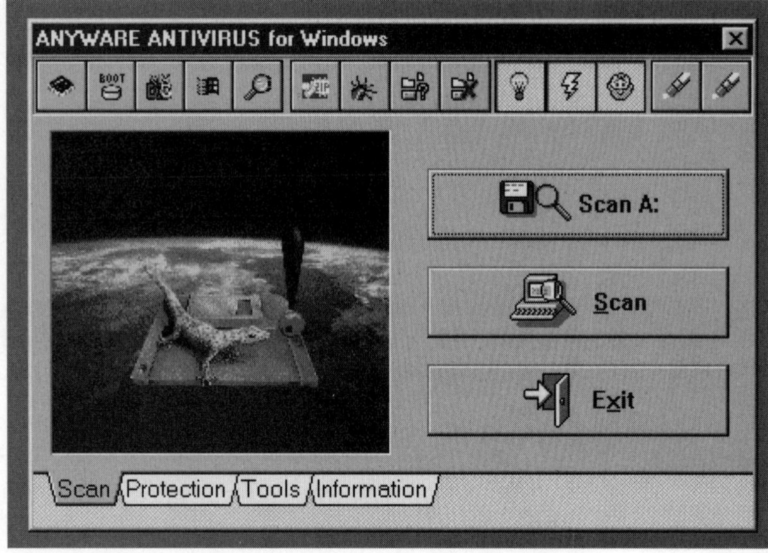

FIG. 16.6
When you open Anyware Antivirus, you are presented with a clean, simple screen. You use this screen to set the program to scan for existing viruses.

Of these, you most often use the Select objects to scan button. If you press the Scan Only/ Automatic removal button, you can toggle between just getting a report on your system and having a discovered virus automatically removed.

NOTE You may also directly launch scans of any one of your drives by selecting that choice from the Anyware group on your Start Menu.

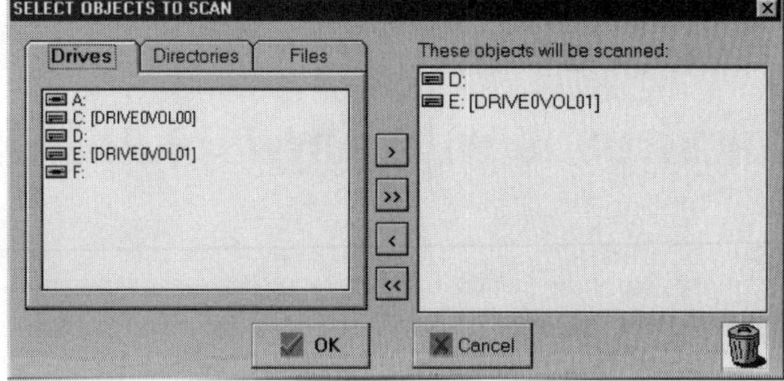

FIG. 16.7
After pressing the Select objects to scan button, you can choose which drive, directory, or file you want to scan.

From the main screen, you can also proceed to the other functions (tab selections at the bottom). These include Scan (what you see when you first start up), Protection (where you set how you want the on-going virus protection to work), Tools (where you can set your Startup Menu Group and delete virus files), and Information (where you can find out about awards Anyware Antivirus has received, and how to get technical support and updates).

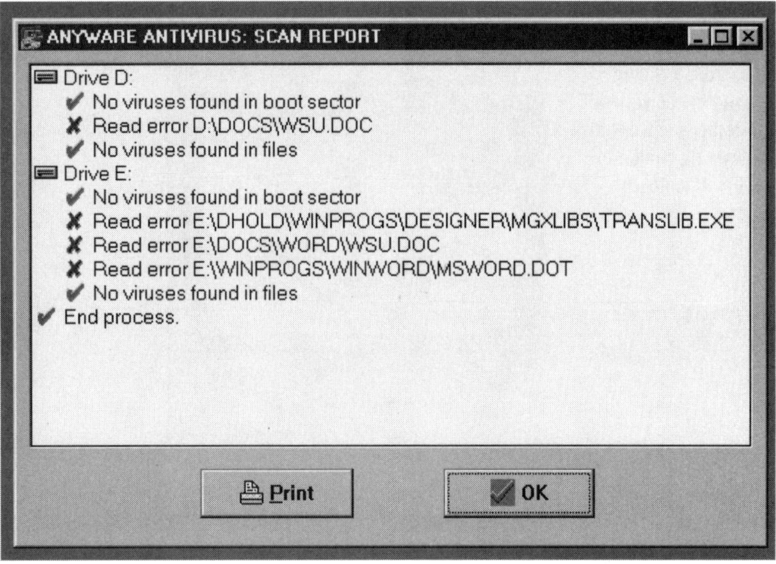

FIG. 16.8
Upon completion of the scan, a readout shows you the results.

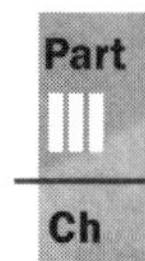

Like other anti-virus tools, it is imperative that you have the latest version(s); to that end, you can get these at their Web site at **http://www.helpvirus.com/**, where they make DOS, Windows 3.x, and Windows 95 versions available.

Choosing Which Vendors You Trust

When your browser downloads an object like an ActiveX control or Java applet to your computer, it looks for information in the object that identifies the publisher. If it finds that information, the browser asks you if you want to install the object. If it doesn't, the browser warns you that installing the object is risky.

When the browser asks you if you want to install the object, it shows you a certificate similar to the one you see in Figure 16.9. The two check boxes at the bottom give you the option of trusting any other object created by that same vendor and certified by a certifying authority (Starfish Software and VeriSign Commercial software Publishers CA in this example).

Shopping Safely at Secured Web Sites

You can safely use your credit card if you're shopping at a Web site that your browser tells you is secure. More than likely, the URL of a secure Web site begins with **https://**. But the real indicator of a secure site is the status bar of the browser. Take a look at the status bar shown in Figure 16.10. Notice that you see a locked padlock on the right-hand side, indicating a secure Web site. In Netscape, you'd see a locked padlock on the left-hand side of the status bar.

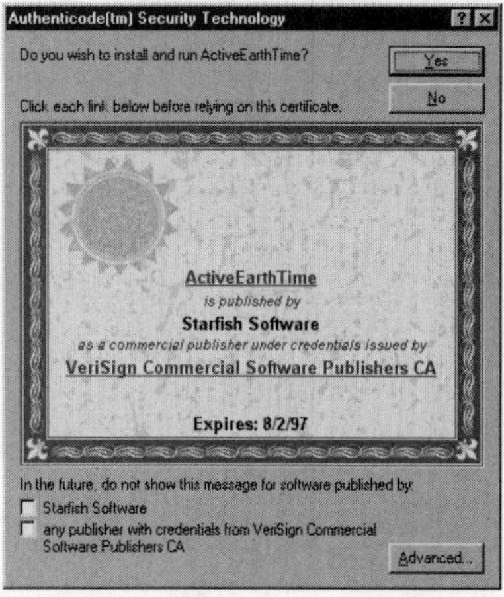

FIG. 16.9
Choose whether you want to trust anything published by the vendor and whether you want to trust anything certified by that certificate authority.

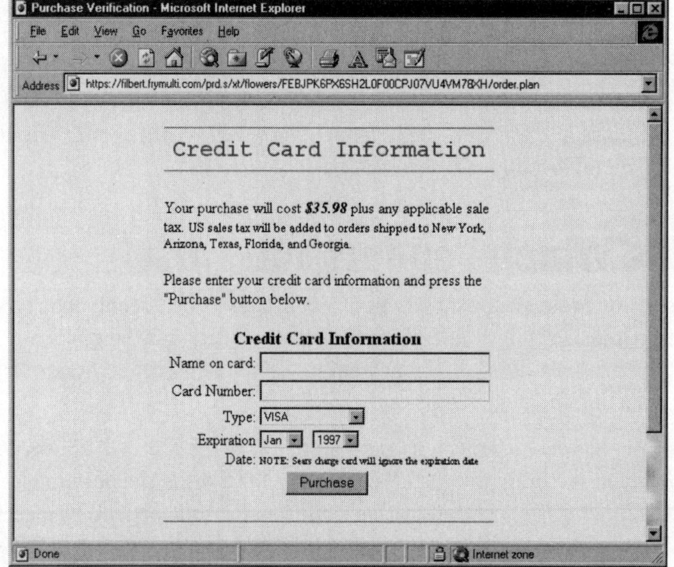

FIG. 16.10
Online shopping is safe, as long as you see the locked padlock in the browser's status bar.

If you have any doubts about whether the site you're visiting is secure, choose File, Properties from Internet Explorer's main menu. Click the Security tab and look for certificate information. In Navigator, choose Communicator, Security Info, and look for certificate information.

CHAPTER 17

Protect Your Kids with CYBERsitter

- The reason for all the fuss
- Using Internet ratings to control access
- Using filtering tools to restrict content
- Installing the CYBERsitter content filter
- Good Web sites for children

The Internet is probably a fact of life for your kids. They may know more about it than you do! And no doubt, as they get older, they will use it more and more for both work and play. They'll use it to communicate with friends and associates. They'll watch movies delivered via the Internet. Voting? Shopping? Entertainment? All on the Internet. A day will come when the Internet will play as central a role in our lives as the telephone and the TV do now. It's not going away.

Still, they are children. You need to take an interest in their experiences with the Internet, and watch over the materials they encounter on it. The Internet has a lot of wonderful things for your kids, but it also has a lot of content that you might feel is inappropriate for them. With just a few precautions, and a bit of parental oversight, you can make sure that your kids have a good time on the Internet, while making sure that the material they encounter is age-appropriate. ■

What Is All the Fuss About?

After your kids go online, they can find just about anything you can think of on the Internet—good and bad. And while it is true that your child has to make a genuine effort to find the adult content on the Internet, it's not that hard to find. Soon enough, your child will learn how to use one of many Internet search engines; this knowledge, and a couple of (in)appropriate search words, and they will be able to link to all kinds of material you may not want them to see.

You need to understand what type of information is out there, if you hope to keep your kid away from it. Thus, take a look at the following list:

- World Wide Web

  There are an abundance of Web sites dedicated to sexual images, and even to live (video) performances of a sexual nature. Most sites such as these cost money, and are impossible to access without a credit card number. But there are also sites (usually of a more moderate nature) that you can access simply by clicking a link.

- Usenet

  On the Internet, you can find many newsgroups that exist solely for the exchange of sexual images. These groups don't just offer nude pictures of men and women; they offer explicit pictures of various sexual acts.

  Newsgroups are for the most part ***unmoderated***, which means that newsgroups dedicated to discussion can also violate boundaries you have set for your children.

- Chat rooms (those on AOL and also on IRC, the non-proprietary Internet chat service) are often the site of conversations of a sexual nature. It is also difficult to ascertain identity truthfully in these chat rooms.
- Denizens of the Internet traditionally have a high respect for freedom of speech, which means that some rather extreme ideas get expressed there. Hate groups, for instance, have established a great many Web sites.
- Internet marketing is also starting to challenge parents. After your child has used the Internet for awhile, his or her e-mail address may come to the attention of Internet marketers, and your child might start receiving unsolicited advertisements in his or her mailbox. Some of these advertisements may be for erotic Web sites.

The very best first step is for you to become sufficiently familiar with the Internet to know what your child is doing with his online time. Talk with your children about the Internet, and try to come up with a set of rules that you are both comfortable with.

Advise your children, for example, not to give out their real name, address, or telephone number to anyone on the Internet. Tell them to let you know if they come across anything on the Net that they feel is inappropriate, or that makes them feel uncomfortable. Certainly, communication between you and your child is the very best first step in heading off any trouble or misunderstanding.

Of course, you'll need some help—no parent can be everywhere at once. Thankfully, help is available. You might start by contacting your Internet service provider and checking to see whether the ISP offers any content-blocking options for you. Some even offer "kid-proof" service, blocking all access to adult sites for you. You might also explore options that you have with various content providers; for example, America Online offers a variety of means to parents to control the content children encounter on that service.

Using Internet Ratings to Control Access

Although the system is still in its infancy, many Web publishers are voluntarily rating their Web sites. Microsoft's Internet Explorer works with these ratings to help you block questionable material. Other browsers haven't added support for this rating system, yet, but soon will.

Here's how to set up rating preferences in Internet Explorer:

1. Choose View, Options from Internet Explorer's main menu, and then click the Security tab.
2. Click the Enabled Ratings button. The first time that you set up the ratings, Internet Explorer asks you for a password. This is for parental control. Type your password in the space provided and click OK. You'll then see the property sheet.
3. Choose the ratings category you want to set from Category: Language, Nudity, Sex, or Violence.
4. Move the slider to the right to allow more explicit material for that category, or move it to the left to prevent explicit material for that category. You'll see a description of what types of material each setting allows.
5. Repeat steps 3 and 4 for each category you want to change, then click OK to save your ratings.
6. Click OK again to save the Security tab settings.

The next time you open the Internet Ratings property sheet, you'll be asked for your password. No one can change these ratings without the password. You can change your password by clicking the General tab in the Internet Ratings property sheet. Then, click Change Password.

If you really want to see what your child has been looking at, check the browser's history folder and sort by date.

NOTE These and all other rating systems depend on the cooperation of the Web content providers. If an adult site doesn't participate in the rating system, your child can still visit that site–even though you configured the ratings to disallow it. You can keep your child from visiting unrated sites by clicking the General tab in the Internet Ratings property sheet; then, deselect Users can see sites that have no rating.

Using Filtering Tools to Restrict Content

A *filtering tool* is a program that prevents a user from seeing certain types of content. SurfWatch and Net Nanny are just two such products.

These filters do the same thing, basically: they keep your child from viewing content you don't want them to see. They work by subscription—the software you install comes with an initial built-in list of "banned" sites. Companies update these sites regularly, adding new adult sites as they appear on the Internet. Your subscription allows you to download these sites from the company, thereby keeping your software current.

If you've recently purchased a new computer, you may already have the SurfWatch content filter. It comes bundled with a variety of machines, including certain Compaq and Packard Bell lines.

Installing the CYBERsitter Content Filter

The CD-ROM that accompanies this book includes an install file for the CYBERsitter content filter program. This program screens content from Web sites, Usenet newsgroups, FTP sites, IRC chat rooms, and e-mail. In addition to the choices programmed into CYBERsitter, the program gives you a chance to shape content blocking yourself—you can add specific Internet addresses to the program's list, as well as any words and phrases you want the program to screen.

The program starts running as soon as you install it, working in the background of your computer until you require its service. You can, however, set many different preferences. After you install the program, open CYBERsitter. A screen that contains the program's toolbar greets you. (See Figure 17.1.)

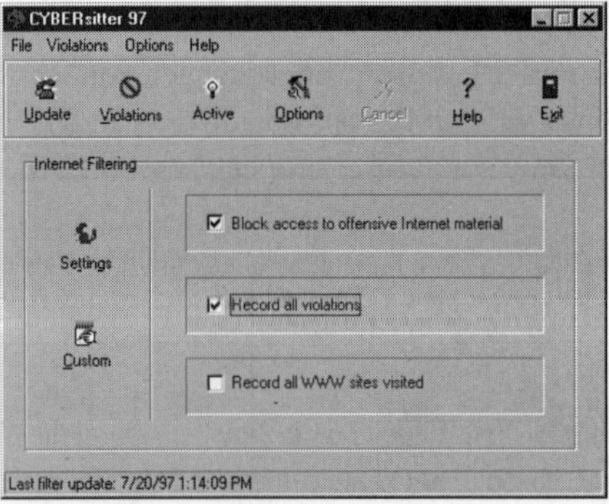

FIG. 17.1
CYBERsitter's opening screen.

The opening screen gives you several immediate choices. You can, if you prefer, turn off CYBERsitter by clicking the Active button. If you render the program inactive, the next time you want to use CYBERsitter, you must open it and manually turn the program back on. You can also uncheck the "Block access to offensive Internet material" box to achieve the same effect.

You can also ask the program to keep a record of all violations of the program's blocking boundaries. Just check the "Record all violations" box. (To view this record of violations, click the Violations button on the toolbar.)

You can obtain updated screening lists for CYBERsitter by clicking the Update button on the toolbar. (Make sure that your modem is on!) The program automatically dials up the company's access site and downloads the latest list of blocked sites to your computer.

You can also access the program's internal Help pages by clicking the Help button on the toolbar.

You can set further options by clicking the Settings icon in the middle left of the opening screen, or by clicking the Options icon on the toolbar.

The Options page opens. This page has five different tabs; each tab provides settings that you can change to alter the way CYBERsitter interacts with your browser:

- **E-mail.** Use this tab to add your e-mail address to the program; CYBERsitter uses this address only when you use its Help function to e-mail the company for technical advice.
- **Connection.** This tab allows you to select a preferred Internet connection when updating CYBERsitter's files. If you have only one Internet connection, you do not need this tab.
- **Security.** You can use this tab to create a password, thereby preventing anyone else from tampering with the CYBERsitter settings that you establish.
- **Filter Files.** Here, you can select between several broad categories of content blocking, letting CYBERsitter know which restrictions to follow and which ones to ignore. The program, by default, screens for "adult/sexually oriented" content, for information on "gay/lesbian activities," and for Internet sites "advocating illegal/radical activities." If you do not want CYBERsitter to screen all of these topics, you must deselect the check box for the respective topic.
- **Blocking Options.** CYBERsitter automatically checks Web sites, but you can control whether it blocks material from other Internet sources as well—IRC chat areas, FTP sites, Usenet newsgroups, e-mail—by selecting or deselecting the appropriate boxes here. (See Figure 17.2.)

As mentioned earlier, you can tailor CYBERsitter's blocking choices to fit your own needs. CYBERsitter allows you to block specific Web site and e-mail addresses, as well as words and phrases of your choice. To do this, click the Custom icon on the bottom left of the main CYBERsitter screen. The Custom Sites page opens. Enter the words, phrases, and addresses that you want to block in this window, enclosing each within brackets. (See Figure 17.3.)

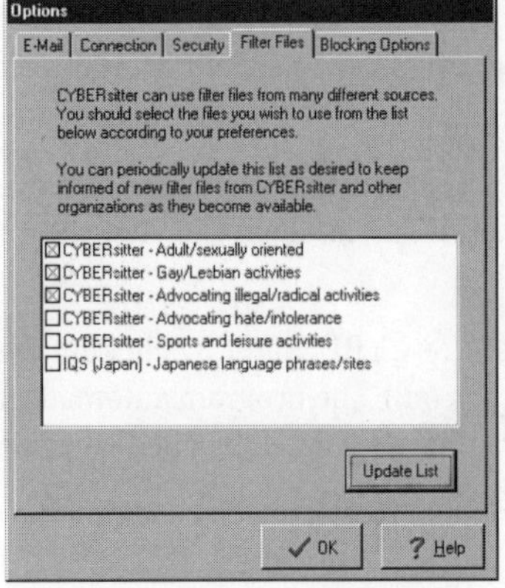

FIG. 17.2
The Options screen, with the Filter Files tab shown.

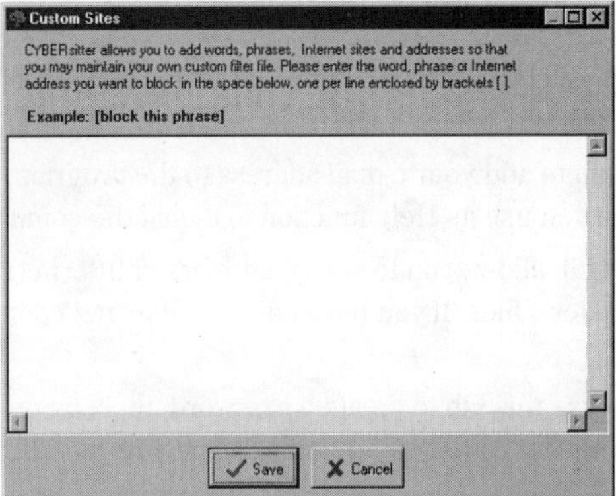

FIG. 17.3
The Custom Sites page.

After you set these preferences for CYBERsitter, you can allow the program to run in the background, where it filters Web content as necessary. Aside from the need to update the program's list of blocked sites occasionally, CYBERsitter is maintenance-free. Pay attention, however, to the way the program interacts with your computer. Content-blocking is in no way a perfect science. Not only does the program often miss sites that you would prefer your children not see, it also blocks sites that may be perfectly harmless. Even a content filter like CYBERsitter ultimately does not absolve you of the parental responsibility to watch over your children. Take some time to view the Internet with your children, and to discuss with them the things you encounter there.

Good Web Sites for Children

Many sites on the Web are made just for kids. These sites are safe, educational, and entertaining. Yahooligans!, for example, is maintained by the same folks who bring you Yahoo!. Open **http://www.yahooligans.com/** in your Web browser to take a look for yourself. It works exactly like the regular Yahoo!, but with links meant just for kids.

You can find many more sites just like this one on the Web. For example:

- Treehouse
  http://www5.zdnet.com/athome/filters/thouse.htm
- GusTown
  http://www.gustown.com/
- Disney's Daily Blast
  http://www.disneyblast.com/

Take some time yourself and look around for more! ●

CHAPTER 18

Enhance Your Web Browser with Plug-Ins

- Learn how to use the multimedia plug-in module
- Learn how to use the VRML plug-in module
- Learn how to use the productivity or business application plug-in module

Although a wide variety of plug-in modules is now available for Netscape and Internet Explorer and more are under development, they all fall roughly into three categories. In this chapter, you will learn about all three types: multimedia, VRML, and productivity or business applications. ■

Installing Plug-Ins for Your Web Browser

Downloading plug-ins couldn't be much easier. Netscape maintains a page that lists many of the currently available plug-ins, with links to the pages from which you can download them. You can find the page at the following address:

http://www.netscape.com/comprod/mirror/navcomponents_download.html

The Plug-Ins Plaza site seems to be even more consistently up-to-date than Netscape's own site. You can find the Plug-Ins Plaza at the following address:

http://www.browserwatch.com

For your convenience, this chapter provides the URL of the download site for each of the plug-ins described.

Before installing a plug-in, you should download the plug-in file into its own temporary directory. You might keep a directory called C:\INSTALL on your hard drive just for this purpose. Then you can download a single plug-in to the INSTALL directory, install the plug-in, then delete the files in C:\INSTALL so that the directory is empty and available for your next installation. (You might make sure that the plug-in is actually installed correctly and working properly before you delete the installation files.)

NOTE The CD-ROM accompanying this book contains numerous Plug-Ins and ActiveX Controls. ■

Each plug-in downloads as a single file. Installation involves one of two procedures:

- If the file is called SETUP.EXE, all you have to do is run it. It will automatically install itself as a plug-in. The installation program might let you specify the directory into which to install the plug-in. Don't change the default unless you already have a directory by that name that contains something else.
- If the file has some obscure name like XX32B4.EXE, it is almost certainly a self-extracting archive. In this case, double-clicking the file in Windows 95 (or opening a DOS shell in Windows 3.1, CDing to the INSTALL directory, and typing the file name) extracts the archive into a whole bunch of files in your INSTALL directory. You then close the DOS window and run the program SETUP.EXE, using the same process described in the preceding prodedure.

In any event, the download page for a plug-in always contains complete instructions on downloading and installation. Read and follow these instructions carefully. Different plug-ins might require different instructions, and you don't want to be caught by surprise.

Determining Which Plug-Ins You Have Installed

Suppose that you have installed several plug-ins and now cannot remember which ones you have and which ones you don't. You installed a nice plug-in for playing an audio, video, or multimedia file, but one plug-in that you installed later seems to have taken over this function, and you don't like that plug-in nearly as much. How can you figure out which plug-ins you have installed, and which ones you still need? Is there any way to get your old plug-in back?

In Netscape 3.0, you need only open the Navigator's Help menu and choose About Plug-Ins. Netscape then displays a nicely formatted table of all the plug-ins that you have installed (see Figure 18.1).

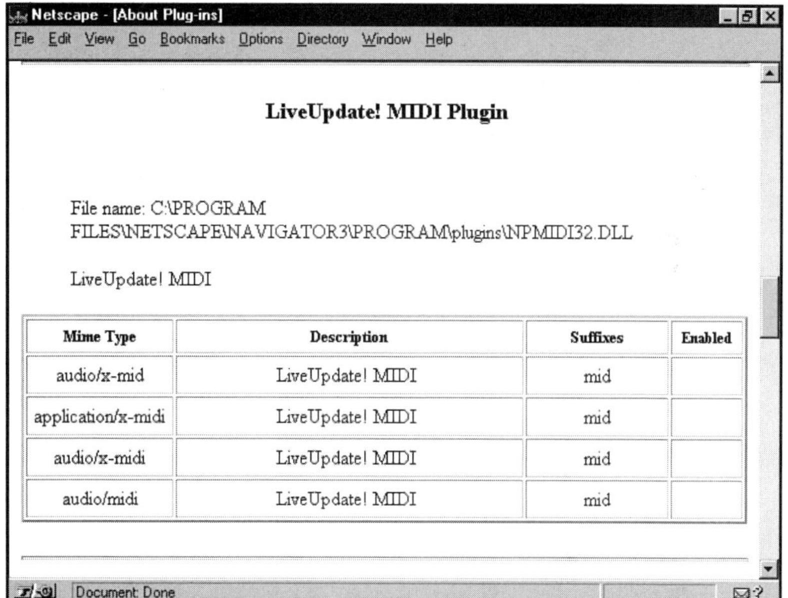

FIG. 18.1
Netscape 3.0 tells you the MIME type, application, and other important information associated with an installed plug-in.

One is the Navigator Help menu's About Plug-Ins command. This command generates a list formatted as follows:

```
File name:
Types:
Description: data
MIME Type: x-world/x-vrml
Suffixes: wrl
etc
```

This output lists the MIME types registered to launch plug-ins. Netscape enters each entry on this list whenever you install a plug-in. Although this list is a good indicator of the file types that launch plug-ins when encountered, the output doesn't tell you exactly which plug-ins the file types will launch.

Running a Plug-In

Running a plug-in is simple; in fact, you don't have to run a plug-in at all. Plug-ins run themselves whenever a Web page or link contains the proper kind of embedded file. You don't have to decide when to run them, and you don't have to figure out how to load the data file.

However, you do have to learn how the controls work. Many of these programs provide on the screen a set of specialized controls for zooming, printing, panning, scrolling, and so on. Each plug-in comes with detailed documentation explaining its specific controls and how they work. (In some cases, you might have to download a separate manual file, or the plug-in's documentation is online in the form of Web pages. Make sure that you get your plug-in's documentation.) Read the documentation so that you know all about a plug-in *before* you encounter any files that it will display. Then you won't have to spend valuable online time trying to figure out your plug-in's behavior.

NOTE Even if you can't install a plug-in for Internet Explorer, all is not lost. Remember, plug-in support is more or less a competitive afterthought for Internet Explorer. Internet Explorer's preferred way of handling innovative Web page content is through ActiveX controls, not plug-ins. The odds are good that, for just about every plug-in, there is an equivalent ActiveX control. In fact, if you are using Internet Explorer exclusively, you probably should stick with ActiveX controls rather than plug-ins where possible. You can download ActiveX controls at **http://www.microsoft.com/activex/controls.**

CAUTION

Don't try to install the NCompass ActiveX plug-in for Internet Explorer. ActiveX support is already built in to Internet Explorer.

Multimedia Plug-Ins

This section lists and describes the sound, graphics, video, animation, and multimedia plug-ins currently being distributed.

Sound

Internet audio is growing like gangbusters. More live audio programs, digitized sound files, and MIDI music files seem to be appearing on the Web each day. With the explosion of plug-ins development in this area, the use of Internet audio is sure to grow even faster in the near future.

In the beginning, the Web was mute. Eventually, some sites began to add a few digitized sounds. To download and play these sounds, you had to use helper applications. Now, several sound plug-ins enable Netscape to play live audio data streams in real time. Audio plug-ins are available for several varieties of digitized sound as well as MIDI music and speech.

LiveAudio Because it ships with Netscape 3.0, the LiveAudio plug-in is essentially the "official" Netscape audio player. Unlike the other audio plug-ins discussed in this chapter, LiveAudio doesn't use a proprietary sound file format, but instead plays standard AIFF, .AU, MIDI, and .WAV files. You can either embed or link sound files in or to a Web page. LiveAudio features an easy-to-use console with play, pause, stop, and volume controls.

RealAudio Progressive Networks' RealAudio plug-in provides live, on-demand, real-time audio over 14.4 kilobytes per second (Kbps) or faster Internet connections. Users with 28.8Kbps or better connections can now hear true FM-quality broadcasting. RealAudio's controls are like those of a CD player—you can pause, rewind, fast-forward, stop, and start play with onscreen buttons.

RealAudio is getting much support on the Internet from diverse sources—from big companies such as the ABC broadcasting network, to small, independent radio stations, to individual users. The plug-in is almost a necessity for browsing the Web. The latest version even has synchronized multimedia playback capabilities.

You also can download the plug-in directly from the RealAudio Web site at the following address:

http://www.realaudio.com/products/ra2.0/

TrueSpeech If nothing else, TrueSpeech is convenient. If you're using Windows 3.1 or Windows 95, the supplied Sound Recorder program can digitize sound files and convert them to TrueSpeech format. You can then use the TrueSpeech player to listen to them on the Web in real time. Despite its name, TrueSpeech can be used for any type of audio file. You don't need a special server. You can download TrueSpeech players for Windows 3.1, Windows 95, Windows NT, Macintosh, and PowerMac from the DSP Group's home page:

http://www.dspg.com

Crescendo and Crescendo Plus Most sound cards go a step beyond merely digitizing and playing back sounds. They also can generate their own sounds. If your sound card is MIDI-compatible (as most are), you have more than a passive record-and-playback system—you have a full-fledged music synthesizer. With a MIDI plug-in, you can experience Web sites with a full music soundtrack.

LiveUpdate's Crescendo plug-in enables Navigator to play inline MIDI music embedded in Web pages. With a MIDI-capable browser, you can create Web pages that have their own background music soundtracks. Because MIDI instruments can be sampled sounds, you can also create sound-effects tracks.

Crescendo is just a 10K self-extracting archive file for Windows 95 and Windows NT, or a 50K file for Windows 3.1. The Windows 95 and Windows NT version is very tiny—you might have to check twice to make sure that you have downloaded it!

You can download Crescendo from the following site:

http://www.liveupdate.com/midi.html

An enhanced version, Crescendo Plus, adds onscreen controls and live streaming (see Figure 18.2). With the live streaming feature, you don't have to wait for a MIDI file to download completely before it starts playing. You can purchase Crescendo Plus also from LiveUpdate's Web site.

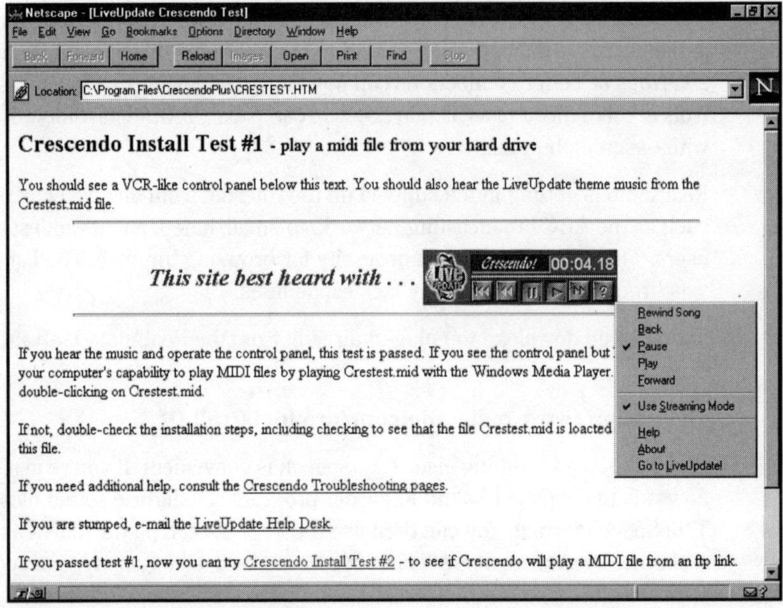

FIG. 18.2
Crescendo Plus features a CD-player style control panel and a convenient pop-up menu.

ToolVox If all you need is speech, three kinds of speech plug-ins are available for Netscape:

- Players for digitized audio that is of less-than-music quality
- Text-to-speech converters, currently available only for the Macintosh
- A speech recognition plug-in, which is also for the Macintosh only

ToolVox provides audio compression ratios of up to 53:1, which creates very small files that transfer quickly over the Internet. Speech can be delivered in real time even over 9,600-baud modems. One unique feature is that you can slow down playback to improve comprehension, or speed it up to shorten listening times without changing voice pitch.

Like the higher-fidelity RealAudio, ToolVox streams audio in real time, so you don't have to wait for a file to download before you can listen to it.

ToolVox Navigator plug-ins are available for Windows 3.1 and Windows 95. Voxware also promises Macintosh and PowerMac versions. You can download these plug-ins from the Voxware site:

http://www.voxware.com/download.htm

EchoSpeech EchoSpeech compresses speech at a ratio of 18.5:1. Therefore, 16-bit speech sampled at 11,025Hz is compressed to 9,600bps. Even users with 14.4Kbps modems can listen to real-time EchoSpeech audio streams. Because EchoSpeech is designed to code speech sampled at 1,1025Hz rather than 8,000Hz, EchoSpeech files sound better than ToolVox.

EchoSpeech is available for Windows 3.1 and Windows 95, and a Macintosh version is promised. You can get EchoSpeech from the following address:

http://www.echospeech.com

Graphics

Although Netscape Navigator displays inline GIF and JPEG images just fine, there's more to graphics than those two file formats. Besides knowing nothing about other bitmap formats such as TIFF and PNG, Navigator is completely ignorant of vector graphics formats like Computer Graphics Metafiles (CGM) and Corel's CMX. Graphics plug-ins fill that void. The real-time demands of the Internet are also pushing graphics compression to the limit, with new high-tech encoders coming out all the time. Netscape plug-ins can handle some of the latest compression techniques.

FIGleaf Inline Bitmaps are the canvas of computer graphics. Every image that you see on your screen is a bitmap, a collection of colorful, lit pixels in a grid. Computers usually also store screen images in bitmap format. This format is, after all, the easiest way to store images, because of the one-to-one relationship between the pixels in the picture and the pixels on the screen. Netscape can handle GIF and JPEG bitmap images all by itself, but they are far from the full range of bitmap formats. Dozens—perhaps hundreds—of different bitmap formats are available on the Web. To view them, you must install the appropriate Netscape plug-ins.

Carberry Technology's FIGleaf Inline plug-in enables you to zoom, pan, and scroll both vector (CGM format) and bitmap graphics, including GIF, JPEG, TIFF, CCITT GP4, .BMP, WMF, Sun Raster, PNG, and other graphics file formats. The plug-in even handles Encapsulated PostScript (EPS) files, as well as the new proposed standard PGM and PBM file types. FIGleaf Inline can even improve the display of your GIFs and JPEGs.

The plug-in can rotate all images to 0, 90, 180, or 270 degrees, and can display multipage files. Scrollbars are available when you zoom in on an image or when the image is too large to display within the default window (see Figure 18.3).

Figure 18.3 shows the FIGleaf Inline version for Windows 95. Carberry also plans to release Macintosh and Windows 3.1 versions. The self-extracting archive is big—1.5M including sample files—but in one fell swoop the plug-in practically eliminates the need for other Netscape graphics plug-ins or helper applications. If the file size disturbs you, a smaller version, FIGleaf Inline Lite, is also available.

FIGleaf Inline is available for free evaluation at the following site:

http://www.ct.ebt.com/figinline/download.html

ViewDirector The ViewDirector Imaging plug-in from TMS displays black-and-white, grayscale, and color raster images in TIFF (uncompressed, modified Huffman, G3 1&2D, and G4), CALS Type 1, JPEG, .PCX/.DCX, .BMP, and other image formats. With ViewDirector, you can zoom, pan, and rotate images embedded in Web pages. ViewDirector even enables you to enhance image quality by turning on scale-to-gray and color-smoothing functions. A professional version adds the capability to view multipage images, magnify them, and more. You can download ViewDirector, which is available for Windows 95 and Windows NT, from the following address:

http://www.tmsinc.com

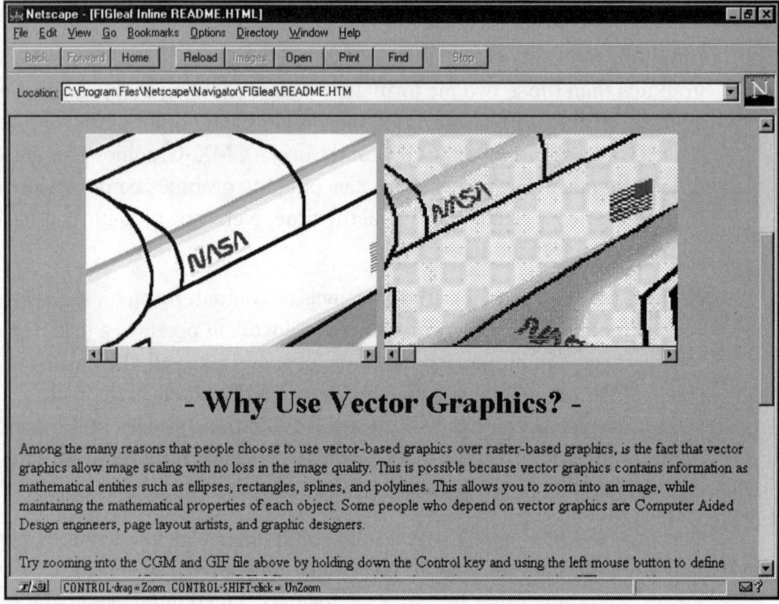

FIG. 18.3 This tight zoom on two graphics being displayed inline by the FIGleaf plug-in demonstrates the superiority of CGM vector graphics (left) versus GIF bitmap graphics (right).

AutoDesk's WHIP! Most architects, engineers, and designers create their masterworks in AutoCAD, the *de facto* standard computer-aided drafting (CAD) program. Just about every modern manufactured object or constructed edifice that you encounter started out somewhere as an AutoCAD drawing. With the rise of the corporate intranet, there is increased interest in making these drawings available for viewing in Web browsers. Thanks to a handful of Netscape plug-ins, achieving this objective is now possible.

Although AutoDesk, the publisher of AutoCAD, was not the first developer to produce a Netscape plug-in for viewing two-dimensional (2-D) AutoCAD drawings on the Web, AutoDesk's plug-in is almost certain to end up being the most popular. AutoDesk based its WHIP! plug-in on the same rendering technology as the WHIP! driver in AutoCAD Release 13. This technology allows for panning, zooming, and embedding URLs in AutoCAD drawings.

WHIP! uses a new DWF (Drawing Web Format) file type, which future versions of AutoCAD will support. Although WHIP! doesn't view current DXF AutoCAD files, the new file type is highly compressed and optimized for fast transfer over the Internet. Although it will take time for existing AutoCAD files to be converted to the new format, AutoDesk's promotion of WHIP! should make the plug-in very popular very quickly.

You can download WHIP! from AutoDesk's Web site:

http://www.autodesk.com/

DWG/DXF Viewer SoftSource's DWG/DXF plug-in is the first Netscape plug-in to enable users to view AutoCAD and DXF drawings on the Web (see Figure 18.4). Zoom, pan, and layer visibility controls make it simple to explore complex CAD drawings online. DWG/DXF Viewer's advantage over WHIP! is that it can view standard AutoCAD DXF or DWG format drawing files. Therefore, you don't have to translate existing libraries of AutoCAD drawings before you can view them.

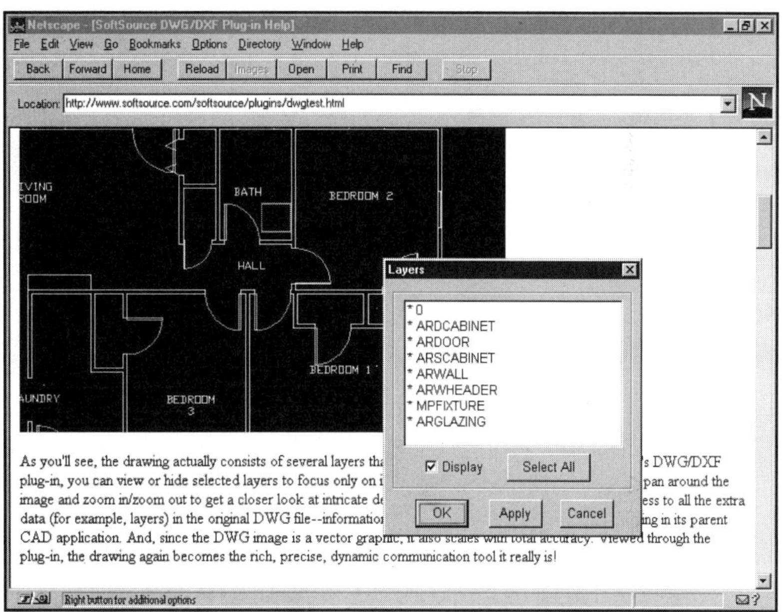

FIG. 18.4
SoftSource's DWG/DXF plug-in makes viewing AutoCAD format drawings an online activity.

You can download DWG/DXF, which is available for Windows 95 and Windows NT, from the following site:

http://www.softsource.com/softsource/plugins/plugins.html

NOTE European users might particularly want to check out NetSlide 95 by Alessandro Oddera, an AutoCAD file plug-in for Windows 95. NetSlide 95 is available at the following site:

http://www.prog.arch.unige.it/~aoddera/Homeao.htm

Corel CMX The problem with bitmaps is that they're chunky. Because they consist of square pixels arranged in a grid, bitmaps aren't really scalable. Where a bitmap is an actual map of a picture, a vector graphics file is more of a description of how to draw a picture. A vector graphics file tells a drawing program how to use lines, curves, fill patterns, rectangles, and other elements to re-create an image. The size at which the program draws the image is an entirely different question. For this reason, vector graphics can be rescaled to any size and retain their good looks, without losing detail.

Many vector graphics formats are available, and with the following plug-ins, Netscape can display quite a few of the formats.

CorelDRAW! is perhaps the most popular vector-graphics creation program for both the PC and the Macintosh. Corel's CMX Viewer plug-in for Navigator 3.0 enables you to view Corel CMX vector graphics in Web pages inline (see Figure 18.5).

FIG. 18.5 Corel's CMX vector graphics viewer enables you to view smooth Corel format vector graphics images inline in Navigator.

There are no special controls or considerations with the CMX Viewer—when installed, the plug-in simply displays CMX images when they are encountered. You'll enjoy watching CMX Viewer draw the pieces of the image onscreen in real time, instead of opening like a window shade as bitmap graphics do.

You can download the Corel CMX Viewer from the following site:

http://www.corel.com/corelcmx/

Other Vector Graphics Viewers SoftSource, the creator of the DWG/DXF AutoCAD plug-in, also has its own vector graphics drawing program. The Simple Vector Format (SVF) plug-in for Netscape Navigator enables you to view vector graphics on the Web. SVF uses an officially registered MIME type and features single-download navigational capabilities and scalable vector graphics. You can pan and zoom an SVF image, and hide and display layers. SVF works similarly to SoftSource's DWG/DXF plug-in. The SVF plug-in also enables you to include HTML hyperlinks (either URLs or textual annotations) in an SVF file. The plug-in is part of SoftSource's Vdraft (Virtual Drafter) suite of Internet CAD tools. You can download both Windows 3.1 and Windows 95 versions of the SVF plug-in from the following address:

http://www.softsource.com

You can create CGMs for use by a wide variety of programs; they're an industry standard. InterCAP Graphics Systems' InterCAP InLine plug-in is an online adaptation of the company's MetaLink RunTime CGM viewer. With InterCAP InLine, you can view, zoom, pan, and magnify an image. Animation of intelligent, hyperlinked CGM graphics is also possible. A Windows 95 and Windows NT version is available at the following site:

http://www.intergraph.com/icap/

FutureSplash's CelAnimator is software for creating vector-based drawings and animations for multimedia and Web pages. You can use CelAnimator to create static or fully animated cartoons, logos, technical drawings, and interactive buttons. You can export these animations as FutureSplash, animated GIF, Windows .AVI, or QuickTime files. From FutureSplash's Web site you can download a free trial version of CelAnimator for Macintosh or Windows 95 and Windows NT. Although not a plug-in, CelAnimator enables you to use animated GIF, .AVI, and QuickTime files with other plug-ins.

The FutureSplash plug-in for Netscape (available for Macintosh and Windows 3.1, Windows 95, and Windows NT) enables you to view FutureSplash format animations as well. These animations are vector-based, and thus zoomable and scalable.

This plug-in is a truly unique product. With the plug-in, you can even display FutureSplash animations as they download, which enables you to begin playing long animation sequences immediately. The plug-in even supports scalable outline fonts and antialiasing to eliminate jagged edges. Interactive buttons enable you to get URLs and play animations. The plug-in is small (90–150K uncompressed). FutureSplash plans to release UNIX and Java versions.

All versions of the plug-in and CelAnimator are available from the following site:

http://www.futurewave.com/

Lightning Strike Graphics files can take up multimegabytes of hard disk space in no time, and seem to take an eternity to load over the Web. JPEG images are better than most graphics files, compressing some images dozens of times smaller than they started. But JPEG has its limitations, and the bandwidth demands of Web browsing have people searching for even better solutions. At least three Netscape plug-ins improve transfer times for graphics considerably.

Infinet Op's Lightning Strike plug-in competes directly with JPEG image compression. Images compressed with Lightning Strike have higher compression ratios, smaller image files, faster transmissions, and improved image quality.

JPEG uses a method based on Fourier analysis, such as discrete cosine transform (DCT). Infinet Op, however, uses a form of the wavelet transform. Lightning Strike images look as good as JPEG images and transfer quickly. It's difficult to predict whether Lightning Strike will gain a following. However, if you are into graphics, you'll definitely want to install Lightning Strike and take a look at some of the sample compressed images on Infinet Op's site. They're awesome.

Infinet Op's plug-ins for Macintosh, Windows 3.1, Windows 95, and Windows NT are available at the following site:

http://www.infinop.com/html/extvwr_pick.html

FIF Viewer Iterated Systems' FIF (Fractal Image Format) viewer plug-in for Navigator displays fractally compressed images inline in the Netscape window. FIF images are smaller and load faster than JPEGs, and you can scale and zoom FIF images on the page. One typical 768-by-512 image in the Iterated Systems gallery compressed from 1.15M to only 47K with remarkable fidelity.

The FIF plug-in is available for Windows 3.1, Windows 95, Windows NT, and Macintosh platforms. You can download the FIF Viewer plug-in from the following address:

http://www.iterated.com/cnplugin.htm

Summus Wavelet Viewer Summus' Wavelet Viewer is another plug-in for decompressing images inline that were compressed with Summus' proprietary wavelet technology.

Versions of this plug-in are currently available for Windows 3.1, Windows 95, and Windows NT at the following site:

ftp://ftp.scsn.net/software/summus/

Special Graphics Formats Sometimes a "standard" graphics format is just not good enough. When you need a graphic to do something special, you turn to proprietary formats.

For example, Freehand is the major competitor to CorelDRAW! as the top illustration program. If your studio or company uses Freehand, you'll be glad to know that Macromedia's Shockwave for Freehand plug-in enables you to put your Freehand drawings on the Web or on your company intranet. (Don't let the name confuse you; Macromedia has given *all* its plug-ins the name Shockwave. The first plug-in was for Macromedia Director; this one is for Freehand.)

The Shockwave for Freehand plug-in enables users to view compact 24-bit vector graphics with panning and zooming up to 25,600 percent. These graphics can contain irregularly shaped hot objects that link to other Web pages.

Delivering Freehand content on the Web actually involves three modules: the Shockwave for Freehand plug-in for Netscape; the Shockwave Afterburner Xtra module, which is installed into the Freehand drawing program to compress Freehand images up to 50 percent for distribution on the Web; and the Shockwave URL Managers, which enable the designer to add URL references to hot spots on drawings. Windows 3.1, Windows 95, Windows NT, and Macintosh versions are available at the following site:

http://www.macromedia.com/Tools/Shockwave/Info/index.html

Although its end result is a graphic image, the Chemscape Chime plug-in from MDL Information Systems is more of a scientific and chemical engineering tool than a graphics plug-in. MDL Information Systems supplies chemical information-management solutions to the pharmaceutical, agrochemical, and chemical industries. The plug-in enables scientists and engineers to display "chemically significant" (that is, scientifically accurate) 2-D and 3-D structures within an HTML page or table. You can download Windows 3.1, Windows 95, Windows NT, Macintosh, and PowerMac versions from the following site:

http://www.mdli.com/chemscape/chime/download.html

Micrografx's QuickSilver is a highly popular business graphics tool. Micrografx now offers the ABC QuickSilver plug-in for Netscape. This plug-in makes QuickSilver files usable over the Web or corporate intranets. You create these vector images with ABC Graphics Suite, which can move drawings, display messages, or link to URLs. The plug-in uses a 32-bit vector graphics rendering engine for fast display. You can download the Windows 95 and Windows NT version of the plug-in at the following address:

http://www.micrografx.com/download/qsdl.html

Johnson-Grace's ART Press program creates ART image format files, which you can view online using Johnson-Grace's ART Press plug-in. The plug-in is available from the following site:

http://www.jgc.com/aip/artpub.html

America Online's TurboWeb browser already uses ART compression. Johnson-Grace claims that ART Press images download and display three times faster than GIF and JPEG images.

Lari Software's Vertigo displays pictures in GX format, which you can create by using LightningDraw GX or any other application that saves files in GX format. This plug-in performs automatic smoothing (antialiasing) and enables you to animate pictures using HTML tag spin, stretch, move, loop, and time attributes. You can download PowerPC and Macintosh versions from the following address:

http://www.larisoftware.com/Products/WebPlugin.html

WebXpresso displays 2-D and 3-D drawings, graphs, and controls. It supports real-time interaction and continuous or periodic updating from a server data stream. In addition, WebXpresso controls objects that can return data to the server. The WebXpresso Drawing Editor creates arbitrary 2-D and 3-D object hierarchies. Java Native Methods enable the client-side to manipulate graphics. Download WebXpresso and view the sample pages. For Windows 95, Windows NT, and UNIX, WebXpresso is available from the following site:

http://www.dvcorp.com

Plastic Thought's Web-Active displays dynamic 3-D images that you can rotate and tumble onscreen. You can download sample Web virtual reality (VR) files and plug-ins for Macintosh and PowerMac from the following site:

http://www.3d-active.com

You can get WebActive 3D (which promises a Windows version) at the following address:

http://www.3d-Active.com/pages/WebUtilities.html

You can create QuickTime VR scenes from photographs, video stills, or computer renderings. Most scenes consist of a series of photographs taken at 30-degree increments while turning the camera in a full circle. These photos are organized into a panorama and combined with multiframe photos of real objects taken at a variety of angles. This technology creates scenes that are quite realistic. You can find out more about the technology from Apple's Web site:

http://qtvr.quicktime.apple.com/

Video

Video plug-ins enable Netscape Navigator to play inline videos in real time. With the right plug-in, you can play Video for Windows, QuickTime, and MPEG movies.

Video for Windows Plug-Ins Video for Windows is the standard for PC platforms. Several programs and video boards can create .AVI format animations or digitized scenes. With the following plug-ins, you can deliver such video as Web page content in Netscape.

LiveVideo Netscape's official plug-in for .AVI video is LiveVideo, which is included with the Netscape distribution. LiveVideo automatically installs and configures as your Video for Windows player of choice. You click a movie image to play the plug-in, and click again to stop it. Right-clicking an image pops up a complete menu of controls, including Play, Pause, Rewind, Fast Forward, Frame Back, and Frame Forward. If you failed to receive this plug-in with Netscape, you can download it by following the links from Netscape's home page:

http://www.netscape.com

VDOLive The VDOLive plug-in for Netscape enables you to include specially compressed inline Video for Windows (.AVI) clips in HTML pages, and play back the clip in real time (see Figure 18.6).

If you are operating over a slow connection, VDOLive intelligently downloads a video file and skips over enough information to retain real-time playback. In cases of severe bandwidth shortage (such as 14.4Kbps PPP connections), you get a low frame rate (approximately one frame every one to three seconds) but can still view videos. In other cases, the VDOLive Player and the VDOLive Server try to converge at the best possible bandwidth, which sometimes might result in a blurry display or low frame rate. Although this technique can also result in jerky playback (especially over a slow modem SLIP or PPP connection), it sure speeds up video over the Web!

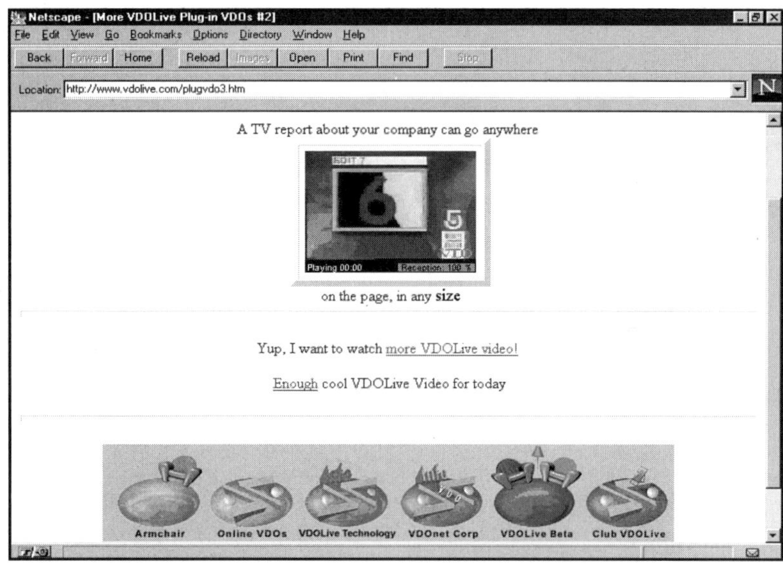

FIG. 18.6
VDOLive displays video files inline and can deliver reasonable performance over even a very slow Internet connection.

Autostart, Stretch, Width, and Height options enable HTML designers to customize inline Web page video for just about any purpose.

To deliver motion video from your Web server, you need the VDOLive Personal Server. The VDOLive Personal Server and Tools 1.0 enable you to deliver as many as two streams of video, to capture, compress, and serve as much as one minute of video and audio, and to scale connections as long as 256Kbps.

VDOLive is available for Windows 3.1, Windows 95, and Windows NT from VDONet's site:

http://www.vdolive.com/download/

CoolFusion Iterated Systems' CoolFusion is a plug-in for Navigator that plays inline Video for Windows (.AVI) movies. Using the plug-in, you can view videos of any size, including full screen. CoolFusion offers a full set of controls for stopping, replaying, and saving the videos.

One self-extracting archive, CF_B6_32.EXE, is for Windows 95 or Windows NT. This archive requires only a 256-color graphics card, although a 24-bit or high-color graphics adapter is recommended. You also need at least 8M of RAM.

Other .AVI Video Plug-Ins Developed as a joint venture between the University of Illinois and Digital Video Communications, Vosaic, or Video Mosaic, is another inline video plug-in. Versions are available for both Netscape and Spyglass Mosaic. Features include the capability to embed hyperlinks within the video stream, and to access other documents by clicking moving objects in the video stream.

The VivoActive Player is a streaming .AVI video plug-in that uses Video for Windows .AVI files compressed up to 250:1 into a new .VIV file format. You can transmit .VIV files using the standard HTTP protocol, and thus don't need special server software to use them on your Web pages. The VivoActive Player plug-in is available for Windows 95 and Windows NT from the following site:

http://www.vivo.com

QuickTime Plug-Ins Where Microsoft's standard video format is Video for Windows (.AVI files), Apple's video standard is QuickTime. Because many creative people use the Macintosh, many QuickTime movies are available on the Web.

Apple (**http://www.apple.com**) has had a QuickTime movie player plug-in for Netscape in the works for some time, although the plug-in still wasn't available as this book was being written. However, quite a few third-party plug-ins are available that can play QuickTime movies in Netscape.

Knowledge Engineering's MacZilla is a Macintosh-only Navigator plug-in. MacZilla is a sort of Swiss Army knife of plug-ins. Besides QuickTime movies, MacZilla plays or displays MIDI background music; .WAV, .AU, and AIFF audio; and MPEG and .AVI movies. Using its own plug-in component architecture, MacZilla can extend and update itself over the Internet with the click of a button. You even get a built-in MacZilla game! You can download MacZilla from Knowledge Engineering's site:

http://maczilla.com

MovieStar by Intelligence at Large is less ambitious—it's only for QuickTime movie playback. Using MovieStar Maker, a multimedia editing application also available for downloading, Webmasters can optimize QuickTime movies so that Navigator users can view them as they download. You can also use autoplay, looping, and many other settings. This plug-in is available for Windows 3.1, Windows 95, and Macintosh from the following site:

http://www.beingthere.com/

MPEG Plug-Ins MPEG is currently the bright and shining star of multimedia. The MPEG2 movie compression standard is destined to provide full-screen, full-motion movies on a highly compressed CD-ROM, among other things. Because of its high compression ratios, MPEG is also a good choice for delivering movies over the Internet.

MPEG works best with a video board capable of doing hardware decompression. But even running in software on fast Pentium systems, MPEG shows promise.

At least four Netscape plug-ins are available for playing inline MPEG videos.

Open2U's Action MPEG player plug-in can also play included synchronized soundtracks, or sound-only files compressed with MPEG. Action doesn't require special hardware or even a special Web server. You can download Windows 95 and Windows NT versions for trial from the following site:

http://www.open2u.com/action/action.html

InterVU's PreVU plug-in also plays streaming MPEG video without specialized MPEG hardware or a proprietary video server. This plug-in gives you a first-frame view inline, streaming viewing while downloading, and full-speed cached playback from your hard drive. PreVU requires a 486 or Pentium processor. Windows 95, Windows NT, and Macintosh versions are available. You can download PreVU from the following site:

http://www.intervu.com/download.html

Xing, well-known for its MPEG applications, will be providing a Navigator plug-in to support live-streaming MPEG and low bit rate (LBR) audio and full-motion MPEG video from Xing StreamWorks Web servers. Check out Xing's Web site for availability information:

http://www.xingtech.com

Animation

Pictures that move—that wonderful concept has brought millions of children (and adults who hold onto their childlike wonder) untold hours of entertainment and enjoyment. When computers got powerful enough, animation made the move to the computer. With the advent of powerful animation-player plug-ins for Netscape, animation is making the transition to the World Wide Web and even to corporate intranets.

Sizzler Totally Hip Software's Sizzler plug-in and companion converter program enable you to create and display Web animation. The Sizzler converter (currently available only in a version for the Macintosh) converts .PIC files or QuickTime movies into sprite files that Navigator can play in real time.

Totally Hip's core technology (Object Scenario) allows for streamed delivery of several media types, including text, animation, video, sound, and interactivity. The company plans to add all these features to Sizzler soon.

The Sizzler plug-in is available as a free download for Windows 3.1, Windows 95, Windows NT, and the Macintosh, from the Totally Hip site:

http://www.totallyhip.com/tools/Win/2f_tools.html

Emblaze GEO Interactive Media Group's Emblaze plug-in is a real-time animation player. It plays a proprietary animation format that GEO says requires only 3M to 4M of disk space for approximately 30 minutes of play time. The animations can display at a rate of 12 to 24 frames per second in 256 colors in real time over a 14.4Kbps connection. You must create the animations with the commercial Emblaze Creator program.

You can obtain Windows 3.1, Windows 95, Macintosh, and PowerMac versions at the following address:

http://www.Geo.Inter.net/technology/emblaze/index.html

Other Animation Plug-Ins Two more animation plug-ins for Netscape are noteworthy: Web Animator and Play3D.

Deltapoint's Web Animator is for the Macintosh only (although Deltapoint plans to release a Windows version). This plug-in combines animation, sound, and live interaction. The authoring tool for creating animations to add to your own site is also available from Deltapoint's Web site:

http://www.deltapoint.com/animate/index.htm

Heads Off's Play3D plug-in supports real-time, interactive 3-D and 2-D sprites, and .WAV and MIDI sound playback. With this plug-in, you can link objects to URLs, media files, or Play3D "scene" files. The free demo version enables you to author and play back files without leaving Netscape. You can download Play3D, which is for Windows 95 only, from the following site:

http://www.headsoff.com

Multimedia

Multimedia is a good buzzword, but what does it really mean? The term literally translates as *more than one medium,* but when most people use the term to refer to a presentation that includes some combination of sound, graphics, animation, video, and even interactivity. Interactivity is an important part of multimedia. It's the part that puts the flow of the whole presentation under the user's control. Although this control can be as simple as an onscreen button that the user clicks to move to the next slide, more often the user has to make selections from multiple choices.

Multimedia currently is the hottest topic on the Web, so it's not surprising that a dozen or more multimedia player plug-ins are already available for Netscape.

Shockwave for Macromedia Director Perhaps one of the most significant and awe-inspiring plug-ins that Netscape supports directly is Macromedia Shockwave for Director (see Figure 18.7). With this plug-in, you can view Director movies directly on a Web page. (Don't confuse Director "movies" with other file types of the same name, such as QuickTime movies.) To create Director movies, you use Macromedia's Director, a cross-platform multimedia authoring program that enables multimedia developers to create fully interactive multimedia applications or titles. Because of its interactive integration of animation, bitmap, video, and sound media, and its playback compatibility with a variety of computer platforms including Windows, Macintosh, OS/2, and SGI, Director is now the most widely used professional multimedia authoring tool.

A Director movie running over the Internet can support the same sort of features as a Director movie running off a CD-ROM, including animated sequences, sophisticated scripting of interactivity, user input of text right into the Director window (or "stage"), sound playback, and much more. Developers can even include hot links through URLs.

FIG. 18.7 The Shockwave for Director plug-in for Netscape plays interactive multimedia Director files inline in the Netscape window. These can range from simple animations to complex interactive games, like this "concentration" game from the *Toy Story* Web site.

Shockwave for Director consists of two main components: the Shockwave plug-in itself, and Shockwave Afterburner, a compressor program that squeezes a Director file by 40 to 50 percent for faster access over the Internet. You can download the plug-in from Macromedia's site:

http://www-1.macromedia.com/Tools/Shockwave/Plugin/plugin.cgi

Shockwave for Authorware Another in Macromedia's series of Shockwave plug-ins, the Shockwave for Authorware plug-in enables users to interact with Authorware interactive multimedia "courses" and "pieces" within the Netscape Navigator window. With Shockwave for Authorware, you can integrate animation, clickable buttons, links to other Web pages, hybrid layout and delivery, streaming .PICs, movies, sound, and more into a piece to deliver an interactive multimedia experience.

Intended for the delivery of large, content-rich multimedia presentations such as courseware and training materials, Authorware can also write viewer data back to a Web server using the File Transfer Protocol (FTP), so the plug-in is useful for creating market surveys, tests and quizzes, and customer service applications.

Like all Shockwave plug-ins, Authorware includes an Afterburner module. You can use this module to compress files for delivery on the Web. Authorware developers package their multimedia pieces without Runtime Project (which Macromedia usually includes with its Shockware products), then drag and drop this file onto the Authorware Afterburner program. Afterburner compresses the Authorware file by 50 to 70 percent and creates one map file and multiple segment files. Developers can optimize the number and size of segment files to the bandwidth of the network. You can also create a single map file referencing both Macintosh and Windows segment files for display in the same Web page, making platform-specific segments transparent to the viewer.

You can download Windows 3.1, Windows 95, Windows NT, and Macintosh versions of Shockwave for Authorware from the Macromedia Web site:

http://www.macromedia.com/Tools/Shockwave/Info/index.html

ASAP WebShow Software Publishing Corporation's ASAP WebShow is a Netscape Navigator 2.0 plug-in presentation viewer for viewing, downloading, and printing presentations created with ASAP WordPower. Similar to PowerPoint presentations, WordPower presentations can contain tables, organization charts, bulleted lists, and other graphics and text elements, in a slide show format. Because the files are compressed, you can transmit them quite quickly over the Internet.

You can embed presentations and reports as icons, as live thumbnails, or in a window on a Web page. Users can view each slide in a small, live window, enlarged to fill the current Web page or zoomed to full screen. You can select one slide at a time or watch a continuously running show.

A Windows 95 and Windows NT version is available, and Software Publishing Corporation also plans to offer a Windows 3.1 version. For a free 30-day trial for creating your own WebShow-compatible presentations, you can download a fully functional copy of ASAP 1.0 or ASAP WordPower 1.95 from the following site:

http://www.spco.com/asap/asapwebs.htm

Astound Web Player Gold Disk's Astound Web Player displays multimedia "greeting cards" and other interactive documents created with Gold Disk's Astound or Studio M programs. These presentations can include sound, animation, graphics, video, and even interactive elements.

Version 1.0 of the Astound Web Player is for Windows 95 and Navigator 2.0. Versions are also available for Windows 3.1 and for Navigator 1.1. You can even get a stand-alone version for use with browsers other than Netscape.

If you already own Studio M or Astound, you can download a "slim" version of the player that omits the chart, texture, and animation libraries. If you plan to include movies in your presentations, you need QuickTime for Windows, which is also available from the Gold Disk site.

With the Astound Web Player, you can actively view one multimedia slide while the plug-in downloads the next slide in the background. However, the main appeal of Studio M and Astound is that they enable nonprogrammers to create multimedia presentations by using predesigned templates that integrate animation, graphics, sound, and interactive elements. If you think that multimedia might be too difficult to integrate into your site, you might want to check the specifications for Studio M and Astound on Gold Disk's site:

http://www.golddisk.com/awp/index.html

Other Multimedia Plug-Ins Although the preceding four plug-ins are arguably the hottest multimedia plug-ins for Netscape, this section describes a few more to keep you busy.

The mBED plug-in for Netscape plays multimedia "mbedlets." The .MBD file format and the built-in mBED players are open and license-free. mBED is available for Windows 3.1,

Windows 95, Windows NT, Macintosh, and PowerMac. You can download mBED and find more information about the plug-in from the following site:

http://www.mbed.com

RAD Technologies offers RAD PowerMedia, a plug-in that plays back multimedia applications. Designed for corporate communicators and Web designers, the RAD PowerMedia plug-in provides authoring and viewing of interactive content, presentations, training, kiosks, and demos. This plug-in is available for Windows 95 and Windows NT at the following address:

http://www.rad.com

Asymetrix's ToolBook is one of the top multimedia authoring tools. With Asymetrix's new Neuron plug-in for Netscape, you can deliver ToolBook multimedia titles over the Internet. The Neuron plug-in supports external multimedia files so that you can access, in real time, either complete courseware or multimedia titles, or just the relevant portions of titles. Content does not download unless you request it, saving you download time and making the application more responsive. Check the following site for more information and the download files:

http://www.asymetrix.com/

The mFactory Netscape plug-in promises streamed playback of and communication between fully interactive multimedia worlds embedded in Web pages. mFactory supports the following file formats: for video, QuickTime, QTVR, and Video for Windows (.AVI); for graphics, PICT; for text, dynamic and editable text; for audio and sound, AIFF, SND, and MIDI; for animation, PICT, .PIC, and QuickTime. Their cel-based proprietary mToon animation format enables you to define and play ranges of cels. To find out information about downloading and more, check the following site:

http://www.mfactory.com/

7th Level offers Top Gun, a multimedia and animation authoring and playback engine for Windows 95. A Macintosh version is planned. You can read all about the plug-in at 7th Level's site:

http://www.7thlevel.com

This site is 7th Level's prototype for an Internet-based educational cartoon network.

Powersoft's media.splash plug-in for Windows 3.1 and Windows 95 resides at the following address:

http://www.powersoft.com/media.splash/product/index.html

The SCREAM inline multimedia player is for Windows 3.1, Windows 95, and Macintosh. You can find it at the following site:

http://www.savedbytech.com/sbt/Plug_In.html

Kaleida Labs also plans to offer a multimedia player plug-in for Navigator. The developer of ScriptX, an object-oriented programming language for multimedia, Kaleida currently offers a free, platform-independent Kaleida Media Player (KMP) for playback of ScriptX applications.

You can configure the player as a helper application. To find out when you can get Kaleida's plug-in, check the following site:

http://www.kaleida.com

VRML Plug-Ins

VRML (Virtual Reality Modeling Language) promises to deliver real-time virtual 3-D worlds over the Web. Although it's arguable whether this objective has actually been accomplished yet, VRML's promise looms great. VRML plug-ins bring 3-D worlds right into the Navigator window.

Live3D

Silicon Graphics and Sony have developed Moving Worlds as a proposed extension to the VRML specification. Netscape and many other online developers, including heavy-hitters like Adobe and IBM, are hoping that Moving Worlds will become the VRML 2.0 standard.

Moving Worlds goes beyond the current VRML standard to include Java and JavaScript integration and support for third-party plug-ins. This integration and support enables developers to incorporate live content, such as video and RealAudio, into 3-D VRML worlds. A key new element is the ability to link to databases.

The Moving Worlds specification allows 3-D data sets to be scaleable for viewing on a variety of computer systems ranging from low-cost Internet PCs to powerful 3-D graphics workstations. You can use integrated Java applets to create motion and enable interactivity.

Advocates claim that the Moving Worlds version of VRML will finally make possible the development of real "cyberspace" applications, such as 3-D shopping malls, collaborative 3-D design, 3-D visual database and spreadsheet display, 3-D interactive real-time online games, and photorealistic geographic landscapes.

Silicon Graphics will make the source code for Moving Worlds application development available to all developers.

Netscape's Live3D Navigator plug-in is a VRML viewer that implements the proposed Moving Worlds VRML extensions. The plug-in is feature-packed, fun, and—best of all—Netscape's official VRML browser. Live3D comes bundled with Navigator 3.0 and installs automatically when you install Netscape 3.0. If you missed installing Live3D somehow, you can download it from the following site:

http://www.netscape.com/comprod/products/navigator/live3d/index.html

VR Scout

Chaco Communications' VR Scout VRML plug-in displays VRML worlds inline. Chaco's viewer implements the full VRML 1.0 standard.

VR Scout uses Microsoft Reality Lab for fast software rendering and hardware acceleration. The plug-in is multithreading, so different aspects of a scene download simultaneously. Toys include a headlight with a brightness control, and Walk/Fly/Examiner viewing modes with a heads-up toolbar. VR Scout also supports textures (GIF, JPEG, .BMP, and SFImage).

The VR Scout 1.22 plug-in is for Windows 95 and Windows NT, and its size is 2.96M. Windows 3.1 users can download a stand-alone viewer to use as a Netscape helper application. You can download VR Scout from the following site:

http://www.chaco.com/vrscout/plugin.html

Other VRML Browser Plug-Ins

Although there are more VRML plug-ins than any other type, most VRML plug-ins are fairly similar. Still, some offer a few special features. Choosing the best VRML browser (like choosing the best Web browser) is pretty much a matter of personal preference. This section lists some other VRML browser plug-ins that you might want to check out.

With SuperScape's Viscape, you can grab objects, do walkthroughs, and hear sounds in VRML worlds. Viscape is available for Windows 95 and Windows NT at the following site:

http://www.superscape.com

Integrated Data Systems' VRealm VRML plug-in also adds some features to VRML worlds, like object behaviors, gravity, collision detection, autopilot, and multimedia support. You can download VRealm, which is available for Windows 95 and Windows NT, from the following site:

http://www.ids-net.com/ids/downldpi.html

Topper supports VRML extensions for dynamic 3-D interactive worlds with keyframe animations and proximity triggers. The plug-in also supports the 3DS and DXF file formats. Windows 95 and Windows NT users can download Topper from the following site:

http://www.ktx.com/products/hyperwire/download.htm

Template Graphics Software adapted its WebSpace/VRML plug-in from Silicon Graphics' VRML browser. WebSpace supports the complete Open Inventor 2.x feature set plus the VRML 1.0 subset. You can download WebSpace, which is available for the Windows platform, from the following site:

http://www.sd.tgs.com/~template

Express VR for the Macintosh resides at the following address:

http://www.cis.upenn.edu/~brada/VRML/ExpressVR.html

You can find Liquid Reality for Windows 3.1, Windows 95, and Macintosh at the following site:

http://www.dimensionx.com/products/lr/index.html

Cybergate for Windows 95 supports multiuser interaction, chat, and avatars in VRML worlds delivered by servers equipped with Cybergate's Cyberhub server. You can find Cybergate at the following address:

http://www2.blacksun.com/beta/c-gate/download.html

Paragraph 3D for Windows 95 enables users to view ParaGraph Virtual Home Space Builder Files, which are VRML worlds that can include animations, sounds, and behaviors. You can find Paragraph 3D at the following site:

http://russia.paragraph.com/vr/d96html/download.htm

Virtus Voyager is currently a stand-alone VRML viewer, but a plug-in is promised for Netscape. You can find Virtus Voyager at the following address:

http://www.virtus.com/voyager.html

TerraForm Free is a VRML browser plug-in for Internet Explorer, although the plug-in should work with Netscape, too. For more information, check out the Brilliance Labs home page:

http://www.brlabs.com/files/terraform.zip

Productivity Plug-Ins

Productivity is a nebulous category that includes real-world tools such as word processors and spreadsheets, development systems that enable you to create your own integrated controls and programs, and miscellaneous tools such as clocks and calculators. Most of these tools are already available as Netscape plug-ins and the rest should eventually follow.

Acrobat Amber Reader

If you're like most Web users, you have many files that you would like to put on the Web. Unfortunately, the files are in a wide variety of formats, and the task of translating that much content into HTML files seems intimidating if not impossible.

Never fear. A broad spectrum of document viewer plug-ins are becoming available for Netscape. Whether your information is in the form of Word documents, Excel worksheets, Adobe Acrobat portable documents, or most any other format, the odds are good that a Netscape plug-in capable of displaying it is available—or soon will be.

Adobe's Amber version of the Acrobat Reader enables you to view and print Acrobat Portable Document Format (PDF) files. In a nutshell, PDF files are viewable documents that have the visual integrity of a desktop-published document that has been printed on paper. PDF viewers are available for UNIX, Macintosh, and Windows platforms, and each displays PDF documents identically. If the integrity of your documents is important to you (as it is, for example, to the Internal Revenue Service, which uses Acrobat to distribute accurate tax forms over the Web), PDF files are for you.

When activated, the Amber plug-in creates a dockable toolbar in the Netscape window (see Figure 18.8). The toolbar provides controls for zooming, printing, and navigating the Acrobat document.

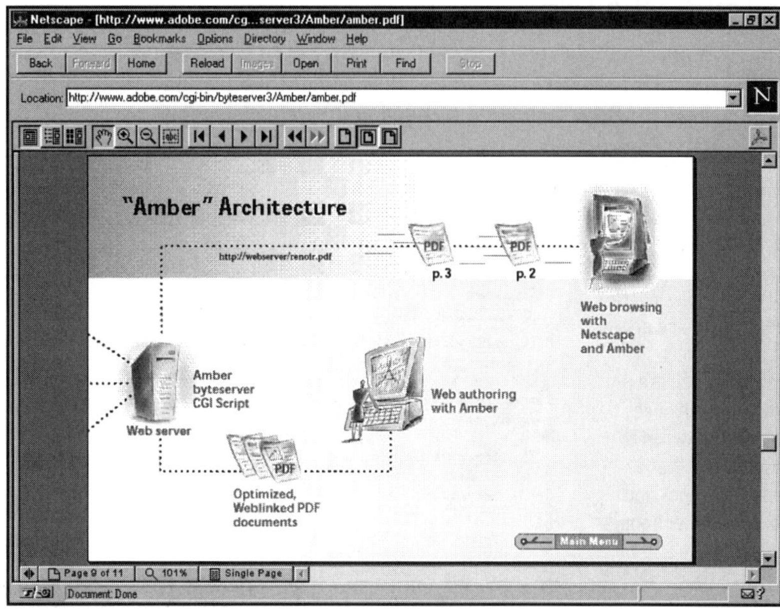

FIG. 18.8
The Adobe Acrobat Amber PDF reader plug-in in action in Netscape Navigator 2.0. Amber provides a full set of Acrobat navigational and viewing controls.

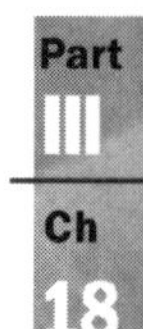

The Amber plug-in is available for Windows 3.1, Windows 95, and Macintosh; a UNIX version is in the wings. You can download Amber from the Adobe Web site:

http://www.adobe.com/Amber/Download.html

Envoy

With Tumbleweed Software's Envoy plug-in, you can view Envoy portable documents in Navigator inline. Envoy documents, like Acrobat PDF files, maintain their look and feel no matter where or how you display them. An Envoy document is usually much smaller than the original document.

Envoy's live hypertext links enable you to jump to other URLs. Zoom features let you fit your document to the width or height of the browser and move in and out of the document from 3 percent to 2,000 percent magnification. Using buttons or the scrollbar, you can scroll or pan the display and jump to different areas of the document. Envoy even enables you to search for text strings within a document. You can use any application to create your document; you publish it in Envoy format using a custom printer driver that translates the content into an Envoy format file.

You can download the Envoy plug-in from the following address:

http://www.twcorp.com/plugin.htm

Formula One/NET

Visual Components' Formula One/NET is an Excel-compatible spreadsheet plug-in for Navigator. The plug-in enables you to display fully functional worksheets that can include live charts, links to URLs, formatted text and numbers, calculations, and clickable buttons and controls (see Figure 18.9).

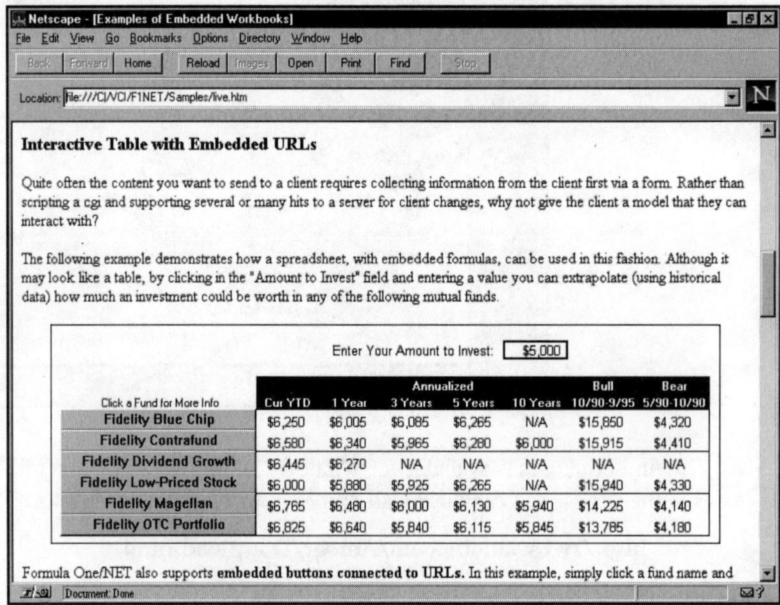

FIG. 18.9
This embedded spreadsheet displayed by the Formula One/NET plug-in looks and acts just like an Excel spreadsheet. Unlike a form, the embedded spreadsheet doesn't require that data be transmitted back and forth to a server if you make changes and want to update your calculations.

The plug-in is absolutely amazing; you can actually place the functionality of a full spreadsheet program inline in Navigator. Formula One/NET has all the fancy formulas, formatting options, and even the charts and graphs that you need to do everything from simple forms to the quarterly taxes for General Motors.

Formula One/NET is the plug-in for viewing spreadsheets, and Formula One/NET Pro adds a pop-up inline designer for creating them. The Pro package also comes with a stand-alone version of the program that adds the capability to read, write, and work with Excel workbook files, all for $39. An even more "professional" version of the whole works with ActiveX controls is available for $249.

Formula One/NET is available for Windows 3.1, Windows 95, or Windows NT. You can download the plug-in from the following site:

http://www.visualcomp.com/f1net/download.htm

Word Viewer

Inso's Word Viewer plug-in displays Microsoft Word for Windows 6.0 or 7.0 documents in Netscape Navigator 2.0 inline. Based on Inso's Quick View Plus viewer, this plug-in enables you to copy and print Word documents with all original formatting intact.

You can find versions for Windows 3.1, Windows 95, Windows NT, and Macintosh at the following site:

http://www.inso.com/plug.htm

KEYview

With FTP Software's KEYview Netscape plug-in, you can view, print, and convert nearly 200 different file formats. Therefore, you can use just about any file format, including Microsoft Word, WordPerfect, Microsoft Excel, EPS, .PCX, and compressed files. You can download Windows 3.1, Windows 95, and Windows NT evaluation versions from the following site:

http://www.ftp.com

The upcoming KEYviews version 5.0 promises to display even more file types, including popular multimedia formats.

Other Document Viewers

This section rounds up some of the other document viewers available as Netscape plug-ins.

PointPlus displays Microsoft PowerPoint presentations within the Netscape browser window. You can view each slide manually or display presentations automatically with the autoplay feature. For more information, check out the PointPlus home page:

http://www.net-scene.com

Not to be outdone by a third party, Microsoft has its own PowerPoint plug-in for Windows 95. This special viewer is for compressed PowerPoint files that can include audio. Microsoft has also made the publisher for these files available, so if you have PowerPoint 95, you can save slides in this new format. Even though this plug-in is from Microsoft and intended for Internet Explorer, it seems to work great with Netscape. You can download this plug-in from the following site:

http://www.microsoft.com/mspowerpoint/internet/player/default.htm

Texture Viewer plays interactive files created with the Texture program. You can find Texture Viewer, which is available for Windows 95, at the following site:

http://www.futuretense.com/viewdown.htm

Techexplorer is an exciting new Netscape plug-in from IBM. Techexplorer processes and displays a large subset of TeX/LaTeX, the professional markup language used for typesetting and publishing in education, mathematics, and many of the sciences. Tuned for onscreen readability, Techexplorer provides many options for formatting and customization. Because it formats on-the-fly, Techexplorer source documents are small, often just one-fourth the size of documents in Acrobat format. Techexplorer can help authors and publishers rapidly. If you publish in TeX, this plug-in enables you to put your files right on the Web. You can find Techexplorer at the following site:

http://www.ics.raleigh.ibm.com/ics/techexp.htm

APPENDIX A

Internet Q & A

This is the part of the book that no one really wants to read because if you have to turn to this part, you must be having a problem. But don't despair! This part contains 101 of the most common Internet-related problems, as well as their solutions. You won't have to fumble through the whole book saying to yourself, "I know I've seen the solution in here somewhere." The solutions are all right here for easy reference.

Connection Frustrations

My modem is not receiving a dial tone.

The dial tone signals that the modem is properly attached to the actual phone line. On occasion, you may not hear a dial tone through the modem speaker, or you may receive an error message, such as "No dial tone" from your communications software. There are two common causes for this problem: a bad connection or a wrong configuration.

Checking to see if the phone line is improperly or incompletely connected to the modem is easy. Check the back of the modem, and be sure that the phone line from the wall is plugged into the modem jack labeled "line" or "in." If you want a telephone or answering machine unit on the same line, it should be connected to the modem's jack labeled "phone" or "out."

Checking the configuration is slightly more difficult. To make sure you've configured your software to use the correct COM port, in Windows 95, open My Computer, select Control Panel, and click Modems. You should see the name of your modem. Click the Properties button. The dialog box shown in the next figure appears. If there is no way to select a COM port and one is already listed, Windows 95 installed your modem as a Plug and Play device and determined the correct COM port on its own. If, on the other hand, you have the option to select a COM port, you may have the wrong one selected. The thick gray cable that connects your modem to your PC plugs into your PC's serial port. Your PC's manufacturer assigned each serial port a COM number between 1 and 4. Most PCs use COM 2 for the serial port; some use 3. If you aren't sure which is correct, try each one, or contact the manufacturer.

Although internal modems are not connected by cable to an external serial port, they are preconfigured to use a particular COM port, such as COM1 or COM2. Windows 95 should be able to automatically detect which COM port the internal modem is on. If it doesn't seem to be right, check the documentation or try each possibility.

If neither of those things seems to fix the problem, make sure the phone line from the wall is functioning properly. Plug a regular phone directly into the wall and check for a dial tone. Maybe you didn't pay your bill! (It happens—as I well know.)

I can't hear the modem dialing.

Most modems have a built-in speaker through which you can hear the dial and connect tones (that series of screeching sounds that would scare away even the most territorial of cats). Whether you listen to the modem's tones is usually a matter of personal preference; however, with some modems, those tones can let you know what is going on. For example, if you have an internal modem that has no other display, you may have to listen for the dial tones to make sure it is actually working.

In Windows 95, you can configure the modem speaker through the Modem Properties settings. Open My Computer, select Control Panel, and click Modems. You should then see the name of your modem. Click the Properties button. In the dialog box is a volume slider that controls the modem speaker (see the following figure). Drag the slider to any position you want, from off to low to medium to full blast.

If you're not using Windows 95, configuring the modem speaker is a bit trickier. Most common modems share a command set, and you can send the modem commands to configure certain characteristics. To do this, you must use software that allows you to send commands directly to the modem. *Terminal programs* are the most common software packages that allow this. If you use a terminal program such as ProComm Plus, Qmodem Pro, ComIT, or even Terminal (which is included with Windows 3.1) to connect to your Internet account, you can send commands directly to the modem before dialing your provider.

Modem commands, often called AT commands, begin with the letters AT. This tells the modem that it should pay attention to the next command. So to disable the modem's internal speaker, for example, you would type the command AT M0 directly into the terminal program and press Enter. The next figure shows an example of using an AT command in HyperTerminal (the terminal program included with Windows 95).

In response to your command, the modem returns OK to let you know that it understood the command. Other speaker-related AT commands include the following:

AT M1	Enable internal speaker
AT L1	Set speaker volume to low
AT L2	Set speaker volume to medium
AT L3	Set speaker volume to high

The line is busy. Can I auto-redial?

Some phone numbers are constantly busy, especially if you attempt to connect at peak hours (such as prime time on weeknights). Most communications software has a feature you can use to redial automatically until a connection is made—which gives you the freedom to make popcorn or eat Ben & Jerry's instead of sitting in front of the modem for 20 minutes trying to make a connection.

Each communications package is different, so it is impossible to describe exactly how each redial feature works; however, it is usually a very basic feature. If you use Windows 95's built-in Dial-Up Networking to connect to the Internet, you may find that you need to configure it to support redialing. To do that, follow these steps.

1. In Windows 95, open **My Computer** and select **Dial-Up Networking**.
2. From the Dial-Up Networking window, select **Connections** and select the **Settings** command.
3. In the configuration window that appears, check the **Redial** option (if it's not already selected). Then enter settings for how many times you want the modem to redial before giving up, and for how much time the modem should wait between attempts.
4. When you finish, click **OK** to save your settings for auto redialing.

For users of Trumpet Winsock with Windows 3.1, the redialing capability is built into the default login script that comes with the software. You'll encounter Trumpet login scripting in a bit more detail later in this section.

The line simply rings and rings.

If the line is ringing—that is, if you hear the traditional dialing sound coming from your modem's speaker—you know that the line is functioning. Actually, when the line just rings and rings, the problem is not on your end, but on the end you are trying to connect to.

A somewhat common problem for Internet Service Providers (ISP) is called *ringthrough*. Your ISP (the people you dial to access the Internet) has a series of modems. Although you dial only one phone number, you're supposed to be connected to the first available modem in the series. Sometimes a modem goes bad, and you're connected to one of these dud modems that doesn't answer the line. It simply rings and rings and rings. That is a ringthrough, and you should certainly notify your provider if this sort of thing is happening. Sometimes they don't realize that a modem is bad; it's tough for them to know because they don't dial into their own modems. Other than that, the only thing you can do is hang up and dial again—and hope that you won't be connected to a dud modem.

The modem is connecting at the wrong speed.

Modem speeds often cause major confusion. All communications software enables you to select a baud rate for your modem connection. The general recommendation is that people with 14.4Kbps modems should select a baud rate of 57,600Kbps, and people with 28.8Kbps modems should select a baud rate of 115,200Kbps. But why?

The 14.4 and 28.8 numbers indicate the speed at which your modem can communicate with the other modem (assuming they both support the same speed). The 57.6 and 115.2 numbers indicate the speeds at which your modem and your own computer communicate. When you see communications software reporting the speed of a connection, it's important that you know which number it is telling you.

Users of Windows 95's Dial-Up Networking should note that once you're connected, a little window pops up saying Connected at *some speed*. This is the modem-to-modem speed. If you have a 28.8Kbps modem and are connecting to another 28.8Kbps modem, you should see a number close to 28,800. People often are confused by this if they know they configured their modem (via the Modem Properties dialog box) to connect at, say, 57,600 or 115,200 baud. Remember that Dial-Up Networking is not reporting that setting.

Now, you do want to pay attention if a reported connection speed is lower than the speed of your modem. For example, if you have a 14.4Kbps modem but receive connection speeds of only, say, 9,600 or 12,000, that is something to take note of. What might be the cause of that trouble? It's most likely a result of difficulties between the two modems attempting to connect. The trouble may lie in modem configuration settings on your end or on the other end.

On your end, the easiest solution is to try resetting the modem to factory defaults—just in case you somehow messed with certain connect speed settings. You usually do this using the

AT &F0 or AT &F1 modem command in a terminal program; however, you should check your modem manual to be sure. If the problem is a modem on the other end, there's little you can do except notify the person who maintains that system. Then you might try dialing in again to see if you get another modem.

Lastly, two modems can connect only at the maximum speed of the slower modem. So a 14.4Kbps modem can only connect at 14.4 if the other modem supports at least 14.4. Similarly, a 28.8Kbps modem can only achieve that speed with another 28.8Kbps modem. When a 28.8Kbps modem connects with a 14.4Kbps modem, however, the fastest possible connection speed is 14.4Kbps. So it's good to know the speed of the modem you are calling (your provider will be able to tell you). If you connect to a modem slower than your own, you'll wind up with a connection at the slower speed.

I never connect at 28.8 even though I paid handsomely for a 28.8 modem.

Because so many variables can prevent a proper 28.8Kbps connection, it's surprising that they occur at all. Analog phone lines (the kind that connect your house and the local phone company) are the remains of older technology: they were not designed for high-speed digital communications. Communication at the speed of 28,800Kbps truly pushes these lines further than they can often handle. To achieve these speeds, the lines need to be of perfect quality and have no noise or interference along the way.

Many factors can cause interference. Poor-quality in-home wiring, the distance of a call, and the quality of phone lines in a general region all affect the amount of interference. In addition, the quality of the modems plays a part. A cheaper 28.8 modem is not likely to achieve 28.8Kbps connections under imperfect conditions; a more expensive one may be better able to maximize your connection speed on lines with minor imperfections.

Real-world results seem to indicate that many people can achieve 28.8Kbps connections on local calls between themselves and a provider who is only a few miles away. Many who can't reach 28.8 can usually reach 26.4, which is fairly close in terms of speed. However, if you are attempting to make long-distance connections, your chances of such speeds drop considerably.

Modems are now available that operate at speeds of 36.6 and even 56,000 Kbps. The problem with these modems is that there are very few service providers that have lines that can connect you at your modem's top speed. For instance, your 36.6 modem will probably only connect at 28.8 even with the most ideal conditions. As service providers update their equipment and connections, you will be able to take advantage of the higher speeds that these new modems offer.

I get garbage characters coming over the line.

Some people, when they are connected to their Internet account via modem, will see some garbage characters on the screen. By garbage characters, I simply mean nonsensical groups of symbols and characters, such as D##$@!~~+ . Garbage characters basically signal errors in data transmission coming over the line. These errors are often caused by noisy phone lines.

Most modern high-speed modems have built in error correction and should be able to detect such errors in transmission *before* you see the results. After they have found an error, these modems request retransmission of the data from the other end. Of course, this error correction only works to a point: If the lines are of absolutely atrocious quality, the modem will not be able to succeed in correcting errors and will probably just disconnect. However, that's a rare exception. Most people's lines are of decent but not perfect quality, in which case, some errors will arise.

Except for some of the cheapest 14.4 and 28.8 models, most modems include built-in error correction features that can handle regular, random errors. Therefore, a properly functioning error-correcting modem should not yield garbage characters. If—as a last resort—you need to disable error-correction, try resetting the modem to its factory settings. You can usually do this with the AT &F0 or AT &F1 command, but check the manual for certain. Some modems use DIP switches to determine factory settings.

Slow modems, especially those as slow as 2,400 baud, may not have any built in error correction. Some do, but many do not. The ones that do not are definitely prone to spewing out garbage characters.

Letters are missing from the words when I use my account.

The problem of missing letters is called *dropping characters*, and it's as simple as it sounds: some of the data is lost on the way. Most often, this happens when you have the connection speed between your modem and the PC set higher than your PC can handle. While it is generally recommended, for example, that you configure your software to 57,600 baud for a 14.4 modem, slower CPUs may not be able to keep up.

The solution is to try lowering the speed of the computer's baud rate. If you have a 14.4Kbps modem, try lowering your baud rate to 38,400. You can lower the baud rate as much as necessary until it quits dropping characters—as long as the baud rate doesn't drop lower than the speed of the modem. Although lowering the baud rate limits the maximum speed at which you can transfer data, it's better than losing characters.

To change the computer's baud rate in Windows 95, open My Computer, select Control Panel, and click Modems. You should then see the name of your modem. Click the Properties button. At the bottom of the window pictured here, notice the setting labeled Maximum Speed.

You can select the baud rate at which you want the modem to *attempt* a connection. I don't advise that you check the box marked Only connect at this speed. If you do enable it and the modem cannot connect at the selected baud rate, it will abort the connection attempt entirely.

Although Windows 3.1 offers a similar configuration in its Control Panel, virtually all communications software written for 3.1 ignores this setting. Instead, they provide their own configurations. So Windows 3.1 users will set the desired baud rate when setting the options of the communications software itself (such as their terminal programs).

Download speed is slower than I expected.

The first way to approach this question is to consider what you're expecting. Although modems advertisements put a lot of emphasis on a speed (such as 28.8Kbps), it's not immediately obvious just how this number boils down into actual data transfer speeds.

Ultimately, data transfer speed depends on two main factors: the method of transfer (what protocols are used), and the data being transferred (how compressible is it). Making a few assumptions about these two factors, one can provide relatively accurate expectations.

Many large downloads consist of precompressed files (such as .ZIP files, .JPG files, and .GIF files). Thus, these files will not benefit much from the modem's built-in compression routines. For these sorts of files (and they are the most commonly transferred types), you can expect the following rough estimates.

Protocol	Modem Speed	Reasonable Expectation
Zmodem	14.4Kbps	1600–1650 cps
Zmodem	28.8Kbps	1.2–1.4 K/sec
FTP/WWW	14.4Kbps	3200–3300 cps
FTP/WWW	28.8Kbps	2.8–3.2 K/sec

Note that in the expected speed column, I've used two different forms to express the same information. Most programs using Zmodem report transfer speeds in the form of cps, while most FTP/WWW programs report transfer speeds in the form of K/sec. As a means of comparison, cps divided by 1,024 equals K/sec.

More compressible files (such as plain text files) will yield higher speeds than those listed above. So if you're pulling in speeds higher than these estimates (some text files can transfer up to four times faster), you don't need to worry at all. However, if you're pulling in speeds slower than these, you have a problem. Read on.

If you are using Zmodem, the most common causes of slow transfers are CRC errors. Skip ahead to the next problem to learn what to do. If you are using FTP or WWW, you face a potentially more confusing scenario. There are three major causes of slow transfers via FTP/WWW.

- **CRC errors.** As with Zmodem, CRC errors can be the problem with FTP/WWW transfers. Again, skip down to the next problem to learn how to banish CRC errors.
- **Poorly tuned MTU/RWIN settings in your TCP/IP software.** These settings essentially fine-tune the flow of data in and out of your computer. These are somewhat complicated settings to explain in a Quick Fix, and what's worse is that Microsoft's Dial-Up Networking makes them difficult to access. First, ask your service provider what MTU setting to use with their system. Then, if you use Trumpet Winsock, read the Trumpet Winsock documentation or the Trumpet Winsock coverage in this book to learn how to adjust these settings. If you use Windows 95, go to the Web site

http://www.windows95.com and follow the links to information on how to modify the settings. You can also find discussions and help on these matters in the Usenet newsgroups at alt.winsock, alt.winsock.trumpet, and comp.os.ms-windows.networking.tcp-ip.

- **Heavy network traffic on the Internet.** The Internet is a place of varying busy-ness, and everyone has to share the same pathways. Thus, it is vulnerable to traffic jams. Even if you have the correct configurations, if you attempt to transfer large files—especially from far-away machines—across the Internet during high usage hours (business hours), you're likely to run into slowdowns. The only solution is to try finding information on geographically closer servers or servers that are less heavily used, or to wait until off-peak hours.

My communications software is reporting many "overrun" or "CRC" errors.

This error occurs when the data flows into your PC too quickly for your PC to process it. It is, in essence, a flood. This data overrun causes the PC to have to request repeat transmission of the lost data. Repeating transmission wastes time. And because you're transferring the same data multiple times, many repeated transmissions result in a slower overall transfer speed for the data.

Overruns (which are called *CRC errors* by some software) are the result of problems unrelated to your software configurations or what protocol you are using. They represent a more fundamental problem in which your computer cannot keep up with the incoming flow of data. Although many factors influence whether your computer is able to keep up, a few specific things cause the majority of all overruns.

- **The UART** This only applies if you use an external modem. Your serial port (which is probably part of your I/O card) has a buffer on it that is intended to prevent data overruns. This buffer is called a UART chip. Old serial cards have a UART model 8250 or 16450. These older UARTs are generally not sufficient for today's high-speed modems of 14.4Kbps and higher. Current I/O cards have model numbers of 16550A or higher (16550AFN, for example), which are capable of higher speed buffering. Thus, the first and foremost recommendation if you experience many overruns is to check your UART.

  Checking your UART is simple. Whether you use Windows 3.1 or Windows 95, you must first exit to DOS; you *cannot* just open a DOS window. In Windows 3.1, then, open the **File** menu and select **Exit**; in Windows 95, click **Start**, select **Shutdown**, and click **Restart the Computer in MS-DOS Mode**. At the DOS prompt, type **msd** and press **Enter**. In that program, select **COM ports**, and it tells you what UART model you have. If it's not 16550A or higher, the simplest solution is to buy a new I/O card. (They cost around $30.) Most new PCs already have proper UARTs, but older ones may not.

  In addition, if you use Windows 3.1, you must tell it to use the UART by adding the line **COM*x*FIFO=1** in the [386enh] section of your windows\system.ini file. Replace ***x*** with the number of the COM port to which your modem is installed. Thus, if your modem is on COM 2 (which is common), the line should read **COM2FIFO=1.**

If you use Windows 95, verify that the UART (also called a FIFO) is functioning by opening **My Computer** and selecting **Control Panel**, **Modems**, **Properties**, **Connection**, and **Port Settings**. Check the **Use FIFO buffers** option if it's not already enabled.

- **Old hardware drivers** Drivers for some video cards and some hard drives use nasty tricks to increase their own performance, and in doing so, they cause Windows to be susceptible to data overruns. If you are still receiving many overrun errors and you've ruled out the UART as the source of the problem, contact the manufacturers of your video card and hard drive (or ask around on the Net) for updated, current drivers. Many manufacturers now offer drivers that will behave themselves.

The modem seems to hang up randomly while connected.

Sometimes you'll be merrily Netting along, when the modem will just hang up—apparently out of the blue. Why? One common cause is call waiting, which is discussed in detail in the problem "I want to disable or enable call waiting." Aside from that, you need to try to determine whether the culprit is on your end of the connection or at the other end. Let's do a little detective work.

Do you only connect to one phone number? Try calling other modems in the area—local BBSs, other service providers, and so forth—and see if it happens with them. This kind of experimentation helps you get an idea of whether the cause is you or your provider.

Next, ask other subscribers to your provider if they have the same problem. More often than not, random disconnects are problems on the provider's end, sometimes due to differing brands of modems. Most modems are supposed to be able to talk to one another regardless of manufacturer, but there are some exceptions. (One particular modem model may have trouble communicating with another particular model, for example.)

Finally, although random disconnects probably are not the result of a configuration problem on your end, if you aren't sure, try the factory reset command. You may have twiddled some esoteric setting that set it off. (Modern modems have hundreds of esoteric settings.)

My #!?@ roommates keep lifting the phone extension and ruining my connection.

This is not an uncommon problem in households or apartments in which multiple devices use the same phone line. Often, both a phone in the kitchen and the modem in the bedroom are on the same line. When someone in the kitchen lifts up the phone and hears the horrible screech of the modem, they have succeeded in ruining the connection. A solution? There are three possibilities.

Obviously, multiple phone lines are a solution, but not everyone can afford that. If it's not an option for you, try talking to the other people in the house to work out some system of knowing who is on the line.

If diplomacy doesn't work, try a technological solution. Most modems have a jack in the back for a phone. Some modems, if they are online, disable the phone hooked to this jack. Thus, although it's a wiring nightmare, if you can connect the aforementioned kitchen phone to the back of the modem, the phone will be disabled when the modem is in use. However, this only works with a modem that does, in fact, disable its phone jack when online.

The only other answer lies at that ubiquitous of gadget stores: Radio Shack. They sell a little doohickey that you can place on the phone line that disables one extension when the other is in use. That doohickey is called a "Teleprotector" (Radio Shack catalog #43-107), and it sells for approximately $10.

I want to disable or enable call waiting.

To many, the bane of telephone conversations is also the bane of modem communications. If you are using the modem when a call waiting beep comes down the lines, your connection will probably be broken. You may or may not appreciate this. Some people who are online frequently but cannot afford a second line may prefer being knocked off the line to having their callers get busy signals all day long. However, most people prefer not to be interrupted while online.

If you don't want those interruptions, you can usually disable call waiting on a per-call basis by inserting *70 into the dial string of your communications software. For example, if you normally dial 555-1515 to access your service provider, change it so your software dials *70,555-1515. The *70 prefix works in most telephone regions. If it does not seem to work for you, contact the local phone company to find out how to disable call waiting. Note that this disables call waiting only during the current call; as soon as you disconnect the modem, call waiting is automatically enabled again.

When I quit my connection, the modem doesn't hang up the line.

Most communications software has some feature to "hang up." This isn't always the same as exiting. With some software, if you quit the software but do not choose to hang up the line, the modem won't disconnect.

The obvious rule is to hang up before you exit the software. However, if you forget to hang up first and the modem doesn't hang up automatically, try running the communications software again. It may hang up the line when it starts in order to clear it for use. If that doesn't work, try to run your terminal program and select hang up. The terminal program should pass the hang up command to the modem.

If you have an external modem, you can flip the power switch (turn it off and back on). Another possibility is to unplug the phone wire from the telephone jack and then plug it back in. Finally, as a last resort, reboot Windows, but only if all else fails.

E-Mail Troubles

The e-mail I sent came back to me undelivered.

This is known as *bounced* mail. It means that the mail could not be delivered to the specified recipient. A couple of things cause mail to bounce.

- **There's no such user.** The recipient you specified doesn't exist. Either you have the wrong e-mail address, or you typed it wrong.
- **The mailbox is full.** There isn't enough room in the recipient's mailbox to hold your e-mail.

When you receive a bounced e-mail, you get your original message back along with a brief explanation of the problem. For example, you might see a message like this at the top of the bounced message:

```
----- The following addresses had delivery problems -----
<markymark@interlog.com>  (unrecoverable error)
   ----- Transcript of session follows -----
... while talking to gold.interlog.com.:
>>> RCPT To:<markymark@interlog.com>
<<< 550 <markymark@interlog.com>... User unknown
550 <markymark@interlog.com>... User unknown
```

As you can see, in this example, the error is described as User unknown. In such a case, check your spelling to see if you made a typo in the address. Note that capitalization does not matter in an e-mail address, so that would not be the cause of a User unknown error.

My e-mail was never delivered to the other party, but it didn't bounce.

An e-mail message travels through several computers on the way to its ultimate destination. Sometimes one of these computers may be down temporarily. Or the destination computer itself might be down. In these cases, there will obviously be a delay in delivery.

There are procedures in place on the Internet that try to account for possible obstacles. If the destination computer is down, delivery will often be attempted periodically (automatically—without your assistance or knowledge) until it's successful. Sometimes, however, it does not succeed after several attempts, usually because of network problems with the destination computer or another computer near that end of the line. In some such cases, after several days you will receive a warning e-mail saying that your message could not be successfully delivered. This is not a bounce, it's a notification. The system will continue to attempt delivery for a specified period of time.

Suppose you have a persistent problem with your e-mail not reaching recipients in various locations. If your e-mail seems to have truly vanished, you need to check two possible suspects: your e-mail software and your outgoing mail server (provided by your service provider).

- Make sure your e-mail software is, in fact, sending the e-mail and not queuing it. Mail applications such as Eudora and Pegasus Mail offer you the option whether to "queue" outgoing mail or send it immediately. If you choose to queue your mail, all of your composed messages are stored on your hard drive to be sent out in one batch when you instruct the program to "send all queued mail." Of course, if you never tell it to send the queued mail, that mail will never leave your PC. Queuing is generally only useful for users who compose mail offline and then dial in to their provider when they're ready to send all their e-mail in one batch. For users who remain online while they write e-mail, it's more sensible to have the mailer actually send it out when you complete the composition.
- Your service provider's outgoing server may not be working properly or reliably. You have two options: to speak to your provider or to use a different outgoing server. The outgoing server is known as the SMTP server, and you can configure it via options in your e-mail application. Often, you can use any SMTP server—not just the one your provider offers. Check around and see if you can find another provider locally, such as at a nearby university. If so, find out the name of their server (often, they are named in the form *mail.providername.com* or something very similar). If you find another SMTP server that's more reliable, stick with it. However, considering you are paying your ISP, it is worth talking to them about their server.

I need to send the same message to multiple people.

This is an easy one! There are two ways you can do this, depending on your needs.

- You can often include multiple e-mail addresses in the To: header, separated by commas. Perhaps more commonly, you can use the CC: header line provided by most e-mail programs to enter one or more addresses. This sends "carbon copies" of the one message to all cc recipients. Thus, you can address your message in either of the following ways:

  To: person1@isp.com,person2@otherisp.com,
  person3@yetanotherisp.com

  or

  To: person1@isp.com
  Subject: Hello
  CC: person2@otherisp.com,person3@yetanotherisp.com

- You can use distribution lists. Some e-mail applications enable you to create a distribution list. A distribution list contains multiple e-mail addresses that you can refer to with one label—very useful if you frequently send memos out to the same group of people. For example, you could create a list of all the people in your immediate department and name the whole group "Co-workers." Then when you compose a message in that e-mail program, you can simply address it **To: Co-workers**, and the message is sent to all the people on the list. Check to see if your e-mail program has this capability.

When I retrieve my e-mail, I keep receiving old messages along with the new.

Many users nowadays have SLIP/PPP accounts. You dial into your provider and check e-mail with a program such as Eudora or Pegasus Mail. These programs retrieve your e-mail from a machine known as a POP server. The POP server holds all the e-mail that is sent to you.

Most e-mail programs allow you to configure at least two options related to retrieving this mail: a "delete mail from server" option and a "download only unread/new mail" option. If you choose to enable mail deletion, the program deletes each message after it is downloaded to your PC. Of course, the only copies of those messages are on your PC, and if you delete or lose them, they're gone for good. On the other hand, deleting from the server might be better, because you probably have a mailbox size limit and don't want all the mail you've ever received to keep piling up on the server.

If you turn on the mail deletion option, the "download only..." option is irrelevant. But if you prefer to leave your mail on the server instead of deleting it after retrieval, you will probably want to enable the download only unread/new mail option. If you don't enable this option, every time you check mail, *all* of your messages will be downloaded, including those you have downloaded in the past. If you do enable this option, only new messages will be downloaded; the rest remain on the server.

Although each e-mail application is different, these options are usually among the Network configurations settings. For Pegasus Mail users, for example, use the File, Network Configuration command to access these options.

How can I have e-mail checked automatically?

Almost all e-mail applications allow for *background polling*. This means that your program can automatically, periodically check your POP server for new e-mail. In many programs, you can configure how often the program polls, setting it to check mail every 10 minutes or—if you're like me—every 45 seconds!

Some mail programs prevent you from doing other tasks while they poll, others do not. If you intend to use the background polling feature, you should consider this when deciding which e-mail program to use. When they perform the background poll, most programs will notify you of new mail by way of either a pop-up window or a sound. This quickly leads to Pavlovian conditioning; you may soon find yourself anxiously awaiting the next "You have new mail" bell to sound.

Sometimes when I check e-mail, I get an error such as "POP server timed out."

This indicates that the e-mail program could not connect to the POP server. In most cases, the POP server is temporarily inaccessible, maybe because that machine (owned by your Internet service provider) has crashed or been taken down for some reason (usually only for a short time). In addition, POP servers usually have a limit of how many people can connect and check for e-mail at one time. So if you happen to attempt a connection when the machine is at its limit, it might refuse you. That could generate this error message or a similar one.

It is possible that you have a problem with your TCP/IP software, but if this were the case, you would always get the above message. If you only get timeout errors some of the time, it's basically not your fault. Just wait a few minutes and check again. If you find that your ISP's POP server times out a lot, complain to them. If there is a problem on your end, you're likely to have problems connecting to virtually anywhere else (FTP, the Web, and so on).

I have a slow connection, and it takes forever to retrieve very large e-mail messages.

Many people check their e-mail from several locations—perhaps from work or school during the day and from home at night. Generally, Internet connections from home are often slower than those at workplaces or school computer centers. Suppose you ask someone to e-mail you a one-megabyte file. You may not really want to download it from home, but if you check e-mail from home and the file is waiting for you, it's going to be downloaded. That is, unless you can configure your e-mail program *not* to download files that are particularly large.

Often, you can set such an option. Some e-mail programs may have a predetermined file size limit; others will let you specify with an option such as "Don't download messages over ___ kB." In Pegasus Mail, for example, choose File, Network Configuration and set the leave mail larger than option to whatever size you want to be the maximum. Messages larger than that will not be deleted from the server when the rest of your e-mail is delivered and deleted. You can retrieve them at a later time—perhaps from work or school.

How can I have e-mail to my old account forwarded to my new one?

Just as people move from one home to another, they sometimes move from one Internet service provider to another. And that usually means a new e-mail account. Of course, the problem is that everyone knows your old address.

First, you should tell everyone you know about your new account. In addition, check with your service provider to see if they offer some form of forwarding. If you are still paying both providers, you definitely should be able to have mail forwarded from one account to another. The exact method varies; ask the provider that you want to forward your messages what method to use. However, if you've stopped paying one service provider and signed up with a new one, you may not be able to cajole the old provider into forwarding mail. After all, you're no longer a paying customer to them. If they won't let you forward mail after leaving them, and it's important that you not miss messages, you might have to pay for both accounts until everyone you know catches up with your new address.

One solution to all of this is to use an e-mail forwarding service. The most popular by far is called Pobox (**http://pobox.com**). Although this is a for-pay service, the fees are low. When you use a forwarding service, you give out the address the forwarding service assigns you as if it were your true e-mail address. All e-mail sent to that address is then forwarded to your "real" address, which you give to the forwarding service. The nice thing about this arrangement is that if you change your "real" e-mail address, you simply reconfigure your account with the forwarding service and give them your new address. And no matter how many times you change accounts or service providers, people can always send your messages to the same address.

Help! I accidentally deleted a message.

The first question is, where did you delete it from? In most cases, deleting a message by accident is not a good thing. If you deleted it from your PC (your mailbox in your e-mail program), it may still be on the POP server if you are not configured to delete messages from the POP server upon download.

Some e-mail packages, such as Microsoft Internet Mail, maintain a "deleted" folder of messages. These e-mail messages are not truly deleted until you clean out this folder. Check to see if your e-mail package has a place where it keeps deleted items. You may be able to find your message.

If you really did, in fact, delete the message and it's no longer on the POP server, it's basically gone. One last resort is to contact the original sender. Many e-mail programs store copies of outgoing mail, and if the sender has a copy of the message saved, he could just resend it. You might also try asking your ISP if they keep backups of the POP server. It is highly unlikely that such a backup could help you, though, because chances would be slim that the backup was made in the time span between when the message was received and when you deleted it from the server.

People keep telling me that my e-mail has "long lines."

Not everyone uses the same size screen, fonts, and so on. You can't assume that text that fits on your screen will fit the same way on someone else's. It is generally considered proper practice to use no more than 75 characters per line in an e-mail message. This ensures that everyone will be able to read it properly, without strange linewrapping that makes the message more difficult to read.

Some e-mail programs let you set the width of a message. If yours does, set it to 75 characters per line, and you won't have to worry about taking note yourself. If you're stuck with a program that doesn't have such an option, try to keep the 75-character limit in mind and hit Enter to break to each new line ...or get a new e-mail program. If you cannot keep your line lengths to 75 characters, you may continue to hear about it from people who have a hard time reading your messages.

How can I make an e-mail signature?

A signature is a little blurb that appears at the bottom of every message. Some people use it as an opportunity to impart some clever witticism or express some personality trait. Others use it for more utilitarian purposes, such as to give their name, address, and contact information.

You do not have to have a signature at all, but if you want one, you can specify it in your e-mail program. For PC-based programs, either you can create a signature from an option directly in the program, or you can configure the program to use a pre-existing signature. Because a signature is just a text file, you can create one in any basic text editor such as WordPad or Notepad (in Windows 95). If your e-mail program doesn't enable you to create a signature, then, at the very least, your e-mail program should let you specify which file to use as the signature.

You should follow one basic rule when creating your signature: don't let the size get out of hand. As you know, you shouldn't use more than 75 characters per line. On top of that, you should keep your signature to no more than 4 lines. A very large signature is considered obnoxious; short and tasteful is recommended.

Can I filter incoming e-mail into separate mailboxes?

Would you believe—maybe? It depends entirely on your e-mail program. First, consider what mail filtering is all about. Suppose you frequently receive messages from a few sources: a mailing list about ferrets, a mailing list about chocolate, and a best friend. Normally, upon retrieval, all these messages would appear in one new-mail folder. Some people move the messages into specific folders, such as "ferrets," "chocolate," and "bestfriend." Filtering allows for the retrieved message to be automatically sorted into their appropriate folders.

Mail filtering is a feature (or lack thereof) of each particular e-mail application. Some do not provide any mail filtering capabilities at all. Some provide moderate capabilities (defined as how complexly you can define the filtering rules), while others provide advanced filtering capabilities (the ability to create detailed filtering rules). Both popular Windows programs Eudora Pro and Pegasus Mail offer mail filtering, although Pegasus Mail is generally considered the most capable in this area.

How do I handle/create messages with attached files?

As e-mail programs' capabilities to deal with attached files have improved, the popularity of attaching files to messages has grown accordingly. An attached file is a file that is sent with an e-mail message. Perhaps you want to send someone a .JPG format graphic file. You might write them a message which says "Here is that picture of my new puppy." Then, you would attach the file (perhaps puppy.jpg) to the message.

"Attach" refers to an e-mail program feature usually called attach. All modern e-mail programs allow you to select one or more files to attach to a given message. This is normally relatively straightforward. In Eudora, there is an Attachments header line where you can click to select files to attach. In Pegasus Mail, when in the message editor, you can select an Attach button and choose the files to attach.

When you receive an e-mail message with an attachment, your e-mail program may handle it in a number of ways. Some programs such as Pegasus Mail will show you that the e-mail contains one message and one attachment. You then have the opportunity to select the attachment and then save it to a file. Other programs such as Eudora will automatically save the attached file(s) upon receipt. From there, you can use them in whatever application they were intended. Some programs such as Eudora allow you to configure an "attachments directory" to where all received attachments are automatically saved.

E-mail packages like Microsoft Internet Mail and Microsoft Exchange actually show the attached file as an icon in your mail message. By double-clicking the attached file, you can open it in the application that it was create in. Then you can save the file to a new directory or with a new name.

The e-mail program won't open a file mailed to me.

Sometimes, you receive an attachment, but it doesn't seem to work properly. Perhaps the e-mail program complains that it cannot read the attachment.

Attached files must be "encoded" before being sent via e-mail. This encoding, to be brief, is used to convert a binary file (such as a document, graphic, sound, or executable program) to a text file suitable for e-mail transmission. There are several encoding schemes, and it's necessary that the encoding scheme used by the originating e-mail program be comprehensible to the receiving e-mail program.

The two major encoding schemes are UUENCODE and MIME. MIME is probably the more common scheme for attached files in e-mail. Some e-mail programs will allow you to select which scheme to use for encoding (sending) a file. Others do not allow a choice and automatically use one (probably MIME). Fortunately, most of this is done automatically: Upon receipt of an encoded file, your mail program will attempt to determine what encoding scheme was used, and then automatically decode the file and save it to disk (or offer you the option of saving it to disk). Of course, if a scheme was used that your e-mail application cannot handle, you'll run into a problem.

The safest bet for all sides is to stick with MIME encoding, if you are offered such configurations. If you receive a file that your e-mail program cannot seem to decode, you have two options:

- Attempt to determine what encoding scheme was used. If you view the attached file as a text file somehow (perhaps by loading the message into Notepad), it might say what encoding scheme was used. There are auxiliary utilities for Windows that can decode most encoding schemes. However, doing this is a pain. Having an e-mail program that can decode on its own is certainly much better.
- Notify the original sender that his attachment is in the wrong format; tell him to use MIME.

I want to get off this mailing list!

Mailing lists can be great sources of information or discussion within a particular interest area. However, they can also generate a lot of e-mail, and you may eventually decide that you can't deal with it anymore. Or perhaps you simply have lost interest in the discussion.

To remove yourself from a mailing list, you have to *unsubscribe*. The confusing part is that many mailing lists have their own method of unsubscribing. It usually entails sending a message to a particular address—but often a different address than one uses to send messages to the list. This message might have various syntaxes depending on the list; usually, you need to at least write unsubscribe, sometimes followed by the list name and/or your e-mail address. It really varies, so you have to find out the specific procedure for your own mailing list.

If at all possible, find information on how to unsubscribe to your list before asking anyone in the list. Often the list has unsubscribe information posted in its signature file and makes it available via online information as well. Asking the list members how to unsubscribe is the most common "annoying question" that pops up in mailing lists. Of course, if the list has not made the information readily available elsewhere, then you have little other choice but to bug the list (in which case, they're asking for it anyway).

Somebody keeps sending me abusive or harassing messages.

Unfortunately, this is not an uncommon problem. Granted, it's not a technical problem, per se, but it's frequent enough to warrant addressing. Regardless of the technologies at their disposal, people aren't always very good at behaving themselves. Especially if you get into an online argument with someone, it is possible (not likely, but possible) to start receiving abusive e-mail from them.

You can simply ignore it, but if you would prefer to take other action, there are some options at your disposal. First and foremost, save all the abusive messages, as well as copies of what you wrote to them. No matter how offensive, if you delete them, you'll be destroying your own evidence.

It's always a move in your favor to keep a cool head and not to sink to the other person's level. Let him know that you plan to contact his system administrator. If that does not stop him, then go through with it; send a polite but detailed messages to his system administrator. To do this, you need to figure out what provider he uses—in many cases, this is relatively easy. It is indicated in the portion of the e-mail address following the @ sign. The rightmost two domains of the address are the best bet, for example:

bobjerk@horribleguy.isp.com

In this example, isp.com is a good bet to be the provider. Every ISP has an account named postmaster. Thus, address your complaint to postmaster@isp.com, in this example. You needn't provide all your collected evidence in the first message to the postmaster, but let him know you have it. If he asks for the evidence, provide it. Although the postmaster of an ISP has no *obligation* to do anything to help you, most—for the sake of their own business—will reprimand and/or cut off service to users on their system who are being abusive to others.

I think someone is forging messages under my name.

A forged e-mail message occurs when someone fakes the From: address, so that it looks as if it originated from someone other than the actual source. This is very devious, although it's not terribly difficult to do. A "bad forgery" is easily traced, because even though the From: address may have been faked, the rest of the e-mail headers give away the actual source of the message. Good forgers cover their tracks.

In any case, sometimes—perhaps as a twisted form of abuse, or perhaps simply to hide his own identity—someone will attack others on the Net with messages forged as if they were from you. The most probably way in which you'll learn of this abuse is through complaint letters sent to you or your postmaster about you. Being totally innocent (presumably!), you will be bewildered as to why these accusations are being laid against you.

If messages are being forged under your name, and you protest against this accusation, you shouldn't have too difficult a case. The forged messages will almost always be traceable to some origin other than you. This isn't a matter your responsibilities if someone is forging your address (he will be found out, or at the least you will be vindicated), it's more a case of understanding why you are being accused of something that you never did. Note that forging is different than someone breaking into your account and sending abusive e-mails from it. That's not forging, since he is, in fact, e-mailing from your account. This is a different matter, in which case, you'd need to provide evidence that your account was broken into. Still, this is often traceable, as well, if your service provider is interested enough in doing so.

How can I find someone's e-mail address?

There is no central directory of all Internet users. The easiest way to find someone's e-mail address is to ask him, if at all possible. Obviously, this is not applicable to many cases, such as searching for an old friend or some other person with whom you have no other pre-existing contact.

Many, if not most colleges and universities provide online directories for their students, and sometimes staff and faculty. The Web pages of a university is a good place to start a search, if you know the person to be so affiliated. Many businesses and commercial Internet service providers do not provide directories of their users. In these cases, there really is no surefire way to locate someone's address.

There are a number of services that attempt to provide directories. A good place to browse is the Yahoo catalog (**http://www.yahoo.com**) in the subject area Reference : White Pages. Some of these directories simply solicit users to enter their name and address, thus creating something of a volunteer phone book. Other directories pull names and addresses from Usenet postings. These can be a very good way to find someone, as long as they have ever participated in Usenet. Most directory services are a combination of these two strategies.

Another excellent resource for finding e-mail addresses is the Four11 Directory at **http://www.four11.com/**. Four11 is basically the equivalent of the Internet white pages. To use the service you must register, but it's free. Every time a new user joins Four11 adds another person and their e-mail address to their database.

World Wide Web Worries

Can I change the startup page for my browser?

Yes. Most browsers come preconfigured to access their own home page upon startup. If you like that, fine. However, many people prefer to choose a different startup page, or in some cases, no startup page. One way to speed startup is to choose a startup page that is saved on your own PC. This way, the browser doesn't immediately have to connect to a remote site to retrieve the startup page. Saves a little time.

In Netscape, choose Options, General Preferences, and Appearance. There is an entry that allows you to select either a blank startup page or a specified location. Enter the location of your choosing. If you have saved a page to a local .htm file on your PC, you may start up with a local page with the URL file:///C|/*yourpath*/*filename*.htm.

In Internet Explorer, choose View, Options, Start and Search Pages. Here, you can select the current page loaded as the search page, by clicking the Use Current button. This is a slightly awkward way to select a start page, because it means you have to go to that page before coming to this options setting.

Netscape *keeps* crashing!

No surprise, it does that to everyone. Netscape is somewhat notorious for crashing, even though it is a very nice browser otherwise. Netscape can be a little finicky, because it's a very complex program, but here are some things to watch for in case of crashes.

- Be sure to use the proper flavor of Netscape for your version of Windows. Navigator comes intwo "flavors"—one for 16-bit operating systems (Windows 3.1), and one for 32-bit operating systems (Windows 95). So, be sure to get the one(16- or 32-bit) appropriate for your operating system. Also make sure that you are using the most up-to-date version of the software. Version 3.0 is now available and Version 4.0 will be available soon.
- I recommend that before you install a new version of Netscape, you uninstall the previous version. Doing this may prevent mysterious crashes. However, it also wipes out your Netscape preferences, including helper application definitions.
- If you do not choose to uninstall before upgrading, try deleting a file called **netscape.hs** from the Netscape directory. It seems to be the cause of crashes when upgrading to a newer version.
- Are you using a Beta version of Netscape? Netscape Corporation likes to release Beta version of their product for users to play with, and they are labeled as Betas (a Beta is a version that is not fully tested or finished). But remember that a Beta version is known to have bugs and, therefore, will most likely crash in certain circumstances. You use Beta software at your own risk, but report crashes to Netscape so that they can investigate. To find out whether your copy of Netscape is a Beta or final version, open the **Help** menu and choose **About Netscape**. You'll see the Netscape logo and the words **Netscape Navigator Version xx;** Beta versions will say **beta** in this message.

The graphics or colors appear all wrong.

The most common cause of messed-up graphic appearance in the Web browser are video card driver incompatibilities. Because browsers and Windows 95 are newer than many video card drivers, problems arise. One solution, then—and this applies to more than simply Web browsing—is to have the latest video card drivers for your video card. These are often made available by the manufacturers via the Web or online.

If colors appear strange, also consider double-checking that you have set your Windows to 256 colors or higher (all new cards have these capabilities). Many images in Web pages have more than 16 colors, and if your Windows is set to only 16 colors, the images will look freaky onscreen. In Windows 95, you can check you screen preferences by right-clicking anywhere on the desktop background. A little menu will pop up, from which you choose Properties and Settings. There you will find a selector named Color Palette that allows you to choose between the varying numbers of colors your video card supports.

My browser redownloads images that have already been retrieved.

Some browsers have what are known as *caches*. The cache stores the files and graphics you retrieve from the Web on your hard drive so that if you return to one of those pages, your computer can quickly load the graphics from your local storage instead of having to download them from the Net again. However, several factors can cause the ideal principle behind a cache to fall short of reality.

The first major factor is size: Be sure your cache is set large enough. You should usually configure your browser's cache to 4–5 megs (4096–5000k). If the cache is too small, it won't have the room to store many graphics. If the cache is very large, it takes up a great deal of hard drive space.

Second, be sure the cache is enabled. In Mosaic, the cache options provide a specific Enable button that should be selected with a check mark.

Third, take note of how the browser is configured to operate with the cache. All three major browsers offer options similar to those listed below to increase cache-reliance. The following figure shows these typical cache settings in Netscape Navigator.

- Once per session: If you attempt to load a page you've already been to, the browser will check to see if the page has changed at all since last time. If so, it will reload the page anew. If not, it will use the files from the cache. With this option, it will only check for page updates one time during this session; subsequent returns to that page will be assumed to draw from the cache.
- Every time: Browser will always check the server to see if the page has been changed at all before drawing from cache.
- Never: If you've been to this page before, the browser will not even check to see if it has changed and will draw the files from the cache.

Understanding these options should help you to understand the logic behind the browser's cache behavior. To access these options in Netscape, use the Options, Network Preferences,

Cache command sequence. In Internet Explorer, choose View, Options, Advanced. In NCSA Mosaic, use the Options, Preferences, Cache sequence.

Lastly, at the risk of really confusing matters, some browsers' cache management just doesn't work properly. Needless to say, if that's what you're up against, there's no good solution except to switch to a new browser. The browsers discussed here should work properly (although Beta versions of each release may not).

All of the letters look like Greek or something.

Probably because you somehow managed to change the browser font to Greek. This seems to happen to people periodically, although it's not clear if the user is doing something wrong or there are some goblins haunting the browsers. In any case, check your font settings.

Each browser allows you to configure which fonts to use to show the Web page contents. You can find the settings in Netscape by selecting Options, General Preferences, and Fonts; in Mosaic, select Options, Preferences, and Fonts. For Internet Explorer, select View, Options, and Appearance. In any case, simply be sure that the selected fonts are, in fact, legible fonts such as Times New Roman and Courier (popular choices). Choosing to change the font will allow you to see what the current fonts look like and help you make a proper selection.

Some Web pages never finish loading.

Isn't this frustrating? You attempt to connect to a Web page, it starts downloading, as indicated by the spinning progress icon or the shooting stars in Netscape, but never seems to finish. You may be left staring at a blank screen waiting for this endless page to complete.

Several factors could be at fault here, although this problem has been recognized as a particular bugaboo for Netscape users who also use Windows 95 Dial-Up Networking. In some cases, the delay may simply be justifiable network traffic. One simple solution is to hit the STOP button in the toolbar of the browser. This will cause it to give up and will probably show the contents that it has retrieved (which may be virtually all of the page minus a picture or three).

Links to sounds are not playing.

That's probably because you don't have an appropriate audio player configured as a helper application. When the Web browser encounters a link to a file that is a sound, it attempts to send that sound to whichever audio player you've chosen—if you've chosen one. Upon installation, some browsers may automatically default to a certain player; others may not.

The key here is to check your viewer or *helper app's* (same thing) configurations. Netscape carries these around in General Preferences (shown in the following figure) and Helpers, while Mosaic tucks them away in Options, Preferences, and Viewers. Internet Explorer bases its helpers on the file associations defined in Windows 95; select View, Options, Filetypes to get there.

Although you may encounter several types of sound files, WAV and AU files are the most common. Be sure you've configured a player for both. (You'll find entries for both in the viewer configurations previously mentioned.) You can certainly use the same player if it can play both types of files. Netscape comes with an AU player but not a WAV player. Windows 95 includes the program mplayer, which can play both types of sound files, so it is a common pick for a sound viewer.

If you want to check out others, you can find a cornucopia of helper apps at Stroud's Consummate Winsock Apps List or Shareware.com. Stroud's is on the Web at **http://cws.iworld.com/**. Shareware.com is at **http://shareware.com**.

Followed links are not remembered.

When you click a link to follow it, the browser may or may not "remember" that you've visited that link before. In some browsers, the link becomes a different color after you select it so you can keep track of which links you've followed in the past and which ones you have not. The following figure shows two different links in Netscape Navigator.

This behavior is determined completely by the browser settings. Every browser that marks followed links allows you to determine how long it remembers the followed links. If you want, you can set this history to "expire" after some number of days (that is, you tell the browser when to forget the followed links).

In Netscape, you change this behavior by selecting Options, General Preferences, Appearance. In Mosaic, select Options, Preferences, Anchors. Internet Explorer offers a slightly more limited version of these settings in View, Options, Appearance.

Keeping track of followed links is only to help you know where you've been. It doesn't affect the browser's functionality.

Java applets are not playing.

Java applets are little programs that can add all manner of useful and/or nifty enhancements to a Web page, such as animated text or images. An increasing number of Web pages now feature Java applets. If you find that professed Java applets are not playing on your system, consider the following factors.

- This may sound obvious, but does your browser support Java? Netscape Navigator, Internet Explorer, and HotJava support Java applets. Check to make sure that your browser does as well; the easiest way to check is to go to the Sun Microsystem home page, **www.sun.com**, and see if the Java applets on this page will play. You can also check your Web browser's documentation or help files to see if it is Java compatible.
- If you are using a Java-compatible browser in Windows 95 but still do not see Java applets, check to be sure Java has not been disabled in your browser. Choose **Options** and **Security Preferences**, where you will find a disable Java check box. Of course, it should be deselected to enable Java.
- Lastly, some TCP/IP software has had trouble when run with Netscape, in playing Java applets. At the time of writing, there are beta versions of Trumpet Winsock 32-bit in release that do not support playing of Java applets. Windows 95's Dial-Up Networking does work with Java.

Sending e-mail from my browser doesn't work.

Most importantly, be sure you have configured a viable SMTP server in your browser's mail preferences. Use the same one that you've configured to use in your e-mail application, if you use one. Often, this will be an address provided by your provider with a name such as mail.yourisp.com or smtp.yourisp.com.

Check your Netscape mail settings by selecting Options, Mail and News Preferences, and Servers. Be sure the Outgoing Mail (SMTP) Server text box contains the name of a working server. You needn't fill in the Incoming Mail (POP) Server text box unless you want to use Netscape to retrieve e-mail as well. Also be sure you choose Options, Mail and News Preferences, and Identity and enter your name and e-mail address.

In Mosaic, you can find this information by choosing Options, Preferences, Services. Internet Explorer does not have a built-in e-mail capability; instead, it uses Microsoft Exchange, which is part of Windows 95.

I cannot convince audio—or video—on demand programs (such as RealAudio) to work.

There are several new breeds of Web applications that provide audio and video in realtime; that is, they are played while they download, rather than having to be fully downloaded first. Some popular examples include RealAudio, Internet Wave, VDO Live, and XingStreamWorks.

As part of the normal installation, the browser needs to be configured to use these helper apps ("viewer"). Often, this is done automatically by the on-demand installation programs. However, if, for example, you select, a RealAudio link and are presented with a query from the browser as to what to do with this type of file, then your helper app is not properly configured. In this case, go into the helper apps configuration of your browser, find the listing for the file type in question, and set the play program appropriately.

For some users, however, the helper app is configured properly; the on demand application simply doesn't work. The most common reason for this is that users are not using "real" SLIP/PPP connections. Many users nowadays use "pseudo-SLIP" connections, provided by such programs as The Internet Adaptor (TIA) and SLiRP. These programs allow users with only dial-up UNIX account to gain much SLIP/PPP functionality. While most Web browsing works fine with these sorts of connection, the multimedia on-demand programs often do not.

To be technical for a moment, the only way to get these programs to possibly work, if you use TIA or SLiRP instead of a "real" SLIP/PPP account, is to use a feature called *port redirection*. Current releases of TIA do not even support port redirection, so the point is moot there. SLiRP does, but it's too complicated to explain here; if you do use SLiRP for your Net connection and want to use one of these programs, check into the newsgroup alt.dcom.slip-emulators. There you can find or initiate discussion on exact port redirection settings for each on-demand application.

This page says "wait to continue" but nothing more ever happens.

Push-pull. What? Some Web servers use something called "push"ing and "pull"ing to automatically cause events to occur on your end, such as moving to a new Web page. Only problem is, not all browsers support caring about the servers pushy demands. In those cases, nothing will happen; the page will simply sit there.

Wise Web authors provide an alternative for those browsers that don't push or pull. Such an alternative might be a link to click to take you where they want you to go. Those who don't offer this alternative may simply leave you hanging without the proper browser. The three main browsers should all handle the pushy-pullies properly. If your browser does not support push-pull, and no alternative traditional link has been provided, then you've no choice but to abandon the page.

I'd like to maximize the usable space in my browser window.

With all window options enabled, a fair amount of desktop space is covered up by the browser's screen elements (see the following figure). Many users—especially those who use smaller sized desktops such as 640 x 480—want all the browser space they can get. Although all those button bars and navigation icons are pretty, they take up screen space.

Each browser's configurations allow you to alter the appearance of the window. If you use the options right, you can maximize the window space. Here are some tips for doing so in each of our three browsers:

- In Netscape, uncheck **Options** and **Show Directory Buttons.** Select **Options**, **General Preference**, **Appearance**, and choose **Show Toolbar as Text**. You can even remove the entire toolbar (but you'll have to use the menus to navigate) and the window that shows your current location by deselecting **Options**, **Show Toolbar** and **Options**, **Show Location**. As you can see in the next figure, such judicious disabling of extra features gives you much more browser window real estate.
- Internet Explorer also lets you hide the toolbar, status bar, and location bar by deselecting those options in the **View** menu.

Lastly, you can fiddle with font sizes in the font configurations discussed previously. Obviously, making fonts smaller allows more text to fit in the window. But making them too small can mean many more visits to the optometrist. Find a healthy balance.

That's a neat picture. How can I save Web page images for my own use?

Many Web pages contain lots of *inline graphics* (images that are part of the page). Sometimes they are pictures or designs, and other times there are buttons, lines, and so on. You just want a picture because you like it, or you may want to capture a design element for your own use. Each browser provides a relatively easy way to grab these images from the page and save them to individual graphic files on your hard drive.

In Netscape, simply click the right mouse button on top of the image you want to save. In the menu that pops up (see the following figure), select Save this image as. Then you can select a location on your hard drive to which you want the image saved for your future pillaging.

You use the same right-click technique in Internet Explorer. When you do, a slightly different menu pops up, giving you the option of saving the image in its original format ("Remote site format") or in a Windows .BMP format. If you plan to use the image in future Web pages, remote site format is probably the better choice for compatibility purposes.

One browser supports some features, another supports others. Just tell me, which browser should I use?

Okay, I admit, this isn't really a "quick fix." But it is a common question, and a reasonable one. As each new browser is developed, it comes up with new nifty features in an attempt to win market share away from the other browsers. Netscape took the early lead in by developing a number of "extensions" to traditional Web page design which allowed for new effects. Thus, people who wanted to design even "cooler" pages started adopting Netscape's extensions. In doing so, this meant Netscape's browser had to be used to view the page, thereby increasing Netscape's market share. At the time of this writing, Netscape is far and away the most popular browser with some 70 percent of the browser market.

Microsoft leapt out of the woodwork to play catch-up when it introduced Internet Explorer, which is probably the closest rival to Netscape. Explorer, in turn, offered its own *extensions*. Now there are pages that are designed for Netscape and some that are designed for Explorer. Most pages can be viewed on either browser, but special features may not be, and certain design elements may appear strange or distorted in the "wrong" browser. Microsoft's release of ActiveX technology has muddied the Web waters further. Now Navigator plays special content via plug-ins and Explorer plays them using ActiveX controls.

While Internet Explorer has increased its market share, Netscape Navigator is still the most-used browser. Many people choose to use both since Internet Explorer and Netscape Navigator are free. So, if you have the inclination, it's not unusual or unreasonable to have more than one browser on your computer.

Usenet News Jams

My news server says "You have no permission to talk. Goodbye."

Most Usenet news servers are configured only to allow certain sites to connect to them. This prevents anyone in the world from connecting and draining the resources of the server. Some servers, as just explained, accept only certain domains to connect, while others require a user name and password.

First, be sure that you are connecting from a valid domain. For example, let's say that you go to school at Kazoo University and want to connect to their news server news.kazoo.edu. If you have a SLIP/PPP account provided by Kazoo, there should be no problem. However, let's say you are using another SLIP/PPP account, perhaps that of a local commercial Internet provider. In that case, Kazoo will not know that you have rights to their machine; thus, be sure you are connecting to the server from an account within its acceptable domain.

Secondly, although less common, if the server requires a user ID and password, be sure you've filled one into your Usenet application's configuration settings.

I'd like to post anonymously.

There are a variety of "noncriminal" reasons why someone would want to submit an anonymous post to a Usenet newsgroup. In any case, doing so simply requires that you submit your post via an anonymous-posting service.

This is done by contacting any one of several anonymous remailers and following their particular instructions, submitting your post. They will then send your post to the Usenet newsgroup(s) you request. Private e-mail replies to your post will come back to you, but the replier will not know who you are (and, often, nor will you know who they are).

Because there are many remailers to choose from, I cannot provide step-by-step instructions here. Most remailers are designed by default to send anonymous private e-mail, and thus they take special commands in the body of the message to make a Usenet post. You can read the help instructions for the popular remailers at the Web site **http://electron.rutgers.edu/~gambino/anon_servers/anon.html**.

Several Web sites offer easy interfaces via which you can compose a message and select a remailer; two worth trying are the Community ConneXion (**http://www.c2.org/remail/by-www.html**) and Noah's Place (**http://www.lookup.com/Homepages/64499/anon.html**).

I want to change my posted name and organization.

Although a non-anonymous Usenet post will always contain your e-mail address, it need not contain your real name. Some prefer to change their listed name, either for personal reasons or cosmetic. If you are using a PC newsreader, such as Agent, Free Agent, News Xpress, and so forth, changing these settings is quite easy.

For example, in Agent (rapidly becoming the most popular newsreader for the PC), simply choose Options, Preferences and click the User folder tab. You can enter any personal name and organization name that you want. Each of the newsreader applications have a similar capability, including the Netscape Navigator built-in newsreader (accessed via Options, Mail and News Preferences, Identity).

After I post, I receive "Post failed" errors.

A post can fail for several reasons. One common cause of a post failing is known as *throttling*, and the error message may indicate this if it's the problem. In short, throttling is a result of your provider's news server being filled to capacity. There is nothing you can do, except complain. If a provider is suffering from many throttling errors, they seriously need to upgrade their storage capacity.

Another cause of post failing errors is a server timeout. Your newsreader will attempt to contact the news server, to send it your post, but the news server may not answer. This may be because the news server machine is down or overloaded with users. The odd server timeout does occur, and you should simply wait a few minutes and then resubmit your post. Again, though, if this problem happens with some regularity, your provider is likely at fault.

Although it is possible that your TCP/IP settings are misconfigured, thus preventing connection to the server, if this were the case, none of your Internet applications would be connecting to anywhere.

Lastly, some newsreaders will attempt to enforce two Usenet customs:

- Signature files longer than four lines are considered a violation of netiquette (waste of network traffic), and although many newsreaders won't object if you break this custom, a few will.
- In another attempt to conserve traffic and improve content, some newsreaders disallow you from submitting a follow-up post, in which you include less new text than you quote from the previous message. This is a dubious "rule," intended to prevent someone from reposting an entire message and only adding "Yes I agree." Again, most newsreaders do not enforce this rule, although the custom is something to keep in mind when composing follow-up posts.

What is a moderated newsgroup? How can I post to one?

Although all Usenet newsgroups are publicly accessible, some are more democratic than others. The vast majority of newsgroups are *unmoderated.* This means that anyone can post anything to that newsgroup. Although this invites the widest possible array of discussion, it also draws a lot of garbage. Some newsgroups are *moderated,* which means that posts are submitted to a moderator, who then may accept or reject the post for the newsgroup.

Nobody is forcing anyone to use moderated newsgroups. In almost every instance, there are unmoderated alternatives in which to discuss the same subject matter. But, there are advantages to participating in moderated newsgroups; specifically, a high discussion content-to-noise ratio. Usually, a moderated newsgroup will be indicated as such in the newsgroup description, although some PC newsreaders don't display the newsgroup description. In other cases, you will usually find a FAQ posted regularly within the newsgroup that explains how to submit posts to the moderator. Besides being a tip-off that this is a moderated newsgroup, it'll also provide the instructions you need. The basic mechanism is that you'll e-mail your post to the moderator, as per his guidelines as outlined in the FAQ, and he will take it from there.

Attempting to post directly to a moderated newsgroup will likely result in a rejected post.

Why are there messages missing from this newsgroup?

Nothing can be more frustrating (well, not *nothing*) than discovering that desired posts are missing from the newsgroup. You may be reading an ongoing discussion and find that reference is made to a post that you don't see. Or perhaps you are attempting to decode a binary file that is posted in multiple parts, and one or more of the parts are missing. Argh!

This isn't your fault and may only indirectly be your service provider's fault. The problem partially lies in the design of Usenet. In brief, Usenet is like a large network of rivers and streams, each feeding into one another at various nodes. In theory, the water from each stream should eventually feed into every other stream, except this doesn't always happen. There are blockages and dams, and sometimes, only partial feeds reach your local server. Ultimately, your service provider subscribes to a feed from another source; if that incoming feed is incomplete, yours will be, too. The only "fix" to this is to complain to your service provider and pressure them to add a new newsfeed from another source (for example, newsfeeds provided to service providers from MCI are known for being quite complete, whereas those from Sprint are notoriously incomplete).

Why does this group have few or no posts anymore?

If a well-trafficked group that you've been reading suddenly starts to plummet in activity, I'd suspect a news feed problem to your provider. Perhaps, the service feeding your provider decided to cut that newsgroup from their feed, for instance.

Other newsgroups are simply low-traffic by nature; there are quite a few newsgroups, especially in the alt.* hierarchy that are either "joke" creations or simply appeal to an extremely limited audience.

What is the best way to practice posting?

Given how many people read Usenet, if you've never made a post before, you might want to be sure that you know how before attempting it. Not only do you risk quite the public faux pas otherwise, but you also want to be sure that your message reaches the intended audience. In other cases, you may have plenty of Usenet experience but want to test new newsreading software to be sure you know how to post with it.

Although it is not uncommon to see messages posted in newsgroups with subject lines such as "TEST – ignore" or "Please ignore," this is the incorrect way to test your posting capabilities. There are several global groups in which you can post test messages; for example, try alt.test and misc.test. Note that if you post to one of these newsgroups, you may receive a flood of e-mail messages from automated news servers, notifying you that your message was successfully received.

You can also test to a local or university test newsgroup, such as ny.test, tor.test, or cornell.test. By doing this, you won't receive a flood of e-mail from servers around the world, but if you reread the newsgroup a few minutes later, you should see whether your post appeared.

When I reply by e-mail, it is never received by the other party.

To successfully reply to a poster via e-mail, your newsreader has to be properly configured for e-mail sending. Normally, this is done by at least choosing an e-mail server, known in technospeak as an SMTP server—the sort of machine which can send e-mail.

For example, in Agent or Free Agent for the PC, you would configure this setting via Options, Preferences and then the System folder tab. Which machine should you choose as your e-mail server? Your best bet is the same one you've chosen in your e-mail program. Your Internet provider should have supplied you with the name of your SMTP server; it is often something such as mail.yourprovider.com, but not necessarily.

Assuming you've set the e-mail server properly, don't forget to fill in your name and return e-mail address in the newsreader's other settings. This was covered briefly in an earlier question about changing your personal name in Usenet posts.

People tell me to read some group "such.and.such" but it doesn't seem to exist.

Again, this is most likely a newsfeed-related problem. Besides the fact that not all newsfeeds provide all the available posts, many do not provide all available newsgroups. If you are interested in a newsgroup that doesn't seem to be carried by your provider, ask them to add it. Often, they will do this upon request.

Note, though, that if your provider adds a new newsgroup, it may take several days to fill up with traffic.

How do I view posted pictures, sounds, and movies?

This question opens up quite the can of worms—creepy, crawly, slimy. Usenet was not originally designed to exchange binary data, which by its nature is 8-bit. Plain text data, such as messages from one human to another, are 7-bit, and thus so is the nature of Usenet. Nonetheless, people tried to devise ways to exchange binary data over this medium, because it is a convenient way of exchanging files publicly.

The most common method of posting binary files to Usenet is known as UUENCODING. UUENCODE is essentially a program that converts 8-bit data into 7-bit data for transport purposes. Once you retrieve this 7-bit data, it must be converted back to 8-bit data before it will be usable for whatever its purpose (video, sound, and so on).

Furthermore, because binary files tend to be of large size, they are often split into several smaller sections before posting. That is why you will often see binary files posted with subject lines such as these:

```
homer.wav (1/3)
homer.wav (2/3)
homer.wav (3/3)
```

Thus another step is added into the decoding process; each of the parts must be retrieved, combined, and then decoded back to 8-bit data. Whew! Over the years, newsreaders have grown increasingly intelligent about automating this entire process. The newest newsreaders such as Free Agent and Agent make life easy as pie; you simply select one of the sections of the posted file, and it finds all of them, retrieves them in order, and then decodes them. You need only select File, Decode Binary Attachment after highlighting the binary messages you want to download.

Other popular newsreaders have similar capabilities, and thus it is recommended that you use the latest versions of your newsreading software, such as the Agent siblings, News Xpress, and so forth. Netscape Navigator 2.0 includes a built-in newsreader that automatically decodes single-part binary files. However, it doesn't do such a good job with multipart binary postings, and so the above-named newsreaders are recommended if you plan on working with many binary posts in Usenet.

How do I post my own binary files?

Of course, the concepts described in the previous Quick Fix hold true in this scenario, too—they're just reversed. The same newsreaders are also capable of taking a specified binary file, chopping it into slices, encoding it, and then posting it. For example, you can configure how Agent manages this task by choosing the Options, Preferences command and clicking the Attachments folder tab. The Preferences dialog box shown here contains options with which Agent can convert a binary file suitable for posting.

In the first half of the window, you select whether Agent should post the whole file in one large piece or chop it up into several pieces. Because some news servers will reject files larger than a certain size, you should slice files into 900-line segments. To do so, enable the Send attachment as multiple messages option and enter 900 in the Lines per Message box.

The bottom half of the settings window deals with any text you may want to include as a preface to the file (such as "This file is an MPG format video of my dog Scrappy in a compromising position"). If you select the option labeled Send text as a preface message (0/N), Agent will post a message numbered part 0 (which contains only the text) before the post(s) containing the UUENCODED binary file. If you choose the second option, Agent will include the text at the beginning of the first part of the binary file post. The second option is inconvenient because the user must download at least one whole chunk of the file just to read your description. The third option here tells Agent not to include any preface text at all.

Again, other newsreaders will have similar configuration capabilities. When you choose to compose a new Usenet post, there will be an Attach file option, which lets you select the particular file to post.

Someone is flaming me; what should I do?

A flame in Usenet is much like a flame in e-mail: a rude, often coarse, derogatory message directed at someone, either for his statements or beliefs. The best strategies for handling flames are those same strategies that work best in the playground: ignore them.

If you cannot, or feel that the flames are damaging to you in a public sphere, publicly ask the flamer to stop. If he does not, privately ask him to stop flaming you. Remember to keep copies of all messages you send to him and those that he sends to you, in case future evidence is needed. Finally, if none of this quiets the storm, write e-mail to his postmaster, in the same manner recommended earlier in this chapter.

The recourse you never want to take is to flame back and become involved in a flame-war. Besides wasting your time, it is also a waste of network traffic, and extremely tedious for everyone else to sift through.

FTP Hangups

How do I log in using anonymous FTP?

Anonymous FTP is a phrase that pops up repeatedly in Internet circles (and books, and articles, and posts). FTP, or File Transfer Protocol is a common method for transferring files from one computer on the Internet to any other. For authorization purposes, passwords are implemented to control who can access the files on what computer.

Anonymous FTP is used for public archives: file storage that may be accessed by anyone in the public, hence anonymous. To access such archives, you connect to the site and log in with the user ID anonymous, and at the password prompt, enter your e-mail address. Thus, if someone told you to ftp some files from ftp.site.com via anonymous FTP, you would do the following (the parts in bold text are what you would type):

```
ftp> open ftp.gated.cornell.edu
Connected to GATED.CORNELL.EDU.
220 comet.cit.cornell.edu FTP server Wed Jun 7 17:22:02
995) ready.
Name: anonymous
331 Guest login ok, send your complete e-mail address
Password: dog@woof.woof.com
230-Please read the file README
230-  it was last modified on Fri Jan 26 09:52:01 1996
230 Guest login ok, access restrictions apply.
```

The estimated time of transfer is inaccurate.

Some FTP programs, such as NcFTP, attempt to estimate how long the transfer will take. Simply keep in mind one rule of thumb for any file transfer time estimates, be they FTP or anywhere else: Salt. Take them with several grains of salt. An estimated time of transfer necessarily assumes consistent transfer speed. This rarely happens, especially when using FTP. Network traffic and bottlenecks anywhere between you and the remote computer can alter the speed of the transfer. Thus, these time estimates are quite like their brethren in the auto repair world: *estimates*.

Can I salvage an interrupted transfer?

Recall that in the UNIX account scenario, downloading a file from the Internet to your PC is a two-step process. First, you must retrieve the file into your UNIX account, such as via FTP. Then, you must download the file from UNIX to your PC, as with Zmodem. For this question, we are considering the first step only: retrieving the file from the Internet to your UNIX account.

Whether you retrieve files to your account with FTP, Gopher, or the World Wide Web (with the program Lynx, for instance), none of these commonly support *resumed transfers*. Resuming transfer is the capability to start a transfer at some mid-way point, picking up where a previously interrupted transfer left off. Quite a convenient feature, but not yet implemented widely enough to be feasible.

Thus, the short answer is "no," you basically cannot salvage an interrupted transfer from the Internet to your UNIX account. The only real solution is to simply retransfer the file again from scratch.

But my FTP program has a "resume transfer" option; why doesn't it work?

The truth is that FTP *can* support resuming transfers. Some FTP programs have implemented support for the reget command, which is the FTP command that can be used to resume a transfer. However, both the FTP program *and* FTP server must support reget, and very few FTP servers do.

So, you have a situation where few FTP servers support reget, and few FTP programs support it. Therefore, it is not a very commonly available feature. So, if your FTP program does support resume transfer, it'll still only work if you've connected to one of the few FTP servers that support it in kind.

I'm trying to access my UNIX account at ftp.myprovider.com but it denies me access.

This is a common error users make. Let's say that your UNIX account is on the provider.com machine. You want to FTP some files from your UNIX account to some other machine. So, naturally, you attempt to connect to ftp.provider.com, but when you log in with your account user ID and password, access is denied. Why?

Because ftp.provider.com is probably not the machine you need to be connecting to. That is their "public" FTP server, meant to serve files for public availability. Your UNIX account resides on provider.com, and so you, in fact, want to open your FTP connection to provider.com. Then, your user ID and password will work, and you'll have access to the contents of your account.

Downloading Difficulties

My download was interrupted partway through!

Recall above the doom and gloom about resume transfer. Now, though, you are considering the second step of the UNIX two-step: transferring the file from your UNIX account to your PC. In this case, you have the benefit of the magical Zmodem.

Zmodem fully supports resuming transfers, although it prefers to term it *crash recovery*—different words, same meaning. Be sure that you have Zmodem crash recovery enabled; check the Zmodem settings in your particular terminal program.

Assuming that it is enabled, if a Zmodem download dies partway through, you can simply begin the download again. Zmodem will automatically recognize that a portion of the file has already been downloaded, and it will pick up from where it left off. Nice!

I try to download the file, but nothing seems to happen.

Now you run into some of Zmodem's other settings. Not all terminal programs allow you to configure all possible Zmodem settings, but assume that yours does.

In many terminal programs, you can determine exactly how crash recovery will behave. For instance, if you attempt to download a file that already exists on your PC, Zmodem can compare them against each other. Suppose that both have the same time and date—which they would if you were attempting to resume a file previously interrupted. Zmodem, upon realizing this, can either crash recover, start over from scratch for that file, or skip transferring that file altogether. Your terminal may allow you to select these behaviors from its Zmodem configuration screen, but this varies from product to product.

If you attempt to Zmodem download a file and nothing happens, a common cause of this is that you already have a file with the same name in your download path on your PC. Your terminal program is probably configured to skip transfers, rather than resume or overwrite them. This is why the settings explained previously are important—this is one of those "easily forgotten" settings.

Strange text started spewing all over my screen.

Ugh! The transfer seemed to be motoring along just fine, and then suddenly the progress window disappeared and illegible goop starting being output to the screen. This is a Zmodem transfer problem that happens from time to time when the connection between you and your provider burps.

There isn't any notable way to prevent this from occurring. Once it has occurred, the file is no longer being properly transferred, so simply hang up the modem. Wait a few minutes, reconnect to your UNIX account, and then you should be able to resume the transfer with Zmodem.

Why do some files download much faster than others?

Your terminal program probably displays a progress window while a transfer is in progress. This figure shows a transfer progress meter from HyperTerminal, the terminal program included with Windows 95.

Speed of transfer is often measured in "characters per second" (cps) or "bytes per second" (bps), although they mean the same thing. If you, for example, have a 14.4Kbps modem, you may have noticed that many files download at around 1600–1650cps, or thereabouts. Owners of 28.8Kbps will generally see twice that speed.

However, some files seem to transfer much faster—perhaps 3000 cps on a 14.4 or 5000 on a 28.8. What's going on? Compression. Your modem always attempts to compress the data that is being transferred. Doing so results in less data to transfer, and thus a shorter transfer time, and thus a faster perceived transfer rate.

Many binary file types, though, such as .ZIP files, are already compressed. Thus, your modem can do no more to help them, and you see the typical speeds of 1650cps. Other files, which are not compressed (such as ASCII text files) gain great benefit from your modem's built-in compression, and thus they appear to transfer much faster.

In the end, it makes little difference where the compression took place. If you compressed the text file in UNIX before transferring it, the cps rate would drop back to 1650, but the file would be a smaller size. After the smoke is cleared, the total amount of time it takes to download the file is no different whether it was compressed before transfer or during.

I downloaded a text file to my PC, and it looks messed up.

Once again, the ASCII versus binary mix-up claims another victim. Don't be a statistic!

The reason the file appears all screwy is that it has improper "end-of-line" markers (EOL). These are special characters that tell the computer where the end of a line of text is. The classic problem is that UNIX uses a different EOL than does MS-DOS/Windows. There are two feasible solutions to this:

- When downloading a file from UNIX to your PC, you are most likely using Zmodem, with the UNIX sz command. In this case, if you are going to transfer a plain text (ASCII) file, use the sz -a command instead; that will automatically convert the UNIX EOLs into PC-compatible ones.
- If you've already downloaded the file with improper EOLs, all is not lost. There are many tiny utilities available for the PC that can convert the file into correct form for you. All are available at a major PC archive site, such as **http://www.winsite.com**. One I especially recommend is the shareware product UltraEdit, also available at any major site for Windows software. UltraEdit is a versatile text editor that includes a built-in option for converting EOLs from UNIX to PC and vice versa.

The program I downloaded to my PC claims to be corrupted.

What if you have ftp'd a file to your UNIX account, and it was not corrupted, but then downloaded the file to your PC only to find that it now is corrupted? Where is the culprit in this scenario?

First, we have to consider whether this is, in fact, true. If you mistakenly ftp'd a binary file in ASCII mode, for instance, it has been corrupted already. Assuming, though, that you did not make this error, what might corrupt a perfectly good file on its way from your UNIX account to your PC?

In my experience, the most common answer to this question, strangely enough is "nothing." I almost bet that if you investigate, you will find that the file was, in fact, corrupted in its original location. That is, the file you ftp'd was *already* in a corrupt state of affairs before you even came around. Of course, this means there is nothing you can do about it, except perhaps notify the administrator of the site from which you ftp'd the file.

Were the above not the case, though, do be sure that you are using a robust transfer protocol between your UNIX account and your PC. By far, the recommended choice is Zmodem, which any good terminal program supports. The sz *filenames* command is used in UNIX to initiate a Zmodem download. A protocol such as Zmodem will not corrupt your files, but do remember to use sz -a *filenames* if you're downloading an ASCII text file.

Miscellaneous Lukewarm Leftover Grumbles

My ISP does not offer an IRC server; how can I connect?

The many available public IRC servers should more than fulfill your global chatting needs. However, because they change often, listing particular servers here would be fruitless. Instead, I can recommend some reliable sources for current information on public IRC servers:

- On Usenet, check the newsgroup alt.irc. There are periodic posts of public servers, or you can post a request.
- On the World Wide Web, go to the Yahoo catalog (**http://www.yahoo.com**). Enter **IRC** in the search box, and it will bring up a list of IRC-related Web sites, some of which contain lists of public servers. Even these Web sites change, which is why they are not listed here. This method, though, will lead you to a list.

When choosing a public IRC server, try your best to use one as geographically close to you as possible. Not only will it reduce network traffic for everyone, but you will see speedier response times as well.

While on IRC, somebody asked me to DCC a file; what is that?

DCC is a form of file transfer for use within the IRC public chat system. Using DCC, users can exchange files with one another. It is quite simple to use; recall that all IRC commands begin with a slash (/).

In your IRC program, to send a file to someone via DCC enter

```
/dcc send theirnick fullfilename
```

Suppose you want to send the file beagle.jpg to the IRC user whose nickname is harry. You would type the following:

```
/dcc send harry c:\pix\beagle.jpg
```

If someone attempts to DCC send a file to you, your IRC program will notify you. Some IRC programs will automatically accept the file and begin receiving it. If yours does not, simply use the command /dcc get *theirnick.* Enter the command /dcc without any other parameters to see the current progress of the transfer.

Do those "Internet telephone" programs really work?

Admittedly, this is not a Quick Fix, but it *is* a common curiosity. Internet telephony has become a hot market in the past year, as several products are competing for your voice (for instance, Internet Phone, WebPhone, DigiPhone). The main attraction of these products is that you can speak to anyone on the Internet, anywhere in the world, without needing to use a traditional long-distance phone call.

But are they as good as a real phone call? Not really, is the answer at this point in time. It takes a great deal of compression technology to push your voice through a typical 14.4 or 28.8Kbps modem. Beyond that obstacle, the Internet is a vast network of shared pathways, wherein data cannot travel at a consistent speed from point A to point B. The result of these factors are that Internet telephone programs tend to produce speech that is slightly fuzzy and noticeably choppy.

Certainly, the closer the two speaking parties are to one another on the Internet, the more fluidly these programs will work (that is, if both users are on the same service provider, speech will work far better than if one is in New York and the other in Melbourne, or even Los Angeles). All is not lost forever, though. As home connections speed up and the Internet itself becomes more robust, these sorts of "telephones" will become much more feasible to use.

Other software packages such as Cu-SeeMe and Microsoft Netmeeting offer the possibility of video conferencing on the Internet. As modem speeds increase, this type of software will become more popular. The efficiency of this products at the present time is related to band-width. The hardware and software available will do the job; hopefully Internet through-put will catch up with the possibilities.

This is costing me; how can I keep track of my time online?

This is an important consideration for many Internet users who are charged by the hour. Most terminal programs have built in online time displays, which are often located on a status line.

However, this is of no help to SLIP/PPP users, who don't use a terminal program. Fortunately, Windows 95 provided a built-in solution for those who use its Dial-Up Networking. After your connection is established, a small window (shown in the next figure) displays the connection speed and online duration. This window remains on the screen unless you choose to minimize it to the taskbar.

My connection disconnects if I am idle for too long.

To prevent users from leaving their modems connected and hogging up the modem resources, some service providers institute an idle-time rule. If you remain connected but don't engage in any activity for longer than, say, 30 minutes, you are automatically disconnected. While this is a reasonable practice, it may be a problem under certain circumstances, such as if you are awaiting an important e-mail message or chat request. As you might expect, there are ways around it.

One little utility program written to work around this idle time disconnect is called Keep Alive. You can find Keep Alive at many major software sites, such as Winsite (**http://www.winsite.com**) or Stroud's Consummate Winsock Apps (**http://cws.iworld.com/**). Keep Alive simply sends a bit of data (known as a *ping*) every so often to keep your connection from being completely idle.

I get a GetHostName() error message, when I try to connect to a reflector using CU-SeeMe.

Setting up the software and hardware for video conferencing on your PC is really quite easy. Both the Cornell and White Pine versions of CU-SeeMe (the most commonly used video conferencing software) provide you with automatic installations. Make sure that you install your camera hardware and the software drivers for the camera before you install the CU-SeeMe software. CU-SeeMe automatically detects the camera drivers that are installed on your PC and sets them up as the default for video conferencing.

One of the most commonly experienced problems related to CU-SeeMe video conferencing is the GetHostName error message, which is related to the IP address that you are assigned by your service provider. When you log onto your service provider's computer you are assigned an Internet protocol (IP for short) address. This IP address consists of four numbers that are separated by periods; an example would be 228.74.88.2. In most cases your service provider will "own" a series of IP addresses. When you log onto your service, you are assigned one of the IP addresses randomly.

When you attempt to connect to a reflector using the Cu-SeeMe software the reflector expects to be able to identify your computer by a name and an IP address. However, if your service provider assigns IP addresses randomly, there is not an IP address that relates directly to your and your computer. Unable to identify you, the reflector returns the GetHostName() error and does not connect you to reflector.

A fairly easy-to-apply fix has been developed to get around the fact that you are not assigned a permanent IP number. By creating a text file called HOSTS. (the file name must end with the period delimiter) you can fool the reflector into thinking that you have a IP number all your own. The HOSTS. file, which will actually contain a range of possible IP addresses (the range is based on the IP addresses used by your service provider), is placed in your Windows directory.

To generate the HOSTS file all you have to do is connect to your service provider and check what IP address you've been assigned. You can do this by starting the CU-SeeMe software. Your IP address will appear in the CU-SeeMe command window. Once you know your current IP address use your Web browser to go to the Cornell CuSeeMe page on the Web at **http://cu-seeme.cornell.edu/~WCW/**. On this page are directions to download a program called MAKEHOST.COM. This freeware software can be used to generate your own HOSTS. file using the IP address that you are currently assigned. Once the GetHostName()error is overcome using the HOSTS. file, you should be able to connect to any of the reflectors listed in the CU-SeeMe software phone book.

I have a color video camera but it doesn't seem to work with CU-SeeMe.

The first thing that you should check is which CU-SeeMe software version you are using. The White Pine version of CU-SeeMe (Enhanced CU-SeeMe version 2.1) supports color. If you are getting a grayscale image in your video box when you start the Enhanced CU-SeeMe software, you may only need to select the appropriate video compression codec (the video protocol for the software) to send color video. To check the current codec select the Edit menu and then select Preferences. A drop down box in the Video tab of the Preferences dialog box allows you to select the grayscale codec or the enhanced color codec.

Unfortunately, users of the Cornell freeware version of CU-SeeMe will not be able to see your video. If you get a message from another user that your video window is blank, it may be due to their choice of CU-SeeMe version.

Index

A

B

F

J-K-L

M

N

O

P

Q–R

S

X-Y-Z

THE SKEPTICS WERE RIGHT: THE WEB WILL FOLD!

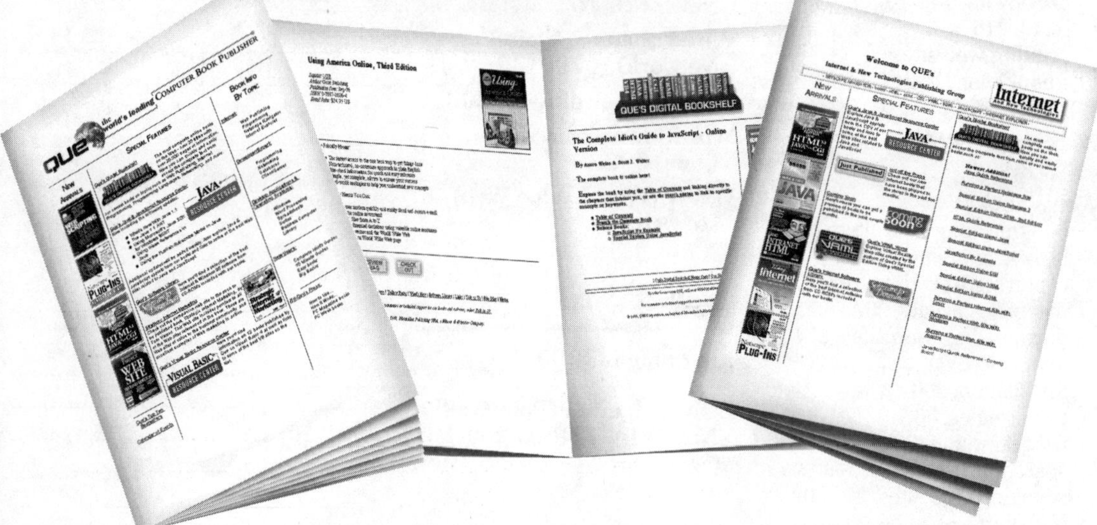

Fold the Web and take it with you. WebPrinter instantly turns Internet, CD-ROM and Windows files into portable, double-sided booklets. With just two clicks, your favorite articles, reference materials, product literature and even photos are transformed into convenient booklets.

WebPrinter is simple to use and works with any laser or inkjet printer. It intercepts standard-sized pages and reduces, rotates and realigns them to print as booklets. WebPrinter even walks you through double-sided printing.

Fold the Web For Free!

Included on this book's CD ROM is a free version of WebPrinter that lets you print any four booklets of your choice. Use it to turn the content of CD ROMs or pages on the Que Web site into handy booklets. The free version is limited to one 4-pack installation per computer.

WebPrinter, the best way yet to print the 'Net.

FOREFRONT™

The ForeFront Group, Inc.
1330 Post Oak Boulevard, Suite 1300
Houston, Texas 77056 http://www.ffg.com

Call us at 1-800-653-4933

Complete and Return this Card for a *FREE* Computer Book Catalog

Thank you for purchasing this book! You have purchased a superior computer book written expressly for your needs. To continue to provide the kind of up-to-date, pertinent coverage you've come to expect from us, we need to hear from you. Please take a minute to complete and return this self-addressed, postage-paid form. In return, we'll send you a free catalog of all our computer books on topics ranging from word processing to programming and the internet.

Mr. ☐ Mrs. ☐ Ms. ☐ Dr. ☐

Name (first) ☐☐☐☐☐☐☐☐☐☐☐ (M.I.) ☐ (last) ☐☐☐☐☐☐☐☐☐☐☐☐☐☐☐

Address ☐☐☐☐☐☐☐☐☐☐☐☐☐☐☐☐☐☐☐☐☐☐☐☐☐☐☐☐☐☐☐☐☐☐☐

☐☐☐☐☐☐☐☐☐☐☐☐☐☐☐☐☐☐☐☐☐☐☐☐☐☐☐☐☐☐☐☐☐☐☐

City ☐☐☐☐☐☐☐☐☐☐☐☐☐☐☐ State ☐☐ Zip ☐☐☐☐☐ ☐☐☐☐

Phone ☐☐☐ ☐☐☐ ☐☐☐☐ Fax ☐☐☐ ☐☐☐ ☐☐☐☐

Company Name ☐☐☐☐☐☐☐☐☐☐☐☐☐☐☐☐☐☐☐☐☐☐☐☐☐☐☐☐☐☐☐☐☐

E-mail address ☐☐☐☐☐☐☐☐☐☐☐☐☐☐☐☐☐☐☐☐☐☐☐☐☐☐☐☐☐☐☐☐☐

1. Please check at least (3) influencing factors for purchasing this book.

Front or back cover information on book .... ☐
Special approach to the content .... ☐
Completeness of content .... ☐
Author's reputation .... ☐
Publisher's reputation .... ☐
Book cover design or layout .... ☐
Index or table of contents of book .... ☐
Price of book .... ☐
Special effects, graphics, illustrations .... ☐
Other (Please specify): ______________________ ☐

2. How did you first learn about this book?

Saw in Macmillan Computer Publishing catalog .... ☐
Recommended by store personnel .... ☐
Saw the book on bookshelf at store .... ☐
Recommended by a friend .... ☐
Received advertisement in the mail .... ☐
Saw an advertisement in: ______________________ ☐
Read book review in: ______________________ ☐
Other (Please specify): ______________________ ☐

3. How many computer books have you purchased in the last six months?

This book only .... ☐ 3 to 5 books .... ☐
2 books .... ☐ More than 5 .... ☐

4. Where did you purchase this book?

Bookstore .... ☐
Computer Store .... ☐
Consumer Electronics Store .... ☐
Department Store .... ☐
Office Club .... ☐
Warehouse Club .... ☐
Mail Order .... ☐
Direct from Publisher .... ☐
Internet site .... ☐
Other (Please specify): ______________________ ☐

5. How long have you been using a computer?

☐ Less than 6 months ☐ 6 months to a year
☐ 1 to 3 years ☐ More than 3 years

6. What is your level of experience with personal computers and with the subject of this book?

	With PCs	With subject of book
New	☐	.... ☐
Casual	☐	.... ☐
Accomplished	☐	.... ☐
Expert	☐	.... ☐

Source Code ISBN: 0-7897-1480-9

7. Which of the following best describes your job title?

Administrative Assistant ☐
Coordinator ☐
Manager/Supervisor ☐
Director ☐
Vice President ☐
President/CEO/COO ☐
Lawyer/Doctor/Medical Professional ☐
Teacher/Educator/Trainer ☐
Engineer/Technician ☐
Consultant ☐
Not employed/Student/Retired ☐
Other (Please specify): ________________ ☐

8. Which of the following best describes the area of the company your job title falls under?

Accounting ☐
Engineering ☐
Manufacturing ☐
Operations ☐
Marketing ☐
Sales ☐
Other (Please specify): ________________ ☐

9. What is your age?

Under 20 ☐
21-29 ☐
30-39 ☐
40-49 ☐
50-59 ☐
60-over ☐

10. Are you:

Male ☐
Female ☐

11. Which computer publications do you read regularly? (Please list)

____
____
____
____
____
____
____
____
____

***Comments*:** ____
____
____

Fold here and scotch-tape to mail.

NO POSTAGE NECESSARY IF MAILED IN THE UNITED STATES

BUSINESS REPLY MAIL

FIRST-CLASS MAIL PERMIT NO. 9918 INDIANAPOLIS IN

POSTAGE WILL BE PAID BY THE ADDRESSEE

ATTN MARKETING
MACMILLAN COMPUTER PUBLISHING
MACMILLAN PUBLISHING USA
201 W 103RD ST
INDIANAPOLIS IN 46290-9042

Check out Que® Books on the World Wide Web
http://www.quecorp.com

As the biggest software release in computer history, Windows 95 continues to redefine the computer industry. Click here for the latest info on our Windows 95 books

Make computing quick and easy with these products designed exclusively for new and casual users

Examine the latest releases in word processing, spreadsheets, operating systems, and suites

The Internet, The World Wide Web, CompuServe®, America Online®, Prodigy®—it's a world of ever-changing information. Don't get left behind!

Find out about new additions to our site, new bestsellers and hot topics

In-depth information on high-end topics: find the best reference books for databases, programming, networking, and client/server technologies

A recent addition to Que, Ziff-Davis Press publishes the highly-successful *How It Works* and *How to Use* series of books, as well as *PC Learning Labs Teaches* and *PC Magazine* series of book/disc packages

Stay on the cutting edge of Macintosh® technologies and visual communications

Find out which titles are making headlines

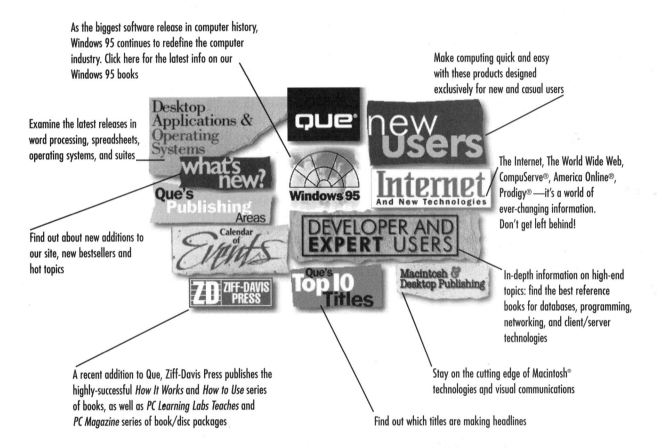

With 6 separate publishing groups, Que develops products for many specific market segments and areas of computer technology. Explore our Web Site and you'll find information on best-selling titles, newly published titles, upcoming products, authors, and much more.

- Stay informed on the latest industry trends and products available
- Visit our online bookstore for the latest information and editions
- Download software from Que's library of the best shareware and freeware

Before using any of the software on this disc, you need to install the software you plan to use. If you have problems with *Using the Internet Starter Kit CD*, please contact Macmillan Technical Support at (800) 545-5914 ext. 3833. We can be reached by e-mail at support@mcp.com or by CompuServe at GO QUEBOOKS.

Read This Before Opening Software